Emerging Information Resources Management and Technologies

Mehdi Khosrow-Pour, DBA
Information Resources Management Association, USA

IDEA GROUP PUBLISHING

Hershey • London • Melbourne • Singapore

Acquisitions Editor:	Kristin Klinger
Development Editor:	Kristin Roth
Senior Managing Editor:	Jennifer Neidig
Managing Editor:	Sara Reed
Assistant Managing Editor:	Sharon Berger
Copy Editor:	April Schmidt
Typesetter:	Amanda Appicello
Cover Design:	Lisa Tosheff
Printed at:	Yurchak Printing Inc.

Published in the United States of America by
      Idea Group Publishing (an imprint of Idea Group Inc.)
      701 E. Chocolate Avenue, Suite 200
      Hershey PA 17033-1240
      Tel: 717-533-8845
      Fax: 717-533-8661
      E-mail: cust@idea-group.com
      Web site: http://www.idea-group.com

and in the United Kingdom by
      Idea Group Publishing (an imprint of Idea Group Inc.)
      3 Henrietta Street
      Covent Garden
      London WC2E 8LU
      Tel: 44 20 7240 0856
      Fax: 44 20 7379 0609
      Web site: http://www.eurospanonline.com

      Library of Congress Cataloging-in-Publication Data

Emerging information resources management and technologies / Mehdi Khosrow-Pour, editor.
    p. cm.
  Summary: "This book supplies the industry leaders, practicing managers, researchers, experts, and educators with the most current findings on undertaking the operation of the latest information technology reforms, developments, and changes. It presents the issues facing modern organizations and provides the most recent strategies in overcoming the obstacles of the ever-evolving information management and utilization industry"--Provided by publisher.
  Includes bibliographical references and index.
  ISBN 1-59904-286-X (hardcover) -- ISBN 1-59904-287-8 (softcover) -- ISBN 1-59904-288-6 (ebook)
  1. Information technology--Management. 2. Management information systems. 3. Information resources management. I. Khosrowpour, Mehdi, 1951-
  HD30.2E47 2007
  004.068--dc22
                    2006032163

Emerging Information Resources Management and Technologies is part of the Idea Group Publishing series named *Advanced Topics in Information Resources Management* Series (ISSN 1537-9329)

British Cataloguing in Publication Data
A Cataloguing in Publication record for this book is available from the British Library.

All work contributed to this book is new, previously-unpublished material. The views expressed in this book are those of the authors, but not necessarily of the publisher.

Advances in Information Resources Management Series

Mehdi Khosrow-Pour, Editor-in-Chief

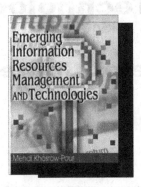

Advances in Information Resources Management features the most current research findings in all aspects of information resources management. From successfully implementing technology change to understanding the human factors in IT utilization, this important series addresses many of the managerial and organizational applications to and implications of information technology in organizations.

Emerging Information Resources Management and Technologies © 2007
1-59904-286-X h/c • 1-59904-287-8 s/c

Advanced Topics in Information Resources Management, Vol 5, © 2006
1-59140-929-2 h/c • 1-59140-930-6 s/c

Advanced Topics in Information Resources Management, Vol 4, © 2005
1-59140-465-7 h/c • 1-59140-466-5 s/c

Advanced Topics in Information Resources Management, Vol 3, © 2004
1-59140-253-0 h/c • 1-59140-295-6 s/c

Advanced Topics in Information Resources Management, Vol 2, © 2003
1-59140-062-7 h/c • 1-59140-099-6 s/c

Advanced Topics in Information Resources Management, Vol 1, © 2002
1-930708-44-0 h/c

For more information, visit www.idea-group.com.

Emerging Information Resources Management and Technologies

Table of Contents

Preface

In the time of constant technological and managerial advancement, firms of the 21st century are faced with an ongoing quest for implementing more effective strategies and methodologies to remain at the apex of the information resources management industry. Considering this, researchers and the pioneers of academia incessantly delve into potential solutions to increase efficacy within technological and information resources management, as well as identify the emerging technologies and trends. *Emerging Information Resources Management and Technologies,* part of the *Advances in Information Resources Management Series,* supplies the industry leaders, practicing managers, researchers, experts, and educators with the most current findings on undertaking the operation of the latest information technology reforms, developments, and changes. This publication presents the issues facing modern organizations and provides the most recent strategies in overcoming the obstacles of the ever-evolving information management and utilization industry.

Chapter I, "The Relevance of Learning Processes for IT Implementation," by *Tanya Bondarouk and Klaas Sikkel, University of Twente (The Netherlands),* discusses the belief that it is neither the quality of the technology, nor that of the individual users, but the interactions among people in groups of users concerning a new system that determines the success or failure of IT implementation. Aiming at conceptualization of the role of group learning in IT implementation, the authors first develop a theoretical framework based on the experiential learning cycle that includes five processes. Second, the authors illustrate the roles of learning processes in three case studies. Analysis of the interviews with 98 users of information technologies has revealed a unique function of group learning in the IT implementation. The chapter elaborates on three organizational conditions important for directing the constructive group learning: managerial support issues, structural and nonstructural group characteristics, and technological features that turn group learning in a positive direction.

Chapter II, "Salary Differences Between Male and Female Software Developers," by *Ronald Dattero, Missouri State University (USA), Stuart D. Galup, Florida Atlantic University (USA), and Jing "Jim" Quan, Salisbury University (USA)*, quantifies differences in the hourly salaries of female software developers with their male counterparts using the human capital model based on economic theory. In addition to the gender factor, the human capital model includes other control variables that may account for the salary differences such as education, experience, and specific skills, such as object-oriented programming and SQL. Our models indicate that gender is a statistically and practically significant factor in assessing a software developer's salary.

Chapter III, "Exploring the Effectiveness of Information Security Policies," by *Neil F. Doherty and Heather Fulford, Loughborough University (UK)*, discusses how ensuring the security of corporate information assets has become an extremely complex, challenging and high-priority activity, due partly to their growing organizational importance, but also because of their increasing vulnerability to attacks from viruses, hackers, criminals, and human error. Consequently, organizations have to prioritize the security of their computer systems, to ensure that their information assets retain their accuracy, confidentiality, and availability. While the importance of the information security policy (InSPy) in ensuring the security of information is widely acknowledged, there has, to date, been little empirical analysis of its impact or effectiveness in this role. To help fill this gap an exploratory study was initiated that sought to investigate the relationship between the uptake and application of information security policies and the accompanying levels of security breaches. To this end a questionnaire was designed, validated, and then targeted at IT managers within large organizations in the United Kingdom. The findings are presented in this chapter.

Chapter IV, "Competing in the Marketplace: Incorporating Online Education into Higher Education: An Organizational Perspective," by *Deirdre A. Folkers, The Pennsylvania State University – York Campus (USA)*, examines the external forces that are challenging higher education. It will further examine the managerial, organizational, and cultural issues that arise as colleges and universities seek to move from the physical "marketplace" to the virtual world of the "marketspace" through the integration of distance education programs.

Chapter V, "Determinant of Information Quality and Use of Executive Information Systems (EIS) in UK," by *Omar E.M. Khalil, Kuwait University (Kuwait)* and *Manal M. Elkordy, Alexandria University (Egypt)*, reports on the findings of a research investigating the influence of information quality on EIS information use as well as the possible impact of ease of use, user involvement, IS maturity, and system sophistication on EIS information quality. To test the research hypotheses, data was collected from 216 U.K.-based executives. A structural equation modeling (SEM) technique for data analysis and model measurement was applied. Information quality was found to influence EIS information use. Also, ease of use, user involvement, the IS integration dimension of IS maturity, and EIS sophistication were found to influence executives' perception of information quality. Further findings, limitations, and implications for researchers and practitioners are discussed.

Chapter VI, "Evidence of Compensatory Adaptation to Unnatural Media in a Field Study of Process Redesign Dyads," by *Ned Kock, Texas A&M International University (USA)*, presents how much of the past research on electronic communication media suggests that those media pose obstacles to communication in collaborative tasks when compared with the face-to-face medium. On the other hand, past research also points at mixed findings in connection with the quality of the outcomes of collaborative tasks, generally suggesting that the use of electronic communication media has no negative effect on those outcomes. A new theoretical framework building on human evolution theory, called compensatory adaptation theory, has been proposed to explain these contradictory findings. This study provides a review and test of compensatory adaptation theory. The study suggests that even though the use of electronic communication media seemed to increase cognitive effort and communication ambiguity, it had a neutral impact on task outcome quality. These results appear to be an outcome of compensatory adaptation, whereby the members of the dyads interacting through the electronic communication medium modified their behavior in order to compensate for the obstacles posed by the medium, which is suggested by a decrease in fluency and an increase in message preparation.

Chapter VII, "Information Technology as a Target, Shield, and Weapon in the Post-9/11 Environment," by *Laura Lally, Hofstra University (USA)*, draws upon normal accident theory and the theory of high reliability organizations to examine the potential impacts of information technology being used as a target in terrorist and other malicious attacks. The chapter also argues that information technology can be used as a shield to prevent further attacks and mitigate their impact if they should occur. A target and shield model is developed, which extends normal accident theory to encompass secondary effects, change, and feedback loops to prevent future accidents. The target and shield model is applied to the Y2K problem and the emerging threats and initiatives in the post-9/11 environment. The model is then extended to encompass the use of IT as a weapon against terrorism.

Chapter VIII, "An Extended Trust Building Model: Comparing Experiential and Non-Experiential Factors," by *D. Harrison McKnight, Michigan State University (USA)* and *Norman L. Chervany, University of Minnesota (USA)*, examines a model of factors influencing system troubleshooter trust in their supervisors, contrasting experiential and nonexperiential factors. System troubleshooters keep important organizational systems operating. Traditional research suggests that trust forms through interactional experience. Recent research indicates that initial interpersonal trust develops through nonexperiential factors that are dispositional (individual differences-related) or institutional (structural/situational). This chapter combines initial and experiential factors to see which remain effective over time. The study shows that both experiential and nonexperiential factors are important to troubleshooter trust even after parties know each other well.

Chapter IX, "A Question of Timing: Information Acquisition and Group Decision Making Performance," by *Souren Paul, Southern Illinois University Carbondale (USA), Carol Stoak Saunders, University of Central Florida (USA), and William David Haseman, University of Wisconsin – Milwaukee (USA)*, explores the impact of information acquisition on decision time and perceived decision quality for groups that used group support systems (GSS) to work on a fuzzy task. The authors found that more information was accessed from a Web-based system in the first part of the group decision-making process, when the decision environment was searched and possible courses of action were analyzed. The authors also found that the proportion of information accessed in the first part of the meeting was significantly related to the decision time. More specifically, when most information was accessed in the first part of the decision-making session, the relationship between decision time and amount of information accessed in early part of the meeting was positive and linear. However, a curvilinear relationship was found between decision time and amount of information accessed in the latter part of the decision-making session. Unlike the findings of a previous study, this earlier access of information is not associated with improved perceived decision quality.

Chapter X, "Progress in Internet Privacy Policies: A Review and Survey of U.S. Companies from 1998 through 2006," by *Alan R. Peslak, Penn State University – Worthington Scranton (USA)*, discusses how on the Internet has been of increasing concern with the explosive growth of electronic commerce. A series of past surveys by the Federal Trade Commission and other organizations measured the implementation of fair information practices and industry self-regulation of privacy. This report includes two important additional factors in the review—enforcement and simplicity. Using historical studies and this more comprehensive analysis, this article reviews the current Internet privacy polices of the 50 largest U.S. companies in 2003 and updates this review for 2006.

Chapter XI, "The Relationship of Strategic Intent to the Enablers and Inhibitors of E-Business Adoption in SMEs," by *Margi Levy, University of Warwick (UK), Philip Powell, University of Bath (UK), and Les Worrall, University of Wolverhampton (UK)*, investigates e-business use and drivers using survey data from 354 small and medium-sized enterprises (SMEs) in the U.K. West Midlands. It first discusses different growth strategies adopted by SMEs and reviews Internet adoption in SMEs. Drivers and inhibitors of e-business are identified. Three research questions are derived—does strategic intent drive e-business adoption and is it a factor of market position or product innovation? Is this consistent across sectors? And how is strategic intent and industry adoption influenced by the enablers and inhibitors of e-business adoption? This research demonstrates that strategic intent influences decisions to invest in e-business. Those SMEs remaining in their existing markets are the least likely to invest, primarily due to the Internet not being seen as necessary for growth. Product innovation rather than market penetration drives e-business and e-business drivers and inhibitors provide insights into this.

Chapter XII, "Understanding Web Site Usability: The Influence of Web Site Design Parameters," by *Monideepa Tarafdar, University of Toledo (USA),* and *Jie (Jennifer) Zhang, University of Toledo (USA)*, analyzes Web site usability from the point of view of Web site design parameters. An analysis of usability and other design characteristics of 200 Web sites of different kinds revealed that design aspects such as information content, ease of navigation, download delay, and Web site availability positively influence usability. Web site security and customization were not found to influence usability. The chapter explains these results and suggests design strategies for increasing Web site usability.

Chapter XIII, "Breaking Out of Lock-in: Insights from Case Studies into Ways Up the Value Ladder for Indian Software SMEs," by *Abhishek Nirjar, Indian Institute of Management, Lucknow (India),* and *Andrew Tylecote, University of Sheffield Management School (UK),* states how small and medium enterprises in the Indian software development industry, like their larger counterparts, are mostly low on the value ladder. This chapter examines the difficulties confronting them in moving up the ladder, and the strategies and circumstances conducive to success, drawing on three case studies. Human resource development emerges as central. Though SMEs have meager resources for moving up, compared to large firms, they have a greater incentive to do so—and this organizational interest accords with the interests and motivations of their employees for career development. It is found that the keys to success are to treat employees as co-investors in their own human capital, to form an effective "community of practice" across the firm, and to find market opportunities which "stretch" the firm in the right direction and to the right extent. For the last of these the main contribution is made by existing clients, but an important role may be played by venture capitalists, particularly those which are U.S.-based.

Chapter XIV, "Comparing Expert Systems and Agent Technology for Knowledge Management," by *Tor Guimaraes, Tennessee Technological University (USA),* presents an overview and comparison of expert system and agent technologies, and shows the latter as a powerful extension in artificial intelligence for systems development. To illustrate, a system developed first using an expert system approach and then an agent-based approach are used to identify the strengths and weaknesses of the agent-based approach. Last, the practical implications of a company adoption of agent-based technology for systems development are addressed.

In the competing business environment of today, strategically managing information resources is at the forefront for organizations worldwide. The adaptation of technological advance has become the key agenda for firms who desire the greatest effectiveness and efficiency of information resources management. Technology, and all it facilitates, has become the axis of the modern world, and thus, having access to the most current findings allows firms the vehicle for the next echelon of success. By investigating transpiring technological movements, researchers, experts, and practitioners alike have the opportunity to implement the highest of emerging standards and grow from that execution. To address this, *Emerging Information*

Resources Management and Technologies, comprises the most current findings associated with utilizing these advancements and applying their latest solutions.

Mehdi Khosrow-Pour, D.B.A.
Editor-in-Chief
Emerging Information Resources Management and Technologies

Chapter I

The Relevance of Learning Processes for IT Implementation

Tanya Bondarouk, University of Twente, The Netherlands

Klaas Sikkel, University of Twente, The Netherlands

Abstract

The starting point of this chapter is the belief that it is neither the quality of the technology, nor that of the individual users, but the interactions amongst people in groups of users concerning a new system that determines the success or failure of IT implementation. Aiming at conceptualisation of the role of group learning in IT implementation, we first develop a theoretical framework based on the experiential learning cycle that includes five processes: collective acting, group reflecting, knowledge disseminating, sharing understanding, and mutual adjustment. Second, we illustrate the roles of learning processes in three case studies. Analysis of the interviews with 98 users of information technologies has revealed a unique function of group learning in the IT implementation. It is shown that group learning emerges immediately after a new IT is introduced to the targeted users; it may take different directions (for or against adoption of the technology); it itself can develop during the IT implementation and either progress or take a turn for the worse. The chapter elaborates on three organisational conditions important for directing the constructive group learning: managerial support issues, structural and nonstruc-

tural group characteristics, and technological features that turn group learning in a positive direction.

Introduction

Almost all modern information technologies (IT) have networked, or collaborative, fragments, and human beings interact with one another while using IT rather than only with the computer, though they might well use computers to do so. These interactions develop within new or existing communities of users, called groups of users in this article. Group interactional processes reflect that groups are developing common understandings of the technology they are forced to (or want to) use. In this chapter, we theorise the multifaceted complexity of IT implementation by looking at it from the perspective of learning processes, specifically from the perspective of experiential learning. We aim to conceptualise how IT implementation develops through learning processes and to provide empirical support for this conceptualisation.

Some aspects of learning have already been discussed in the IT implementation literature, such as reflective group processes (Hettinga, 2002; Schippers, 2003; Tucker, Edmondson, & Spear, 2001); sharing understanding (Mulder, Swaak, & Kessels, 2002); and collaborative knowledge building (Stahl, 2000). In an extended version of the structurational perspective, Orlikowski (2000) proposes looking at "communication, mutual coordination, and storytelling" as important sources for engagement with the system (p. 411).

Although some feeling for the topic now exists, and recent research has emphasised the importance of certain elements of learning for IT implementation, systematic insights are still poor.

We start from a definition. Learning in IT implementation is understood as all the interaction processes through which users develop their understandings about a newly introduced system, and that help them in adopting it (Bondarouk & Sikkel, 2005). With this we emphasise that we look at the implementation of IT from its introduction to the targeted employees and until its successful use. Therefore, our main research question is formulated as: What is the role of learning processes in the implementation of IT from its technical installation until its successful use?

To answer this question, in the following subsections we elaborate on the conceptualisation of learning in IT implementation from the perspective of experiential learning (Kolb, 1984). After that we discuss the research methodology and present empirical results from three case studies. We finalise with discussion, conclusions, and remarks about future research.

Conceptualising Learning in
IT Implementation

Examination of the existing studies has convinced us that there is not much theoretical or empirical research yet completed with a particular focus on the role of learning in explaining and resolving the problems of implementing and using information technologies in organisations.

Learning and IT Implementation: Looking for a Theory

The studies that address both organisational learning and information technology consider learning an alternative antidote to the organisational struggles with IT. The overview of the literature about IT and organisational learning by Robey, Boudreau, and Rose (2000) supports this idea; they state: "the link between IT and learning has only begun to be explored" (p. 127).

In the literature about learning in IT implementation, two major streams can be distinguished. First, much has been done in the field of formal training in IT implementation. Such studies deal directly or indirectly with overcoming barriers to acquiring new knowledge in IT use (Robey et al., 2000; Salaway, 1987).

The second, and the main, stream about learning and IT implementation is research on experience-based organisational learning. Strong evidence indicates that an organisation's own experiences provide a knowledge base to guide future actions (Ang, Thong, & Yap, 1997; Caron, Jarvenpaa, & Stoddard, 1994; Robey & Newman, 1996; Robey et al., 2000; Yetton, Johnston, & Craig, 1994).

However, although research validates importance of learning through experience, there is a lack of theoretical conceptualisation and therefore generalisations are rare.

Experiential Learning: A Closer Look

From the models of experiential learning (Kegan, 1994; Torbert, 1972), we have chosen the learning theory of Kolb (1984). It is grounded in the concept that people have a natural capacity to learn, and experiences act as a catalyst for engaging in this process (Kayes, 2002).

According to Kolb (1984), learning involves the interplay between two interdependent dimensions of knowledge: acquisition and transformation. Knowledge acquisition demands the resolution of the tension between apprehension (concrete experience) and comprehension (abstract conceptualisation). Another dimension of knowledge is transformation which also shows a dialectical tension: between intention (reflective observation) and extension (active experimentation). The learning cycle includes four steps: doing, reflecting, thinking, and deciding.

Kolb's (1984) concept combines impulsiveness, feelings, and individual insights with rational thoughts, reflection, and actions. "It maintains the humanistic belief in every individual's capacity to grow and learn, so important for lifelong learning" (Miettinen, 1998, p. 170). All of this makes the theory comprehensive, fully generalisable, and attractive to both proponents and opponents.

Opponents of Kolb's model suggested that the emphasis on individual experience should be expanded to include social aspects of learning (Holman, Pavlica, & Thorpe, 1997; Kayes, 2002; Reynolds, 1999; Vince, 1998). Overall, limitations of Kolb's model are mainly related to the centrality of individual experience in learning. If we understand learning as changing knowledge and behaviour, then we should acknowledge the importance of social experience for learning.

Towards a Research Framework

Kolb's cycle describes learning on the individual level. In IT implementation, however, learning is usually a group process in which users communicate, share experiences, and learn from and with each other. For describing learning at the group level, a similar learning cycle can be used. To accommodate the exchange of knowledge between group members (not present in individual learning), it has five steps, instead of four. In earlier research (Bondarouk & Sikkel, 2005) we have proposed and validated the learning cycle on the group level consisting of the following steps: collective actions, group reflecting, knowledge disseminating, sharing understanding, and mutual adjusting (Figure 1).

Figure 1. Experience-based learning

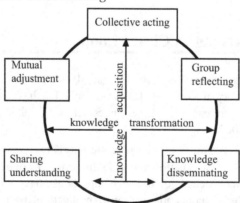

The central challenge lies in the knowledge domain. The group learning cycle is more than multiplying individual learning processes, or "rephrasing" individual to group activities.

Following from Kolb (1984), the knowledge acquisition dimension involves the tension between "doing" processes, or actions (apprehension), and "thinking" (comprehension). Group thinking, in this cycle involves two processes: knowledge disseminating and sharing understanding.

The knowledge transformation dimension of learning is also characterised by a dialectical movement between knowledge intention (group reflecting) and knowledge extension (group deciding, or adjustment and activities).

Collective Acting

A learning cycle begins with *collective experiences and actions* when a group of people is given a certain task to perform. This step reflects apprehension of knowledge: when a group is expected to accept new knowledge through perceptions and direct experiences.

We define collective acting in IT implementation as the task-related operations with a system undertaken by members of a group. When a new technology is introduced to targeted employees who are networked together, they will start to operate with the system in order to execute tasks. This can develop through various activities, including operating with basic modules in everyday task performance, or searching for new techniques in the system. The employees can simply replicate the techniques they have learnt during instruction, or they can try to uncover new functionality in using the system. The more experienced members of a group may take an initiative to test new techniques.

Group Reflecting

The next stage is *group reflection*—the communications upon the extent to which the system supports the performance of tasks (Schippers, 2003). A group is expected to look inward to reflect upon previously acquired knowledge. Reflection takes place through a variety of activities: discussions, asking questions, declaring difficulties, collective debates, and presentations that aim at knowledge externalisation. This is considered crucial in learning from experience because it can help to neutralise biases and errors in group decision making.

In the situation of the introduction of new IT, group reflecting can take place at various stages: after first operations with the system, or when the implementation is well on its way—but it can also happen even before the system is introduced, when future users discuss design issues of the technology. In each case, group reflecting includes communicating about the extent to which the system supports the performance of tasks. Discussions, open dialogue, focus groups, and meetings with a project team might all concentrate on raising difficulties with using the system, comparing it with other software experiences, and with other IT, or raising individual problems in system use. Users might express doubts and suspicions, or trust and beliefs, in the existing ways of solving IT-related difficulties; consider possible reasons for, and outcomes of, mistakes made during operating with the system; or discuss errors in working with various IT functionalities.

Knowledge Disseminating

The *knowledge disseminating* step introduces the key difference between individual and group learning. It is understood as behaviours of group members that aim at the externalisation of ideas about the IT in order to improve its usage. In transferring individual learning into a cooperative one, the act of knowing becomes more complicated. In a group environment, people would have to "think together" —that is, they would share the results of their individual thoughts. However, knowledge is not something that can be easily passed around (Hendriks, 1999).

Certainly, some information can be codified, stored, and reused to enable effective action at a later stage, but representation is not equivalent to knowledge (Sutton, 2001). There are four modes to the knowledge conversion process that can take place in group learning: externalisation—from tacit knowledge to explicit knowledge; combination–from explicit knowledge to explicit knowledge; internalisation–from explicit knowledge to tacit knowledge; and socialisation – from tacit knowledge to tacit knowledge (Kwok, Lee, & Pi, 2002; Nonaka, 1994).

In other words, to break experiences down into meanings, a group would have to go through two phases: first, the reconstruction and codifying of knowledge (externalisation and combination); and, only then, could the knowledge be shared, or transformed, to a tacit form (internalisation and socialisation) (Hendriks, 1999).

Knowledge disseminating during the implementation process of a new IT includes behaviours by the group members that aim to externalise ideas about the system in order to improve its usage. It might emerge in demonstrating the operation of technical modules in both formal (workshops) and informal situations (work breaks), proposing new actions to improve the usage, clarifying difficulties, and peer questioning.

Sharing Understanding

The cycle then moves to *sharing understanding,* creating a common meaning of the system in terms of the role of the system and its functionality. This involves using insights to help people better see their own situations (Kim, 1993). This internalisation also takes in a great variety of forms: learning by doing, reading books, and so forth. It is oriented towards those people who look to acquire knowledge. It implies the informal mutual acceptance and respect of diverse ideas and suggestions. Nelson and Cooprider (1996) define sharing understanding as the appreciation of knowledge amongst group members that affects their mutual performance (p. 410).

Knowledge internalisation concerning new technology will lead to a shared meaning of the system amongst the users. They will share their understanding of the global role of the IT in their company and its intentions for every member of a group, and the design intentions of the developers of the system. An understanding of the technical possibilities and various functionalities (essential and optional) can also be considered a result of this stage. A group will arrive at a common attitude towards the technical and content functionality of the IT: whether the technology helps to accomplish job tasks and personal responsibilities, and to what extent.

Mutual Adjustment

The final step in cooperative learning is *mutual adjustment*, activities that aim for collective agreements on the use of the system within a group. In Kolb's model, this step ("deciding") is related to the extension of knowledge when learners move beyond themselves to interact with an external environment. In this stage, a group will engage in activities that lead to a choice to make decisions together, to evaluate, to reject or adopt, or to ignore, tasks, strategies, and new rules.

Some adaptations need to occur: joint regulations, planning, arrangements, and decisions are activities that need to be undertaken by group members in order to move the learning cycle forward. In this phase, goals are presented and ways to achieve them are planned. Adjustment takes place not only before task execution, but also during it (Schippers, 2003).

In a situation involving new technology, this step in the group learning cycle will include activities aimed towards collective agreements to improve the use of the system in the group. Group members may take initiatives to arrange (or request) additional training, instructions, manuals, and other learning activities. Developing regulations in order to improve the use of technology can become a crucial issue, especially if the users have never worked before as a group. For example, this could involve decisions about dividing responsibilities for making inputs, and schedules for making outputs. Decisions may be also made about the sorts of documents to be submitted, or about data traffic and classification. The IT might also concern group process issues such as developing regulations for intermediate evaluations of the IT project, supporting online chat about topical issues in the project, and news overviews.

The new learning cycle will build upon the existing group experience and knowledge. Planning can also take place during the action or execution of a task, when plans are developed and shaped by seeking feedback, and group reflecting processes. This increases the importance of group reflexivity (Bondarouk, 2006).

We finalise the theoretical discussion by recapitulating the research focus: we are looking at the roles of five learning processes: collective acting, group reflecting, knowledge disseminating, sharing understanding, and mutual adjustment—in the adoption of a newly introduced IT by the users.

Research Methods

We should also look at the larger picture surrounding IT implementation. Learning is not an isolated process, and it may be interrelated with many social and technical issues in an organisation. In order to make our research operational, we will limit it to the, in our view, most important organisational conditions for learning. This

Table 1. Operationalisation scheme

Constructs/definitions	Dimensions/definitions
Technological prerequisites – the visible, technical properties of the system that users are offered.	1. The role of the system in a company – the intended goal and managerial reasons for introducing the system.
	2. Specification of the system – domain-based services that the system is supposed to deliver.
Group support factors – characteristics that maintain interactional processes in the group.	1. Structural devices – designs that facilitate competent group work (Hackman, 1987) through the significance and interdependence of job tasks supported by the system, and how a group is staffed (Campion et al., 1996).
	2. Nonstructural devices of the group – interpersonal understanding and psychological safety shared by the group (Edmondson, 1999).
	3. Software experience – the level of workmanship in software use in the group.
Managerial support for group learning in IT implementation.	1. Organisational arrangements and managerial behavioural patterns for technology implementation aimed at encouraging use of the system.
Learning in IT implementation – all the interactional processes through which users of IT develop interpretive schemes about a newly introduced technology that helps them with its implementation.	1. Collective acting – task-related operations with the system undertaken by members of a group.
	2. Group reflecting – communicating upon the extent to which the system supports them in performing tasks.
	3. Knowledge disseminating – behaviours of the group members that aim at the externalisation of ideas about the system in order to improve its usage.
	4. Sharing understanding – common meaning of the system regarding the role of the system and its functionality.
	5. Mutual adjustment – activities that aim at collective agreements on use of the system in the group.

Table 2. Type and number of interviews conducted

Job position	Number of interviews	Main responsibilities of interviewees
Policymakers	11	Strategic policymaking in organisations, selecting information systems.
Members of the IT project team	10	Steering the IT implementation, providing support for end-users, performed help-desk duties, maintaining functional and technical administration of the system, and sometimes analysing ongoing use of the system.
End users	67	Working with the newly introduced technologies on a daily basis.
Technical personnel	10	Technical administration of the systems.
Total	98	

will include the characteristics of the information technology, groups of users, and managerial support issues. The operationalisation scheme is shown in Table 1.

Three cases studies were conducted in order to explore the role of the learning processes. The goal of the case studies in this research was to exemplify the theoretical discussion on the implementation of IT through learning, and clarifying the contents of the learning processes.

Three companies were selected: a hospital, an insurance company, and a governmental organisation. These are referred to as Medinet, InsurOrg, and AcademCentre. The case study techniques included document analysis, interviews, and participatory observation of IT project activities. We have conducted 87 interviews, each lasting from 45 minutes to 2 hours, and totalling around 121 hours. 98 employees were interviewed (Table 2). Transcripts of all interviews were checked and corrected by the interviewees.

Organisational Contexts

Medinet Case Study

Medinet is a general hospital, founded by the merger of three smaller local hospitals and two polyclinics, one of the largest general hospitals in The Netherlands, with 1,070 beds and around 3,800 employees. Five clusters, distributed over three different locations, comprise 64 departments. In 2001 Beaufort, a module-based workflow system was introduced as a personnel and salary administration system in Medinet. The introduced technology aimed at increasing the efficiency of personnel administration by restructuring the HRM processes, creating shared information files, leading to the use and exchange of personnel information amongst users, and incorporating all the various personnel information systems in Medinet. The users of Beaufort were personnel managers in 64 departments. Nineteen of them participated in the pilot and in this research, of whom 80% were female. The average age was 36 years; 65% of them were educated to high school level. Users never worked together before; their main tasks were to advance HRM policy. The administration tasks were considered secondary, and even tedious, within the general field of personnel management. The software skills of the users varied; 16 of the 19 were familiar with working with IT. Users worked with seven modules for administering documents: Personnel Management, Salary Administration, Sick Leave Administration, Formation and Organisation, Time Registration, Office Link, and Report Generator. In every module users could publish, compose, structure, and store personnel data—but in different manners. Every module required special numerical codification of inputs. Working with Beaufort was obligatory.

The project history included different stages: preparation, negotiation with an external consultancy firm, design, training, piloting, and technical adaptation in the period February 1998–May 2001. In June 2001 Beaufort (one of the modules) was introduced to 19 personnel managers. In July–August 2001 internal evaluations and discussions took place, as well as negotiations with the supplier. A decision was taken to stop the project in September 2001.

InsurOrg Case Study

InsurOrg is one of the largest insurance companies in The Netherlands, with 12.500 full-time employees. It unites about 30 formerly independent insurance companies. The main strategy of InsurOrg was to unify all the subcompanies but keep their business images. That forced a knowledge management strategy as one of the approaches to achieve unification of subcompanies. In 2001 KennisNet, built on top of Lotus Notes, was introduced as a knowledge management system. It had three main goals: providing technical support for gathering and disseminating professional information; developing common knowledge, as compared to shared information; and supporting community building through the development of common knowledge. The users of KennisNet were 39 product managers in nonlife insurance: 38% female; the average age was 34 years; 74% of the employees had been educated at the university level. Users were distributed geographically across five locations. The users had two years of collaborating experience. Their main tasks concerned the development and monitoring of the terms, policies, and changes in nonlife insurance products. All users were highly skilled in using IT. They could work with the system at four different levels of operation, ranging from passive to active-creative: reading, searching, getting information from the data bank; publishing, or submitting new items; editing, commenting, discussing the existing information; discussing, asking, answering questions; requesting information from colleagues. Working with KennisNet was discretionary. The history of the KennisNet project shows that in April 2001 a first draft of the project plan was ready, followed by the approval by the future users in May 2001. In June/August 2001 the future users intensively discussed the design of the technology. In October 2001 KennisNet was introduced to all members of the group. It took one week for the whole group to get familiar with the specifications of the system. After November 2001 the employees did not use the system.

AcademCentre Case Study

AcademCentre is one of the largest universities in The Netherlands, with more than 23,000 students, more than 7,000 employees (academic personnel 53%, support and administrative personnel 47%), and a yearly turnover of €612 million. There are 14 faculties and 15 support units. In 2002 SAP_HR was introduced in the organisation as a part of the packet SAP_HR/Employee Transaction Management. It provided the possibility to process personnel information management and handle reports. It had two main goals: replacing an outdated technology and integration with the already working Financial Model from SAP. The users of SAP_HR were 50 personnel and salary administrators from different units: 65% female; the average age was 35.7; 72.4% were educated to high school level.

Users never worked as a group before. Their main tasks concerned processing changes in the personnel files of the AcademCentre employees. About 40 tasks were performed through SAP_HR like appointment of an employee (subtasks concern appointment of a new employee or an external worker, intern, and *various categories of freelance workers*; modification of basic information, payment information, working time registration, and other data, and so forth. Software skills were not high but sufficient to run SAP_HR. Working with SAP_HR was strictly obligatory. The history of the SAP_HR project developed in several steps: December 2000–October 2001: preparation, negotiations with an external consultancy firm, design, identification of the requirements; in November 2001 training of the users took place. On January 1, 2002, SAP_HR was introduced in 12 faculties and in all the support and administrative services in the AcademCentre. The period of January–November 2002 saw dramatic difficulties experienced by the users in working with SAP_HR.

Findings from the Case Studies

We present the findings from the empirical research in three settings. First, the roles of learning processes are identified. Second, we discuss the findings about organisational conditions for learning in IT implementation: technological prerequisites and group support factors. And we finalise with the discussion about managerial support necessary to promote learning in IT implementation.

The Roles of Learning in IT Implementation

As a result of our research, we propose six statements on the roles of learning in IT implementation:

1.   *Learning emerges immediately after a new technology is introduced to the targeted networked users.*

We saw in all the case studies that the users began to talk about the system, spread their interpretations of it, joked, communicated their attitudes towards the system's functionality, or ignored it, complained to each other, and blamed the system—immediately after they had the opportunity to operate it.

2.   *Learning may take different directions from the very beginning: for or against adoption of the technology.*

Beaufort brought many changes to the tasks of the decentralised users in the Medinet case study: greater responsibilities for secondary tasks, new content in those tasks, and the necessity to be highly interdependent with other users whom they hardly knew before. They did not want to accept a sudden increase in the importance of tasks that were formerly considered boring. Some users did not even try to work with Beaufort after the stories they heard from those who had. As a result, this group created a consensus of Beaufort as useless from the beginning.

In the InsurOrg case study, KennisNet did not result in changes to the job tasks of the nonlife insurance professionals. A lack of clarity about what kind of information to input and share, and with whom and why, lowered the job relevance of KennisNet in the users' perceptions. The following all created disappointment with the system from the beginning: it seemed to work too slowly; the unsophisticated interface required additional efforts to operate KennisNet; overlaps between the insurance subjects that appeared on the screens of KennisNet caused confusion; and there were technical limitations in searching information. As a consequence, the group of KennisNet users developed negative attitudes to the implementation process and the job relevance of the system.

In the AcademCentre case study, personnel and salary administrators experienced significant changes in their daily tasks following the introduction of the SAP_HR system: greater responsibilities for making online inputs, stronger control over these inputs, the necessity to be interdependent, and a need to collaborate across the users of the entire group, many of whom they had not known before. Stress and uncertainty linked to making incorrect inputs to SAP_HR stimulated a negative interpretation of the technology amongst the users from the start: they did not want to invest a lot of effort and were disappointed with the technology. Further, from the beginning, the users assumed that the system was not useful for their job tasks. These negative feelings about SAP_HR were reinforced daily by accumulation of many disappointments, including small details and misunderstandings with the project team and the communication of these throughout the user group.

These observations support the findings elsewhere that show that one of the main bases for users' interpretations about an information technology is its perceived usefulness for the job tasks (see the findings of Adams, Nelson, & Todd, 1992; Brown, Massey, Montoya-Weiss, & Burkman, 2002; Davis, Bagozzi, & Warshaw, 1989; Joshi, 1991; Morris & Venkatesh, 2000; Venkatesh, 2000). We have added to these earlier findings by observing that the usefulness of the technology steers the initial direction of the group learning processes, either positively or negatively.

3. *Learning itself can develop during the implementation process and either progress or take a turn for the worse.*

The existing literature does not elaborate on how and why it can develop and, in contrast, our research has shown that group learning is not a fixed matter but can improve or falter as users work with a technology.

We have observed that learning *can* continue its development in the direction that it took soon after system introduction. In the InsurOrg case study, learning faltered amongst the KennisNet users once the system was introduced, and it continued in the same direction with the group attitudes going from highly enthusiastic, before the KennisNet introduction, to an indifference towards the system within two months of using it.

We have also seen that learning may change its initial direction. In the AcademCentre case study, learning progressed through many difficulties amongst the SAP_HR users, and changed the group interpretations of the system from extremely negative to optimistic.

4.   *Learning has the potential to speed up or slow down the IT implementation process.*

We saw that that learning became an unplanned mechanism for speeding up or slowing implementation, or even for the termination of an IT project (the Medinet case study).

If a group of users appreciates the technological help provided for their tasks, share positive attitudes, help each other, and attribute growth in performance to the system, then, in such a scenario, people will learn the relevant issues about a technology. In so doing, the system is discovered, studied, and better understood; and, with this, the technology becomes more relevant for the job tasks and easier to work with. This will lead to a better and quicker acceptance by the users. In other words, a positive development in group learning will signal quick progress that positively influences interpretations of the technology and leads to constructive action—a quicker acceptance.

The opposite scenario was observed when the users together only complained about the system, perceived it negatively, and convinced each other of its uselessness. Even small details, that in other situations would be ignored, received group attention. In such a scenario, employees learn issues that oppose previous ones. They increase their negative views about the relevance of the system for their tasks and see the technology as too complex to operate. So, the technology becomes less relevant for the job in the opinions of the users, and the learning reinforces the motivation not to accept the system.

We saw that the failure or success of the IT project is magnified in the direction of learning: whether this is oriented towards or against adoption of the technology.

5.   *Most progress/regression in learning was observed during the knowledge acquisition processes. Signs of learning progress or regression can be recognised during the first one to two months of the implementation process.*

The analysis has revealed that, in all the case studies, the developments in learning were mainly related to the progress (or lack of) in the knowledge acquisition processes (collective acting, knowledge disseminating, and sharing understanding), and less so by the knowledge transformation processes (group discussions and mutual adjustment). Signs of positive development in the knowledge acquisition dimension in learning were:

•   increasing activities involving searching for new possibilities in the system;

- an increasing number of proposals from end users for improvements to the system and its implementation (we classified those proposals into three types: technical properties of the system, organisation of information to be input, and group regulations concerning use of the system);

- improving conceptual understanding of the technology (especially understanding the why and the what of the technology, and not only the how);

- discovering, recognising, and acknowledging individual user needs in the technology.

6. *The development of the knowledge acquisition processes was promoted by structural arrangements in the groups of users, and in practice this took less effort than the promotion of knowledge transformation processes.*

We saw that the knowledge acquisition processes were flexible and dynamic. Therefore, we assert that those responsible for the implementation of a new system should pay special attention to the collective acting, knowledge disseminating, and sharing of understanding processes. We also noted that progress was achieved by shaping the structural group characteristics and arrangements such as task reassignment, offering learning possibilities, and setting up discussions. We will elaborate more on this topic in the section on managerial support for IT implementation.

We observed that the group reflecting and mutual adjustment processes were related to the nonstructural characteristics of the group such as psychological safety, knowing each other, trust, and experience in working together. These devices take more time and effort to establish in new groups of users, and therefore the knowledge transformation processes will develop more slowly in new groups.

Technological Prerequisites

In the case studies we observed the implementation of three different technologies: an ERP system (Beaufort), Document Sharing systems (KennisNet), and a WorkFlow system (SAP_HR in AcademCentre). Despite the differences in the architectural design and specifications of the technical parts of these systems, they all have what we call collaborative fragments, that is, modules that require collaboration amongst the users. In all the case studies, the users had to share information and communicate, but with varying intensities and responsibilities, and in different sequences.

We also observed that the greater the level of task interdependence required by the system, the greater the effort that is needed to establish collaboration amongst the users, to redirect group learning towards the level of the entire group of users, and achieve the stable use of the technology.

There was an interesting finding with respect to the freedom given to the employees in their use of the technology. In two cases, the use of the system was mandatory (Beaufort and SAP_HR), while in another it was optional (KennisNet). The case study findings suggest that if system use is voluntary then it must have very clear job relevance to be adopted; that is, the technology has to demonstrate its own value. In the "obligatory" cases we saw a need for appropriate conditions to support group learning in the implementation process. These conditions concerned a strong task interdependency through the technology.

Groups Support Factors

We have divided the group characteristics which are important for "appropriate" learning in IT implementation into two sets: structural and nonstructural. We saw that the structural group characteristics influenced the knowledge acquisition processes in group learning, and the nonstructural ones the knowledge transformation processes.

The findings show that there is only one structural characteristic relevant for IT implementation—task interdependence. We observed that the clarity of the task interdependence (division and definitions) affected the process of shaping a group of users during the implementation process. For example, the tasks for the users of KennisNet were not divided and clarified prior to the introduction of KennisNet and, as a consequence, the employees did not collaborate through the system. The implication is that task operationalisation (division, definitions) should be settled and clarified for the users before the introduction of a technology.

There was a lack of empirical support to suggest that other structural characteristics of user groups influence the success of implementation. We observed different types of groups: large vs. small (50 users of SAP_HR and 17 users of Beaufort), manager-led vs. autonomous (nonlife insurance specialists and the decentralised users), and a virtual team (the group of KennisNet users). We did not find any relationship between the type and size of a group and group learning.

The second set of group characteristics is related to such nonstructural devices like trust, knowing each other's strengths, and open, risk-taking conversations. These characteristics were seen to develop during an IT project. The largest improvement in the nonstructural group features we witnessed took place amongst the users of SAP_HR. At the beginning, they hardly knew each other; but after a couple of months they felt safe enough to speak up. This finding makes it clear that a group can develop during the implementation of a technology.

Those responsible for IT implementation, in our view, have two options in respect of building groups of users in advance. First, they can ignore team building activities on the grounds that it will take too much effort to convince future users of the necessity to become a team before they can sense it for themselves. However, stimulating group discussions and other team building actions must then be undertaken after the system goes live. We saw this scenario in all three situations. The alternative is to begin building nonstructural mechanisms such as trust, and knowing and understanding each other during the preparation stages in IT projects, that is, before the introduction of the system to the users. We did not see this scenario in practice, although we believe that establishing strong nonstructural devices within a potential group of the users may lead to a good start in the group reflecting processes when the technology becomes live.

Managerial Support for Group Learning in IT Implementation

Since the 1970s, information technologies have been viewed as "competitive weapons" in organisations (Parsons, 1983) and, since the same period, social issues have been perceived to be of paramount importance in IT implementation. However, the research by Doherty and King (1998) suggests that there is no relationship between the perceived importance of social issues and their treatment. The authors note that such a pronouncement is worrying as it indicates that many practitioners (especially those responsible for IT implementation) who perceive social issues to be of greater importance than technical ones in IT implementation, are treating those issues only implicitly, or in many cases not at all. No matter how important they think they are, their treatment is often woefully inadequate. Consequently, in many cases, the treatment is simply left to chance (Doherty & King, 1998).

If we look at the reality of IT projects, we must acknowledge that the project teams see various complicating circumstances surrounding IT implementation, including budget limitations, political games in a company, agreements with a consultancy firm, availability of resources, and technological infrastructure. Having acknowledged the importance of the specific circumstances, our research suggests that project leaders should realise that these complications are explicitly or implicitly transferred to the work reality of the end users who are forced to, or want to, work with a new technology. Therefore, we would propose that project leaders acknowledge the range of complex issues that groups of users might face. Having accepted this, it should not be a big step to be honest and inform future users about the difficulties foreseen in a project, and at the same time encourage strong teamwork instead of promising a quick fix. There is a need to realise that interaction processes amongst the users can either speed up or kill the implementation, as we have seen in the case studies. Therefore, it is important to appreciate the role of group learning in IT implementation. This is the first managerial precondition.

In our view, before introducing a system, it is crucial to conceptualise its importance for the users, and to convince them of its relevance. Technology may have, as we saw, a high-level strategic mission. However, this mission must be modified to the language and needs of the end users, and therefore transferred to the users' motives. For example, a system's mission to restructure a company will become visible, touchable, and relevant if it is broken down into subgoals for the users such as making their concrete tasks easier, improving the quality of report generation, and speeding up information searching.

It is also important to fulfil another precondition: the introduction of technology should only start once there is a clear picture about all the job processes that are to be automated. In practice, we saw that managers realised the importance of task operationalisation rather late, when users could not overcome their difficulties with the system, and so we would emphasise this precondition.

When these conditions are met, it is time to think about further project management support. We observed a number of good practices in the three cases that did stimulate constructive group learning. These were:

- Having a help desk or front/back office service on system functionality available for the users at any time,
- Creating and distributing a list of experts on the system's functionality within the group (usually these were the advanced users amongst the targeted employees whose experience can be very helpful to others),
- Introducing an e-mailing list that includes all the users (or setting up a hot-line chatroom),
- Scheduling informal meetings (such as coffee breaks) for the group of users,
- Agreeing how to involve new employees in the use of the system (what to explain to them, who is responsible, etc.),
- Distributing special notebooks for ideas, proposals, and complaints amongst the users,
- Collecting the proposals that come from the users and reacting to them (negotiating),
- Organising regular evaluation sessions with the users about progress in the project.

This list is not exhaustive, it includes only those practices we saw in real life projects.

Promoting learning possibilities is directly related to group learning as it provides the basis for knowledge and skills exchange. However, the findings show that only "customised," user-centred, learning opportunities lead to an improvement in group learning. In our view, users do not need the standard large technical manuals that resemble telephone guides. Rather, the users need task-based, job-related manuals on *why*, *when*, and *how* they should use the various services (modules) in the system. The same holds true for the standardised instruction sessions often provided to the users long before they actually work with the system. Training should be designed on the basis of the concrete tasks of the users, with examples from their own work situations, and provided just-in-time when they are required to complete a task.

If we were to advise a management style for those responsible, we would suggest that they remain constantly "on duty" during the implementation, and keep an eye on the group learning processes to ensure that these develop in the right direction, and that users discuss how to improve the usage of the system rather than how to terminate it. If learning develops impulsively, the adoption of IT may result in complications and high risks for a project as a whole.

Conclusion

The starting point of this research is the belief that it is neither the quality of the technology, nor that of the individual users, but the interactions amongst people in groups of users concerning a new system that determines the success or otherwise of IT implementation. Specific focus of this study is a part of the implementation trajectory that starts after the technology goes live and until its successful use by the targeted employees.

This chapter has presented a lens for looking at IT implementation through developments of collective acting, group reflecting, knowledge disseminating, sharing understanding, and mutual adjustment processes. It is not this chapter's purpose, however, to state that all the problems in IT projects are resolved with the group learning. But it is the purpose to claim that group learning is a (usually unnoticed) mechanism for speeding up or slowing IT implementation, or even for the termination of an IT project.

It is shown that if a group of users appreciates the technological help provided for their tasks, share positive attitudes, and attribute growth in the performance to the technology, then, in such a scenario, people learn relevant issues about a technology. In so doing, the system is discovered, studied, and better understood; and, with this, the technology becomes more relevant for the job tasks and easier to work with. This leads to a better and quicker acceptance of technology by the users. The opposite scenario is when the users together only complain about the system, perceive it negatively, and convince each other of its uselessness. They increase their negative views about the relevance of the system for their tasks and see the technology as too complex to operate. So, the technology becomes "even less relevant" for the job in the opinions of the users, and they learn issues that do not motivate them to accept the system.

Having recognised the importance of the group learning in IT implementation, it is argued that it is vitally important is to stress and accept its role by those who are responsible for IT projects. If managers attempt to advance group learning, then it might become a catalyst for the success of a project. Otherwise the group learning might start an impulsive and unpredicted development that in the end might harm the project.

We have observed conditions that are necessary for group learning to take place such as task interdependence, trust in groups, and certain project management activities. However, to stop at this point misses an important aspect of organisational life. The employees studied (users of technology) went to work and did what they had to do to get their usual jobs done. Their leaders, departments, and the corporate culture, all essential ingredients, were excluded from this research in order to keep the focus on the group and project level. However, further research could greatly contribute to the understanding of the origins and differences in group learning by taking into account different work environments. We suggest that insights could be gained by exploring IT implementation in different types of work and work environments (such as process-, product-, and logistics-based work, and administrative work). Determining whether there is a link between the type of work environment and the type of organisation, and group learning in IT implementation, would add to our research findings.

References

Adams, D.A., Nelson, R.R., & Todd, P.A. (1992). Perceived usefulness, ease of use and usage of information technology: A replication. *MIS Quarterly, 16*(2), 227-247.

Ang, K.-T., Thong, J.Y.L., & Yap, C.-S. (1997, December 15-17). IT implementation through the lens of organizational learning: A case study of INSUROR. In K. Kumar & J.I. DeGross (Eds.), *Proceedings of the 18th International Conference on Information Systems (ICIS'97)* (pp. 331-348). Atlanta, Georgia.

Bondarouk, T. (2006). Action-oriented group learning in the implementation of information technologies: Results from three case studies. *European Journal of Information Systems, 15*(1), 42–53.

Bondarouk, T., & Sikkel, K. (2005). Explaining groupware implementation through group learning. *Information Resource Management Journal, 18*(1), 364-381.

Brown, S.A., Massey, A.P., Montoya-Weiss, M.M., & Burkman, J.R. (2002). Do I really have to? User acceptance of mandated technology. *European Journal of Information Systems, 11*, 283-295.

Campion, M.A., Papper, E.M., & Medsker, G.J. (1996). Relations between work team characteristics and effectiveness: A replication and extention. *Personnel Psychology, 49*, 429-452.

Caron, R.J., Jarvenpaa, S.L., & Stoddard, D.B. (1994). Business reengineering at CIGNA Corporation: Experiences and lessons learnt from the first five years. *MIS Quarterly, 18*(3), 233-250.

Davis, F.D., Bagozzi, R.P., & Warshaw, P.R. (1989, August). User acceptance of computer technology: A comparison of two theoretical models. *Management Science, 35*(8), 982-1004.

Doherty, N.F., & King, M. (1998). The importance of organisational issues in systems development. *Information Technology & People, 11*(2), 104-123.

Edmondson, A. (1999). Psychological safety and learning behaviour in work teams. *Administrative science quarterly, 44*(2), 350-383.

Hackman, J.R. (1987). The design of work teams. In J.Lorsch (Ed.), *Handbook of organisational behaviour* (pp. 315-342). Englewood Cliffs, NJ: Prentice Hall.

Hendriks, P. (1999). Why share knowledge? The influence of ICT on the motivation for knowledge sharing. *Knowledge and Process Management, 6*(2), 91-100.

Hettinga, M. (2002). *Understanding evolutionary use of groupware*. Doctoral thesis, Telematica Instituut Fundamental Research Series, No. 007 (TI/FRS/007), Telematica Instituut, Enschede, The Netherlands.

Holman, D., Pavlica, K., & Thorpe, R. (1997). Rethinking Kolb's theory of experiential learning: The contribution of social constructivism and activity theory. *Management Learning, 28*, 135-148.

Joshi, K. (1991, June). A model of users' perspective on change: The case of information systems technology implementation. *MIS Quarterly, 15*, 229-242.

Kayes, D.C. (2002). Experiential learning and its critics: Preserving the role of experience in management learning and education. *Academy of Management, Learning & Education, 1*(2), 137-150.

Kegan, R. (1994). *In over our heads: The mental demands of modern life*. Cambridge, MA: Harvard University Press.

Kim, D.H. (1993). The link between individual and organizational learning. *Sloan Management Review, 35*(1), 37-50.

Kolb, D.A. (1984). *Experiential learning. Experience as the source of learning and development*. Englewood Cliffs, NJ: Prentice Hall.

Kwok, R.C.-W., Lee, J.-N., & Pi, S.-M. (2002). Role of GSS on collaborative problem-based learning: A study on knowledge externalisation. *European Journal of Information Systems, 11*, 98-107.

Miettinen, R. (1998). About the legacy of experiential learning. *Lifelong learning in europe*, 3, 165-171.

Morris, M.G., & Venkatesh, V. (2000). Age difference in technology adoption decisions: Implications for a changing work force. *Personnel Psychology, 53*, 375-403.

Mulder, I., Swaak, J., & Kessels, J. (2002). Assessing group learning and shared understanding in technology-mediated interaction. *Educational Technology and Society, 5*(1), 35-47.

Nelson, K.M., & Cooprider, J.C. (1996). The contribution of shared knowledge to IS group performance. *MIS Quarterly, 20*(4), 409-429.

Nonaka, I. (1994). A dynamic theory of organizational knowledge creation. *Organization Science, 5*(1), 41-60.

Orlikowski, W.J. (2000). Using technology and constituting structures: A practice lens for studying technology in organisations. *Organization Science, 11*(4), 404-428.

Parsons, G.L. (1983, Fall). Information technology: A new competitive weapon. *Sloan Management Review, 25*, 3-13.

Reynolds, M. (1999). Critical reflection and management education: Rehabilitating less hierarchical approaches. *Journal of Management Education, 23*, 537-553.

Robey, D., Boudreau, M.-C., & Rose, G.M. (2000). Information technology and organisational learning: A review and assessment of research. *Accounting Management and Information Technologies, 10*, 125-155.

Robey, D., & Newman, M. (1996). Sequential patterns in information systems development: An application of a social process model. *ACM Transactions on Information Systems, 14*(1), 30-63.

Salaway, G. (1987). An organisational learning approach to information systems development. *MIS Quarterly, 11*(2), 245-264.

Schippers, M. (2003). *Reflexivity in teams*. Doctoral thesis. Amsterdam: Ridderprint offsetdrukkerij b.v.

Stahl, G. (2000, June 14-17). A model of collaborative knowledge building. In B. Fishman & S. O'Connor-Divelbiss (Eds.), *Proceedings of the 4th International Conference of the Learning Sciences (ICLS2000)* (pp. 70-77). Mahwah, NJ: Erlbaum.

Sutton, D.C. (2001). What is knowledge and can it be managed? *European Journal of Information Systems, 10*, 80-88.

Torbert, W.R. (1972). *Learning from experience, toward consiousness.* New York: Columbia University Press.

Tucker, A.L., Edmondson, A.C., & Spear, S. (2001). *When problem solving prevents organizational learning* (Working Paper No. 01-073). Harvard Business School.

Venkatesh, V. (2000, December). Determinants of perceived ease of use: integrating control, intrinsic motivation, and emotion into the technology acceptance model. *Information Systems Research, 11*(4), 342-366.

Vince, R. (1998). Behind and beyond Kolb's learning cycle. *Journal of Management Education, 22*, 304-319.

Yetton, P.W., Johnston, K.D., & Craig, J.F. (1994, Summer). Computer-aided architects: A case study of IT and strategic change. *Sloan Management Review, 35*, 57-67.

Chapter II

Salary Differences Between Male and Female Software Developers

Ronald Dattero, Missouri State University, USA

Stuart D. Galup, Florida Atlantic University, USA

Jing "Jim" Quan, Salisbury University, USA

Abstract

In this chapter, we quantify the differences in the hourly salaries of female software developers with their male counterparts using the human capital model based on economic theory. In addition to the gender factor, the human capital model includes other control variables that may account for the salary differences such as education, experience, and specific skills, such as object-oriented programming and SQL. Our models indicate that gender is a statistically and practically significant factor in assessing a software developer's salary.

Introduction

U.S. Department of Labor (2002) data indicate that currently full-time female computer programmers make $867 per week (median) compared to their male counterparts who make $975 per week (median). Equivalently, female computer programmers make, on average, only 88.92% of what their male counterparts make or conversely, male computer programmers make, on average, 112.46% of what their female counterparts make. The question addressed in this chapter is the extent to which the salary differences between male and female software developers (we prefer using this term rather than computer programmers) can be attributed to human capital differentials. For most professions, the significant human capital factors include work experience and education. In addition, specific skills may contribute to the human capital of software developers.

To address this question, we analyze the differences in current salaries between female and male software developers by factoring in the effects of education, experience, and specific skills. We fit the human capital model based on economic theory to provide a quantitative assessment of the salary differences attributed to gender. While the human capital model quantifies the salary differences based on gender, it also controls for the effects of different amounts of technical experience and different levels of education that software developers possess. Further, salary data are adjusted to account for the average number of hours worked per week. In addition, we consider other human capital factors that impact the salaries of software developers. If a set of human capital factors is found that make the gender factor insignificant, this will provide support to the viewpoint that human capital differentials are responsible for salary differences. On the other hand, if the gender factor is still significant, the model results will provide a quantitative assessment of salary differences for software developers attributed to gender.

In the next section, the relevant literature on gender inequality and discrimination is reviewed. Then, the human capital model, which we employ to assess potential gender discrimination, and its theoretical rationale, the human capital theory, are detailed. Following this, the nature of our survey is discussed briefly and some summary statistics are presented. The human capital model results are then presented and discussed. To provide confirmatory evidence for our human capital models, our sample is divided into female and male subsets, then Chow (1960) tests and Oaxaca (1973) decompositions are applied. The chapter concludes with a discussion of the results and managerial implications.

Gender Inequality and Discrimination

In the United States of America, Title VII makes it unlawful for employers, labor organizations, and employment agencies to discriminate against employees and applicants on the basis of their race, color, sex, religion, and national origin. Enacted in 1964, Title VII was designed to achieve equality of employment opportunities and to eliminate discriminatory impediments to that equality (Reinsmith, 2002).

Gender discrimination in the workplace can be divided into two types: access and treatment (Levitin, Quinn, & Staines, 1971). Access discrimination occurs when members of a certain gender are not hired into certain jobs because of policies and procedures (written or unwritten) that bar or discourage their recruitment. Treatment discrimination occurs when qualified members of a certain gender receive lower salaries, lower status, or lower positions than comparable members of the opposite sex. In this chapter, treatment discrimination will be examined using human capital theory so further discussion of treatment discrimination will be deferred until that section.

In terms of access discrimination, Truman and Baroudi (1994) indicated that there was lower female participation in the Information Technology (IT) occupations than in other business occupations, such as accountants and auditors, personnel and labor relations managers, and financial managers. They concluded that this was *not* a result of access discrimination as the percentage of females in IT jobs roughly matched the percentage of females graduating from computer science programs. However, Truman and Baroudi (1994) did conclude that, given the relatively low numbers of women graduating from computer science programs, access discrimination was occurring at some earlier stage.

Gender inequality in the IT profession can also be traced to the segregation of labor markets. This segregation can affect labor supply by encouraging or dissuading women in their selection of preferred work. There is an image of the computing culture as male-gendered work which makes the profession unattractive to women (Panteli, Stack & Ramsay, 1999). The segregation of labor markets also impact the type and status of IT jobs that women are employed in. Von Hellens, Pringle, Nielsen, and Greenhill (2000) indicate that women in IT jobs are increasingly concentrated in low status job classifications and interface strictly with customers while their male counterparts are employed in higher status and higher paying IT jobs where they interface predominantly with other IT professionals and with managers. This strengthens the social network for males working in IT while segregating or isolating female IT workers. Ahuja (2002) proposes the use of social network analysis to study the different networks of men and women in organizations.

Human Capital

Human capital theory is the dominant economic theory of wage determination (Berndt, 1991). Its origins trace back to the 18th century writings of Adam Smith (1937). Schultz (1960, 1961) popularized the idea of "human capital"—the idea of treating educational spending as an investment. Berndt (1991) states that educated workers are (hopefully) more productive than their less educated counterparts. As a result, they are more likely to command higher wages. This is a straightforward extension of Smith's idea of equalizing differences. This theory also provides an economic explanation as to why a person will forego earnings and incur additional expenses to undertake an education. In addition to formal education, on-the-job training is also important in the accumulation of one's human capital because many job skills are acquired through training sessions, apprenticeships, and similar efforts (Becker, 1962, 1964; Mincer, 1958, 1962, 1974).

Gender treatment discrimination occurs when qualified members of one gender receive lower salaries, lower status, or lower positions than comparable members of the opposite sex (Levitin, Quinn, & Staines, 1971). Treatment discrimination represents a situation in which the treatment of employees is based more on their subgroup membership than on their merit or achievements (Greenhaus, Parasuraman, & Wormley, 1990; Moyes, Williams, & Quigley, 2000).

Economists take the position that some part of the gender gap in earnings is due to average group differences in productivity-linked characteristics (a human capital gap) and some part is due to average group differences in treatment (a discrimination gap). Gaps that can be explained by human capital differences (such as education, experience, and specific skills) make it easier to assert that labor markets function in a nondiscriminatory manner (Darity & Mason, 1998).

The econometric literature on wage determination based on human capital has for the most part been based on regression models of the following form: the natural logarithm of earnings is a function of a measure of schooling, a measure of experience, possibly other factors, and a random disturbance term. Roy's (1950) research showed that there is a relationship between earnings distributions and the underlying abilities of the employee (such as intelligence, physical strength, etc.). Roy (1950) also showed that if each of the underlying abilities is normally distributed than the logarithm of earnings will be normally distributed.

Mincer (1974) showed that the regression equation for wages is linear in education but quadratic in experience. That is:

$$\log Y_i = \log Y_0 + \beta_1 S_i + \beta_2 X_i + \beta_3 X_i^2 + u_i \tag{1}$$

where Y_i is the wages, S_i is education, X_i is experience, and u_i is the random disturbance. Because earnings cannot increase indefinitely as experience increases, estimates of β_2 should be positive while estimates of β_3 should be negative.

Survey Details and Summary Statistics

We obtained our data from the voluntary Web-based survey on salary and skills of IT workers conducted by Dice Incorporated (http://www.dice.com), an online placement company from June 7, 2000 to April 13, 2001. One caveat can be raised regarding the representation of the respondents of this survey: the survey sample was not random since the respondents were self-selecting and voluntary, making nonrepresentativeness and the self-reporting bias a possibility. Further, the online nature of the survey may introduce a bias towards younger workers. However, we argue that these two sets of potential biases would introduce little, if any, bias in our comparative analysis towards female or male software developers because it is likely that these biases, if present, would be equally distributed for both subgroups of the sample.

In the online survey, a respondent could select from 38 different job titles. To identify software developers, we used seven of these job titles—developer: applications, developer: client/server, developer: database, developer: systems, mainframe systems programmer, software engineers, and Web developer/programmer. Any problematic data was removed from our sample using the rules listed in the Appendix. This resulted in a sample of 5,547 software developers used in this analysis.

Females were somewhat underrepresented in this sample as only 17.3% of the survey respondents were female compared to recent U.S. Department of Labor (2002) data indicating that 27.2% of computer programmers are female. In addressing this issue, the following explanations are offered. Since the survey was placed on an online placement company's Web site, the survey respondents were more likely to be actively seeking new employment than typical software developers. Research on gender differences and job searches provide a possible explanation on why the percentage of female survey respondents is low—women conduct a job search with less intensity than men (Keith & McWilliams, 1999) and women are less likely to separate from an existing job (Kulik, 2000). Therefore, these differences would impact only the relative number of respondents and would have little, if any, impact on our comparative analysis of female and male software developers.

In Table 1, the respondents were categorized by (technical) experience level (six categories) and gender. The modal and median experience group for male, female, and overall is Level 3 (3 to 5 years experience). For the first two experience level categories, females constituted 26.9% and 21.5% of the respondents which is

Table 1. Experience and gender percentages

Experience Level	Experience (in years)	Number of Respondents	Males	Females
1	less than 1	413 (7.4%)	302 (73.1%) (6.6%)	111 (26.9%) (11.6%)
2	1 or 2	989 (17.8%)	776 (78.5%) (16.9%)	213 (21.5%) (22.3%)
3	3 to 5	2,042 (36.8%)	1,721 (84.3%) (37.5%)	321 (15.7%) (33.5%)
4	6 to 10	1,088 (19.6%)	929 (85.4%) (20.2%)	159 (14.6%) (16.6%)
5	11 to 14	422 (7.6%)	358 (84.8%) (7.8%)	64 (15.2%) (6.7%)
6	15 or more	593 (10.7%)	504 (85.0%) (11.0%)	89 (15.0%) (9.3%)
Overall		5,547	4,590 (82.7%)	957 (17.3%)

Table 2. Education and gender percentages

Education Level	Number of Respondents	Males	Females
High School	158 (2.8%)	141 (89.2%) (3.1%)	17 (10.8%) (1.8%)
Military	29 (0.5%)	29 (100.0%) (0.6%)	0 (0.0%) (0.0%)
Vocation/Tech School	158 (2.8%)	126 (79.7%) (2.7%)	32 (20.3%) (3.3%)
Some College	876 (15.8%)	745 (85.0%) (16.2%)	131 (15.0%) (13.7%)
College Grad	2,893 (52.2%)	2,382 (82.3%) (51.9%)	511 (17.7%) (53.4%)
Master's Degree	1,256 (22.6%)	1,012 (80.6%) (22.0%)	244 (19.4%) (25.5%)
Doctoral Degree	102 (1.8%)	93 (91.2%) (2.0%)	9 (8.8%) (0.9%)
Professional Degree (MD, JD)	75 (1.4%)	62 (82.7%) (1.4%)	13 (17.3%) (1.4%)
Overall	5,547	4,590 (82.7%)	957 (17.3%)

considerably more than their overall percentage of only 17.3%. For the 6x2 contingency table, the chi-square test statistic is 51.6 (p-value < .0001). So the pattern of experience clearly indicates that females have less experience than their male counterparts.

Table 2 presents the percentage of males and females for the different education levels. The modal education group for male, female, and overall is college grad with over half the respondents falling into this category for all three groups. Gender differences are not as pronounced as was the case for experience. 81.2% of females have a college degree (college grad, master's degree, doctoral degree, or professional degree) compared with only 77.3% of males. For the 8x2 contingency table, the chi-square test statistic is 24.53 (p-value 0.0009). So the pattern of education indicates that females have different educational backgrounds than their male counterparts but the practical differences may not be substantial enough to make the claim that female software developers are better educated.

In terms of reported yearly salary, males reported making an average of $65,948 per year while their female counterparts made only $59,336 per year. (As expected, the test for mean differences was statistically significant with a p-value < 0.0001.) So in our sample, females make 89.98% of what their male counterparts make which is very close to the U.S. Department of Labor (2002) statistic of 88.92% for computer programmers.

In contrast, the U.S. Department of Labor (2002) data indicate that currently full-time female computer programmers make $867 per week (median) compared to their male counterparts who make $975 per week (median). This converts into female computer programmers making only $45,004 ($865x52) per year and male computer programmers making only $50,700 ($975x52) per year. In addressing the issue of why our average yearly salaries are higher, the following argument can be made. Since the survey was placed on an online placement company's Web site, the survey respondents were more likely to be actively seeking new employment than typical software developers. Given the time frame of the survey (before the demand for software developers dropped off), these software developers were probably better qualified than their nonresponding counterparts. Again, we argue that this potential bias would have little impact on our comparative analysis of female and male software developers because it is appears that this bias is equally distributed for male and female software developers.

Human Capital Model Results

Model Preliminaries

Mincer (1974) showed that the regression equation for wages is linear in education but quadratic in experience as given in equation 1. Berndt (1991) suggested that rather than using annual salaries, the hourly salary rate should be employed. Since the respondents also indicated the average number of hours worked per week, we fit the human capital model by taking the annual salary and dividing it by the estimated hours worked per year. The estimated hours worked per year is the number of weeks per year (365/7) times the average hours worked per week.

Since the respondents indicated a technical experience level rather experience in years, the experience level was scaled as follows: (1) 0.5 for less than 1 year, (2)

1.5 for 1-2 years, (3) 4.0 for 3-5 years, (4) 8.0 for 6-10 years, (5) 12.5 for 11-14 years, and (6) 17.5 for more than 15 years. The highest education level attained by each respondent was scaled into education years as follows: (1) 12 for high school, (2) 14 for military, (3) 14 for vocational/tech school, (4) 14 for some college, (5) 16 for college grad, (6) 18 for master's degree, (7) 20 for doctoral degree, and (8) 20 for professional degree (MD, JD).

Simple Multiplicative Model

Before proceeding with the human capital model results, we present a simple multiplicative model to assess gender differences in software developers that does not take into account any human capital factors.

$$\log Y_i = \log Y_0 + \beta_1 G_i + u_i \tag{2}$$

This model is equivalent to:

$$Y_i = Y_0 e^{\beta_1 G_i + u_i} \tag{3}$$

Fitting this model using our data indicates that males make 107.97% more than females, or conversely, females make only 92.62% of what their male counterparts make. This model is highly significant with a p-value less than 0.0001. This increase from 89.98% to 92.62% can probably be attributed to the number of hours worked per week as males reported working an average of 42.8 hours per week while their female counterparts reported working only an average of 41.5 hours per week. The fact that female software developers work, on average, less hours per week compared to their male counterparts is not that surprising as U.S. Labor Statistics, over the last 20 years, indicate that full-time female employees consistently work less than their male counterparts (Ehrenberg & Smith, 1997; U.S. Department of Labor, 2002).

Base Human Capital Model

Next, we present overall results for the base human capital model. Equation (1) is modified to account for the gender factor indicator—G_i which is equal to 1 for males and 0 for females. This model is given in equation 4. Similar to equation 2, this model is multiplicative so e^{β_4} gives the percentage (after converting this number to a percentage) that males make more than their female counterparts. In all the hu-

16

32 Dattero, Galup, & Quan

Table 3. Base human capital model: Overall results

Coefficient or Statistic of Interest	Value	t-value	p-value
Base	2.17496	40.70	< 0.0001
Education	0.04695	14.82	< 0.0001
Exp	0.09076	23.89	< 0.0001
Exp^2	-0.00344	-16.78	< 0.0001
Gender	0.04551	3.34	0.0009
Adjusted R^2	0.1984		< 0.0001

man capital model results presented, the coefficients will be referred to as the base (intercept term), education (β_1), Exp (β_2), Exp^2 (β_3), and Gender (β_4).

$$\log Y_i = \log Y_0 + \beta_1 S_i + \beta_2 X_i + \beta_3 X_i^2 + \beta_4 G_i + u_i \qquad (4)$$

The results given in Table 3 indicate that males make 104.66% (e$^{(Gender)}$) more than females, or conversely, females make only 95.55% (1/e$^{(Gender)}$) of what their male counterparts make. This increase from 92.62% to 95.55% indicates that education and experience are two significant factors that help explain some of the gender differences for software developers. This model is highly significant with a p-value less than 0.0001 and an associated Adjusted R^2 of 0.1984. All coefficients are also highly significant with the highest (least significant) p-value at 0.0009 for the gender coefficient. As expected by the human capital model, experience has a positive coefficient while Exp^2 has a negative coefficient.

Human Capital Model with Specific Skills

The results of a study by Dattero and Galup (2004) indicated that choice of programming language differs between genders. For example, males have a greater than expected representation when considering object-oriented languages, such as Java and C++, while females have a greater than expected representation when considering more traditional programming languages, such as COBOL. In exploring the dataset used in this study, software developers with objected-oriented skills had greater salaries than their counterparts without this skill. Hence, the object-oriented programming skill seems to be a very likely human capital factor. This difference may explain some of the differences in salaries since 54.2% of males in our sample have this skill while only 41.3% of females have it.

To balance the advantage of the object-oriented programming skill, programmers with only COBOL skills make substantially less. Similarly, programmers with only Visual Basic skills make substantially less than their object-oriented programming counterparts. If one also included these two factors in a human capital model, fitting the regression would produce negative coefficients for these two factors. Since losing human capital is not a logical consequence of adding an additional ability, these two factors were not included in the model even though the two factors would be significant and slightly increase the Adjusted R^2.

In exploring the dataset used in this study, SQL was the one other skill factor that had a significant effect and produced a positive regression coefficient. In our sample, 55.3% of males have this skill and 53.2% of females have it.

Incorporating the SQL and objected-oriented programming skills factor into the human capital model with the gender effect (equation 4) produces the following human capital model (equation 5) where O_i is equal to 1 if the developer indicated knowledge of Java, C++, Smalltalk, or OOP (and 0 otherwise), and Q_i is equal to 1 if the developer indicated knowledge of SQL (and 0 otherwise). Similar to equation 4, this model is multiplicative so $e^{\beta 5}$ gives the human capital increase produced by possessing the object-oriented skill while $e^{\beta 6}$ gives the human capital increase produced by possessing SQL skills. In the human capital model results presented, the two new coefficients will be referred as OOP (β_5) and SQL (β_6).

$$\log Y_i = \log Y_0 + \beta_1 S_i + \beta_2 X_i + \beta_3 X_i^2 + \beta_4 G_i + \beta_5 O_i + \beta_6 Q_i + u_i \qquad (5)$$

The results given in Table 4 indicate that females make only 96.58% $(1/e^{(\text{Gender})})$ of what their male counterparts make. This increase from 95.55% to 96.58% indicates that objected-oriented programming and SQL are two significant human capital skill factors that help explain some of the gender differences for software developers. This model is highly significant with a p-value less than 0.0001 and an associated Adjusted R^2 of 0.2106. All coefficients are also highly significant with the highest (least significant) p-value at 0.0108 for the gender coefficient. The OOP skill produces a 107.71% increase in salary while the SQL skill produces a 103.25% increase in salary.

Table 4. Human capital with skills model: Overall results

Coefficient or Statistic of Interest	Value	t-value	p-value
Base	2.19670	41.00	< 0.0001
Education	0.04276	13.35	< 0.0001
Exp	0.08972	23.72	< 0.0001
Exp^2	-0.00336	-16.48	< 0.0001
Gender	0.03479	2.55	0.0108
OOP	0.07428	7.11	< 0.0001
SQL	0.03196	3.11	0.0019
Adjusted R^2	0.2106		< 0.0001

Chow Test

In economics, an alternative to employing a gender indicator variable in the human capital model is to fit the overall model (with both male and female data) and then fit the model to each of the two disjoint subsets (a model with only male data and another model with only female data). In assessing and testing differences between two or more disjoint subsets (such as male and female) using the same econometric regression model, Chow (1960) is credited with developing a test of coefficient equality between the two subsets by fitting the regression model to each of the two subsets and the entire or pooled set of data.

The Chow test is conducted as follows. First, fit the model (with k parameters—not counting the intercept term) using the entire set of data and compute the (restricted) residual sum of the squares denoted by RRSS. Second, fit the model using only the first subset of data (of size n_1) and compute the residual sum of the squares denoted by RSS_1. Third, fit the model using only the second subset of data (of size n_2), and compute the residual sum of the squares denoted by RSS_2. Next, compute the unrestricted residual sum of the squares denoted by URSS by summing RSS_1 and RSS_2. The test statistic is distributed according to an F-distribution with $(k + 1)$ and $(n_1 + n_2 - 2k - 2)$ degrees of freedom and is computed as follows:

$$F = \frac{(RRSS - URSS)/(k+1)}{URSS/(n_1 + n_2 - 2k - 2)}$$

(6)

The results for the base human capital model for the three sets are given in Table 5. The Chow test indicates a significant difference between the male and female

Table 5. Base human capital models and Chow test results

Coefficient or Statistic of Interest	All	Male	Female
Base	2.21488*	2.29213*	1.76777*
Education	0.04660*	0.04244*	0.07238*
Exp	0.09174*	0.09111*	0.08784*
Exp^2	-0.00348*	-0.00346*	-0.00323*
Adjusted R^2	0.1970	0.1859	0.2454
Model p-value	< 0.0001	< 0.0001	< 0.0001
N	5,547	4,590	957
Residual Sum of Squares	810.62536	677.41909	129.90515

* Coefficient significantly different from 0 at < 0.0001 level
Chow Test statistic = 5.66 with a p-value = 0.0002

Table 6. Human capital with skills models and Chow test results

Coefficient or Statistic of Interest	All	Male	Female
Base	2.22806***	2.29799***	1.81804***
Education	0.04235***	0.03864***	0.06650***
Exp	0.09043***	0.09015***	0.08632***
Exp^2	-0.00339***	-0.00339***	-0.00311***
OOP	0.07704***	0.07700***	0.05325**
SQL	0.03227***	0.02758**	0.04711*
Adjusted R^2	0.2062	0.1946	0.2509
Model p-value	< 0.0001	< 0.0001	< 0.0001
N	5,547	4,590	957
Residual Sum of Squares	801.03222	669.89718	128.68867

*** *Coefficient significantly different from 0 at 1% level*
** *Coefficient significantly different from 0 at 5% level*
* *Coefficient significantly different from 0 at 10% level*
Chow Test statistic = 2.83 with a p-value = 0.0095

models with a p-value equal to 0.0002. This Chow test assumes equal variance for the male and female subsets.

Examining the models closely, the base coefficient for males is substantially higher (130%) than for females indicating that males have a substantial initial advantage in salary. Females get a substantially greater increase from education than their male counterparts which somewhat lessens the base impact. Males benefit slightly more from experience than females. With the strong results for the Chow test and the substantially larger base coefficient for males, one could make a strong argument that the difference in wages appears to be based considerably on gender.

The results for the human capital model with the added OOP and SQL skills for the three sets are given in Table 6. Most of the values in Table 6 are similar to those in Table 5. Surprisingly, males get a greater increase (108%) from possessing OOP skills than their female counterparts (105%) while females get a greater increase (105%) from possessing SQL skills than their male counterparts (103%).

Oaxaca Decomposition

The Chow test provides only an indicator on whether the gender models are significantly different in structure. The Oaxaca (1973) decomposition breaks up the salary gender differences into two components: explained and unexplained (or residual). The explained portion is due to the differences in human capital while the unexplained portion can be attributed to discrimination. However, when using Oaxaca decompositions to explain discrimination, some reservations must be made. An often unstated or hidden assumption in the presentation of an Oaxaca decomposition is that the human capital model contains the significant human capital factors—if the human capital model is seriously lacking in significant human capital factors, the unexplained portion is not really a measure of discrimination but merely a measure of the poorness of the human capital model. Gosse (2002) expands this criticism of stating without question that the unexplained portion should be attributed to discrimination as follows. First, there is an imperfect collection of variables used to model the gender pay gap, and it is likely that one or more important variables are missing from even the best model. Second, the variables used in this model likely contain some error in measurement. Third, misspecification of even one variable in the model can considerably impact the decomposition results.

By the definition of least squares regression, the mean of the outcome (dependent variable) for each group is equal to the sum of the mean of each observed variable (independent variable) times the estimated coefficient of that variable. In the Oaxaca decomposition, the equation of one of the groups is subtracted from the other group producing the "difference equation." If one "accidentally" uses the set of means for males with the female model (or the set of means for females with the male model), this "accidental set of terms" (on the right-hand side of the equation) is precisely what is added to and subtracted from the difference equation. Algebraically rearranging this result produces the explained and unexplained components. Employing this process to the base human capital model (equation 1) produces the following decomposition process. Equation 7a is the fitted male human capital model with the corresponding male averages plugged in. Equation 7b is the fitted female human capital model with the corresponding female averages plugged in. Equation 7c is the fitted female human capital model with the corresponding male averages "accidentally" plugged in so the set of three terms on the right-hand side will be added to and subtracted from the difference equation. Equation 8 is the final result with the explained component on the line above the unexplained component.

$$\overline{\log Y}_m = b_{m0} + b_{m1}\overline{S}_m + b_{m2}\overline{X}_m + b_{m3}\overline{(X_m^2)} \tag{7a}$$

$$\overline{\log Y}_f = b_{f0} + b_{f1}\overline{S}_f + b_{f2}\overline{X}_f + b_{f3}\overline{(X_f^2)} \tag{7b}$$

$$\overline{\log Y}_f = b_{f0} + b_{f1}\overline{S}_m + b_{f2}\overline{X}_m + b_{f3}\overline{(X_m^2)} \tag{7c}$$

$$\overline{\log Y}_f - \overline{\log Y}_m =$$
$$b_{f1}(\overline{S}_f - \overline{S}_m) + b_{f2}(\overline{X}_f - \overline{X}_m) + b_{f3}(\overline{(X_f^2)} - \overline{(X_m^2)}) +$$
$$(b_{f0} - b_{m0}) + (b_{f1} - b_{m1})\overline{S}_m + (b_{f2} - b_{m2})\overline{X}_m + (b_{f3} - b_{m3})\overline{(X_m^2)} \tag{8}$$

Table 7. Oaxaca decomposition for base human capital model

Coefficient or Statistic of Interest	Male	Female
Average Hourly Salary	29.90006	27.65833
Average of Log(Hourly Salary)	3.32256	3.24604
Base Coefficient	2.29213	1.76777
Education Coefficient	0.04244	0.07238
Average Education	16.06100	16.19018
Exp Coefficient	0.09111	0.08784
Average Exp	6.30196	5.52612
Exp^2 Coefficient	-0.00346	-0.00323
Average Exp^2	65.16362	55.46003

The results in Table 7 show the values needed for the Oaxaca decomposition for the base human capital model. In our sample, females make only 92.50% of what their male counterparts make which is a difference of $2.24 per hour. Females have a slightly higher education average while males have a higher number of average years of technical experience. Since the human capital model is in terms of the log of hourly salary, the left-hand side of the decomposition is the difference between the average of the log of hourly salary for males and the average of the log of hourly salary for males. So 0.07652 is decomposed into explained and unexplained components which are 0.03163 and 0.04494, respectively (the minor differences in the sum of the component parts and the whole is attributed to calculation of the logs and rounding error). Therefore, 58.7% of the salary differences are unexplained by education and experience and could be potentially attributed to gender discrimination. But since the Adjusted R^2 of this model is only around 0.2, this statement probably overstates the actual difference attributed to discrimination because the model may be missing one or more important explanatory variables.

The results in Table 8 show the values needed for the Oaxaca decomposition for the human capital model with OOP and SQL skills. For each skill indicator variable, the average value is simply the proportion possessing this skill. A much greater proportion of males possess the OOP skill but only a slightly higher proportion of males possess the SQL skill. So 0.07652 is decomposed into explained and unexplained components which are 0.04258 and 0.0339494, respectively. Therefore, 44.4% of the salary differences are unexplained by education, experience, OOP skills, and SQL skills and could be potentially attributed to gender discrimination.

If one reviews the earlier human capital model with OOP and SQL skills with the gender indicator (no decomposition) to check for logical consistency with the Oaxaca decomposition, females made only 96.58% compared to their male counterparts. So for the initial 7.5% (100% to 92.5%) difference in hourly salary, 3.4% of this difference can be viewed as "unexplained." This means 45.6% (3.42/7.50) of the

Table 8. Oaxaca decomposition for human capital with skills model

Coefficient or Statistic of Interest	Male	Female
Average Hourly Salary	29.90006	27.65833
Average of Log(Hourly Salary)	3.32256	3.24604
Base Coefficient	2.29799	1.81804
Education Coefficient	0.03864	0.06650
Average Education	16.06100	16.19018
Exp Coefficient	0.09015	0.08632
Average Exp	6.30196	5.52612
Exp^2 Coefficient	-0.00339	-0.00311
Average Exp^2	65.16362	55.46003
OOP Coefficient	0.07700	0.05325
Proportion with OOP Skill	0.54205	0.41275
SQL Coefficient	0.02758	0.04711
Proportion with SQL Skill	0.55251	0.53187

salary differences could be potentially attributed to gender discrimination which is quite close to the 44.4% figure from the Oaxaca decomposition.

Discussion and Concluding Remarks

Education and experience are two well-known major factors that impact salary. Similarly, knowledge of object-oriented programming and SQL also contribute to a software developer's human capital. No additional skills were found that had positive coefficients (contributed to one's human capital) and significantly contributed to the human capital model.

In our sample, males reported making an average of $65,948 per year while their female counterparts made only $59,336 per year. So females make 89.98% of what their male counterparts make which is very close to the U.S. Department of Labor (2002) statistic of 88.92% for computer programmers. Converting the annual figures in our sample to hourly rates (the respondent indicated the average number of hours worked per week), females make only 92.5% of what their male counterparts make which is a difference of $2.24 per hour. Accounting for human capital factors (education, experience, and specific skills) reduces the gender difference to 96.58%. Despite this difference being substantially less (3.42% instead of 10.02%), females making only 96.58% compared to their male counterparts has practical significance given that this difference translates into a few thousand dollars per year for female software developers. To provide validation of this result, the sample was split into male and female subsets. The results for the human capital models, Chow test, and Oaxaca decomposition provides confirmatory evidence of this result.

Some economists may have reservations about our human capital models. If there are salary differences between female and male software developers, these economists might argue that, on average, male software developers are simply more productive than female software developers so they should be paid more, on average. Another plausible explanation for the observed salary differences by gender is that if males generally had greater job responsibilities, they would receive greater salaries. Since no explicit productivity or job responsibility factors are included in our survey, these factors do not appear in our human capital models. So these factors may be responsible for a portion of the unexplained component of the Oaxaca decomposition.

Some concerns about how well-representative our sample is to the population of software developers can be raised. Throughout the chapter, we tried to point out any potential bias or shortcomings in our sample. In final defense of our sample, we feel that our sample is sufficiently good for our analysis by reiterating what Berndt (1991, p. 160) said: "the practicing econometrician in labor economics is typically forced to make use of data that are considerably less than ideal." Of course, it would be desirable to repeat this study with a random sample from the population of software developers and a more extensive questionnaire that may identify additional human capital factors that determine the salary of software developers. This suggests an avenue for future research.

Despite some concerns about our sample and some reservations about our human capital models, we feel that our study provides a good indication of gender/salary differences for software developers. Unfortunately, our best efforts in finding a good human capital model for software developers indicate that gender is still a statistically significant factor in assessing one's human capital.

Our human capital models indicate that education is an important determinant in salary so female software developers (and aspiring female software developers) should be strongly encouraged to increase their educational background by pursuing degrees in IT programs (such as computer science, computer information systems, etc.). In addition, female software developers should be encouraged to acquire specific higher paying skills such as OOP and SQL skills. When entering the workforce, it is vital that women do not underestimate their value (salary). Orazem, Werbel, and McElroy (2003) found that women have lower starting pay expectations than men with similar credentials because women engage in less intensive career planning than men.

References

Ahuja, M.K. (2002). Women in the information technology profession: A literature review, synthesis and research agenda. *European Journal of Information Systems, 11*, 20-34.

Becker, G.S. (1962). Investment in human capital: A theoretical analysis. *Journal of Political Economy, 70*(5, Part 2), S9-S49.

Becker, G.S. (1964). *Human capital: A theoretical and empirical analysis with special reference to education.* National Bureau of Economic Research.

Berndt, E.R. (1991). *The practice of econometrics: Classic and contemporary.* Addison-Wesley.

Chow, G.C. (1960). Tests of equality between subsets of coefficients in two linear regression models. *Econometrica, 28*, 591-605.

Darity, D., & Mason, P. (1988). Evidence on discrimination in employment: Codes of color, codes of gender (in Symposium: discrimination in product, credit and labor markets). *The Journal of Economic Perspectives, 12*(2), 63-90.

Dattero, R., & Galup, S.D. (2004). Programming languages and gender. *Communications of the ACM, 47*(1), 99-102.

Ehrenberg, R.G., & Smith, R.S. (1997). *Modern labor economics: Theory and public policy* (6th ed.). Addison-Wesley.

Gosse, M.A. (2002). *The gender pay gap in the New Zealand Public Service* (Working Paper No. 15). New Zealand State Services Commission.

Greenhaus, J., Parasuraman, S., & Wormley, W. (1990). Effects of race on organizational experiences, job performance evaluations, and career outcomes. *Academy of Management Journal, 33*(1), 64-86.

Keith, K., & McWilliams, A. (1999). The return to mobility and job search by gender. *Industrial and Labor Relations Review, 52*(3), 460-477.

Kulik, L. (2000). A comparative analysis of job search intensity, attitudes toward unemployment, and related responses. *Journal of Occupational and Organizational Psychology, 73*, 487-500.

Levitin, T., Quinn, R.P., & Staines, G.L. (1971). Sex discrimination against the American working women. *American Behavioral Scientist, 15*(2), 238-254.

Mincer, J. (1958). Investment in human capital and personal income distribution. *Journal of Political Economy, 66*(4), 281-302.

Mincer, J. (1962). On-the-job training: Costs, returns, and some implications. *Journal of Political Economy, 70*(5, Part 2), S50-S79.

Mincer, J. (1974). *Schooling, experience and earnings.* Columbia University Press for the National Bureau of Economic Research.

Moyes, G., Williams, P., & Quigley, B. (2000). The relation between perceived treatment discrimination and job satisfaction among African-American accounting professionals. *Accounting Horizons, 14*(1), 21-49.

Oaxaca, R. (1973). Male-female wage differentials in urban labor markets. *International Economic Review, 14*(3), 693-709.

Orazem, P.F., Werbel, J.D., & McElroy, J.C. (2003). Market expectation, job search, and gender differences in starting pay. *Journal of Labor Research, 24*(2), 307-321.

Panteli, A., Stack, J., & Ramsay, H. (1999). Gender and professional ethics in the IT industry. *Journal of Business Ethics, 22*, 51-61.

Reinsmith, L. (2002). Proving an employer's intent: Disparate treatment discrimination and the stray remarks doctrine after Reeves v. Sanderson Plumbing Products. *Vanderbilt Law Review, 55*(1), 219-260.

Roy, A. (1950). The distribution of earnings and of individual output. *Economic Journal, 60*(3), 489-505.

Schultz, T.W. (1960). Capital formation by education. *Journal of Political Economy, 68*(6), 571-583.

Schultz, T.W. (1961). Investment in human capital. *American Economic Review, 51*(1), 1-17.

Smith, A. (1937). *The wealth of nations* (reprinted ed., originally published in 1776). Random House.

Truman, G., & Baroudi, J. (1994). Gender differences in the information systems managerial ranks: An assessment of potential discriminatory practices. *Management Information Systems Quarterly, 18*(2), 129-141.

U.S. Department of Labor. (2002). *Bureau of Labor Statistics, Employment and Earnings.* Author.

Von Hellens, L., Pringle, R., Nielsen, S., & Greenhill, A. (2000). People, business and IT skills: The perspective of women in the IT industry. In *Proceedings of the Association for Computing Machinery Special Interest Group on Computer Personnel Research,* April 8, 2000, Chicago IL, (pp. 152-157).

Appendix: Data Treatment

We have adopted the following rules in attempting to make the self-selected dataset clean. By doing so, some legitimate observations, in addition to the obvious outliers, may have been removed. But it is our belief that it is better to stay on the safe side.

Items	Exclusion Rules	Rational
Age	Age 1 (18 under), 7 (60-64) and 8 (65 and over)	Lack of representation
Education	Education 1 and Education 10	1 is default value and 10 is Other, which is unknown to us.
Job Title	35: Non-IT: Executive/Corporate 36: Non-IT: Financial 37: Non-IT: Manufacturing/Operations	Our interest is limited to ITP.
Hours per Week	Category 1 (< 20 hours/week)	This is the default value and if not careful enough respondents would have unintentionally selected it.
Country	Non-USA countries	Our Intention is to focus on USA
Age * Exp	(Age 18-24) AND (Experience of 11 years or more)	It is unlikely for young people to acquire this many years of experience

Chapter III

Exploring the Effectiveness of Information Security Policies

Neil F. Doherty, Loughborough University, UK

Heather Fulford, Loughborough University, UK

Abstract

Ensuring the security of corporate information assets has become an extremely complex, challenging and high-priority activity, due partly to their growing organisational importance, but also because of their increasing vulnerability to attacks from viruses, hackers, criminals, and human error. Consequently, organisations are having to prioritise the security of their computer systems, to ensure that their information assets retain their accuracy, confidentiality, and availability. Whilst the importance of the information security policy (InSPy) in ensuring the security of information is widely acknowledged, there has, to date, been little empirical analysis of its impact or effectiveness in this role. To help fill this gap an exploratory study was initiated that sought to investigate the relationship between the uptake and application of information security policies and the accompanying levels of security breaches. To this end a questionnaire was designed, validated, and then targeted at IT managers within large organisations in the United Kingdom. The findings, presented in this chapter, are somewhat surprising, as they show no statistically significant relationships between the adoption of information security policies and the incidence or severity of security breaches. The chapter concludes by exploring the possible interpretations of this unexpected finding, and its implications for the practice of information security management.

Introduction

For the past two decades it has been argued that an "*information revolution*" is taking place within organisations, which has made information the critical input to strategic planning and decision making, as well as the day to day control of organisational operations. Indeed, it is often contended that information is now analogous to an organisation's lifeblood: should the flow of information become seriously restricted or compromised, then the organisation may wither and die. However, if applied effectively as a strategic resource, information investments can result in the realisation of significant corporate benefits. As McPherson (1996) argues, "information is vital to the success of the business and will be accountable for a significant share of the business's various indicators of success, including its cash flow and market value." Consequently, organisations must make every effort to ensure that their information resources retain their accuracy, integrity, and availability. However, ensuring the security of corporate information assets has become an extremely complex and challenging activity due to the growing value of information resources and the increased levels of interconnectivity between information systems, both within and between organisations (Garg, Curtis, & Halper, 2003). Indeed, the high incidence of security breaches suggests that many organisations are failing to manage their information resources effectively (Dhillon, 2004b). One increasingly important mechanism for protecting corporate information, and in so doing reducing the occurrence of security breaches, is through the formulation and application of a formal information security policy (InSPy) (e.g., Baskerville & Siponen, 2002; Doherty & Fulford, 2006). Rees, Bandyopadhyay, and Spafford (2003, p. 101) provide a useful overview of the role of the information security policy, when they suggest that it should be "high-level, technology-neutral, concern risks, set directions and procedures, and define penalties and counter-measures, if the policy is transgressed."

The role and importance of information security policies and the incidence and severity of security breaches are both topics that have attracted significant attention in the literature, but there is little evidence that these topics have been explicitly linked. Consequently, there has been little empirical exploration of the extent to which information security policies are effective, in terms of reducing security breaches. The aim of this chapter is to help fill this gap by reporting the results of a study that sought to empirically explore the relationship between the uptake and application of information security policies and the incidence of security breaches. The remainder of this chapter is organised into the following five sections: a review of the literature and a description of the conceptual framework; a discussion of the research methods employed; a presentation of the findings; a discussion of their importance; and finally the conclusions and recommendations for future research.

Conceptual Background

This section aims to present a discussion of the literature with regard to the role and importance of the InSPy and the common security threats, which such policies are intended to prevent. The section concludes with a critique of this literature, and the presentation of the conceptual framework for our study.

The Role of the Information Security Policy

The broad aim of the information security policy is to provide the "ideal operating environment" for the management of information security (Barnard & von Solms, 1998), by defining: "the broad boundaries of information security" as well as the "responsibilities of information resource users" (Hone & Eloff, 2002b, p. 145). More specifically a good security policy should "outline individual responsibilities, define authorized and unauthorized uses of the systems, provide venues for employee reporting of identified or suspected threats to the system, define penalties for violations, and provide a mechanism for updating the policy" (Whitman, 2004, p. 52). The InSPy also has an important role to play in emphasising management's commitment to, and support for, information security (Hone & Eloff, 2002b; Kwok & Longley, 1999). Whilst the InSPy provides the framework for facilitating the prevention, detection, and response to security breaches, the policy document is typically supported by standards that tend to have a more technical or operational focus (Dhillon, 1997).

In recent years, a consensus has emerged—both within the academic and practitioner communities – that the security of corporate information resources is predicated upon the formulation and application of an appropriate information security policy (e.g., Rees et al., 2003). As Hinde (2002, p. 315) puts it, the information security policy is now the "sine qua non (indispensable condition) of effective security management." In a similar vein, von Solms and von Solms (2004, p. 374) note that the information security policy is the "heart and basis" of successful security management. However, whilst an InSPy may play an important role in effective information security management, there is growing recognition that the policy is unlikely to be a successful security tool unless organisations adhere to a number of important prescriptions in their policy implementation (e.g., Hone & Eloff, 2002b). The following are probably the most commonly cited examples of best practice guidelines:

1.   The policy must be widely and strongly disseminated throughout the organisation (Hone & Eloff, 2002a, b; ISO, 2000; Sipponen, 2000);

2.   The policy must be frequently reviewed and revised (Higgins, 1999; Hone & Eloff, 2002a; Hong, Chi, Chao, & Tang, 2003).

It has also been suggested that policies must be tailored to the culture of the organisation (Hone & Eloff, 2002b; ISO, 2000); well aligned with corporate objectives (ISO, 2000; Rees et al., 2003); and rigorously enforced (David, 2002). While the literature with respect to the facilitators of effective information security policy utilisation is undoubtedly growing, no previous studies could be found that sought to empirically explore the importance of different success factors. More importantly, there is a very significant gap in the literature with respect to empirical studies that explicitly seek to explore the role of the InSPy in the prevention of common security threats. Indeed, given the recent concerns that some commentators have expressed (e.g., Hone & Eloff, 2002b; Karyda, Kiountouzis, & Kokolakis, 2005), with respect to the InSPy's effectiveness, the need for well-focused, empirical research in this domain has probably never been greater.

Threats to the Security of Information Assets

Information resources can only retain their integrity, confidentiality, and availability if they can be protected from the growing range of threats that is arrayed against them (Garg et al., 2003). It has been noted that security threats come both from within and from outside the organisation (Hinde, 2002). For example, common internal threats include "mistakes by employees" (Mitchell, Marcella, & Baxter, 1999) and some categories of computer-based fraud (Dhillon, 1999), whilst attacks by hackers (Austin & Darby, 2003) and viruses (de Champeaux, 2002) are the most commonly cited types of external threat. The increasing vulnerability of computer-based information systems is underlined by the growing cost of security breaches (Austin & Darby, 2003). For example, Garg et al. (2003) estimate the cost of significant security breaches, such as "denial of service attacks" to be in the range of "$17-28 million." Given the growing cost of security breaches, many surveys have been undertaken that have sought to quantify the range and significance of threats that face computer-based information systems. A review of these surveys (e.g., Loch, Carr, & Warkentin, 1992; Mitchell et al., 1999; Whitman, 2004), suggest that the

Table 1. Common types of security breaches

Type of Breach	Description
Computer Virus	Computer programs that have the capability to automatically replicate themselves across systems and networks.
Hacking Incidents	The penetration of organisational computer systems by unauthorised outsiders, who are then free to manipulate data.
Unauthorised Access	The deliberate abuse of systems, and the data contained therein, by authorised users of those systems.
Theft of Resources	The theft of increasingly valuable hardware, software, and information assets.
Computer-based Fraud	Information systems, especially financial systems, are vulnerable to individuals who seek to defraud an organisation.
Human Error	The accidental destruction, or incorrect entry, of data by computer users.
Natural Disasters	Damage to computing facilities or data resources, caused by phenomena such as earthquakes, floods, or fires.
Damage by Employee	Disgruntled employees may seek revenge by damaging their employer's computer systems.

breaches presented in Table 1 are probably the most common and the most significant threats. Whilst the threats to the security of information systems are both well documented and well understood, there is a continuing worry that such issues have not been successfully countered, because as Watson (2004) suggests, the security of IT systems is still the most pressing problem facing IT directors. There is, therefore, a pressing need for more research that can highlight any strategies or approaches that might reduce the incidence and severity of security breaches.

Conceptual Framework and Research Hypotheses

The summary of the literature suggests that there are growing literatures both with regard to the role of the information security policy and the nature and incidence of security breaches. Moreover, there is a general acceptance that the information security policy is an important, if not the most important, means of preventing such breaches (e.g., Loch et al., 1992; Mitchell et al., 1999; Whitman, 2004). It is perhaps surprising that, to date, there has been little conceptual or empirical scrutiny to determine whether the incidence and severity of security breaches can be reduced through the adoption of an information security policy. The aim of the remainder of this section is to describe the study designed to fill this gap, before articulating the specific research hypotheses and presenting the research framework. It should be noted that a full discussion of the design of the questionnaire, and the operationalisation of the constructs discussed in this section, is deferred to the following section. Given the lack of empirical research in the area, it was felt that an exploratory piece of work that embraced a wide range of issues would be most appropriate. To this end the aim of the study was to explore how a variety of issues relating to the uptake and application of information security policies impacted upon the incidence of security breaches within large organisations. Based upon our review of the literature, it is possible to hypothesise that a number of distinct aspects of the InSPy might influence the incidence of security breaches. Each of these areas is represented as a significant construct on the conceptual framework (see Figure 1), and each can be linked to a research hypothesis, as described now:

The Existence of an InSPy

The review of literature highlighted the strength of the consensus with regard to the importance of information security policy in countering security breaches (e.g., Loch et al., 1992; Mitchell et al., 1999; Whitman, 2004). It is therefore reasonable to propose the following hypothesis:

- **H1:** Those organisations that *have a documented InSPy* are likely to have fewer security breaches, in terms of both frequency and severity, than those organisations that *do not*.

The Age of the InSPy

The literature has relatively little to say about the longevity of information security policies. However, the following hypothesis articulates the assumption that organisations with a long history of utilising such policies might be more experienced, and therefore effective in security management:

- **H2:** Those organisations that have had an InSPy in place for *many years* are likely to have fewer security breaches, in terms of both frequency and severity, than those organisations that *have not*.

The Updating of the ISP

There is a growing—yet empirically untested—view within the literature (e.g., Higgins, 1999; Hone & Eloff, 2002a) that the InSPy should be updated regularly. Consequently, the following hypothesis can be proposed:

- **H3:** Those organisations that update their InSPy *frequently* are likely to have fewer security breaches, in terms of both frequency and severity, than those organisations that *do not*.

The Scope of the ISP

It has been suggested that the scope of an InSPy might vary greatly, depending upon which national or international information security standard has been adopted (Hone & Eloff, 2002b). What is less clear is how the scope of a policy might effect its successful deployment. However, it seems reasonable to propose the following relationship between the scope of the InSPy and the effectiveness of an organisation's security management:

- **H4:** Those organisations that have a policy with a *broad scope* are likely to have fewer security breaches, in terms of both frequency and severity, than those organisations that *do not*.

The Adoption of Best Practice

The International Standard (ISO, 2000) has some very clear advice about the factors that are important in ensuring the successful application of an InSPy, most of which have not been explicitly covered by the previous hypotheses. The corollary of this, as presented in the following hypothesis, is that the adoption of these success factors should lead to a reduction in security breaches:

- **H5:** Those organisations that have adopted a wide variety of *best practice factors* are likely to have fewer security breaches, in terms of both frequency and severity, than those organisations that *have not*.

It should be noted that the original intention was to explore whether the active dissemination of an information security policy affected the incidence or severity of security breaches (e.g., ISO, 2000; Hone & Eloff, 2002a, b). However, as 99% of our sample reported that they actively disseminated their policies, it was not possible to test this hypothesis. Whilst the hypotheses have been formulated to represent the outcomes that the researchers believed to be the most likely, it was recognised that in some cases, alternative yet equally plausible results might be produced. For example, it might be that the existence of an InSPy is associated with a high incidence of security breaches, in circumstances in which the policy has been implemented in direct response to a poor security record. The possibility of alternative hypotheses is further considered in the fifth section.

The urgent need for more research and new insights in the information security domain was recently highlighted by Dhillon (2004b, p. 4), who noted: "information security problems have been growing at an exponential rate." In a similar vein, Kotulic and Clark (2004, p. 605) argue that "the organizational level information security domain is relatively new and under researched. In spite of this, it may prove to be one of the most critical areas of research, necessary for supporting the viability of the firm." It was therefore envisaged that our study might provide some important new insights, at the organisational level, as to how the incidence and severity of security breaches might be controlled.

Figure 1. Conceptual model of study

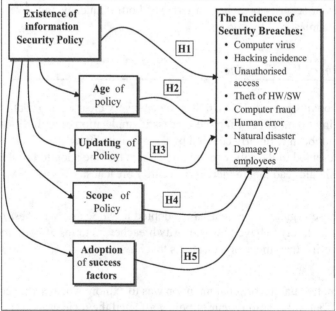

Research Design

To successfully explore the five research hypotheses described in the previous section, it was necessary to employ survey methods, so that the resultant data could be subjected to a rigorous statistical analysis. The aim of this section is to review how the questionnaire was designed, validated, and ultimately executed, and then to describe the characteristics of the sample.

Questionnaire Development, Validation, and Targeting

A detailed questionnaire was used to collect the data necessary to explore the research hypotheses proposed in the previous section. The questionnaire was organised into the following four sections:

- **Security Breaches:** Respondents were asked to report on the incidence and severity of each of the eight most common types of security breach (see Table 1), that their organisations had experienced over the previous two years. The incidence variable was operationalised as a four point ordinal scale (0; 1-5; 6-10; >10), whilst the severity of breaches was measured using a five-point Likert scale.

- **The Existence and Updating of the Information Security Policy:** This section sought to determine whether a responding organisation had a documented InSPy, and if it did, how old it was, and how often it was updated.

- **The Scope of the Information Security Policy:** This section of the questionnaire was designed to evaluate the coverage of the information security policy. The respondent was presented with a list of eleven distinct issues, such as "disclosure of information", "Internet access," and "viruses, worms, and trojans" that an information security policy might reasonably be expected to cover. These items have all been explicitly derived from the International Standard (ISO, 2000), or from a "white paper" published by the SANS Institute (Canavan, 2003). For each of these issues, the respondent was invited to indicate whether the issue was covered in "the policy document only", through the "policy document and a supplementary procedure," or "not explicitly covered" through the InSPy.

- **Best Practice in Information Security Policy Adoption:** The International Standard on information security management (ISO, 2000) suggests that there are ten distinct factors that might influence the success of an information security policy, such as "visible commitment from management" and "a good understanding of security requirements." For each of these factors, the respondents were asked to indicate the extent to which their organisation was successful in adopting that factor, using a five-point Likert scale.

As there are few previous survey-based, empirical studies that explicitly address the application of information security policies, it was not possible to adapt specific questions and item measures from the existing literature. Consequently, once a draft questionnaire had been created, it was necessary to subject it to a rigorous validation process. More specifically, the draft questionnaire was initially validated through a series of pretests, first with four experienced IS researchers, and then, after some modifications, it was retested with five senior IT professionals, all of whom had some responsibility for information security. The pretesters were asked to critically appraise the questionnaire, focusing primarily on issues of instrument content, clarity, question wording, and validity, before providing detailed feedback, via interviews. The pretests were very useful, as they resulted in a number of enhancements being made to the structure of the survey and the wording of specific questions. Having refined the questionnaire, a pilot study exercise was also undertaken, which provided valuable insights into the likely response rate and analytical implications for the full survey.

As the InSPy is essentially a managerial "direction-giving" document (Hone & Eloff, 2002b, p. 14), rather than a technical document, it was recognised that the most appropriate individuals to target would be executives with a high degree of managerial responsibility for information systems and technology. Senior IT executives were, therefore, explicitly targeted, as it was envisaged that they could provide the required organisational and managerial perspective. A list of the addresses of IT directors, from large UK-based organisations, was purchased from a commercial research organisation. The decision to target only larger firms (firms employing more than 250 people) was based on the premise that small firms have few, if any, dedicated IT staff (Prembukar & King, 1992). A total of 219 valid responses were received from the 2,838 questionnaires mailed out, representing a response rate of 7.7%. Whilst this response rate is rather disappointing, it is not perhaps surprising given the increasingly sensitive nature of information security. For example, in an article titled "Why Aren't There More Information Security Studies?" Kotulic and Clark (2004, p. 604) concluded that "it is nearly impossible to extract information of this nature (relating to information security) by mail from business organisations without having a major supporter." Consequently, whilst the sample was smaller than had been originally hoped, it was probably as good as could be expected, under the circumstances.

Sample Characteristics and Response Bias

The sample could be characterised in terms of both the size of the responding organisations and the sectors in which they are primarily operating. Of the valid respondents, 44% were employed in organisations having less than 1,000 employees, 33% were based in organisations with between 1,000 and 5,000 employees, and the remaining 23% in larger organisations with over 5,000 employees. Whilst the responses were also found to have come from a wide variety of industrial sectors, four were particularly well represented: manufacturing (24% of sample), public services (20%), health (7%), and wholesale/retail (6%). Respondents were also asked to indicate the geographical spread of their organisation as it was envisaged that this might have an impact on their need for a formal information security policy. The majority of responding organisations (50%) operated from multiple locations within the UK, while a further 33% of organisations operated from multiple sites, both within the UK and abroad, and the final 17% of the sample were located at a single site within the UK.

When undertaking survey-based research, there is always the danger that the results will be undermined, or even invalidated, through the introduction of bias. It is, therefore, important that active measures are taken to reduce the likelihood of bias having any such negative effects. In this research the content validity of the constructs has been established through the process of initially linking the variables to the research literature and then refining them through an extensive and comprehensive process of pretesting and pilot testing. Any sample bias introduced through the loss of data from nonrespondents is often harder to establish, as these data are not easily obtainable. However, it is possible to approximate this bias by comparing the answer patterns of early and late respondents (Lindner, Murphy, & Briers, 2001). Consequently, in this study, "early" and "late" responses were compared along key dimensions, such as the existence of policy, the age of the policy, the frequency of updating, and severity of breaches, to test for nonresponse bias. An independent samples t-test indicated that there were no significant differences in the profile of responses at the 5.0% level. These results imply that no detectable response bias exists in the sample and that the results are generalisable within the boundary of the sample frame.

Research Findings

This section explores the five research hypotheses, as presented in the second section, through a quantitative analysis of the survey data. Before reviewing the evidence relating to each of these hypotheses, it is important to summarise and discuss the data relating to both the incidence and significance of security breaches, as these two data items are used as the dependent variable throughout the analyses. It is

Table 2. The incidence and severity of security breaches

Type of breach	Incidence of breaches				Severity of worst breach					
	Approximate no. of breaches in last 2 years				*Fairly Insignificant*				*Highly Significant*	*Mean value*
	0	**1-5**	**6-10**	**> 10**	**1**	**2**	**3**	**4**	**5**	
Computer virus	6	111	23	77	45	65	47	35	19	2.59
Hacking incident	142	66	1	5	42	21	10	5	4	1.92
Unauthorised access	106	83	13	10	32	42	21	5	7	2.23
Theft of resources	50	123	24	19	43	52	48	20	8	2.38
Computer-based fraud	187	23	0	2	15	10	3	6	2	2.15
Human error	41	85	19	65	32	61	43	23	10	2.48
Natural disaster	160	54	2	1	16	24	9	11	5	2.52
Damage by employees	185	28	0	0	20	8	7	2	2	1.82

beyond the scope of this chapter to present a detailed, descriptive analysis of the data relating to the uptake and application of information security policies. However, this information is available in a previous paper by the authors (Fulford & Doherty, 2003). Table 2 presents a simple descriptive analysis of the data relating to the incidence and severity of security breaches.

It is interesting to note that all eight potential types of security breach have been experienced within our sample and that there appears to be a relationship between the incidence of breaches and their perceived impact. For example, the computer virus and human error are both a very common type of breach and both have a significant impact, when they do strike. At the other end of the scale, damage by disgruntled employees, hacking incidents, and computer-based fraud all occur infrequently and have a relatively insignificant impact where they do occur. The only type of breach to obviously break this pattern, is natural disasters, which despite occurring rarely, do have a significant impact.

The Impact of the Adoption of an InSPy on Security Breaches

The vast majority of respondents (77%), in our sample, reported that their organisation had a formal, documented InSPy, with the remaining 23% of organisations confirming that they did not. It was therefore both possible and desirable to explore the degree of association between the adoption of an InSPy and the resultant level of security breaches. The results of a series of chi-squared tests suggest that there is no statistical association between the adoption of an InSPy and the incidence of

Table 3. Relationship between the adoption of an InSPy and the incidence and severity of security breaches

Type of breach	Incidence of breaches (Chi-squared analysis)			Severity of worst breach (One-way ANOVA)			
	Pearson Value	Deg. of freedom	2-sided Prob.	Yes	No	F Ratio	F prob.
Computer virus	0.730	3	0.878	2.59	2.69	0.215	0.644
Hacking incident	5.733	3	0.111	1.92	1.72	0.422	0.518
Unauthorised access	3.090	3	0.378	2.23	2.00	0.730	0.395
Theft of resources	1.905	3	0.607	2.38	2.51	0.429	0.513
Computer-based fraud	1.892	2	0.300	2.15	2.25	0.036	0.851
Human error	5.388	3	0.144	2.48	2.67	0.743	0.390
Natural disaster	6.469	3	0.089	2.52	2.32	0.361	0.550
Damage by employees	0.003	1	1.000	1.82	2.30	1.210	0.279

Note: A chi-squared test was used to test the association between the four categories of incidence (0, 1-5, 6-10, >10) and the two classes of InSPy existence (yes, no), whilst ANOVA was used to compare the mean severity of breaches and the two classes of InSPy existence.

security breaches (see Table 3, columns 2-4). An analysis of variance (ANOVA) was also used to determine whether there was any association between the adoption of InSPys and the severity of each of the distinct types of security breaches (see Table 3, columns 5-8).

An inspection of the data in Table 3 indicates that there are no statistically significant associations between the existence of an information security policy, and either the incidence or the severity of any of the eight types of security breach. This is a particularly surprising result, given the prevailing orthodoxy that the InSPy is the primary mechanism for preventing security breaches (e.g., Rees et al., 2003). However, based upon this analysis, hypothesis H1 must be rejected.

The Impact of the Age of an InSPy on Security Breaches

It was envisaged that the greater experience of those organisations that had utilised an information security policy for many years might be manifested in more effective security management practices, and thus fewer security breaches. As the respondents had been asked to estimate the number of years that their organisations had actively used an InSPy, as a simple integer, the degree of association between the age of a policy and the incidence/severity of security breaches was explored using ANOVA (Table 4, columns 2-7) and correlation (Table 4, columns 8-9). The findings

Table 4. Relationship between the age of an InSPy and the incidence/severity of security breaches

Type of breach	Incidence of breaches (One-way ANOVA)						Severity of worst breach (correlation)	
	0	1-5	6-10	>10	F Ratio	F Prob.	Pearson Value	2-sided Significance
Computer virus	2.0	3.7	3.0	5.1	2.3	.08	-0.05	0.501
Hacking incident	3.7	4.7	5.0	5.0	.77	.51	-0.05	0.718
Unauthorised access	3.5	3.9	4.5	10.1	6.4	.00**	-0.08	0.443
Theft of resources	4.1	3.7	3.4	7.27	3.7	.01*	-0.20	0.025*
Computer-based fraud	3.9	6.14	-	3.00	2.8	.07	-0.13	0.513
Human error	3.9	3.5	3.7	4.9	1.2	.31	-0.00	0.963
Natural disaster	4.1	3.8	2.8	-	.23	.80	-0.15	0.335
Damage by employees	7.8	8.9	-	-	2.9	.09	-0.19	0.332

*Note: * Result significant at the 5% level; ** Result significant at the 1% level*

(see Table 4) indicate that there are two significant associations between the age of the policy and the incidence of security breaches. However, an inspection of this data suggests that in both cases, where there is a significant result, the decreased incidence of security breaches is associated with recently deployed policies, rather than those that have been in existence for a long time. Consequently, these findings are important, as they suggest that there may be some complacency creeping into the security practices of those organisations with a longer history of policy utilisation. When it comes to associations between the age of the policy and the severity of breaches, there is only one case (theft of resources) where there is a significant association. In this case, there is some support for hypothesis H2, as the Pearson correlation value is negative, indicating that older policies are associated with less severe breaches. However, given that there is no strong or consistent evidence in support of the hypothesis, H2 must also be rejected.

The Impact of the Frequency of Updating an InSPy on Security Breaches

The relationship between the frequency of updating an information security policy and the incidence and severity of security breaches was explored using a chi-squared analysis (Table 5, columns 2-4) and ANOVA (Table 5, columns 5-8). The frequency with which InSPys were updated was measured using a five item categorical scale

*Table 5. Relationship between the frequency of updating an InSPy and the inci-
dence/severity of security breaches*

Type of breach	Incidence of breaches (Chi-squared analysis)			Severity of worst breach (One-way ANOVA)			
	Pearson Value	Deg. of freedom	2-sided Prob.	< once a year	≥ once a year	F Ratio	F prob.
Computer virus	3.157	3	0.368	2.42	2.75	2.71	0.101
Hacking incident	1.679	3	0.642	2.00	1.92	0.065	0.799
Unauthorised access	3.108	3	0.375	2.21	2.25	0.030	0.864
Theft of resources	2.219	3	0.528	2.35	2.42	0.117	0.733
Computer-based fraud	1.098	2	0.577	2.08	2.20	0.052	0.821
Human error	5.253	3	0.154	2.67	2.42	1.467	0.228
Natural disaster	3.237	2	0.198	2.29	2.72	1.450	0.235
Damage by employees	1.198	1	0.274	1.73	1.87	0.087	0.770

(< *every 2 years; every 2 years; every year; every 6 months;* > *every 6 months*).
To use this variable in a chi-squared analysis, with the "incidence of breaches"
variable, it was necessary to compress the five original categories into just two ("<
once a year" and "≥ once a year"), to ensure that the expected frequencies in every
cell of the contingency table were greater than five, a prerequisite of the chi-squared
approach. Having used a two-category measure of "frequency of updating" for
the chi-squared analysis, it made sense to also use it for the ANOVA, to make the
results more comparable.

The results of the two analyses (see Table 5) indicate that there are no statistically
significant associations between the frequency with which the InSPy is updated
and the incidence and severity of any of the eight types of security breach, and
hypothesis H3 must therefore also be rejected. This result is also surprising in the
face of the prevailing orthodoxy that the InSPy will be more effective if updated
regularly (e.g., Hone & Eloff, 2002b).

The Impact of the Scope of an InSPy on Security Breaches

The scope of information security policies can vary greatly, in terms of the numbers
of issues covered, so it was important to explore whether the scope of the policy
was associated with the incidence and severity of security breaches. As discussed
in the third section, the scope of the policy was investigated by asking respondents
to indicate which issues, from a list of 11 separate issues, were covered in their
policies. Consequently, it was possible to create a new variable—"total issues
covered"—that was the sum of the individual issues covered. This new variable,

Table 6. Relationship between the range of issues covered by an InSPy and the incidence/severity of security breaches

Type of breach	Incidence of breaches (One-way ANOVA)						Severity of worst breach (correlation))	
	0	1-5	6-10	>10	F Ratio	F Prob.	Pearson Value	2-sided Significance
Computer virus	8.0	7.8	7.6	8.4	.79	.49	0.05	0.530
Hacking incident	8.0	7.9	10.0	6.5	.41	.75	-0.04	0.779
Unauthorised access	7.9	8.0	7.9	9.4	.86	.46	0.15	0.169
Theft of resources	7.4	8.0	8.2	9.3	2.4	.10	-0.05	0.536
Computer-based fraud	7.8	9.3	-	5.00	3.4	.04*	0.31	0.122
Human error	8.1	7.9	7.8	8.2	.29	.88	0.02	0.838
Natural disaster	7.9	8.5	3.5	-	3.8	.02*	0.24	0.105
Damage by employees	7.8	8.9	-	-	2.9	.09	0.08	0.678

*Note: * Result significant at the 5% level*

which was in the range 0-11, had a mean of 8.01, and a standard deviation of 2.61. The relationship between the "total issues covered" and the incidence and severity of security breaches was explored using an ANOVA (Table 6, columns 2-7) and a bivariate correlation (Table 6, columns 8-9).

The results, relating to hypothesis H4 are quite interesting as there are some statistically significant results. For example, the range of issues covered is significantly associated with the incidence of both "computer-based fraud" and "natural disasters." However, an inspection of the data (Table 6, columns 2-5) is inconclusive; whilst the incidence of breaches is highest, in both these cases, where the issues covered are lowest, the lowest incidence of breaches is not associated with the highest numbers of issues covered. With regard to the severity of threats, there are no statistically significant associations between number of issues covered by the policy and the severity of security breaches. In summary, given that only 2 out of the 16 individual tests conducted resulted in statistically significant outcomes, there is little in the way of strong evidence in support of hypothesis H4, and it must therefore be rejected.

The Impact of the Adoption of Best Practice on Security Breaches

In order to effectively explore the relationship between the adoption of success factors, and the incidence and severity of security breaches, it was necessary to derive a summated scale for the 10 success factors. An underlying assumption and fundamental requirement for constructing a summated measure of a metric construct is that the item scales all measure the same underlying construct. This was confirmed by undertaking internal reliability tests, using the Cronbach alpha measure, which yielded a statistically significant score of 0.87. Having derived the overall measure for the adoption of best practice, ANOVA and correlation analyses were conducted to explore its association with the incidence and severity of security breaches (see Table 7).

The results of these analyses indicate a statistical association between the summated success factors and security breaches, for 2 out of the 16 individual tests conducted. Moreover, an inspection of the data provides some evidence in support of hypothesis H5. For example, success in adopting best practice is associated with a low occurrence of hacking incidents, whereas low success in adopting best practice is associated with a high incidence of hacking incidents. In a similar vein, success in adopting best practice is associated with low severity breaches due to "human error," whereas low success in adopting best practice is associated with high severity incidents of "human error." However, given that only 2 of the 16 individual tests were significant, there is insufficient evidence to support hypothesis H5, and it must, therefore, be rejected.

Table 7. One-way ANOVA between the successful adoption of success factors and the incidence/severity of security breaches

Type of breach	Incidence of breaches (One-way ANOVA)						Severity of worst breach (correlation)	
	0	1-5	6-10	>10	F Ratio	F Prob.	Pearson Value	Two-sided Significance
Computer virus	3.17	2.95	2.85	2.85	0.42	0.74	0.031	0.699
Hacking incident	2.94	2.93	2.50	1.55	3.05	0.03*	0.120	0.365
Unauthorised access	2.99	2.82	2.76	2.75	1.01	0.39	-0.070	0.529
Theft of resources	2.87	2.89	3.01	2.91	0.40	0.75	-0.149	0.097
Computer-based fraud	2.89	2.87	-	2.40	0.27	0.76	0.305	0.138
Human error	2.98	2.87	3.12	2.81	0.99	0.39	-0.189	0.035*
Natural disaster	2.92	2.82	3.20	-	0.50	0.60	0.171	0.255
Damage by employees	2.91	2.86	-	-	0.09	0.76	-0.088	0.655

*Note: * Result significant at the 5% level*

Discussion

It was established in the literature review that the information security policy is now viewed as the basis for the dissemination and enforcement of sound security practices, and as such should help to reduce the occurrence of security breaches (e.g., Loch et al., 1992; Mitchell et al., 1999; Whitman, 2004). Indeed, as Wadlow (2000) notes: "if you ask any security professional what the single most important thing is that you can do to protect your network, they will unhesitatingly say that it is to write a good security policy." It therefore came as something of a surprise, in the present study, to find almost no statistically significant relationships between the adoption of information security policies and the incidence or severity of security breaches. Consequently, it is important to explore the possible interpretations of this unexpected finding. The implications of this study for the practice of information security management are reviewed in this section, and then its limitations are explored.

Although there is little evidence of any formal empirical studies, focusing on the effectiveness of information security policies, the published literature does provide some clues as to why InSPys might be failing to stem the level of security breaches. Amongst these, the following are the most plausible reasons for deficient policies:

- **Difficulties of Raising Awareness:** Sipponen (2000) highlights the problems of policy dissemination in the workplace. If employees are not made aware of a policy, then there is a danger that it will become a "dead" document, rather than an active and effective security management tool. Given that nearly all the respondents in our study claimed to be actively disseminating their policies, questions must be raised about the effectiveness of their dissemination strategies, given the consistently high levels of security breach witnessed. As Hone and Eloff (2002b, p. 15) note, "a common failure of information security policies is that they fail to impact users on the ground."

- **Difficulties of Enforcement:** As David (2002, p. 506) notes, "having a policy and being able to enforce it are totally different things." Hinde (2002) provides evidence that the problem of policy enforcement might primarily stem from the difficulties of getting employees to read and take heed of policies. As Wood (2000, p. 14) notes, the expectation that "users are going to look at a centralized information security policy is just unrealistic and bound to lead to disappointing results."

- **Policy Standards are too Complex:** Many organisations will lack the skills and experience to formulate an information security policy. They will, therefore, typically refer to one of the many international information security standards, such as ISO17799, COBIT, or GMITS (Hone & Eloff, 2002a). Whilst such standards are recognised as a "good starting point for determining what an InSPy should consist of" (Hone & Eloff, 2002a, p. 402), in practice, they can be complex and time consuming to apply (Arnott, 2002).

- **Inadequate Resourcing:** In too many cases, there are "insufficient resources available to devote to the monitoring and enforcement of policies" (Moule & Giavara, 1995, p. 8). Effective security management requires a great deal of time, effort, and money, which many organisations are not prepared to commit.

- **Failure to Tailor Policies:** It has been argued that the security requirements of an organisation will be dependent upon the types of information being processed (Pernul, 1995) and the culture of the organisation (Hone & Eloff, 2002a, p. 402). Consequently, the InSPy must be tailored to its organisational context. However, because many organisations rely on international standards as the point of departure for developing a policy, they often apply a generic solution, rather than tailoring it to their own circumstances.

It is very likely that the factors reviewed here provide at least a partial explanation as to why InSPys are failing to have a significant impact on the incidence and severity of security breaches. However, the drivers for adopting or enhancing an information security policy might also help to explain why all five of our hypotheses were ultimately rejected. Our basic thesis was that organisations that had formulated a policy, which was regularly updated, broad in scope, and adhered to best practice, would have fewer security breaches than those organisations that had not. An alternative thesis might be that rather than deploying policies to prevent breaches, many organisations might be adopting or enhancing a policy in response to a spate of security breaches. However, if there was any significant evidence in support of this alternative thesis, in which the direction of causality is simply reversed, then a large number of statistically significant associations might still have been expected. Consequently, one plausible explanation of our findings is that there is a mixture of drivers: in some instances, policies are doing their job and preventing breaches; in other cases, policies are being implemented or enhanced in response to a high incidence of breaches. It may also be that many organisations are following Dhillon's (2004a) advice that they need to tailor their policies to organisational circumstances, in which case there may be few generalisable rules as to what makes an effective information security policy.

Whilst the discussion might help to explain the apparent ineffectiveness of information security policies, any manager with responsibility for the formulation of an organisation's information security policy needs to heed the messages inherent in these findings. First, the findings suggest that there is no room for complacency; it is not enough simply to produce a policy, even if that policy has a broad scope, adheres to best practice, and is regularly updated. Steps must be taken to ensure that the policy is tailored to its organisational context and then enforced, which in turn means that the policy must be appropriately disseminated and well resourced. Moreover, the results suggest that organisations need to be more proactive in evaluating the effectiveness of their policies: when security breaches occur, the policy should be reviewed to determine how such incidents can be avoided in the future. It is particularly important for those organisations who already deploy an appropriate policy, and who appear to be following best practice in its application, yet who still suffer a high incidence of security breaches, to critically evaluate their security policy and security practices.

This research should also be of interest to the information management research community. As it is one of the first empirical studies to explicitly tackle the relationship between the information security policy and the level of security breaches, many new variables and item measures have been identified and validated; these might be usefully incorporated in future research. The study also has highlighted the need for far more research in this area to further explore the relationship between the information security policy and security breaches and to determine what steps are needed to improve its effectiveness. Furthermore, this study helps to overcome one of the most common criticisms of information security research that it is too technical in its orientation (e.g., Besnard & Arief, 2004; de Paula, Ding, Dourish, Nies, Pillet, Redmiles, Ren, Rode, & Filho, 2005; Wiant, 2005).

Research into the adoption of sophisticated policies, within the organisational context, is an ambitious undertaking, and therefore contains a number of inherent limitations. In particular, the adoption of the survey format restricts the range of issues and constructs that can be explored, the selection of a very narrow sampling frame reduces the generalisability of the results, and finally there is potential response bias associated with the "single-informant." Moreover, the survey approach cannot help to provide meaningful explanations of why no statistically significant findings were derived from our analyses. Consequently, whilst the study provides many interesting insights, these limitations do highlight the need for follow-up studies to be conducted employing different methods, and targeting different populations. When considering future studies, it will be important for researchers to be creative in finding ways of securing organisational buy-in to their studies, to avoid the difficulties of response, witnessed on this and other information security projects (Kotulic & Clarke, 2004)

Concluding Remarks

The work presented in this chapter makes an important contribution to the information security literature as it presents the first empirical study of the relationship between the application of information security policies and the incidence and severity of security breaches. The key result of this research is the finding that there is no statistically significant relationship between the existence and application of information security policies and the incidence or severity of security breaches. Whilst a number of plausible explanations have been proffered to help understand this, a somewhat surprising finding, there is an urgent need for follow-up studies to explore what can be done to improve the effectiveness of information security policies. To this end, a series of follow-up interviews and focus groups to help interpret and explain the results of the quantitative analysis are currently being planned. As the project unfolds, it is anticipated that the findings will help organisations to better understand the value of security policies and to pinpoint the policy areas for prioritisation.

Acknowledgments

The provisional version of the research framework upon which this chapter is based was presented at the IRMA Conference (Doherty & Fulford, 2003). The authors would like to thank the chapter reviewers and conference participants for their helpful comments, as these greatly shaped our thinking with regard to this chapter.

References

Arnott, S. (2002, February 28). Strategy paper. *Computing*, p. 16.

Austin, R.D., & Darby, C.A. (2003, June). The myth of secure computing. *Harvard Business Review*, 121-126.

Barnard, L., & von Solms, R. (1998). The evaluation and certification of information security against BS 7799. *Information Management and Computer Security*, 6(2), 72-77.

Baskerville, R., & Siponen, M. (2002). An information security meta-policy for emergent organisations. *Information Management and Computer Security*, 15(5/6), 337-346.

Besnard, D., & Arief, B. (2004). Computer security impaired by legitimate users. *Computers & Security*, 23, 253-264.

Canavan, S. (2003). *An information security policy development guide for large companies*. Retrieved July 9, 2006, from SANS Institute, http://www.SANS.org

David, J. (2002). Policy enforcement in the workplace. *Computers and Security, 21*(6), 506-513.

De Campeaux, D. (2002). Taking responsibility for worms and viruses. *Communications of the ACM, 45*(4), 15-16.

de Paula, R., Ding, X., Dourish, P., Nies, K., Pillet, B., Redmiles, D.F., Ren, J., Rode, J.A., & Filho, R.S. (2005). In the eye of the beholder: A visualization-based approach to information security. *International Journal of Human-Computer Studies, 63*, 5-24.

Dhillon, G. (1997). *Managing information systems security*. London: Macmillan Press.

Dhillon, G. (1999). Managing and controlling computer misuse. *Information Management and Computer Security, 7*(4), 171-175.

Dhillon, G. (2004a). Realizing benefits of an information security program. *Business Process Management Journal, 10*(3), 21-22.

Dhillon, G. (2004b). Guest editorial: The challenge of managing information security. *International Journal of Information Management, 24*, 3-4.

Doherty, N.F., & Fulford, H. (2003). Information security policies in large organisations: Developing a conceptual framework to explore their impact. In *Proceedings of the Information Technology and Organizations: Trends, Issues, Challenges and Solutions IRMA International Conference*, Philadelphia, pp.1052-1053.

Doherty, N.F., & Fulford, H. (2006). Aligning the information security policy with the strategic information systems plan. *Computers & Security, 25*, 55-63.

Fulford, H., & Doherty, N.F. (2003). The application of information security policies in large UK-based organizations. *Information Management and Computer Security, 11*(3), 106-114.

Garg, A., Curtis, J., & Halper, H. (2003). Quantifying the financial impact of information security breaches. *Information Management and Computer Security, 11*(2), 74-83.

Higgins, H.N. (1999). Corporate system security: Towards an integrated management approach. *Information Management and Computer Security, 7*(5), 217-222.

Hinde, S. (2002). Security surveys spring crop. *Computers and Security, 21*(4), 310-321.

Hone, K., & Eloff, J.H.P. (2002a). Information security policy: what do international security standards say. *Computers & Security, 21*(5), 402-409.

Hone, K., & Eloff, J.H.P. (2002b). What makes an effective information security policy. *Network Security, 20*(6), 14-16.

Hong, K., Chi, Y., Chao, L., & Tang, J. (2003). An integrated system theory of information security management. *Information Management and Computer Security, 11*(5), 243-248.

ISO. (2000). *Information technology. Code of practice for information security management—ISO 17799*. International Standards Organization.

Karyda, M., Kiountouzis, E.A., & Kokolakis, S. (2005) *Information systems security policies: A contextual perspective Computers and Security, 24*(3), 246-260.

Kotulic , A.G., & Clark, J.G. (2004). Why there aren't more information security research studies. *Information & Management, 41*, 597-607.

Kwok, L., & Longley, D. (1999). Information security management & modelling. *Information Management and Computer Security, 7*(1), 30-39.

Lindner, J.R., Murphy, T.H., & Briers, G.E. (2001). Handling non-response in social science research. *Journal of Agricultural Education, 42*(4), 43-53.

Loch, K.D., Carr, H.H., & Warkentin, M.E. (1992). Threats to information systems: Today's reality, yesterday's understanding. *MIS Quarterly, 16*(2), 173-186.

McPherson, P. K. (1996). The inclusive value of information. *International Federation for Information and Documentation—48th Congress,* pp. 41-60, Graz.

Mitchell, R.C., Marcella, R., & Baxter, G. (1999). Corporate information security. *New Library World, 100*(1150), 213-277.

Moule, B., & Giavara, L. (1995) Policies, procedures and standards: an approach for implementation. *Information management and computer security, 3*(3), 7-16.

Pernul, G. (1995). Information systems security: Scope, state of the art and evaluation of techniques. *International Journal of Information Management, 15*(3), 165-180.

Premkumar, G., & King, W.R. (1992). An empirical assessment of information systems planning and the role of information systems in organizations. *Journal of Management Information Systems, 19*(2), 99-125.

Rees, J., Bandyopadhyay, S., & Spafford, E.H. (2003). PFIRES: A policy framework for information security. *Communications of the ACM, 46*(7), 101-106.

Siponen, M. (2000, August). Policies for construction of information systems' security guidelines. In *Proceedings of 15th International Information Security Conference (IFIP TC11/SEC2000)* (pp. 111-120), Beijing, China.

Von Solms, B., & von Solms, R. (2004). The ten deadly sins of information security management. *Computers & Security, 23*, 371-376.

Wadlow, T.A. (2000). *The process of network security*. Reading, MA: Addison-Wesley.

Watson, J. (2004, August 26). CIO's feel the strain of business alignment. *Computing*, p. 5.

Whitman, M.E. (2004). In defense of the realm: understanding threats to information security. *International Journal of Information Management, 24,* 3-4.

Wiant, T.L. (2005). Information security policy's impact on reporting security incidents. *Computers & Security, 24*(6), 448-459.

Wood, C.C. (2000). An unappreciated reason why information security policies fail. *Computer Fraud & Security, 10,* 13-14.

Chapter IV

Competing in the Marketplace:
Incorporating Online Education into Higher Education:
An Organizational Perspective

Deirdre A. Folkers, The Pennsylvania State University – York Campus, USA

Abstract

Higher education has traditionally been very slow moving, with change being measured in years or even decades. Recently, external forces have combined to challenge higher education's resistance to change. These forces range from the growth of the Internet, to the emergence of a new student population, to a continued decline in governmental support. Together these changes have caused institutions to reexamine both how they function and how they interact with the outside world. Distance education has become a concrete manifestation of the changes in higher education; however, the incorporation of online education often has far-reaching effects, impacting the organization financially, structurally, and culturally. This article will examine the external forces that are challenging higher education. It will further examine the managerial, organizational, and cultural issues that arise as colleges and universities seek to move from the physical "marketplace" to the virtual world of the "marketspace" through the integration of distance education programs.

Introduction

Few would describe higher education as fast paced. To the contrary, higher educa-tion has traditionally been very slow moving, where change can often be measured in years or even decades. As one article describes it, higher education is "highly democratic, yet glacial in its pace" (Levine & Sun, 2002, p. 6). Nonetheless, in the last 10 years, what some might see as higher education's resistance to change has been tested by a number of external forces. While these forces do not necessarily challenge higher education as a fundamental provider of knowledge, they do strongly challenge the ways in which this role is manifest (Duderstadt, 1997).

The external factors that have come to bear on higher education represent a conver-gence of forces. These include technological changes, the most significant of which is the phenomenal growth in the Internet. They include changes within the student population—specifically the emergence of the adult, nontraditional student and the new competitors that have materialized to serve these students (Twigg, 2002). They also include significant changes in the level of funding and support provided to higher education (Selingo, 2003). Taken together, these forces have caused those within higher education to begin to look at how higher education functions, and in many cases to begin to change how it interacts with the greater world. In some cases, these responses have been successful; in others they have not.

The growth of distance (online) education has been a manifest change that has oc-curred in response to these environmental challenges. This article will examine the external forces that are challenging higher education. It will further examine the managerial, organizational, and cultural issues that arise as colleges and universities seek to respond to these challenges by moving from the physical "marketplace" to the virtual "marketspace" through the implementation and integration of distance education programs.

External Changes in the Marketplace

The Need for Lifelong Learning

Increasingly, the acquisition of knowledge has become key to attaining an enhanced standard of living and (to the extent that it is possible) job security (Duderstadt, 1997). Today, approximately 70% of high school graduates in the U.S. go on to attend postsecondary education (Kirst & Venezia, 2001). However, as the pace of change continues to increase, education can no longer end at graduation. It has been estimated that the functional life of a technical degree (i.e., the elapsed time until skills must be updated in order to remain current) is now less than five years (Twigg, 2002); thus today's graduates will need to continually update their skills (O'Donoghue, 2000; Twigg, 2002). This means that adults will have an ongoing relationship with higher education as they seek to learn new information and improve their career opportunities.

This new focus on lifelong learning occurs at a time when many colleges and universities are already experiencing or anticipating large increases in student applications. For example, public institutions in California, Indiana, North Carolina, and Washington are struggling to cope with significant growth in enrollment (Arnone, Hebel, & Schmidt, 2003). These are just some of many states that anticipate more students than current facilities can accommodate (Oblinger & Kidwell, 2000).

The New Majority Student

The emphasis on continual re-education has created a new student population. These students are older and more diverse than their younger counterparts. They are typically part-time students, who live off-campus and have full-time jobs and families (O'Donoghue, 2000). Unlike traditional age students, they do not consider the educational setting to be of great importance. Instead, they concentrate on issues of convenience, with a focus on flexible schedules (Oblinger & Kidwell, 2000; O'Donoghue, 2000); quality (which they are likely to evaluate in terms of customer satisfaction) (Twigg, 2002); cost (low); and service (Duderstadt, 1997). With little loyalty to any one educational institution, these students show a willingness to use their purchasing power in order to attain their goals.

In contrast to traditional students (who account for only 20% of the United States higher education market) (Twigg, 2002), these new students have increasingly turned to distance education. The "typical" online student is over the age of 25, with prior college experience. She (the majority of online students are female) is usually employed, and is highly motivated and disciplined (Blustain, Goldstein, & Lozier, 1999; NEA, 2002). For these students, distance education presents a positive alternative. One distance education student summarized the appeal of distance education by saying, "The flexibility provided by the distance learning format and convenience of schooling at home allowed me to continue to learn and remain in touch with my family" (W. Pauley, personal communicationi, January 24, 2004).

Growth of New Competitors
In response to this new market for distance education, new educational competitors have come into being. These new competitors include for-profit universities such as the University of Phoenix, which now claims more than 150,000 online students (Fair Disclosure Wire, 2006). They also include virtual universities, such as the United Kingdom's Open University (O'Donoghue, 2000). Additionally, corporate

universities such as Motorola Corporation's Motorola University have begun to compete for a share of the new higher education market.

These new competitors specifically target working adults, and offer a great deal of flexibility in their course offerings. For example, Rio Salado College (based in Phoenix, Arizona) begins new online courses every two weeks (Rio Salado, 2003). The University of Phoenix teaches classes on a very compressed schedule. Students schedule a single course at a time, and complete an undergraduate course within five weeks. While some educators might question this as a pedagogical approach, the University of Phoenix reported a 70% growth rate in its online division for 2002 (Olsen, 2002).

Recently, for-profit online institutions received assistance from Congress when it rescinded a long-held rule that required that institutions must offer at least half of their classes in a face-to-face mode in order for the institution's students to be eligible for financial aid. Known as the "50 percent rule," this restriction was originally intended to ameliorate problems encountered with some for-profit trade schools that were seen as little more than diploma mills (Dillon, 2006). The elimination of the requirement followed intense lobbying efforts by for-profit institutions.

Global Competition

The growth of new, flexible competitors offering online courses has created the potential for global competition for students. This has caused a weakening of the geographic barriers that used to exist in student recruitment. Colleges are no longer protected by geographic constraints or the concept of service areas (Twigg, 2002), as competing institutions (private and public, non-profit and for-profit) expand their definitions of geographic boundaries through the establishment of distance education and satellite campuses (Duderstadt, 1997).

Technological Changes

Much of the growth in competition has been fueled by advances in technology, specifically the profound growth of the Internet, which provides the newfound ability to offer instruction to individuals anywhere, at anytime (Duderstadt, 1999; Oblinger & Kidwell, 2000). With the growth of the Internet and the World Wide Web, there has been a vast increase in the number of Web-based resources, and with them the new potential for teaching and learning across the Internet. This new capability presents both an opportunity and a challenge for higher education and its (perhaps more nimble) competitors.

Cost and Funding Concerns

American colleges and universities face these challenges at a time when governmental support for higher education has taken a drastic downturn. The federal government, with its new focus on fighting terrorism and enacting large tax cuts, is unlikely to serve as an increased source of revenue for higher education (Levine & Sun, 2002). Faced with their own budget shortfalls, states have decreased (sometimes dramatically) their appropriations for higher education. The decreases mark an acceleration of a trend that has been active for a number of years. For the last decade, the increases in higher education support by states have been smaller than the increases in the overall state budgets (Hovey, in Jones, 2003). In other words, higher education has increasingly received a smaller share of state budgets. Decreased funding appears to be the manifestation of a general trend on the part of lawmakers whereby higher education is seen as less of a public service deserving of taxpayer support, and more of a private good, to be supported by students and other funding (Selingo, 2003).

Taken together, the external changes noted provide a significant set of challenges for higher education. Colleges and universities, with their long history of slow and considered change, find themselves attempting to serve a new and demanding group of students, who place convenience and cost above campus life. These new students are increasingly being served by new competitors to higher education. Unfettered by tradition (and sometimes, it could be argued, concern for quality), these new for-profit and virtual centers have shown an ability to successfully compete for students on a global basis.

At the same time that institutions of higher education must confront these new challenges, they find themselves faced with waning public support. As public funding decreases, higher education administrators may find themselves approving large tuition increases which must be used not for new competitive initiatives, but for maintaining programs for an increasing number of students. This may further limit the ability of colleges and universities to rise to the new challenges, as they struggle to sustain existing programs in the face of rising costs and declining support (Duderstadt, 1999).

These challenges will not go away, however. In fact, they are likely to grow. Many in the business community see higher education as a potential investment, citing similarities between higher education and the health care industry. Higher education is viewed as poorly run, with high costs and inefficient use of technology (Levine & Sun, 2002; Passmore, 2000). Nonetheless, it provides an appealing investment, as it represents an increasing (and increasingly global) market that generates a significant amount of income (Oblinger & Kidwell, 2000). Unlike many industries, it is counter-cyclical, meaning that historically, enrollments increase during poor economic times (Levine & Sun, 2002). For these reasons, competition within the area of higher education will continue to rise.

As institutions of higher education seek to compete under these changing circumstances, they are not without resources of their own. Colleges and universities have a long history and many have strong reputations. They have established cultures of teaching, research, and service. Nonetheless, institutions of higher education must rapidly develop new business capabilities if they wish to take advantage of the opportunities afforded by distance education. The need for relatively rapid development of distance education programs represents a significant departure from the typically slow decision-making process in higher education (Carr, 2000), and the fast pace may itself present a significant barrier.

An Overview of the Higher Education Response

It has been hypothesized that the growth of distance education will ultimately cause higher education to be divided into three different types of institutions (Levine, 2000). One segment will consist of traditional, campus-based schools that focus solely on face-to-face instruction. These institutions will exist to serve the traditional student aged 18 to 22. Despite the somewhat dire predictions of the previous section, residential instruction will remain. The campus-based educational experience has a long history of meeting both the developmental as well as the educational needs of traditional students. These schools provide the structure within which adolescents can thrive (Farrington, 1999). In the United States, according to Hawkins (2000), "demand for residential instruction programs at the nation's upper- and middle-tier institutions has been increasing in the last decade and is likely to continue to do so."

The second segment of the higher education market is likely to be comprised of virtual institutions that exist primarily to serve the nontraditional population described earlier. These institutions will focus on the delivery of selected certificates and degree programs designed to serve the ongoing educational needs of adult students.

The third segment has been hypothesized as the "brick-and-click" institution—those schools that attempt to bring together both traditional and distance education. This is the model that may become prevalent, particularly among the nation's major universities. In e-commerce terms, these brick-and-click organizations have strong "brand recognition," and may engender a higher level of trust among constituents, as the flexibility of distance education is combined with the stability and reputation of the physical institution (Turban, 2002). A member of the University of Maryland

Baltimore County (UMBC) online master's program supports this assertion. She indicates that "The reputation was the biggest factor for me. I did not know of many programs and felt that UMBC was a more respectable institution than say, the University of Phoenix" (T. Emas, personal communication, January 28, 2004).

In other words, not all colleges and universities will need to offer distance education in order to survive in the new competitive environment. Institutions whose missions stress personal interaction between faculty and students, and who have a strong reputation for traditional residential instruction may find that they are able to thrive without entering the world of online instruction. Indeed, at least one author contends that competition from new institutions such as the University of Phoenix may in fact allow colleges and universities to return to their original focus and responsibility of introducing adolescent students to higher learning (Wolfe, 1998).

Distance Education:
An Overview of Successes and Failures

It is highly likely that not all of the institutions that choose to enter the world of distance education will survive. More than one author has predicted that the distance education market will ultimately be served by a relatively small group of major providers (Hawkins, 2000; Levine & Sun, 2002). Already a number of competitors have come and gone. In March 2003, Columbia University closed Fathom, its for-profit online education wing, after investing millions of dollars in the venture. Fathom was created as a partnership between a number of prestigious institutions, including the American Film Institute, the British Library, The London School of Economics and Political Science, and the University of Chicago, but was never profitable (Carlson, 2003).

Similarly, the United States Open University, the American wing of the British Open University, terminated its operations in the summer of 2002, after investing approximately $20 million (Arnone, 2002a). The University indicated an inability to attract enough students, citing problems with name recognition among Americans, as well as lack of regional accreditation (although the school was in the process of receiving accreditation through the Middle States Association of Colleges and Schools at the time that the decision was made to close).

Despite these well-publicized failures, successful entries into distance education can also be found. The University of Maryland's University College is often cited as an example of a successful online venture by a traditional university, and currently claims more than 143,544 online course enrollments (UMUC, 2005). The majority of UMUC students are pursuing bachelor's programs; online students have a median age of 32 years (UMUC, 2005).

Similarly, the Pennsylvania State University's non-profit World Campus is seen as a successful transition by a major research university to distance education (NEA, 2002). Launched in 1998, the World Campus draws its teaching faculty primarily from the ranks of full-time Penn State faculty (both tenure-track and fixed-term) (G. Miller, personal communication, January 20-21, 2004). The World Campus student body is comprised chiefly of working adults who are studying part-time. More than two thirds of the World Campus student population lives outside the state of Pennsylvania (G. Miller, personal communication, January 20-21, 2004).

Selected Issues of Integration of Online Education

Determining the Market

It is difficult to obtain an accurate estimate of the actual size of the distance education market. Clearly, the trends discussed earlier point to a potentially large body of students who are open to distance education, particularly since distance education may make a college education accessible to students who might not otherwise be able to attend due to their geographical locations or work-related constraints. However, some of the estimates that have been provided are based upon optimistic assumptions that have been applied to much of the industrialized world, including those for whom an English-based curriculum may not be appropriate (Hawkins, 2000). Further, many of these assumptions do not consider the issue of cost barriers. It is not certain just how many of the new population of students, already dealing with the costs of families (and possibly undergraduate education loans) will have the discretionary income available for education (Twigg, 2002).

What does seem to be clear is that these new students are focused on attaining degrees or professional certificates, rather than disconnected courses (Blustain, Goldstein, & Lozier, 1999; Carnevale, 2005). The most successful ventures thus far appear to be those that serve very specific needs, such as enhancing technical skills (NEA, 2002). Online masters programs in high demand areas such as information technology and business appear to have been successful investments for schools initiating distance education programs (Twigg, 2002). For example, Penn State's World Campus offers an "iMBA"—an online version of its resident MBA program, with courses taught by full-time graduate school faculty (World Campus, 2003).

The pricing of distance education programs can be problematic for institutions entering the online arena. Some universities charge online students the same per-credit fees as their face-to-face courses (even though online students do not necessarily have access to the same facilities and resources as their face-to-face counterparts). For public institutions, the distinction between "in-state" and "out-of-state" can pose a challenging question (Hawkins, 1999).

Estimating Costs of Implementation

The move to distance education requires that institutions effectively utilize business plans to a greater extent than many administrators are used to doing. There are already multiple examples of institutions that have invested millions of dollars in launching online operations only to terminate these ventures without ever becoming profitable (e.g., Columbia University's Fathom).

It is critical that institutions recognize and estimate the complete costs of implementing online education within the organization. The costs of integration extend well beyond the development of the courses themselves. Costs will be incurred within a number of different areas, including course design, course delivery, ongoing faculty development and support, and student support services (Sjogren & Fay, 2002). The last issue cited (student support services) is not insubstantial. Institutions that choose to retain student support services such as registration and billing may be faced with the potentially substantial costs of modifying legacy IT systems to allow online processing (NEA, 2002). There may be spill-over benefits from such modifications (for example, allowing traditional students to register online); nonetheless these can represent real and significant costs. This is an area where many organizations within higher education are still lagging. The 2002 National Survey of Information Technology in Higher Education conducted by the Campus Computing Project found that only 40.5% of the colleges and universities surveyed were capable of processing credit card payments from campus Web sites (although this did represent an increase from 27.6% in 2001) (Green, 2002).

Technological Infrastructure

The use of course management software for course delivery represents a critical decision when implementing distance education. Institutions may choose to develop their own proprietary software, or to lease one of the commercially available packages such as Blackboard, WebCT, or ANGEL—software that supports both synchronous and asynchronous online delivery of courses. Either of these decisions typically represents considerable expense. Developing a proprietary program provides the greatest potential for customization, but requires a significant commitment of personnel and other resources. Leasing a course management program (CMS) can minimize the initial costs, but can involve multiyear commitments. Universities may run the risk of committing to products at an initially low cost, but with increasing costs over time (Reid, 1999). As the industry evolves, learning management programs are beginning to be more complex, and therefore more expensive, sometimes significantly so (Young, 2002).

In either case, institutions need to carefully consider the issue of extensibility of the software to other areas of the organization. This allows the organization to provide a consistent online interface to users, and minimizes the learning curve for all users. For example, the Pennsylvania State University adopted a product called ANGEL (A New Generation of e-Learning), which is used both for its online division, The World Campus, as well as technology enhanced face-to-face classes (Arnone, 2002b). Of equal importance is the ability of the course management product to interface with existing information systems (Reid, 1999).

The issue of student support services represents one of the more problematic areas of developing the technological infrastructure for distance education. The addition of students that will complete coursework electronically brings the related requirement that these students access support services electronically as well. Online students require the same services as residential students—registration, accounting, advising, and library services, to name just a few. Given the 24-hour nature of course access, these students will frequently have an expectation of similar access to student support services, and the costs to provide such access and support are not insubstantial.

Of particular importance is the provision of library services to online students. Colleges and universities face a significant challenge in providing online students with online access to research materials (Hawkins, 1999). If all of a student's academic coursework is completed online, there will be an expectation that these services will be available online as well (Sjogren & Fay, 2002).

The ability of colleges and universities to successfully shoulder the costs of the technological infrastructure required for distance education is closely tied to the issue of financial support. Approximately one third of the colleges and universities surveyed for the 2002 National Survey of IT in Higher Education indicated that campus computing budgets had been reduced. Two-fifths of all schools surveyed had seen midyear cuts to computing budgets. More than 40% of all public institutions experienced midyear decreases (Green, 2002). This emphasizes the importance of developing a clear business plan prior to the creation of a distance education program. Penn State's World Campus, for example, was organized as a nonprofit, cost recovery unit, to be primarily funded through tuition (G. Miller, personal communication, January 20-21, 2004).

Staffing Issues

While technology presents an obvious expense when integrating distance education, the move to online course offerings also requires new expertise. Distance education can bring a collaborative element to what was once the solitary process of creating a course, and thereby create the need for new staff positions within the organization. For example, the Pennsylvania State University's World Campus employs instructional designers, who work with faculty members to create online versions of traditional classes. The instructional designers are in fact part of a larger team, which can include a graphics designer, a technical typist, and a production specialist (Carnevale, 2000).

Higher education institutions can face challenges not only in attracting applicants to these new positions, but also in retaining those applicants. It can be difficult for colleges and universities, who are already experiencing budgetary pressures, to offer the salaries and the technological environment that will allow higher education institutions to compete with industry for this expertise (Reid, 1999).

Faculty Development and Training

The incorporation of distance education brings many new challenges to higher education faculty. The move to online education requires a new level of technological skill for many academics. At a minimum, faculty members teaching online courses must be thoroughly familiar with the use of the chosen course management software (Carmean & Haefner, 2002). For most faculty members, achieving familiarity will require that institutions develop, promote, and present formalized training programs.

In actuality, faculty training needs extend well beyond the mechanics of working with course development software. Most faculty members will require training and mentoring in the new pedagogies needed to effectively implement online courses if they are to avoid simply transferring print materials to the Web (a process that has been referred to as "shovelware") (Sparrow et al., in Wallace, 2002). Though some faculty may attempt to teach online courses using a traditional approach, most will require new technology skills in order to effectively communicate with online students (Howell, Saba, Lindsay, & Williams, 2004). This new approach to course development can be challenging for many traditional educators.

The issue of faculty development, however, can be a complex one—with ramifications well beyond the relatively simple task of training faculty to use a new application. In fact, as colleges and universities contemplate the incorporation of distance education, the interpersonal and cultural issues may well overshadow the simple (by comparison) issues of funding and technological infrastructure.

Issues of Organizational Culture

Overview of the Higher Education Culture

As detailed in the opening paragraph, institutions of higher education have a long and rich history, where change (if any) occurs only after lengthy, time-consuming debate. Colleges and universities are not typically run like businesses. Instead, they are characterized by strong traditions and norms (Jaffee, in Harris & DiPaolo, 1999). Traditionally, faculty wield a relatively large amount of power, including the ability to set (or at least influence) organizational processes.

Distance education is perceived by many as being diametrically opposed to this traditional vision of the university (Levine & Sun, 2002). Thus, the incorporation of online education threatens to bring with it changes that have ramifications far beyond the issue of technology (Reid, 1999). Change within an organization brings with it the potential for resistance; change that involves technology and which may lead to the redistribution of both knowledge and power is highly likely to engender resistance within the organization (Laudon & Laudon, 2000). This has frequently been the case with the incorporation of distance education into traditional institutions.

Faculty Resistance

Without the support of higher education faculty, true reform within an institution is unlikely to take place (Jaffee, 1998; White & Myers, 2001). Faculty have often openly resisted the concept of distance education. There have been many reasons postulated for this resistance. Some faculty members have expressed concerns over the pedagogical quality of online courses, or the difficulty of reliably assessing student progress. Others have openly voiced unease about the potential impacts on faculty workload. Still others have questioned the possible rewards (if any) for incorporating distance education. Whether consciously stated or unconsciously held, faculty beliefs about the institution, education, and distance education must be examined if change within the higher education organization is to be successful (Jaffee, 1998).

Issues of Pedagogy and Place

Traditionally, graduate students do not receive instruction on how to teach; the university structure is based upon the assumption that if a person takes a significant number of classes, and gains a significant amount of knowledge in a given area, this person will be able to teach this information to others (Levine & Sun, 2002). Much of a professor's knowledge of how to teach is gained "on the job"—through trial and error, and visual, written, and verbal feedback from students and colleagues (Passmore, 2000). Historically, this instruction has taken place within the four walls of a classroom.

Distance education challenges both the notion of the classroom as a place of learning, as well as the approach by which information is traditionally imparted within the classroom. Additionally, it involves the use of technology. As may be self-evident, the degree of comfort a faculty member feels regarding the use of technology within the classroom is related to that faculty member's comfort with technology in general (Passmore, 2000). In other words, distance education brings the potential to remove teaching from its traditional location, to alter the traditional approach to instruction, and to introduce technology with which faculty members may not be familiar or comfortable.

Issues of Control/Power

Online education not only alters the physical location of education; it can also alter the relationships between faculty members and students. Historically, faculty members have been in the role of conveyors of knowledge, with students acting as receivers. Distance education has the potential to shift power and control from faculty members to students (Jaffee, 1998). Online education can directly challenge the way educators currently carry out their work, and therefore is likely to cause resistance (Wallace, 2002).

Similarly, distance education can provide the opportunity for higher education administration to gain greater control as well. The increased visibility of course material through online education allows administrators to gain instant access to a faculty member's curriculum. The potential for greater scrutiny and supervision of course content by administration is seen by many administrators as justifiable and appropriate; the greater potential for control and even censorship by higher education administration is seen by faculty members as a strong threat to academic freedom (Passmore, 2000; Wallace, 2002).

The development of distance education courses can also alter the perception of a faculty member's role within the learning and curriculum development process. Traditionally, faculty members have created courses as a solo occupation. As noted previously, distance education often becomes a collaborative effort between faculty and new staff members, for example, instructional designers. This can cause a blurring of the roles between traditional academics and a new professional staff. While this can be empowering for staff, it can bring into question faculty roles and the issue of just who "owns" courses (Wallace, 2002).

Issues of Ownership/Intellectual Property

The legal question of ownership of materials is actually covered by federal copyright law. Typically, this law provides the creator of "original works of authorship" with the exclusive right to reproduce and display these materials. An exception to this right has been "work for hire," for example, "work prepared by an employee within the scope of his or her employment" (U.S. Copyright Office, 2000).

The issue of ownership is a critical one for both faculty and administration. Notwithstanding the work for hire rules, faculty members have historically owned the "products" of curriculum development, including course syllabi and notes, and articles and books (Kelley & Bonner, 2002; Levine & Sun, 2002; Passmore, 2000). These policies have either been defined explicitly by administration, or recognized implicitly.

Ownership comes into question with distance education. Online courses have the potential to become a source of financial gain, thus both faculty and higher education institutions have a vested interest in control (Wallace, 2002). The issue involves more than finances, however. Control of a course is related to the quality of a course. One concern is that administrators may require the alteration of course content to make it less controversial, or more commercially viable. Or, alternatively, course content that was originally up to date could be allowed to become dated, even as the faculty member's name remains associated with the course (but out of the faculty member's control) (Kelly & Bonner, 2002). Faculty members have a related concern that institutional ownership may result in their replacement by less qualified (and less expensive) instructors once they have developed an online course (Passmore, 2000; Wallace, 2002).

Not surprisingly, many higher education administrators see this issue differently. Many colleges and universities point out that distance education courses involve a much more collaborative development effort than traditional courses. As noted previously, the development of an online course can entail a number of professional staff members in addition to the faculty member. Furthermore, these staff members utilize university resources in the production of the course (Levine & Sun, 2002; Passmore, 2000). Thus, many administrators argue that ownership of collaboratively developed courses belongs to the college or university.

Different organizations have proposed or adopted different policies related to the issue of intellectual property. For example, the University of Vermont Faculty Senate has proposed that course ownership be divided into content (controlled by the faculty member) and instructional design (controlled by staff) (Carnevale, 2001). This is in line with similar proposals for "unbundling" ownership of online course materials. This concept divides courses into instructional objects that can be owned by different individuals or organizations (Ubell, 2001). The University of North Texas stipulates that faculty members who develop courses will receive royalties when their courses are taught by other North Texas faculty, or if another institution pays to license the course (Klein, in Dahl, 2005).

As of this writing, there appears to be no final consensus on the issue of online course development and online course ownership, nor is it clear whether online courses truly represent potential financial gain for either faculty or administration (Dahl, 2005). What is clear, however, is that intellectual property represents one of the thornier issues that must be clarified as an institution moves toward the integration of distance education programs within the larger organization. Without clarification, faculty members are likely to remain reluctant to participate in online course development (Passmore, 2000).

Issues of Workload

Issues of intellectual property aside, faculty contemplating distance education often express concerns about the time involved to develop and teach an online course (Ellis, 2000; Passmore, 2000; Wallace, 2002; White & Myers, 2001). Institutions contemplating the integration of distance education need to develop a clear policy that motivates faculty to engage in the additional effort required by online courses. Faculty workload is typically defined in terms of the number of courses they teach per semester. Given the time that may be required to develop and refine an online course, it can be difficult to determine the equivalencies between an online course and a traditional face to face course. For example, a survey conducted of 60 Arkansas State University faculty members found that 90% of those surveyed asserted that they needed more time to develop an online course than a face-to-face course (Dickinson, Agnew, & Gorman, in Palloff & Pratt, 2001). The problem of equivalency can be further complicated if, as at some institutions, an online course is not tied to the traditional semester structure (Hawkins, 1999).

Strategies exist for overcoming some of these issues. Penn State University's World Campus typically develops new online degrees with the support of specific departments, and solicits long-term departmental commitment to the program. The World Campus encourages faculty participation by funding faculty release time from teaching assignments both for course development and for teaching World Campus programs (G. Miller, personal communication, January 20-21, 2004). In some cases, this allows departments to acquire additional faculty to manage the increase in overall teaching load.

However, it is difficult to deny faculty perceptions that online teaching is more time consuming than teaching students face-to-face (Ellis, 2000; Levine & Sun, 2002; Thompson, 2002; Wallace, 2002; White & Myers, 2001). Part of the concern over time commitments comes from the nature of the technology itself. When students have 24-hour access to course material, they develop the concurrent expectation of round-the-clock faculty access. Faculty members engaged in distance education report struggles to keep up with the demands for prompt feedback and communication from students (Brown, 2002; Levine & Sun, 2002; Wallace, 2002). As one author has noted, the flexibility afforded by online education can actually serve to enmesh those who teach online courses with student expectations of continual availability (Wallace, 2002). This feeling is echoed by an experienced educator who teaches both face-to-face and online courses. "For a quality online program, the instructor must deal with a much greater density of deliverables by the student—almost in a teacher-student mentoring relationship. That takes far more time in an online course than it does in a comparable face-to-face course, and in the online approach, the instructor is literally continuously available to the student" (H. Emurian, personal communication, January 22, 2004).

Additionally, faculty members experience a learning curve as they first begin the move to distance education. Not only must faculty learn how to effectively utilize the software platform that is being used to deliver the course, but they must learn a new pedagogy as they seek to translate a face-to-face course design to an effective online curriculum (Thompson, 2002). Distance education faculty have indicated that the incorporation of technology requires extensive time (White & Myers, 2001). Even as one experienced and comfortable with the use of technology, this author invested a significant number of hours in the process of utilizing course management software—including the development of the course structure, as well as the sheer mechanics of transferring and developing materials for Web-based presentation. How effectively less technologically aware faculty members are able to accomplish these challenging tasks can be directly related to the support provided by the institution.

Reward

Institutions in the process of integrating distance education often spend a great deal of time promoting the efficacies of online education to often reluctant faculty members. However, higher education institutions have not been as quick to modify the reward structures to reflect this new emphasis on online education. This dichotomy between what is verbally encouraged and what is actually rewarded remains a major source of faculty members' reluctance to embrace and participate in distance education (Ellis, 2000; Passmore, 2000; Thompson, 2001). For example, the Kellogg Commission on the Future of State and Land Grant Universities issued a series of reports on the reforms needed in order for public universities to successfully move into the future. The Commission was chaired by the president of the Pennsylvania State University, and consisted of presidents of more than two dozen public universities, including Clemson, Purdue, Ohio State, and Michigan State (Kellogg Commission, 2001). Contained within the report was a statement of guiding principles, which included the importance of meeting new student needs, and a commitment to developing distance learning techniques as one way to serve these needs. The Pennsylvania State University in particular has successfully developed a distance education program (the previously mentioned World Campus). Nonetheless, more than one writer specifically noted faculty's (perhaps accurate) perception of lack of reward for distance teaching within the university (Ellis, 2000; Passmore, 2000). Clearly, even when endorsed by top-level administration, cultural change is not easy to enact.

This issue is by no means isolated to one university. As one author states, "Too often, faculty are paid for teaching, but rewarded for scholarship" (Farrington, 1999, p. 93)—thus, research often becomes the focus of faculty energy. The question of promotion and tenure looms large in the lives of many faculty members, and the fear of a negative review due to participation in distance education remains a barrier for many (Ellis, 2000).

It is critical that higher education institutions consider alterations in existing faculty reward structures to reward excellence in teaching (including online teaching) if faculty members are to be persuaded to invest the time required to become proficient educators in the new medium of distance education (Harris & DiPaolo, 1999; Passmore, 2001; Sjogren & Fay, 2002).

Conclusion

While higher education can be viewed as a large industry, in actuality it is significantly different from other areas of endeavor. Higher education is founded upon a much loftier ideal than the simple pursuit of profit. With a long and rich history and culture, higher education is characterized by slow, deliberate change. New faculty members join an institution that has long respected the power and knowledge of the professor in the classroom.

Distance education, with its emphasis on nontraditional ways of teaching nontraditional students, provides a significantly different view of higher education, and potentially brings with it a significantly different role for faculty. The speed with which distance education ventures have been developed and deployed is diametrically opposed to the decision-making approach that has been a part of academia for hundreds of years. Distance education challenges higher education partly because its successful deployment can require an attention to business plans, budgets, and strategies in a way to which higher education is not accustomed. More importantly, however, it challenges higher education professionals to reach beyond their comfort zones and to question how and why they teach. Distance education also challenges higher education administrators to question how and why they reward faculty.

If distance education required "only" the development and implementation of a business plan, its integration into higher education would represent a relatively simple task. Instead, it represents a challenge to an entire culture, a need to rethink the essence of higher education. Does higher education take place only within the confines of the classroom? If a student is physically located beyond the walls of the university, is the student still learning? And if the professor no longer interacts with the class in a face to face manner, is the professor still teaching?

For some institutions, particularly those that have a strong reputation for traditional undergraduate education, distance education provides an interesting academic discussion. However, for those institutions that are seeking to serve the nontraditional students that reside within (or without) their traditional service areas, the issue of online education may be one of institutional survival. These organizations will be faced not just with the cost and implementation challenges of distance education, but with the cultural upheaval that may result.

Thus, the integration of distance education into higher education represents both a threat and an opportunity. While it provides the potential to reach a new audience in a new way, it also brings the possibility that it will radically alter the institution in which it is implemented. Some educators will argue that these changes represent a positive adaptation and forward movement; others will contend that these changes will serve to undermine and even destroy the foundations upon which higher education has been built (Croy, 1998). It is clear that the issues bringing about the growth of distance education—nontraditional students; a growing technological infrastructure; the need for lifelong education; decreasing public and governmental support—are unlikely to go away. Institutions of higher education cannot avoid choosing how they will respond to these issues, and the "right" response will vary across organizations. What is equally clear is that for most institutions, competing in the "marketspace" will be a significant challenge.

References

Arnone, M. (2002a). United States Open U. to close after spending $20 million. *The Chronicle of Higher Education, 48,* p. A33.

Arnone, M. (2002b). Mixing and matching distance-education software. *The Chronicle of Higher Education, 48,* p. A44.

Arnone, M., Hebel S., & Schmidt, P. (2003, January 3). Another bleak budget year. *The Chronicle of Higher Education,* p. A21.

Blustain, H., Goldstein, P., & Lozier, G. (1999). Assessing the new competitive landscape. In R.N. Katz & Assoc. (Eds.), *Dancing with the devil: Informa-*

tion technology and the new competition in higher education (pp. 51-71). Educause.

Brown, D. (2002). Please learn from my mistakes. *Syllabus* (8/1).

Carlson, S. (2003, January 7). After losing millions, Columbia U. will close its online-learning venture. *The Chronicle of Higher Education*, p A30.

Carmean, C., & Haefner, J. (2002, November-December). Mind over matter: Transforming course management systems into effective learning environments. *Educause,* pp. 27-34.

Carnevale, D. (2000). Turning traditional classes into distance education. *The Chronicle of Higher Education, 46*, p. A37.

Carnevale, D. (2001, June 8). U. of Vermont considers intellectual property policy to foster distance education. *The Chronicle of Higher Education*, p.A34.

Carnevale, D. (2005, February 4). Offering entire degrees online is one key to distance education, survey finds. *The Chronicle of Higher Education*, p.A31.

Carr, S. (2000). Faculty members are wary of distance-education ventures. *The Chronicle of Higher Education, 46*, p.A41.

Croy, M. (1998). Distance education, individualization, and the demise of the university. *Technology in Society, 20*, 317-326.

Dahl, J. (2005). Who owns the rights to online courses? *Distance Education Report, 9*(22), 4-7.

Dillon, S. (2006). Online colleges receive a boost from congress. Retrieved July 9, 2006, from *The New York Times,* http://www.nytimes.com/2006/03/01/national/01educ.html?_r=1&th&emc=th&oref=slogin

Duderstadt, J. (1997). The future of the university in an age of knowledge. *Journal of Asynchronous Learning Networks, 1*, 78-87.

Duderstadt, J. (1999). Can colleges and universities survive in the information age? In R.N. Katz & Assoc. (Eds.), *Dancing with the devil: Information technology and the new competition in higher education* (pp. 1-25). Educause.

Ellis, E. (2000). Faculty participation in the Pennsylvania State University World Campus: Identifying barriers to success. *Open Learning, 15*, 233-242.

Fair Disclosure Wire. (2006, February 28). Preliminary fiscal 2006 second quarter Apollo Group earnings conference call—final. Retrieved July 9, 2006, from http://proquest.umi.com.ezaccess.libraries.psu.edu/pqdweb?did=100434266 1&sid=3&Fmt=3&clientId=9874&RQT=309&VName=PQD

Farrington, G. (1999). The new technologies and the future of residential undergraduate instruction. In R.N. Katz & Assoc. (Eds.), *Dancing with the devil: Information technology and the new competition in higher education* (pp. 73-94). Educause.

Green, K. (2002). The 2002 national survey of information technology in U.S. higher education. *The Campus Computing Project*. Retrieved July 9, 2006 from http:// www.campuscomputing.net/

Harris, D., & DiPaolo, A. (1999). Institutional policy for ALN. *Journal of Asynchronous Learning Networks, 3*. Retrieved July 9, 2006, from *http://www.aln. org/publications/jaln/v3n1/pdf/v3n1_harris.pdf*

Hawkins, B. (1999). Distributed learning and institutional restructuring. *Educom Review, 34*. Educause, pp. 12-18.

Hawkins, B. (2000, November-December). Technology, higher education, and a very foggy crystal ball. *Educause* [Journal], pp. 64-73.

Howell, S., Saba, F., Lindsay, N., & Williams, P. (2004). Seven strategies for enabling faculty success in distance education. *The Internet and Higher Education, 7*, 33-49.

Jaffee, D. (1998). Institutionalized resistance to asynchronous learning networks. *Journal of Asynchronous Learning Networks, 2*. Retrieved July 9, 2006, from http://www.aln.org/publications/jaln/v2n2/pdf/v2n2_jaffee.pdf

Jones, D. (2003). State shortfalls projected throughout the decade: Higher ed budgets likely to feel continued squeeze. Retrieved July 9, 2006, from *The National Center for Public Policy and Higher Education*, http://www.highereducation. org/pa_0203/index.html

Kelly, K., & Bonner, K. (2002). Courseware ownership in distance education: Issues and policies. *Sloan_C View, 1*, 3-5. Retrieved July 9, 2006, from http://www. aln.org/publications/view/v1n1/pdf/SloanCView_vol1_iss1.pdf

Kellogg Commission on the Future of State and Land-Grant Universities, The. (2001). *Returning to our roots: Executive summaries of the reports of the Kellogg Commission on the Future of State and Land-Grant Universities*. Washington, DC: National Association of State Universities and Land-Grant Colleges.

Kirst, M., & Venezia, A. (2001). Bridging the great divide between secondary schools and postsecondary education. *Phi Delta Kappan, 83*, 92-97. Retrieved July 9, 2006, from http://www.stanford.edu/group/bridgeproject/greatdivide.pdf

Laudon, K., & Laudon, J. (2000). *Management information systems: Organization and technology in the networked enterprise* (6th ed.). Upper Saddle River, NJ: Prentice Hall.

Levine, A. (2000). The future of colleges: 9 inevitable changes. Retrieved July 9, 2006, from *The Chronicle of Higher Education*, http://education.gsu.edu/ctl/ Programs/Future_Colleges.htm

Levine, A., & Sun, J. (2002). *Barriers to distance education*. American Council on Education Center for Policy Analysis/Educause.

NEA. (2002). The promise and reality of distance education. *NEA Higher Education Research Center Update, 8*, 1-4.

Oblinger, D., & Kidwell, J. (2000, May-June). Distance learning: Are we being realistic? *Educause Review*, pp. 31-39.

O'Donoghue. (2000). IT developments and changes in customer demand in higher education. *ALN Magazine, 4*. Retrieved July 9, 2006, from http://www.aln.org/publications/magazine/v4n1/odonoghue.asp

Olsen, F. (2002). Phoenix rises. *The Chronicle of Higher Education, 49*, p. A29.

Palloff, R., & Pratt, K. (2001). *Lessons from the cyberspace classroom: The realities of online teaching.* CA: Jossey-Bass.

Passmore, D. (2000). Impediments to adoption of Web-based course delivery among university faculty. *ALN Magazine, 4*. Retrieved July 9, 2006, from http://www.aln.org/publications/magazine/v4n2/passmore.asp

Reid, I. (1999). Beyond models: Developing an institutional strategy for online instruction. *Journal of Asynchronous Learning Networks, 3*. Retrieved July 9, 2006, from http://www.aln.org/publications/jaln/v3n1/v3n1_reid.asp

Rio Salado College. (2003). Course schedule. Retrieved July 9, 2006, from http://www.riosalado.edu/ci/schedule/

Selingo, J. (2003, February 28). The disappearing state in public higher education. *The Chronicle of Higher Education*, p. A22.

Sjogren, J., & Fay, J. (2002). Cost issues in online learning. *Change, 34*, 52-57.

Thompson, M. (2002). Faculty satisfaction. *Sloan-C View, 1*, 6-7. Retrieved July 9, 2006, from http://www.aln.org/publications/view/v1n2/pdf/vln2.pdf

Turban, E. (2002). *Electronic commerce: A managerial perspective 2002.* Upper Saddle River, NJ: Pearson Education.

Twigg, C.A. (2002). The impact of the changing economy on four-year institutions of higher education: The importance of the Internet. In P.A. Graham & N.G. Stacey (Eds.), *The knowledge economy and postsecondary education: Report of a workshop* (pp. 77-104). Washington, DC: National Academy Press.

Ubell, R. (2001). Who owns what? Unbundling Web course property rights. *Educause Quarterly, 1*, 45-47.

UMUC. (2005). *UMUC at a glance.* Retrieved July 9, 2006, from http://www.umuc.edu/ip/umucfacts_02.html

U.S. Copyright Office. (2000). *Copyright basics.* Retrieved July 9, 2006, from The Library of Congress, http://www.copyright.gov/circs/circ1.html#wci

Wallace, M. (2002). Managing and developing online education: Issues of change and identity. *Journal of Workplace Learning, 14*, 198-208.

White, J., & Myers, S. (2001). You can teach an old dog new tricks: The faculty's role in technology implementation. *Business Communications Quarterly, 64*, 95-101.

Wolfe, A. (1998, December 4). How a for-profit university can be invaluable to the traditional liberal arts. *The Chronicle of Higher Education*, p. B4.

World Campus. (2003). Admissions fact sheet. Retrieved July 9, 2006, from http://www.worldcampus.psu.edu/pub/imba/afs_benefits.shtml

Young, J. (2002). Pricing shifts by blackboard and WebCT cost some colleges much more. *The Chronicle of Higher Education, 48*, p. A35.

Chapter V

Determinant of Information Quality and Use of Executive Information Systems (EIS) in UK

Omar E. M. Khalil, Kuwait University, Kuwait

Manal M. Elkordy, Alexandria University, Egypt

Abstract

This chapter reports on the findings of research investigating the influence of information quality on EIS information use as well as the possible impact of ease of use, user involvement, IS maturity, and system sophistication on EIS information quality. To test the research hypotheses, data were collected from 216 U.K.-based executives. A structural equation modeling (SEM) technique for data analysis and model measurement was applied. Information quality was found to influence EIS information use. Also, ease of use, user involvement, the IS integration dimension of IS maturity, and EIS sophistication were found to influence executives' perception of information quality. Further findings, limitations, and implications for researchers and practitioners are discussed.

Introduction

Information use is important for organizational learning and competitive advantages, and an understanding of the factors that affect such usage is critical (Low & Mohr, 2001). Managers receive information in various forms (e.g., printed, graphics, verbal, visual, etc.) and from different internal and external sources (e.g., memos and letters, scheduled and unscheduled meetings, telephone, office visits, computer reports, periodicals, conventions, social/civic activities, etc.). Earlier research findings indicated that executives relied more heavily on informal sources of information, compared to formal sources. Of the written media, memos and noncomputer reports were considered more valuable than computer reports (Jones & McLeod, 1986; McLeod, Jones, & Poitevent, 1984). However, later research findings show an improvement in managers' ranking of computer-based information sources, compared to noncomputer-based sources, and more emphasis on external sources, compared to internal resources (e.g., Benard & Satir, 1993; Lan & Scott, 1996).

Executive information systems (EIS) are systems that provide executives with information that is relevant to their work (Amott & Pervan, 2005; Basu, Poindexter, Drosen, & Addo, 2000; Oggier, 2005; Walstrom, Kent, & Wilson, 1997, p. 77). EIS are assumed to provide improvements in the quantity and quality of information made available to executives. This includes providing timelier, concise, relevant, and accessible information. However, since an EIS is one of many information sources available to managers to support their work activities, the extent to which managers use this source is expected to vary. Among other factors, EIS use may be influenced by its users' perceptions of information quality (Leidner, 1996, 1998; Seddon & Kiew, 1994). In earlier investigations, EIS information quality was ranked as the most important characteristic of an executive information system (Bergeron, Raymond, & Lagorge, 1991), and the frequency of EIS use was best explained by the quality of information (Leidner, 1996).

Understanding the factors that possibly influence EIS information quality is crucial to EIS development and organizational information management. However, most of the prior EIS research focused on the reasons and methods of EIS development and implementation (e.g., Bergeron et al., 1991; Poor & Wagner, 2001; Rainer & Watson, 1995; Rockart & Delong, 1988; Watson & Carte, 2000; Watson, Rainer, & Houdeshel, 1997). In addition, much of the limited prior research on EIS use focused on the mode, benefits, and impact of use on decision making (e.g., Elam & Leidner, 1995; Frolick, Parzinger, Rainer, & Ramarapu, 1997; Nord & Nord, 1995). In addition, the literature on information quality is generally prescriptive and empirical evidence that links information quality to EIS information use is rather limited.

Little is known about the factors that influence systems-related perceptions (Agarwal, Prasad, & Zanino, 1996; Igbaria, Guimaraes, & Davis, 1995; Venkatesh & Davis, 1994), including the perception of EIS information quality. This study investigates the relationship of EIS information use to EIS information quality and the possible impact of ease of use, user involvement, information systems (IS) maturity, and system sophistication on EIS information quality using UK-based data.

The chapter is organized accordingly. The first section presents the study background, followed by the research model and hypotheses, data analysis and results, discussion, research limitations, and the chapter ends with conclusions.

Background

EISs are viewed as visual reporting systems, which provide managers with real-time information in a graphical, easy-to-use format. They support managerial learning about an organization, its processes, and its interaction with the external environment. Nevertheless, failure stories of EIS in organizations have been documented in the literature on information systems effectiveness (e.g., Glover, Watson, & Rainer, 1992; Liang & Miranda, 2001; Nandhakumar & Jones, 1997; Rainer & Watson, 1995; Xu & Lehaney, 2003; Young & Watson, 1995). Such failures can be linked to organizational, management, social, cultural, behavioral, psychological, and technological factors (McBride, 1997; Nandhakumar & Jones, 1997; Poon & Wagner, 2001; Xu & Lehaney, 2003). Executives are often disappointed by the quality of information received from EIS and get frustrated when trying to operate them (Pervan & Phua, 1997).

Information quality is believed to be one of the most important characteristics that determine the degree to which information is used (O'Reilly, 1982). Salmeron (2002) argues that an EIS is only as useful as the data/information it utilizes. Managers refuse to use a system if it does not respond to their immediate information needs or is too difficult to learn and use. The rather limited previous empirical research on information quality and information systems effectiveness suggests a positive relationship between perceived information quality and information use. In particular, information quality was found to be central to EIS success (e.g., Bergeron, Raymond, Rivard, & Gara, 1995; Koh, Chang, & Watson, 1998; Leidner, 1996; Rainer & Watson, 1995; Rockart & Delong, 1988). Also, managers were found to likely trust information of high quality and, hence, are more likely to rely on such information in making decisions or evaluating performance (Low & Mohr, 2001).

Quality is viewed as the fitness for use or the extent to which a product/service successfully serves the purposes of its consumers (Juran, Gryna, & Bingham, 1974). Information quality refers to the extent to which the available information meets the information requirements of its users (Seddon & Kiew, 1994). Kahn, Strong, and Wang (2002) draw distinctions between the quality dimensions of information as a product and information as a service. Information product quality includes dimensions such as the tangible measures of accuracy, completeness, and freedom from errors. Service quality, on the other hand, includes dimensions related to the service delivery process as well as the intangible measures of ease of manipulation, security, and added value of the information to consumers. Although the conventional view of information quality is product-oriented, both product and service quality are important aspects of information quality (Pitt, Watson, & Kavan, 1995; Wang & Strong, 1996).

The information quality literature suggests the existence of a number of views on what constitutes the dimensions (attributes) of information quality. Raghunathan (1999), for instance, used accuracy as a measure of information quality. Clikeman (1999) identified information quality to include the dimensions of relevance, reliability, timeliness, and cost. From a consumer's perspective, a framework was developed to capture the underlying information quality in four groups (Huang, Lee, & Wang, 1999; Strong, Lee, & Wang, 1997; Wang & Strong, 1996): (1) intrinsic (e.g., accuracy, reliability, believability), (2) contextual (e.g., relevancy, completeness, timeliness), (3) representational (e.g., conciseness, consistency, interpretability), and (4) accessibility (e.g., access, security). Also, Cambridge Research Group (1997) developed an instrument to assess information quality across 17 dimensions, hence, providing a benchmark of the information quality status of an organization.

Nevertheless, the growing body of knowledge on information quality is mostly prescriptive. It focuses primarily on information quality definitions, dimensions and attributes, and quality measurement and improvement approaches (e.g., Ballou & Pazer, 1985, 1995; Firth & Wang, 1996; Huang et al., 1999; Madnick & Wang, 1992; Orr, 1998; Redman, 1992; Strong et al., 1997; Wang & Strong, 1996; Yang, Strong, Kahn, & Wang, 2002). Yet, empirical evidence that links information quality to systems use is somewhat limited.

On the other hand, information systems effectiveness research models and frameworks—(for example, Ives, Hamilton, & Davis, 1980; Fuerst & Cheney, 1982; Raymond, 1990); the technology acceptance model (TAM) (Davis, 1989; Davis, Bagozzi, & Warshaw, 1989); diffusion of innovations (e.g., Rogers, 1995); the theory of planned behavior (TPB) (e.g., Taylor & Todd, 1995a); social cognitive theory (SCT) (e.g., Compeau, Higgins, & Huff, 1999)—and past relevant research produced useful insights to individuals' behavioral reactions to information systems and the factors that may influence such reactions. However, despite a substantial body of empirical evidence linking user perceptions to use, little is known about the factors that influence systems-related perceptions (Agarwal et al., 1996; Igbaria et al., 1995; Venkatesh & Davis, 1994), including perceptions of information quality.

There are few empirical studies (e.g., Bajwa, Rai, & Brennan, 1998; Bergeron et al., 1995; El-Kordy, 2000; Hung, 2003; Hung & Liang, 2001; Kim, 1996; Koh & Watson, 1998; Leidner, 1996, 1998; Rainer & Watson, 1995; Young & Watson, 1995) that investigated EIS effectiveness and its determinants. Although recognized as a major determinant of EIS success, information quality received little attention as a construct in the past empirical research on information systems effectiveness. Specifically, information quality was often treated as a component of a general measure of user satisfaction in past empirical research. As a result, empirically-driven evidence on the possible influence of information quality on EIS information use and the factors that may influence users' perception of EIS information quality should be of interest to both IS researchers and practitioners.

Although the literature on information systems effectiveness suggests a number of technical, managerial, and organizational factors that are believed to influence perceived information quality, only ease of use (e.g., Davis et al., 1989; Igbaria, Zinatelli, Cragg, & Cavaye Angele, 1997; Straub, Limayem, & Karahanna-Evaristo, 1995), user involvement (e.g., Barki & Hartwick, 1989; Khalil & Elkordy, 1997; Srivihok, 1999; Watson et al., 1997), IS maturity (e.g., Cheney & Dickson, 1982; Igbaria et al., 1997; King & Sabherwal, 1992; Millet & Mawhinney, 1992), and EIS sophistication (e.g., Bergeron et al., 1995; Davis et al., 1989; Rainer & Watson, 1995) are investigated in this study. The selection of these research variables was guided by (1) the findings of the prior research that investigated their influence on information systems use and user satisfaction (e.g., Khalil & Elkordy, 1999; Kraemer, Danziger, Dunkle, & King, 1993; Leidner, 1996; Seddon & Kiew, 1994), and (2) the restricted research resources that were available to the researchers.

Research Model and Hypotheses

The proposed research model (Figure 1) suggests that the use of EIS information is a function of EIS perceived information quality. The review of the literature reveals that user satisfaction with information systems was studied from three perspectives: attitudes toward the information system, information quality, and effectiveness (Kim, 1989). One of those dimensions, information quality, was found to be an important factor for EIS success (Bergeron et al., 1995; Leidner, 1996; Koh & Watson, 1998; Rainer & Watson, 1995; Rockart & Delong, 1988). Consequently, information quality was included in the proposed model as a direct determinant of EIS information use.

Figure 1 depicts ease of use, user involvement, IS maturity, and EIS sophistication as possible determinants of EIS information quality. The information of an EIS that is perceived to be easier to use and less complex has a higher chance to be perceived positively by its users. User participation in EIS development efforts is expected to enhance the user's perceived information quality through the intervention of a need-based psychological component (i.e., user involvement) (McKeen, Guimaraes & Wetherbe, 1994; Rainer & Watson, 1995). Also, a more mature IS function should

Figure 1. The research model

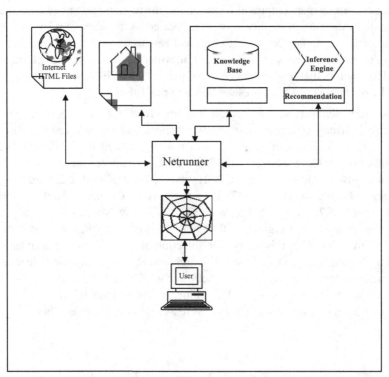

be in a better position to plan, design, implement, and operate effective EIS; and, consequently, users are expected to have more positive beliefs about their information quality. In addition, system sophistication—the availability of EIS functions (e.g., status access, exception reporting, drill down, etc.)—is expected to positively influence the perceived information quality of the systems. These expectations are put together in proposed hypotheses.

EIS Information Use and Information Quality

Perceived information quality is defined as the extent to which users believe that the information systems available to them meet their information requirements in terms of timeliness, accuracy, format, and relevance of the information generated by the system (Leidner, 1996; Seddon & Kiew, 1994). The direct link between different facets of user satisfaction and usage is supported with a big body of empirical research (e.g., Baroudi, Olson, & Ives, 1986; Ein-Dor & Segev, 1986; Elkordy, 1994; Lucas, 1975, 1978; O'Reilly, 1982; Raymond, 1985; Robey, 1979; Torkzadeh & Dwyer, 1994).

The investigation of the possible link between information quality and computer-based information use is particularly important in the context of EIS, which are mainly designed to provide managers with the timely, precise, and relevant information they need. Previous research suggests a positive relationship between information quality and information use (Low & Mohr, 2001; Maltz & Kohli, 1996). DeLone and McLean's (1992) and Seddon's (1997) models for information systems success posit that information quality and system quality affect user satisfaction and system use. Rai, Lang, and Welker (2002) tested the two models and reported reasonable support for both. In more recent tests of the DeLone and McLean's (1992) model, Livari (2005) found information quality to be predictive of user satisfaction with the system but not of system use; and Almutairi and Subramanian (2005) found information quality to impact system quality and user satisfaction in the Kuwaiti private sector. Furthermore, information quality was found to be positively related to the use of information in assessing marketing communications productivity (Low & Mohr, 2001), an important factor to Web site quality (Webb & Webb, 2004), and to affect the intention to use the system and overall satisfaction (Bharati & Chaudhury, 2006). However, McGill, Hobbs, and Klobas (2003) found information quality to have no direct impact on intended use of user-developed applications.

On the other hand, a number of investigations focused on information quality as a determinant of EIS use. Bergeron et al. (1995) defined affect towards EIS in terms of satisfaction with the EIS information quality, accessibility, and services provided by the EIS staff. Their study found that affect of EIS has a positive influence on its use. This finding is consistent with the finding of a prior study that information quality is the most important characteristic of an EIS (Bergeron et al., 1991). Also, Leidner (1996, 1998) found that frequency of EIS use was best explained by the quality of the EIS information. Kraemer et al. (1993) reported that information quality has a significant positive influence on perceived usefulness of computer-based information.

The inclusion of perceived information quality as a direct determinant of information use is based on Delone and Mclean's (1989, 1992, 2003) and Seddon's (1997) models of IS success, which propose information quality is a direct antecedent of systems use. Also, the technology acceptance model (TAM) (Davis et al., 1989) and theory of reasoned action (TRA) (Fishbein, 1980) imply that beliefs about the systems' quality is expected to influence its use. Accordingly, the following hypothesis is proposed:

H1. *EIS perceived information quality positively influences EIS information use.*

Determinants of Perceived Information Quality

Ease of Use

Perceived ease of use is defined as the degree to which a person believes that using a certain system is effort free (Davis, 1989, p. 320). Usually, managers have little time to invest in learning the system, a low tolerance for errors, and may have very little incentive to use it. Even if the information in the system is useful, a difficult interface with the system will discourage the managers from using it.

A significant research investigated the influence of perceived ease of use on actual use or the intention to use (e.g., Adams, Nelson, & Todd, 1992; Compeau & Higgins, 1995; Davis, 1989; Davis et al., 1989; Gefen & Straub, 1997; Hung, 2003; Hung & Liang, 2001; Igbaria et al., 1997; Sjazna, 1996; Straub et al., 1995) with mixed results. Perceived ease of use was also found to explain a considerable variance in perceived usefulness (Adams et al., 1992; Igbaria et al., 1997; Mathieson, 1991; Sjazna, 1996).

However, little attention was given to the influence of ease of use on perceived information quality in the past empirical research. For example, Doll and Torkzadeh (1988) reported significant relationships between ease of use and information quality dimensions, namely, content, timeliness, and accuracy. Also Srinivansan (1985) reported a positive relationship between system quality in terms of perceived reliability and information quality. Thus, one can argue that a system, which is perceived as "easy to use," has a better chance to be perceived as providing high quality information. Therefore, the expected relationship of perceived ease of use to perceived information quality will be tested using the following hypothesis:

H2-1. *EIS ease of use positively influences EIS information quality.*

User Involvement

Following Barki and Hartwick (1989) and Santosa, Wei, and Chan (2005), involvement is defined as the degree to which the user believes that the system possesses two characteristics: relevance and importance. In contrast with participation, involvement refers to a psychological state of the individual rather than a set of activities during systems development. Kappelman and McLean (1991) suggested involvement to mediate the influence of user participation on systems success. In the context of EIS, user participation is reported to increase the chances of user acceptance and successful implementation because it helps tailor the system to meet users' perceptions (Franz & Robey, 1986; Watson et al., 1997).

Santosa et al. (2005) found user involvement to influence user satisfaction in the context of information seeking activities. A study on 52 EIS users found that participation in EIS development is positively related to EIS information quality (Srivihok, 1999). Barki and Hartwick (1994) reported a positive influence of involvement on user attitudes. No prior studies, however, have directly tested the influence of user involvement on perceived information quality. Higher levels of user involvement are likely to lead to better perceptions of information quality; similarly, a system which is seen to be unimportant and irrelevant to the person stands little chance of being perceived as high quality output. This expectation will be tested via the following hypothesis.

H2-2. *User involvement positively influences EIS information quality.*

IS Maturity

IS maturity is defined as the overall status of the IS function within the organization (King & Sabherwal, 1992). The level of IS maturity reflects the progress of the information systems function in the organization from the era of data processing to the strategic IS era (Wastell & Sewards, 1995). Raymond (1990) reported a positive relation between the organization's managerial and technical sophistication in implementing, operating its information systems, and systems usage and satisfaction. Results from a survey of senior IT managers found that managerial IT knowledge is a dominant factor in explaining the extent of IT use (Boynton, Zmud, & Jacobs, 1994). Selim (1997) found IS maturity to be the main determinant of user satisfaction with information systems. IS maturity was also found to correlate with the success of strategic IS applications (King & Sabherwal, 1992).

Millet and Mawhinney (1992) argue that if the MIS structure is not well developed, management should consider postponing the investment in EIS until the MIS can adequately support such a system. This implies that the chances of EIS application to succeed are expected to increase with the maturation of the overall organizational IS function. Prior studies (Igbaria et al., 1997; Taylor & Todd, 1995a, b) recommended that future studies should clarify the relationship between systems success/failure and the development stage of IS in the organization. Thus, the researchers believe that the possible influence of IS maturity on EIS information quality warrants investigation, particularly when past investigations are lacking. As the IS function matures, the organization's managerial and technical sophistication in planning, implementing, operating, and using its information systems improves. Subsequently, experienced IS staff are expected to build and manage better quality systems, especially strategic systems such as EIS. Therefore, IS maturity is expected to have a positive impact on the perceived quality of EIS. Such an expectation is formulated in the following hypothesis:

H2-3. *IS maturity positively influences EIS information quality.*

EIS Sophistication

Raymond and St-Pierre (2005) found the sophistication of the advanced manufacturing systems (AMS) to significantly impact the operational and business performance of the small- and medium-sized companies (SMEs). In the EIS context, the availability of EIS capabilities/functions was found to positively influence EIS use (Bergeron et al., 1995; Rainer & Watson, 1995; Raymond, 1985). It can be argued as the managerial activities and roles vary, it is expected that an EIS which addresses a greater number of the executive problems (through the availability of more functions) will be perceived as of higher quality output, compared to the output of a less sophisticated system. Based on the Triandis' (1980) model of behavior and attitude and TAM (Davis et al., 1989), EIS sophistication is expected to directly influence perceived information quality as well as EIS-based information use. The possible influence of system sophistication on information quality is formulated in the following hypothesis:

H2-4. *EIS sophistication positively influences information quality.*

Methodology

Sample

The unit of analysis in this investigation is the executive (respondent) who uses an EIS in an organization. A cross-section mail survey was used to collect data in order to test the research hypotheses. The study population consisted of potential users who had EIS available to them in support of their work. The lack of information on the EIS user population precluded random selection and made the use of a purposive sampling design acceptable. Judgment was used to select units (respondents) that are representative or typical of the target population (Singleton, Royce, Straits, & Straits, 1993). Customer lists of major EIS vendors are considered one of the most direct sources of information regarding EIS users (Elam & Leidner, 1995).

Data were collected from UK-based EIS users working in organizations that were included in the customer list of a major EIS vendor. 960 surveys were sent out to all managers on the vendor's customer list. The authors and the EIS vendor made the necessary arrangement in order to conduct the survey while maintaining the confidentiality of the data and the anonymity of the respondents. Out of the 960

Table 1. Response bias analysis: Demographic data

Sample Characteristics	Mean (first 35 /first mail)	Mean (last 35 /second mail)	ANOVA	
			F	P
Age of respondents	41.4000	39.0588	1.484	0.227
Years of education	15.9143	16.3793	0.035	0.853
Managerial experience (years)	11.5429	9.9714	0.326	0.570
Company size (no. of employees)	9362.5806	6206.0938	1.586	0.213
Number of EIS functions	4.7143	4.8286	1.332	0.252

Table 2. Sample characteristics

Industry Sector	Frequency	%	Number of employee	Frequency	%
Finance/Banking/ Insurance	44	20.4	≤ 500	21	9.7
Pharmaceuticals, Chemicals	22	10.2	501-1000	19	8.8
Health Service	21	9.7	1001-5000	91	42.1
Retail, Trade	35	16.2	5001-10000	31	14.4
Government	4	1.9	10001-25000	23	10.6
Public Utilities	9	4.2	More than 25000	19	8.8
Manufacturing, Engineering	48	22.2	Missing	12	5.6
Publishing, Media, Information	5	2.3	Total	216	100
Airline, Transportation, Leisure	8	3.7			
Logistics, Distribution	15	6.9			
Others	5	2.3			
Total	216	100			

distributed surveys, only 216 completed (usable) surveys (22.5% response rate) were returned after an initial mailing, reminder letters, and a second mailing.

An analysis of the questionnaires received at different points of the data collection might be used to estimate the nonresponse bias (Babbie, 1990, p. 180). Analysis of variance was used to compare the mean value of five demographic characteristics between the first 35 respondents from the first mail and the last 35 respondents from the second mail. The results (Table 1) indicate that there are no statistically significant differences between the respondents from the first wave and those from the second. This test suggests that respondents to the survey are representative of the population and that their responses could be aggregated across the two response waves.

The respondents represented a broad cross-section of different industries and different sized firms (Table 2). The sample consisted of 13.9% one managerial level below the CEO, 47.7% two levels below the CEO, 13.4% three levels below the CEO, and 22.8% four levels or more below the CEO. They also came from different functional areas, 53.7% of the respondents coming from finance and accounting. Managers from IT/IS functional area constituted 19% of the respondents, 15.3% reported from general management positions, 10.2% from marketing, sales, and advertising, and only 1.4% reported from production.

Variables Definitions and Measures

The scales used to measure the constructs included in the research model are presented in Table 3 and are discussed subsequently.

EIS Information Use

Dependence on the system describes the extent to which the information system has been integrated into the individual's work routine. The more the information is consumed to fulfill job requirements, the more the information system is integrated into the user's work. Following Goodhue and Thompson's (1995) "dependence on the system" approach, this study measures EIS information use (info-use) by asking the respondents to determine the extent of their dependence on EIS-based information compared to other information sources (Elkordy, 1994). The respondents were asked to report on the percentage of their information needs satisfied through four sources: personal contacts, paper-based sources, direct use of EIS, and EIS output provided by others. The extent of EIS information use is the sum of the percentages of the information needs satisfied through the direct and the indirect use of EIS.

Perceived Information Quality

This study measured perceived information quality (IQ) using a subset of the end-user computing satisfaction (EUCS) instrument developed and tested by Doll and Torkzadeh (1988). The end-user computing satisfaction instrument consists of five subscales: content, accuracy, format, ease of use, and timeliness. A confirmatory factor analysis of the instrument revealed that it can be used as a standardized measure of user satisfaction with a specific application, and that researchers can use these subscales with confidence as they have adequate validity and reliability (Doll, Xia, & Torkzadeh, 1994). The researchers followed the recommendations of Seddon and Kiew (1994) to eliminate the perceived ease of use related items from the instrument in order to measure only satisfaction with information quality. Respondents were asked to answer nine questions concerning the information quality of their EIS on a five-point scale ranging from hardly ever, 25% of the time, 50% of the time, 75% of the time, to always.

Perceived Ease of Use

Perceived ease of use (PEOU) is defined as the degree to which a person believes that using a certain system is effort free (Davis, 1989). The study used the perceived ease of use instrument developed and tested by Davis (1989) and verified by other researchers (e.g., Adams et al., 1992, Chin & Todd, 1995). Respondents were asked to indicate on a five-point scale their agreement or disagreement with four statements pertinent to EIS perceived ease of use.

User Involvement

User involvement (INV) is defined as the degree to which the user believes that the system possesses two characteristics: relevance and importance (Barki & Hartwick, 1989). This construct is measured using the instrument developed and tested by Barki and Hartwick (1994). The respondent is asked to describe the importance and relevance of EIS to the respondent's job on a seven-point scale using six pairs of adjectives.

IS Maturity

IS organizational maturity (MAT) refers to the overall status of the IS function within the organization. Prior studies used various criteria to measure information systems maturity. This study measures IS maturity using the nine-item instrument developed by King and Sabherwal (1992). This measure was based on previous scales of organizational maturity (Benbasat, Dexter, & Mantha, 1980) and was able to display high levels of reliability and validity. Respondents were asked to describe nine aspects of the overall information systems environment of their organisation on a six-point scale ranging from no extent to a very great extent.

EIS Sophistication

In accordance with Bergeron et al. (1995), this study measured EIS sophistication by ascertaining the presence of various technical features associated with EIS applications. The study adapted this measure by asking the respondent to choose the EIS capabilities available in the EIS out of a list of eight capabilities. Those were standard reporting, exception reporting, ad-hoc/unscheduled query, drill down capability, simple analyses (e.g., spreadsheets), what-if-analyses/modeling, external databases, and soft data (e.g., news and forecasts).

Table 3. Constructs measures

Information quality (IQ): IQ1. Do you think the output is presented in a useful format? IQ2. Is the information clear? IQ3. Is the information accurate? IQ4. Does EIS provide the critical information you need? IQ5. Does EIS provide sufficient information? IQ6. Does EIS provide up-to-date information? IQ7. Do you get the information you need in time? IQ8. Does EIS provide reports that are about exactly what you want? IQ9. Does the system provide the precise information you need?
Ease of use (EOU): EOU1. I find EIS easy to interact with EOU2. I find it easy to get EIS to do what I want it to do EOU3. My use of EIS requires a lot of mental effort EOU4. I find it is easy to become skillful at using EIS
User involvement (INV): INV1. Important/unimportant INV2. Essential/nonessential INV3. Trivial/fundamental INV4. Of no concern to me/of concern to me INV5. Relevant to me/irrelevant to me INV6. Matters to me/does not matter to me
IS maturity (MAT): MAT1. Extent to which IS staff are informed about business plans and operations MAT2. Extent to which top management is informed about information technology MAT3. Extent to which information technology impacts the organization's performance MAT4. Extent to which IS supports many functions in the organization MAT5. Extent to which information technology is available throughout the organization's premises MAT6. Extent to which IS performance is evaluated in terms of contribution to the organization's overall objectives rather than cost savings MAT7. Extent to which IS planning is formalised MAT8. Extent to which IS planning takes the business plans into consideration MAT9. Extent to which top management is involved in IS planning
EIS sophistication (SOFIS): Number of functions available in your EIS
EIS information use (INFOUSE): The percentage of information needs satisfied via the use of EIS (directly and through others)

The research instrument was pilot tested on 22 respondents, who were participants in the executive MBA evening program at City University Business School. Most of the students were full time executives and part time students. The participants were considered representative of the real world managers. Using the feedback from the pilot test, a number of the questions were reworded for clarity, and the final questionnaire was shortened.

Table 4. Levels of use of EIS information and other information sources

Information sources available to the EIS user	Mean	Std. Deviation	Minimum	Maximum
EIS information use (direct)	29.08%	0.2283	0%	100%
EIS information use (indirect)	15.15%	0.1653	0%	80%
Paper-based sources	29.97%	0.1888	0%	85%
Personal contacts	25.27%	0.1906	0%	90%

Analysis and Results

Descriptive Statistics

Table 4 describes the managers' use of various information sources available to them. The results show that EIS is used to satisfy only 44% of the executives' information needs: 29% through direct use and 15% through indirect use. The results also show that executives in the sample still satisfy 56% of their information needs through other conventional information sources such as paper-based sources (29%) and personal contacts (25%).

These results are consistent with previous research on managers' use of computer-based information. Many executives today still depend on paper summaries or information provided by administrative staff while those who use personal computers often receive data heavily manipulated by others in the organization (Bartholomew, 1997). The dependence on personal contacts may be explained by the nature of this source as a rich communication channel able to convey both hard and soft information (Watson et al., 1997).

The means and standard deviations for the constructs are reported in Table 5. EIS information quality is calculated as the average score (3.57) of nine quality attributes on a five-point scale. This result indicates that, on average, EIS are perceived to provide a satisfactory level of information quality. The relatively low standard deviation (0.71) is an indicator of a relatively low dispersion of the responses around their mean. In addition, the means of the individual items (dimensions) of information quality reveal that the executives' satisfaction with the accuracy, clearness, and timeliness dimensions of EIS information was higher than their satisfaction with the precision, relevancy, and format dimensions. Although this result reflects a higher than average perception of EIS information quality, more efforts are needed in order to improve EIS information quality and meet executives' information needs.

Table 5. Descriptive statistics

Construct	Mean	S.D.
1 - EIS information use (INTOUSE)	0.4423	0.2599
2 - Information quality (IQ)	3.5653	0.7078
3 - Easy of use (EOUA)	3.6551	0.7019
4 - User involvement (INV)	5.7901	1.0211
IS maturity (MAT)	3.3762	0.5734
5 - EIS sophistication (SOFIS)	4.5324	1.5578

Also, the results in Table 5 show that EIS is perceived to be moderately easy to use (mean = 3.66 on a 5-point scale). This result is consistent with the finding of an earlier study of UK organizations (Fitzgerald & Murphy, 1994), indicating a moderate level of ease of use. However, this finding somewhat differs from the high level of ease of use (mean = 4.5 on a 5-point scale) reported by the Finnish and English EIS users in Partanen and Savolainen (1995).

User involvement was calculated as the average score of the respondents' evaluation of the importance and relevance of EIS to their job using six adjectives on a seven-point scale. The mean of user involvement score is 5.79 (on a 7-point scale), which indicates that users perceived EIS as being highly relevant and important to their jobs. The standard deviation of 1.02 reflects a relatively low dispersion of the values around their mean.

IS maturity is the average score of nine items corresponding to different aspects of the IS function on a six-point scale, ranging from no extent to a very great extent. The total maturity score has a mean of 3.38 and a standard deviation of 0.57, which reflects a moderate overall IS maturity status. The questionnaire items related to the

Table 6. Frequency of reported availability of EIS functions

EIS Functions	Frequency (N = 216)	Valid Percent
Standard Reporting	214	99.1%
Ad-hoc/Unscheduled Query	165	76.4%
External Databases	54	25.0%
Simple Analyses/Spreadsheets	178	82.4%
Exception Reporting	116	53.7%
Drill-down Capability	150	69.4%
What-if Analyses/Modeling	60	27.8%
Soft data (e.g., news, forecasts)	41	19.0%

extent of information technology (IT) penetration in the various functions in the organization received higher ratings than the items related to IT management and systems evaluation based on their impact on the organizational goals. Although this finding reflects only a relatively moderate level of IS maturity, it is higher than the generally low IS maturity level in the small to medium sized UK manufacturing organizations reported in Wastell and Sewards' (1995) study.

As to EIS sophistication, the results in Table 6 show that, on average, EIS provide from four to five capabilities to their users (mean = 4.56). Table 6 displays the distribution of the EIS capabilities in the sample. More than 99% of the executives had access to ad-hoc query capabilities, and more than 82% had access to simple information analyses (i.e., spreadsheets) capabilities. However, only 19% of the executives reported to have access to soft data (i.e., news, forecasts), and only 27% were found to have access to what-if analysis and modeling capabilities. Such findings echo the results of an earlier similar survey in the UK (Perera, 1995).

Hypotheses and Model Testing

The exogenous variables in this study include ease of use, user involvement, IS maturity, and EIS sophistication. The two endogenous variables are information quality and information use. A structural equations modeling (SEM) technique was applied to test the research model, which incorporates linkages between all exogenous variables in order to detect any partial or full mediation by information quality (e.g., Kowtha & Choon, 2001). The AMOS 3.61 package was used since it has the ability to test relationships between constructs with multiple indicators. It provides maximum likelihood estimates of paths, assessment of measurement model, and modification indices that can help in model identification.

The Measurement Model

To assess the measurement model, Table 7 illustrates the standardized loading of the indicators on their corresponding constructs, their critical ratios (the parameter estimate divided by its standard error), the coefficient of determination as an indicator of composite reliability, and the variance extracted estimate.

From Table 7, the standardized factor loadings, which are indicators of the degree of association between a scale item and a construct, are highly significant (with critical ratio ranging from 6.41 to 17.42), where critical values greater than 0.2 indicate loading significance at $p < 0.05$. With the exception of IS maturity, all items loaded clearly on their corresponding constructs demonstrating both convergent and discriminant validity.

Table 7. Standardized loadings, critical ratio composite reliability, and variance extracted

Constructs	Scale items	Standardized loading	Critical ratio	Composite reliability	Variance extracted
IS Maturity:					
IS Integration	MAT1	0.59*			
	MAT2	0.56	6.48		
	MAT6	0.58	6.62		
	MAT7	0.68	7.39	0.80	0.42
	MAT8	0.77	7.96		
	MAT9	0.68	7.41		
IT Penetration	MAT3	0.65	6.41		
	MAT4	0.78	6.53	0.71	0.45
	MAT5	0.58*			
Ease of Use	EOU1	0.81*			
	EOU2	0.77	11.95		
	EOU3	0.82	12.67	0.87	0.63
	EOU4	0.78	12.07		
Involvement	INV1	0.82*			
	INV2	0.84	15.1		
	INV3	0.87	15.85		
	INV4	0.90	16.86	0.95	0.77
	INV5	0.91	17.05		
	INV6	0.92	17.42		
Information Quality	IQ1	0.69*			
	IQ2	0.65	8.91		
	IQ3	0.56	7.76		
	IQ4	0.80	10.84		
	IQ5	0.76	10.29	0.91	0.53
	IQ6	0.65	8.97		
	IQ7	0.72	9.78		
	IQ8	0.83	11.20		
	IQ9	0.85	11.50		

* Indicates parameters fixed at 1.0 in the original solution, thus no critical ration is provided.

The results of the analysis suggest that the IS maturity construct includes two dimensions. The first dimension is *IS integration* (MAT1, MAT2, MAT6, MAT7, MAT8, and MAT9), which reflects the extent of IS alignment and integration with the organization. The second dimension is *IT penetration* (MAT3, MAT4, and MAT5), which reflects the extent of IT dissemination within the organization. A comparison between the means of the two dimensions of IS maturity shows a significantly higher IT penetration mean (4.02) than the IS integration mean of 3.07 (p < 0.001). This result suggests that the technological focus of the IS functions in the surveyed companies is stronger than their business alignment and integration focus. The two dimensions of IS maturity (IS integration and IT penetration) are included in the structural equation modeling analysis.

Figure 2. The revised model and path coefficient

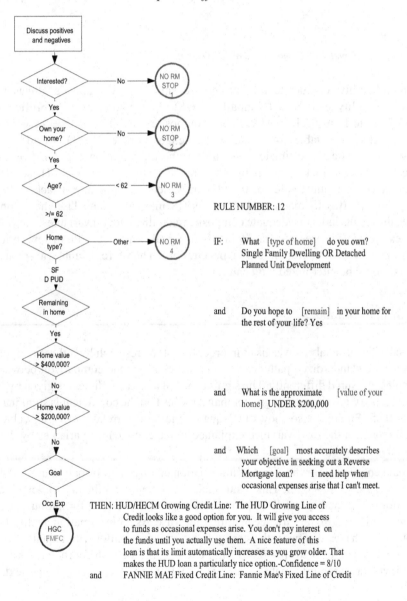

RULE NUMBER: 12

IF: What [type of home]   do you own? Single Family Dwelling OR Detached Planned Unit Development

and   Do you hope to   [remain]   in your home for the rest of your life? Yes

and   What is the approximate   [value of your home]   UNDER $200,000

and   Which   [goal]   most accurately describes your objective in seeking out a Reverse Mortgage loan?   I need help when occasional expenses arise that I can't meet.

THEN: HUD/HECM Growing Credit Line: The HUD Growing Line of Credit looks like a good option for you. It will give you access to funds as occasional expenses arise. You don't pay interest on the funds until you actually use them. A nice feature of this loan is that its limit automatically increases as you grow older. That makes the HUD loan a particularly nice option.-Confidence = 8/10

and   FANNIE MAE Fixed Credit Line: Fannie Mae's Fixed Line of Credit

Table 8. The results of path analysis

Hypothesis	Path		Standardized Path Coefficient	Critical Ratio (CR)[1]	Variance Explained SMC
	From To				
H1	Information Quality	Information use	0.47	6.56	0.22
H2-1	Ease of use	Information Quality	0.40	5.55	
H2-2	User Involvement	Information Quality	0.27	4.13	
H2-3a	IS Integration	Information Quality	0.25	2.93	0.45
H2-3b	IT Penetration	Information Quality	-0.03	-0.35	
H2-4	EIS Sophistication	Information Quality	0.18	3.00	

[1] *CR > 2 indicates path coefficients significant at p < 0.05*

As to reliability, composite reliabilities are similar to Cronbach's alphas internal reliability estimates (Nunnally, 1978). The composite reliabilities in Table 7 range from 0.71 to 0.91, and a composite reliability of 0.70 or greater is considered acceptable for research (Fornell & Larcker, 1981). In addition, the variance extracted estimates, which describe the variation explained by the indicators relative to measurement error, range from 0.77 to 0.42. These estimates exceed the cutoff value of 0.50 (Hair, Anderson, Tatham, & Black, 1998), except for the two IS maturity dimensions (IS integration and IT penetration). While the results indicate adequate composite reliabilities for all variables, the variance extracted estimates adequately justify using all constructs with the exception of IS maturity (IS integration and IT penetration). Therefore, IS maturity-related results should be interpreted with caution.

The Structural Model

Path coefficients analysis was used in order to test the research hypotheses. Figure 2 shows the standardized path coefficients, which allow the comparison between variables measured differently. The significance of a path coefficient is given by its critical ratio (CR) where a CR greater than 2 means that the coefficient is significant at p < 0.05. Figure 2 also shows the squared multiple correlation (SMC) values, which represent the total variance explained in the endogenous variables by their respective determinants.

The path coefficient for the effect of information quality on information use is 0.47 (p < 0.001) and CR = 6.56. This result indicates a positive influence of perceived EIS information quality on EIS based information use. However, information quality explains only 22% of the variance in information use. As for information quality, the results show that ease of use is the strongest determinant of information quality with a path coefficient of 0.40 (p > 0.001) and CR = 5.55. The path coefficient of 0.27 from involvement to information quality (p < 0.001) and CR = 4.13 comes next.

Table 9. The fit indices for the tested research model

Fit Indices	Guidelines	Model Testing Results
Chi-square Significance	P < 0.05	P < 0.001
Chi-square/Degrees of Freedom (CMIN/DF)	< 2 – 5	1.9
Goodness of Fit (GFI)	> 0.90	0.80
Adjusted Goodness of Fit (AGFI)	> 0.80	0.77
Root Mean Square Error of Approximation (RMSEA)	< 0.1	0.07
Comparative Fit Index (CFI/RNI)	> 0.90	0.90
Tucker-Lewis Coefficient (TLI/NNFI)	> 0.90	0.89

Also, only one dimension of IS maturity has illustrated a significant positive impact on information quality. IS integration with the organization was found to influence perceived information quality (path coefficient = 0.25, CR = 2.9, P < 0.01). This result suggests that the integration and the alignment of the IS function within the organization may be more influential on the perceived information quality of EIS than the mere IT penetration of the organization is. Finally, EIS sophistication shows a positive significant impact on perceived EIS information quality (path coefficient = 0.18, CR = 3.0, P < 0.01).

Table 8 summarizes the results of path analysis. With the exception of *H2-3b*, the test results support the acceptance of all hypotheses.

The Fit of the Structural Model

To test the goodness of fit of the structural model, several indices were computed and are summarized in Table 9. A statistically significant chi-square (chi-square = 756; df = 391; p < 0.001) was found, which suggests that the hypothesized model is sufficiently close to the observed data. However, the chi-square statistic is marginally useful when used alone, due to its sensitivity to sample size and departure from multivariate normality. Alternatively, the ratio of the chi-square to the degrees of freedom CMIN/DF (e.g., Sharma, 1996) was used. CMIN/DF was found to be approximately 1.9 (below the thresholds of 2-5), which suggests an acceptable model fit.

Furthermore, although both values are lower than desired, the goodness of fit index (GFI = 0.80) and the adjusted goodness of fit index (AGFI = 0.77) indicate a reasonable model fit. The root mean square error of approximation (RMSEA = 0.07) is at an acceptable level. Finally, the comparative fit index (CFI = 0.90), which is identical to McDonald and March's relative noncentrality index (RNI), and the Tucker-Lewis coefficient (TLI = 0.89), also known as Bentler-Bonett non-normed fit index (NNFI) (Arbuckle, 1997), suggests a good model fit. Overall, the indices in Table 9 indicate that the hypothesized model exhibits a satisfactory fit with the observed data.

Discussion

The research model of this study was designed to investigate the possible impact of user involvement, ease of use, IS maturity, and system sophistication on users' perception of information quality on one hand, and the possible impact of information quality on EIS information use on the other hand. With the exception of the relationship of the IT penetration dimension of IS maturity on EIS information quality, the data analyses support all the hypothesized relationships between the independent and dependent variables in the research model. EIS information quality was found to positively influence EIS information use; and EIS information quality, in turn, was found to be positively influenced by ease of use, user involvement, the IS integration dimension of IS maturity, and EIS sophistication.

The finding of a positive impact of EIS information quality on information usage is consistent with the findings of a number of past similar studies. For instance, Bergeron et al. (1995) found the satisfaction with information content to have a positive influence on the frequency of use and on the level of EIS internalization in the user's work. Also, Leidner (1996) reported EIS information quality to be the main determinant of frequent use of EIS. The positive impact of information quality on EIS usage was expected, since the quality of EIS information output was reported to be a key to EIS information use (Rainer & Watson, 1995). Furthermore, information quality was found to be the most important attributes of EIS from the top managers' point of view (Bergeron et al., 1991).

When information is perceived as relevant to their needs, reliable in terms of accuracy and content, managers are more likely to use it (Low & Mohr, 2001). However, EIS were found to satisfy only 44% of the executives' information needs, of which only 29% are satisfied through direct use of EIS. Improvement in EIS information quality is likely to increase the proportion of information needs that can be satisfied via direct use of EIS. Additionally, the analysis of the data on EIS information quality suggests that the executives were satisfied with EIS information accuracy, clearness, and timeliness but less satisfied with its relevancy, precision, and format. Therefore, managers and EIS developers need to cooperate effectively in order to improve the overall quality of EIS information, consequently, enhancing its use.

Ease of use was found to be the strongest determinant of EIS information quality, followed by user involvement, IS maturity, and system sophistication. The finding of a strong, positive impact of ease of use on EIS information quality is logical and lends further support to the literature suggesting accessibility as an important information quality attribute (Huang et al., 1999; Strong et al., 1997; Wang & Strong, 1996). It is also consistent with those of the prior studies that investigated accessibility and information use (O'Reilly, 1982) and ease of use and perceived usefulness (Adams et al., 1992; Igbaria et al., 1997; Mathieson, 1991; Sjazna, 1996). Inaccessible EIS information has no value to users, and its quality will be negatively perceived. Consequently, in order to boost users' positive beliefs in EIS information quality, EIS must be easy to interact with, flexible, and easy to learn. Continuous user training and orientation programs along with investments in flexible and easy to learn EIS should improve information quality, and consequently, its use.

The positive impact of user involvement on EIS information quality comes in accordance with our expectation. Effective managers' participation in EIS planning and implementation is expected to develop positive beliefs concerning the relevancy and importance of the systems (Barki & Hartwick, 1989) to their decision making and activities. In this context, the finding of this study is consistent with those of Srivihok (1999), where a positive correlation was detected between participation in EIS development and EIS information quality. This particular finding implies that user participation results in an accurate assessment of the users' information needs and avoids the development of unnecessary features and, therefore, creates a higher user perception of the system's information quality. Therefore, top management should consider providing an environment that is conducive to users' participation and involvement in EIS planning and implementation.

The factor analysis yielded two dimensions of the IS maturity construct: IS integration and IT penetration. IS integration was found to influence information quality. This finding emphasizes the importance of the organizational context in which EIS are introduced on the information quality of such applications. The insignificant influence of IT penetration on information quality implies that higher levels of IT dispersion in the organization may not be conducive to providing higher quality information output. When properly aligned and managed in an organization, the IS function should be capable of planning, designing, and implementing EIS applications that are likely to be perceived to offer useful and quality information to their users.

The impact of IS maturity on EIS information quality was not previously investigated. Research on information systems has treated satisfaction with information quality as an important component of user satisfaction with information systems. Likewise, the finding of a positive impact of the IS integration dimension of IS maturity on EIS information quality seems to be consistent with the findings of those studies that investigated the relationship of IS maturity to user satisfaction (e.g., Cheney & Dickson, 1982; Mahmood & Becker, 1985; Raymond, 1990). However, the IS maturity related findings of this study should be cautiously interpreted since the results of the measurement model analysis (Table 7) suggests that the measurement of the IS maturity construct may be problematic.

Higher levels of EIS sophistication were found to contribute to stronger positive beliefs concerning information quality. Standard reporting, simple analysis, ad hoc queries, drill-down analyses, and exception reporting are the most common EIS capabilities reported by managers. The data also suggest that access to external and soft information data is still a scarce occurrence in the UK-based EIS applications. In other words, UK-based EIS applications provide internal reporting and control capabilities rather than environmental scanning capabilities. This finding lends support to Perera's (1995) findings in an earlier UK-based EIS study.

The limited access to external and soft information seems prevalent in the surveyed U.K.-based EIS applications. Such applications are likely used to support the internal reporting and control managerial functions rather than to support the more important planning and environmental scanning functions of executives. Designers and implementers of EIS applications need to ensure the availability of the reportedly lacking soft data and modeling capabilities to managers. However, EIS designers and implementers should also be aware of the possible negative impact of adding or enhancing the technical capabilities of the systems (i.e., provision of drill down) on ease of use as a strong determinant of perceived information quality.

Research Limitations

The implications from this study should be considered in light of its main limitations. First, information quality was investigated in this study as a strong determinant of EIS information use and, consequently, EIS effectiveness. The implicit assumption here is that using more information is associated with improved decisions. Such an assumption, however, is strongly supported by past research demonstrating positive effects of information use on improved organizational outcomes (e.g., Low & Mohr, 2001).

Second, the key informant methodology was used to collect the research data and to measure the research variables. Although this method is the most frequently used technique in IS research, it raises concerns about the respondent's ability to accurately answer questions (Low & Mohr, 2001). To address such a measurement limitation, future information systems effectiveness research could add to our understanding of the factors that affect managers' use of EIS information by relying on qualitative research or experimental methods in order to complement the results reported in this investigation.

Third, the variance extracted estimates for the two IS maturity dimensions—IS integration and IT penetration—are 0.42 and 0.45, respectively. These two estimates—the variation explained by the indicators relative to measurement error—are below the recommended cutoff value of 0.50 (Hair et al., 1998), which justifies using the construct related data in the analysis. Therefore, our IS maturity related results should be interpreted with caution. Future research may verify this measurement problem of IS maturity before searching for an alternative measure to operationalize the construct.

Finally, the objective of this study was to investigate the impact of information quality on EIS information. Therefore, the analysis focused on measuring only the direct path (influence) from EIS information quality to EIS information use, and no direct paths from the exogenous variables to EIS information use were measured. While the structural model exhibits a satisfactory fit with the observed data, only 22% of the variance in EIS information use are explained by EIS information quality. Having only information quality as a determinant of EIS information use weakens the explanatory power of our model. In an attempt to explain more variance in EIS information use, future research may be designed to measure the indirect as well as the direct paths from the exogenous variables of ease of use, user involvement, IS maturity, and EIS sophistication to EIS information use. Similar future research models may include other variables (e.g., perceived usefulness, facilitating conditions, user attitudes, user training) that are believed to affect EIS information use in order to explain more variance in both perceived information quality and EIS information use. In addition, since there is an evident transition from traditional EIS to Web-based EIS (e.g., Basu et al., 2000), future research designs may also focus on exploring the possible impact of these factors on the information quality and use of the Web-based EIS.

Conclusion

Faced with an abundance of data, executives are expected to assess EIS information quality in order to determine whether they should use them. This raises the question of what can be done to improve information quality. The results of this investigation concerning EIS information quality influence on information use by UK managers, and EIS information quality determinants (ease of use, user involvement, IS maturity, and system sophistication) contribute to IS literature on information systems success. The findings of this investigation suggest that information quality is an important determinant of information use, which ultimately leads to effective managerial decisions and improved organizational performance. EIS information quality, in turn, can be enhanced by fully or partially manipulating factors such as ease of use, user involvement, IS maturity (integration), and EIS sophistication.

UK executives were found to satisfy 55% of their information needs from sources other than EIS (i.e., personal contacts, paper-based sources). This finding may be explained by the fact that managers' perception of EIS information quality was found to be just above average. As such, it is important to develop and implement EIS that are capable of providing managers with information that better suits their information needs. Improvement efforts may focus on the installation of flexible and easy to learn EIS, enhancement of EIS capabilities to include soft and external data analysis and modeling, provision of an environment that is conducive to users' involvement in EIS planning and implementation, and strong commitment to achieving IS alignment and integration with business strategies and plans.

Given the limitations of this investigation, future research may be designed in order to replicate and extend this investigation using other exogenous variables, different sampling frames, and other EIS forms (e.g., Web-based EIS) and information systems applications in order to verify our findings and enhance their external capacity to be generalized. The development of future research models and the selection of new variables should be guided by the models and frameworks available in the literature on information systems effectiveness.

References

Adams, D.A., Nelson, R.R., & Todd, P.A. (1992). Perceived usefulness, ease of use, and usage of information technology: A replication. *MIS Quarterly, 16*, 227-248.

Agarwal, R., Prasad, J., & Zanino, M.C. (1996). Training experience and usage intentions: A field study of a graphical user interface. *International Journal of Human-Computer Studies, 45*, 215-241.

Almutairi, H., & Subramanian, G.H. (2005). An empirical application of the DeLone and McLean model in the Kuwaiti Private Sector. *The Journal of Computer Information Systems, 45*(3), 113-122.

Amott, D., & Pervan, G. (2005). A critical analysis of decision support systems research. *Journal of Information Technology, 20*(2), 67.

Arbuckle, J.L. (1997). *AMOS user guild version 3.6*. Chicago: Small Waters Corporation.

Babbie, E. (1990). *Survey research methods* (2nd ed.). Belmont, CA: Wadsworth.

Bajwa, D.S., Rai, A., & Brennan, I. (1998). Key antecedents of executive information systems success: A path analytic approach. *Decision Support Systems, 22*, 31-43.

Barki, H., & Hartwick, J. (1989). Rethinking the concept of user involvement. *MIS Quarterly, 13*(1), 53-63.

Barki, H., & Hartwick, J. (1994). Measuring user participation, user involvement, and user attitude. *MIS Quarterly, 18*(1), 59-82.

Ballou, D.P., & Pazer, H.L. (1985). Modeling data and process quality in multi-input, multi-output information systems. *Management Science, 31*(2), 150-162.

Ballou, D.P., & Pazer, H.L. (1995). Designing information systems to optimize the accuracy-timeliness trade off. *Information Systems Research, 6*(1), 51-72.

Baroudi, J.J., Olson, M.H., & Ives, B. (1986). An empirical study of the impact of user involvement on system usage and information system satisfaction. *Communications of the ACM*, (29) 3, 232-238.

Bartholomew, D. (1997, March). When will EIS deliver? *Industry Week, 3*, 37-39.

Basu, C., Poindexter, S., Drosen, J., & Addo, T. (2000). Diffusion of executive information systems in organizations and the shift to Web technologies. *Industrial Management + Data Systems, 100*(6), 271.

Benard R., & Satir, A. (1993). User satisfaction with EISs: Meeting the needs of the executive users. *Information Systems Management, 10*(4), 21-29.

Benbasat, I., Dexter, A.S., & Mantha, R.W. (1980). Impact of organizational maturity on information system skill need. *MIS Quarterly, 4*(1), 21-34.

Bergeron, F., Raymond, L., & Lagorge, M. (1991). Top managers evaluate the attributes of EIS. In I. Zigurs (Ed.), *DSS-91 transactions* (pp. 6-12).

Bergeron, F., Raymond, Rivard, S., & Gara, M. (1995). Determinants of EIS use: Testing a behavioral model. *Decision Support systems, 14*(2), 131-146.

Bharati, P., & Chaudhury, A. (2006). Product customization: An empirical study of factors impacting choiceboard user satisfaction. *Information Resources management Journal, 19*(2), 69-81.

Boynton, A.C., Zmud, R.W., & Jacobs, G.C. (1994, September). The influence of IT management practice on IT use in large organizations. *MIS Quarterly*, 299-318.

Cambridge Research Group (CRG). (1997). *Information quality survey: Administrator's guide*. Cambridge, MA: CRG.

Cheney, P., & Dickson, G.B. (1982). Organizational characteristics and information systems: An exploratory investigation. *Academy of Management Journal, 25*(1), 170-148.

Chin, W.W., & Todd, P.A. (1995, June). On the use, usefulness, and ease of use of the use of structural equation modeling in MIS research: A note of caution. *MIS Quarterly*, pp. 237-246.

Clikeman, P.M. (1999). Improving information quality. *The Internal Auditor, 56*(3), 32-33.

Compeau, D., & Higgins, C. (1995). Computer self-efficacy: Development of a measure and initial test. *MIS Quarterly, 19*(2), 189-211.

Compeau, D., Higgins, C.A., & Huff, S. (1999). Social cognitive theory and individual reactions to computing technology: A longitudinal study. *MIS Quarterly, 23*(2), 145-158.

Davis, F.D. (1989). Perceived usefulness, perceived ease of use, and user acceptance of information technology. *MIS Quarterly, 13*(30), 319-339.

Davis, F.D., Bagozzi, R.P., & Warshaw P.R. (1989). User acceptance of computer technology: A comparison of two theoretical models. *Management Science, 35*(8), 982-1003.

DeLone, W.H., & McLean, E.R. (1989). Information systems success: The quest for the dependent variable. *Information Systems Research, 3*(1), 60-94.

DeLone, W.D., & McLean, E.R. (1992). Information systems success: The quest for the dependent variable. *Information Systems Research, 3*(1), 60-95.

DeLone, W.D., & McLean, E.R. (2003). The DeLone and McLean model of information systems success: A ten-year update. *Journal of Management Information Systems, 19*(4), 9-30.

Doll, W.J., & Torkzadeh, G. (1988). The measurement of end-user computing satisfaction. *MIS Quarterly, 12*(2), 259-274.

Doll, W.J., Xia, W., & Torkzadeh, G. (1994, December). A confirmatory factor analysis of the end-user computing satisfaction instrument. *MIS Quarterly,* 453-461.

Ein-Dor, P., & Segev, E. (1986). Attitudes, associations, and success of MIS: Some empirical results from research in the context of a business game. *The Computer Journal, 29*(3), 212-221.

Elam, J.J., & Leidner, D.G. (1995). EIS adoption, use, and impact: The executive perspective. *Decision Support Systems, 14*(2), 89-103.

El-Kordy, M. (2000). *Understanding the utilization of executive information systems using an integrated technology acceptance model: Theoretical base and empirical validation.* Unpublished Doctoral Dissertation, City University London.

Elkordy, M. (1994). *Analyses of some personal and environmental variables and their relation with MIS effectiveness: An applied study in the banking sector.* Master's thesis (in Arabic), Alexandria University, Egypt, Department of Business Administration.

Firth, C.P., & Wang, R.Y. (1996). *Data quality systems: Evaluation and implementation.* Cambridge Market, London: Intelligence Ltd.

Fishbein, M. (1980). *A theory of personal action: Some applications and implications.* In Nebraska Symposium on Motivation, 1979: Beliefs, Attitudes and Values (pp. 65-116). University of Nebraska Press.

Fitzgerald, B., & Murphy, C. (1994). Introducing executive information systems into organizations: Separating fact from fallacy. *Journal of Information Technology, 9*, 288-297.

Fornell, C., & Larcker, D.F. (1981). Evaluating structural equations models with unobservable variables and measurement error. *Journal of Marketing research, 18*(1), 39-50.

Franz, C.R., & Robey, D. (1986). Organizational context, user involvement, and the usefulness of information systems. *Decision Sciences, 17*, 329-355.

Frolick, M.N., Parzinger, M.J., Rainer, R.K., Jr., & Ramarapu, N.K. (1997). Using EISs for environmental scanning. *Information Systems in Management, 14*(1), 35-40.

Fuerst, W., & Cheney, P. (1982). Factors affecting the perceived utilization of computer-based information systems in the oil industry. *Decision Science, 13*, 554-569.

Gefen, D., & Straub, D.W. (1997). Gender differences in the perception and use of e-mail: An extension of the technology acceptance model. *MIS Quarterly, 21*(8), 389-400.

Glover, H., Watson, H.J., & Rainer, K. (1992, Winter). 20 ways to waste an EIS investment. *Information Strategy: The Executive's Journal, 8*(Part 2), 11-17.

Goodhue, D.L., & Thompson, R.L. (1995, June). Task-technology fit and individual performance. *MIS Quarterly, 19*, 213-236.

Hair, J.F., Anderson, R.E., Tatham, R.L., & Black, W.C. (1998). *Multivariate data analysis* (5th ed.). Upper Saddle River, NJ: Prentice Hall.

Huang, K., Lee, Y., & Wang, R. (1999). *Quality information and knowledge.* Upper Saddle River, NJ: Prentice Hall.

Hung, S. (2003). Expert versus novice use of the executive support systems: An empirical study. *Information & Management, 40*(3), 177.

Hung, S., & Liang, T. (2001). Effect of computer self-efficacy on the use of executive support systems. *Industrial Management + data Systems, 101*(5/6), 227-236.

Igbaria, M., Guimaraes, T., & Davis, G.B. (1995). Testing the determinants of microcomputer usage via a structural equation model. *Journal of Management Information Systems, 11*(4), 87-114.

Igbaria, M., Zinatelli, N., Cragg, P., & Cavaye Angele, L.M. (1997). Personal computing acceptance factors in small firms: A structural equation model. *MIS Quarterly, 21*(3), 279-305.

Ives, B., Hamilton, S., & Davis, G. (1980). A framework for research in computer-based management information systems. *Management Science, 20*(9), 47-53.

Jones, J.W., & McLeod, R. (1986). The structure of executive information systems: An exploratory analysis. *Decision Sciences, 17*, 220-248.

Juran, J.M., Gryna, F.M.J., & Bingham, R.S. (1974). *Quality control handbook* (3rd ed.). New York, NY: McGraw-Hill Book Co.

Kahn, B.K., Strong, D.M., & Wang, R.Y. (2002). Information quality benchmarks: Product and service performance. *Communications of the ACM, 45*(4), 184-192.

Kappelman, L.A., & McLean, E. (1991). The perspective roles of user participation and user involvement in the information systems implementation success. In *Proceedings of the 12th International Conference on Information Systems* (pp. 339-349), New York.

Khalil, O., & Elkordy, M. (1999). The relationship between user satisfaction and systems usage: Empirical evidence from Egypt. *Journal of End User Computing, 11*(2), 21-28.

Khalil, O.E., & Elkordy, M.M. (1997). The relation of some personal and situational factors to IS effectiveness: Empirical evidence from Egypt. *Journal of Global Information Management, 2*(5), 22-33.

Kim, J. (1996). *An empirical investigation of factors influencing the utilization of executive information systems*. Unpublished Doctoral Dissertation, University of Nebraska.

Kim, K.K. (1989, Fall). User satisfaction: A synthesis of three different perspectives. *Journal of Information Systems*, pp. 1-12.

King, W., & Sabherwal, R. (1992). The factors affecting strategic information systems applications. *Information & Management, 23*, 217-235.

Koh, C.E., & Watson, H.J. (1998). Data management in executive information systems. *Information & Management, 33*, 301-312.

Kowtha, N.R., & Choon, T.W.I. (2001). Determinants of Website development: A study of electronic commerce in Singapore. *Information & Management, 39*, 227-242.

Kraemer, K.L., Danziger, J.N., Dunkle, D.E., & King, J.L. (1993). The usefulness of computer-based information to public managers. *MIS Quarterly, 17*(2), 129-148.

Lan, Z., & Scott, G.R. (1996). The relative importance of computer-mediated information versus conventional non-computer mediated information in public managerial decision making. *Information Resource Management Journal, 9*(1), 27-37.

Leidner, D.E. (1996). Modern management in the developing world: The success of EIS in Mexican organizations. In *Proceedings of the International Conference on Information Systems* (pp. 290-306), Cleveland, Ohio.

Leidner, D.E. (1998). Mexican executives' use of information systems: An empirical investigation of EIS use and impact. *Journal of Global Information Technology Management, 1*(2), 19-36.

Liang, L.Y., & Miranda, R. (2001). Dashboards and scorecards: Executive information systems for the public sector. *Government Finance Review, 17*(6), 14-26.

Livari, J. (2005). An empirical test of the DeLone-Mclean model of information system success. *Database for Advances in Information Systems, 36*(2), 8-27.

Low, G.S., & Mohr, J. (2001). Factors affecting the use of information in the evaluation of marketing communications productivity. *Academy of Marketing Science Journal, 29*(1), 70-88.

Lucas, H.C. (1975). *Why information systems fail?* Columbia, New York.

Lucas, H.C. (1978). The use of an interactive information storage and retrieval system in medical research. *Communications of the ACM, 21*(3), 197-205.

Madnick, S., & Wang, R.Y. (1992*). Introduction to total quality management (TDQM) research program* (No. TDQM-92-0). Total Data Quality Management Program, MIT Sloan School of Management, Sloan.

Mahmood, M.A., & Becker, J.D. (1985). Effect of organizational maturity on end-users' satisfaction with information systems. *Journal of Management Information Systems, 11*(3), 37-65.

Maltz, E., & Kohli, A.K. (1996, February). Market intelligence dissemination across functional boundaries. *Journal of Marketing Research, 33*, 47-61.

Mathieson, K. (1991). Predicting user intention: Comparing the technology acceptance model with the theory of planned behavior. *Information Systems Research, 2*(3), 173-191.

McBride, N. (1997). The rise and fall of an executive information system: A case study. *Information Systems Journal, 7*, 277-287.

McGill, T., Hobbs, V., & Klobas, J. (2003). User-developed applications and information systems success: A test of DeLone and McLean's model. *Information Resources Management Journal, 16*(1), 24-45.

McKeen, J.D., Guimaraes, T., & Wetherbe, J.C. (1994, December). The relationship between user participation and user satisfaction: An investigation of four contingency factors. *MIS Quarterly*, pp. 427-451.

Mcleod, R., Jones, J.W., & Poitevent, J.L. (1984). Executives' perceptions of their information sources. In W. Robert (Ed.), *Transactions of the Fourth International DSS.84 Conference on Decision Support Systems* (pp. 2-14), Dallas, Texas.

Millet, I., & Mawhinney, C.H. (1992). Executive information systems: A critical perspective. *Information & Management, 23*, 83-92.

Nandhakumar, J., & Jones, M. (1997, December 15-17). Designing in the dark: The changing user-development relationship in information systems development. In *Proceedings of the Eighteenth International Conference on Information Systems* (pp. 75-87), Atlanta, Georgia.

Nord, J.H., & Nord, G.D. (1995). Executive information systems: A study and comparative analysis. *Information & Management, 29*, 95-106.

Nunnally, J.C. (1978). *Psychometric theory* (2nd ed.). New York: McGraw-Hill.

Oggier, C. (2005). Nestle improves its financial reporting with management science. *Interface, 35*(4), 271-281.

O'Reilly, C.A. (1982). Variations in decision maker's use of information sources: The impact of quality and accessibility of information. *Academy of Management Review, 24*(4), 756-771.

Orr, K. (1998). Data quality and systems theory. *Communications of the ACM, 41*(2), 66-71.

Partanen, K., & Savolainen, V. (1995). Perspectives on executive information systems. *Systems Practice, 8*(6), 551-575.

Perera, K. (1995). *An investigation into the changing definition of EIS.* Master's Thesis, City University Business School, Department of Management Systems and Information.

Pervan, G., & Phua, R. (1997). A survey of the state of executive information systems in large Australian organizations. *Information Technology, 29*(2), 65-73.

Pitt, L.F., Watson, R.T., & Kavan, C.B. (1995). Service quality: A measure of information systems effectiveness. *MIQ Quarterly, 19*(2), 173-188.

Poon, P.P., & Wagner, C. (2001). Critical success factors revisited: Success and failure cases of information systems for senior executives. *Decision Support Systems, 30*, 393-418.

Raghunathan, S. (1999). Impact of information quality and decision-maker quality on decision quality. A theoretical model and simulation analysis. *Decision Support Systems, 26*(4), 275-286.

Rai, A., Lang, S.S., & Welker, R.B. (2002). Assessing the validity of IS success models: An empirical test and theoretical analysis. *Information Systems Research, 13*(1), 50-69.

Rainer, R.K., & Watson, H.J. (1995, Fall). The keys to executive information systems success. *Journal of Management Information Systems*, pp. 83-98.

Raymond, L. (1985). Organizational characteristics and MIS success in the context of small business. *MIS Quarterly, 9*(1), 37-52.

Raymond, L. (1990). Organizational context and information system success: A contingency approach. *Journal of Management Information Systems, 6*(4), 5-20.

Raymond, L., & St-Pierre, J. (2005). Antecedents and performance outcomes of advanced manufacturing systems sophistication in SMEs. *International Journal of Operations & Production Management, 25*(5/6), 514-533.

Robey, D. (1979). User attitudes and management information use. *Academy of Management Journal, 22*(3), 527-538.

Redman, T.C. (1992). *Data quality: Management and technology.* New York: Bantam Books.

Robey, D. (1979). User attitudes and management information use. *Academy of Management Journal, 22*(3), 527-538.

Rockart, J.F., & DeLong, D. (1988). *Executive support systems: The emergence of top management computer use.* New York: McGraw-Hill Book Company.

Rogers, E.M. (1995). *Diffusion of innovations* (4th ed.). New York: The Free Press.

Salmeron, J.L. (2002). EIS data: Findings from an evolutionary study. *The Journal of Systems and Software, 64*(2), 111.

Santosa, P.I., Wei, K.K., & Chan, H.C. (2005). User involvement and user satisfaction with information-seeking activity. *European Journal of Information Systems, 14*(4), 361.

Seddon, P., & Kiew, M. (1994). A partial test and development of the Delone and McLean model of IS success. In *Proceedings of the International Conference on Information Systems (ICIS 94)* (pp. 99-109). Vancouver, Canada.

Seddon, P.B. (1997). A respecification and extension of the Delone and McLean model of IS success. *Information Systems Research, 8*(3), 240- 253.

Sharma, S. (1996). *Applied multivariate techniques.* John Wiley & Sons, Inc.

Singleton, R.A., Straits, B.C., & Straits, M.M. (1993). *Approaches to social research* (2nd ed.). New York: Oxford University Press, Inc.

Sjazna, B. (1996). Empirical evaluation of the revised technology acceptance model. *Management Science, 42*(1), 85-92.

Srinivansan, A. (1985, September). Alternative measures of systems effectiveness: Associations and impact. *MIS Quarterly*, pp. 243-253.

Srivihok, A. (1999). Understanding executive information systems implementation: An empirical study of EIS success factors. In *Proceedings of the 32nd Hawaii International Conference on System Science*, Hawaii. IEEE Computer Society.

Straub, D., Limayem, M., & Karahanna-Evaristo, E. (1995) Measuring system usage: Implications for IS theory testing. *Management Science, 41*(8), 1328-1342.

Strong, D.M., Lee, Y.W., & Wang, R.Y. (1997). Data quality in context. *Communications of the ACM, 40*(5), 103-110.

Taylor, S., & Todd, P. (1995a). Understanding information technology usage: A test of competing models. *Information Systems Research, 6*(2), 144-176.

Taylor, S., & Todd, P. (1995b, December). Assessing IT usage: The role of prior experience. *MIS Quarterly,* pp. 561-570.

Torkzadeh, G., & Dwyer, D.J. (1994). A path analytic study of determinants of information systems usage. *Omega, International Journal of Management Science, 22*(4), 339-348.

Torkzadeh, R., Pelughoeft, K., & Hall, L. (1979). Computer self-efficacy, training effectiveness and user attitudes: An empirical study. *Behavior and Information Technology, 18*(4), 299-309.

Triandis, H.C. (1980). Values, attitudes, and interpersonal behavior. In *Nebraska Symposium on Motivation, Beliefs, Attitudes and Values* (pp. 195-259). University of Nebraska Press.

Venkatesh, V., & Davis, F.D. (1994). Modeling the determinants of perceived ease of use. In *Proceedings of the International Conference on Information systems* (pp. 213-227), Vancouver, Canada.

Walstrom, K.A., & Wilson, R.L. (1997). An examination of executive systems users. *Information & Management, 32*, 75-83.

Wang, R.Y., & Strong, D.M. (1996). Beyond accuracy: What data quality means to data consumers. *Journal of Management information Systems, 12*(4), 5-34.

Wastell, D., & Sewards, A. (1995). An information systems profile of the UK manufacturing sector. *Journal of Information Technology, 10*, 179-189.

Watson, H.J., & Carte, T.A. (2000). Executive information systems in government organizations. *Public Productivity & Management Review, 23*(3), 371-382.

Watson, H.J., Rainer, K., & Houdeshel, G. (1997). *Building executive information systems and other decision support applications.* New York: John Wiley and Sons, Inc.

Webb, H.W., & Webb, L.A. (2005). SitQual: An integrated measure of Web site quality. *Journal of Enterprise Information Management, 17*(6), 430-440.

Xu, X., & Lehaney, B. (2003). Some UK and USA comparisons of executive information systems in practice and theory. *Journal of End User Computing, 15*(1), 1-19.

Yang, W.L., Strong, D.M., Kahn B.K., & Wang, R.Y. (2002). AIMQ: A methodology for information quality assessment. *Information & Management, 40*, 133-146.

Young, D., & Watson, J.W. (1995). Determinants of EIS acceptance. *Information & Management, 29*, 153-164.

Chapter VI

Evidence of Compensatory Adaptation to Unnatural Media in a Field Study of Process Redesign Dyads

Ned Kock, Texas A&M International University, USA

Abstract

Much of the past research on electronic communication media suggests that those media pose obstacles to communication in collaborative tasks when compared with the face-to-face medium. On the other hand, past research also points at mixed findings in connection with the quality of the outcomes of collaborative tasks, generally suggesting that the use of electronic communication media has no negative effect on those outcomes. A new theoretical framework building on human evolution theory, called compensatory adaptation theory, has been proposed to explain these contradictory findings. This study provides a review and test of compensatory adaptation theory. It investigates the impact of the use of an electronic communication medium on 20 business process redesign dyads involving managers and professionals at a large defense contractor, with a focus on cognitive effort, com-

munication ambiguity, message preparation, fluency, and task outcome quality. The study suggests that even though the use of electronic communication media seemed to increase cognitive effort and communication ambiguity, it had a neutral impact on task outcome quality. These results appear to be an outcome of compensatory adaptation, whereby the members of the dyads interacting through the electronic communication medium modified their behavior in order to compensate for the obstacles posed by the medium, which is suggested by a decrease in fluency and an increase in message preparation. The results generally support predictions based on compensatory adaptation theory.

Introduction

Research on the effects of technologies on people in business settings has a long history. Within that research tradition, few research topics have received so much sustained attention over such a long period of time as "electronic communication"— that is, the study of communication through electronic media created by artifacts such as the telephone, fax, and computer. This area of inquiry has taken different forms and different names over the years, such as computer-supported cooperative work, computer-mediated communication, groupware, group support systems, and, more recently, a variety of "e" combinations (where "e" stands for "electronic") such as e-collaboration and e-commerce (Davenport, 2000; Dennis, Carte, & Kelly, 2003; Fingar, Aronica, & Maizlish, 2001; Grudin, 1994; Kock, Hilmer, Standing, & Clark, 2000; Kock, Davison, Ocker, & Wazlawick, 2001; Standing & Benson, 2000). While these different varieties present unique characteristics that identify them as distinct "research schools," they all share the same common interest in electronic communication tools and their effects on human behavior. The advent of the Internet, e-business, and the proliferation of low cost computer networks and electronic communication tools have led to increased interest in research on how electronic communication media affect collaborative work in organizations.

This interest is shared by the U.S. Department of Defense (DoD), where Internet-based computer networks have removed geographical and time constraints to collaboration among distributed process teams engaged in defense acquisition activities. With the growth of distributed acquisition process teams also comes the challenge of improving defense acquisition processes in a distributed manner, since new technologies, regulatory modifications, and other change drivers constantly push the DoD into rethinking and redesigning the way it procures, purchases, and internally distributes products and services. This can be accomplished through distributed and asynchronous process redesign groups supported by Internet-based electronic communication tools. Yet little is known about the effects of electronic communication media on process redesign groups, particularly in the defense sector. This study tries to fill this gap by conducting a preliminary investigation of the effects of electronic communication media on process redesign dyads (i.e., pairs) targeting defense acquisition processes.

This chapter is organized as follows. It first reviews different theoretical perspectives that seem contradictory, and that pertain to the adequacy of electronic communication as a full or partial replacement to face-to-face communication in organizational settings. Next, it discusses a new theory that tries to address those contradictions, namely, compensatory adaptation theory. The theory is discussed particularly in connection with its two main theoretical principles of *media naturalness* and *compensatory adaptation*. The chapter then develops a set of hypotheses that are empirically tested through a field study of 20 business process redesign dyads involving managers and professionals at a large defense contractor, with a focus on cognitive effort, communication ambiguity, message preparation, fluency, and task outcome quality. The chapter concludes with a discussion of the findings and implications for practitioners.

Research Background

It has long been theorized that the face-to-face communication medium possesses inherent characteristics that make it more appropriate for the conduct of a variety of collaborative tasks (Daft & Lengel, 1986; Graetz, Boyle, Kimble, Thompson, & Garloch, 1998; Sallnas, Rassmus-Grohn, & Sjostrom, 2000; Short, Williams, & Christie, 1976; Warkentin, Sayeed, & Hightower, 1997). This has led to the conclusion that the use of electronic communication media, which usually do not incorporate all of the elements present in the face-to-face communication medium (e.g., synchronicity, ability to convey tone of voice, and facial expressions) will lead to decreased *effectiveness* in communication interactions and thus to decreased quality of outcomes in collaborative tasks.

In the human-computer interaction literature, one field study in the early 1990s (Nardi, Schwarz, Kuchinsky, Leichner, Whittaker, & Sclabassi, 1993) and two more recent experimental studies (Basdogan, Ho, Srinivasan, & Slater, 2000; Sallnas et al., 2000) provide compelling evidence supporting in part the above conclusions. The field study conducted by Nardi et al. (1993) on the use of video and audio conferencing systems in the operating room of a hospital is particularly interesting because it sheds new light on previous claims that the addition of a video channel (usually in the form of what the authors refer to as "talking heads") to an existing audio channel in an e-communication medium usually does not significantly enhance performance in collaborative tasks (see their paper for a review of previous research on the topic). Nardi et al. (1993) suggest that the results of previous studies might have been biased by technology operation and experimental design problems, and provide unequivocal evidence of the usefulness of video in addition to audio as a "cognitive effort reducer" in a variety of complex and fast-paced interactions between individuals involved in surgical procedures.

The experimental studies conducted by Basdogan et al. (2000) and Sallnas et al. (2000) provide additional support for the notion that the face-to-face communication medium possesses characteristics that make it particularly appropriate for the conduct of a variety of collaborative tasks. They examined the role of touch, or "haptic" feedback, in the execution of collaborative tasks in distributed virtual environments. Both studies involved data collection and analysis regarding several pairs of individuals collaborating through a shared virtual environment to perform simple tasks with and without haptic feedback. Sallnas et al.'s (2000) study involved more subjects and higher task variety and complexity than Basdogan et al.'s study (2000). The similarity of their findings is remarkable. Both studies found that haptic feedback significantly improved task performance, with Sallnas et al.'s (2000, p. 474) study offering additional evidence linking a reduction in cognitive effort with haptic feedback: "[The analysis of the perceptions by subjects] suggests that it was easier to manipulate and understand the interface when the interaction was supported by haptic force feedback."

Two theories that are well aligned with the above conclusions in connection with the advantages offered by the face-to-face medium over electronic media (particularly media that suppress many of the elements found in face-to-face communication) in connection with variety of collaborative tasks. Those two theories are the social presence theory (Short et al., 1976) and the media richness theory (Daft & Lengel, 1986; Daft, Lengel, & Trevino, 1987).

Social presence theory (Short et al., 1976) conceptualizes different communication media along a one-dimensional continuum of "social presence," where the degree of social presence is equated to the degree of "awareness" of the other person in a communication interaction. According to social presence theory, communication is effective if the communication medium has the appropriate social presence required for the level of interpersonal involvement required for a task. On a continuum of social presence, the face-to-face medium is considered to have the most social presence, whereas written, text-based communication, the least.

Similarly to the social presence theory, media richness theory (Daft & Lengel, 1986; Daft et al., 1987) classifies communication media along a continuum of "richness" where richness is based on the ability of media to carry nonverbal cues, provide rapid feedback, convey personality traits, and support the use of natural language. A reasonable interpretation of the media richness theory's core argument is that decisions regarding matching media to collaborative tasks are based on the need to reduce discussion ambiguity. The face-to-face communication medium is generally considered among the richest and most effective media for reducing discussion ambiguity (Daft & Lengel, 1986). In contrast, electronic communication media in general are not considered rich because of their inherent limitations in, for example, carrying nonverbal cues (Daft et al., 1987; Lee, 1994).

Many past empirical findings, particularly from the organizational research literature, have supported in part the social presence and media richness theories (Daft et al., 1987; Fulk, Schmitz, & Steinfield, 1990; Rice, 1993; Rice & Shook, 1990). However, among the key problems with the social presence and media richness theories, was that they proposed theoretical links between low social presence and low richness, respectively, in communication media, and either (a) avoidance by users to use those media for collaborative tasks or (b) low quality of the outcomes of collaborative tasks, if the users decide to use those communication media (Daft et al., 1987; Lengel & Daft, 1988; Short et al., 1976).

Several empirical studies have suggested that these hypothesized theoretical links are wrong, particularly because other factors such as social influences and geographic distribution can both lead users to choose "lean" communication media and modify their behavior in ways that are independent of the degree of social presence or richness of those media and that compensate for problems associated with media "leanness" (Fulk et al., 1990; Lee, 1994; Markus, 1994; Ngwenyama & Lee, 1997). Other empirical studies led to mixed findings. For example, Baker's (2002) study, which compared the performance of 64 virtual teams utilizing four different types of communication media (text-only, audio-only, text-video, and audio-video), found no significant difference in the quality of decisions reached by teams interacting through text-only and audio-only media. However, the same study found that the addition of video to audio-only communication resulted in a significant improvement in the quality of teams' strategic decisions.

Inconsistencies such as the ones mentioned above led, over the years, to several attempts to develop more robust theoretical frameworks combining theoretical elements of the social presence and media richness theories with theoretical elements of theories that take into account other factors, such as social influences (Carlson & Zmud, 1999; Trevino, Webster, & Stein, 2000; Webster & Trevino, 1995). Other attempts tried to review the foundations of the social presence and media richness theories and create more robust theories that could provide an alternative to the social presence and media richness theories. One such attempt led to the development of compensatory adaptation theory.

Compensatory Adaptation Theory

Compensatory adaptation theory (Kock, 1998, 1999, 2001a, 2001b, 2005) has been developed in part to explain the inconsistent findings discussed in the previous section, and in part to provide an alternative theory that could overcome the limitations of the social presence and media richness theories. Compensatory adaptation theory argues that electronic communication media in general offer certain advantages, such as that of allowing for asynchronous and distributed group interaction, and, at the same time, pose obstacles for communication in groups. In this respect, compensatory adaptation theory is similar to the social presence and media richness theories. The key difference is that compensatory adaptation theory attempts to provide a scientific basis for the existence of those obstacles, by arguing that they are primarily due to the fact that our biological communication apparatus, which includes specialized organs and brain functions, has been optimized by Darwinian evolution for face-to-face communication incorporating five main elements—o-location, synchronicity, and the ability to convey body language, facial expressions, and speech.

Evidence about the evolution of our biological communication apparatus suggests that during over 99% of our evolutionary cycle our ancestors relied on collocated and synchronous forms of communication through facial expressions, body language, and sounds (including speech, which uses a large variety of sound combinations) to exchange information and knowledge among themselves (Boaz & Almquist, 1997; Cartwright, 2000). According to evolutionary principles, a plausible conclusion from this is that our biological communication apparatus was designed primarily to excel in face-to-face communication (Kock, 2005b; Kock, Hassell, & Wazlawick, 2002). That is, since we have communicated only face-to-face during the vast majority of our evolutionary cycle, then our biological communication apparatus (which includes the brain modules involved in the sensing and control of our communication organs) must have been designed for face-to-face communication.

The above conclusion is supported by the presence of obvious face-to-face communication adaptations in our biological communication apparatus. For instance, evolution endowed human beings with a complex web of facial muscles (22 on each side of the face; more than any other animal) that allow them to generate over 6,000 communicative expressions; very few of these muscles are used for other purposes, such as chewing (Bates & Cleese, 2001; McNeill, 1998). The existence of such a complex web of muscles would appear to have been a major waste, had we not been designed to use them extensively while communicating with others.

The evolutionary path that led to our species also suggests a noticeable evolutionary direction over millions of years toward the development of a biological communication apparatus that supported ever more sophisticated forms of speech, culminating with the development of complex speech approximately 100,000 years ago. The advent of complex speech was enabled by the development of a larynx located relatively low in the neck and an enlarged vocal tract—key morphological traits that differentiate modern humans from their early ancestors and that allow modern humans to generate the large variety of sounds required to speak most modern languages (Laitman, 1984, 1993; Lieberman, 1998). The morphology of the human ear also suggests a specialized design to decode speech (Lieberman, 1998; Pinker,

1994). The adaptive importance of speech for human beings is highlighted by the fact that our enlarged vocal tract also makes us the most likely among all primates to choke on food and ingested liquids.

The Media Naturalness Principle

The evolution of closely matched brain and body functions, which follows from the widely held brain-body co-evolution law of modern evolution theory (Lieberman, 1998; Wills, 1989, 1993), provides a scientific basis for the apparent bias toward face-to-face communication hypothesized by the social presence and media richness theories, and is reflected in compensatory adaptation theory's *media naturalness principle*. The principle states that individuals who choose to use electronic communication tools experience increased cognitive effort and communication ambiguity proportionally to the degree to which the tools suppress elements that are present in face-to-face communication (e.g., synchronicity, ability to convey/perceive nonverbal communication cues). The principle is task independent; that is, it applies to all collaborative tasks, even though it acknowledges that the link is less noticeable in tasks that do not involve intense communication, which are seen as tasks that involve little knowledge sharing among collaborators (Kock, 2001b, 2005b).

The media naturalness principle links the use of electronic communication media with high cognitive effort and communication ambiguity, but not necessarily with specific task-related outcomes. In doing so, it explains empirical findings that supported in part the social presence and media richness theories (Daft et al., 1987; Fulk et al., 1990; Rice, 1993; Rice & Shook, 1990), while at the same time avoiding the problems associated with making predictions about media choice or task-related outcomes based on communication media traits, which led to criticism by social researchers (El-Shinnawy & Markus, 1998; Kinney & Watson, 1992; Kock, 1998; Lee, 1994; Markus, 1994). For example, the media naturalness principle is compatible with the notion that social influences can lead users to modify their behavior (Lee, 1994; Markus, 1994; Ngwenyama & Lee, 1997) in ways that are independent of the apparent degree of naturalness of a medium, even though the cognitive effort required for this to happen will be higher than if a more "natural" communication medium (i.e., the face-to-face medium) were used.

The above discussion is compatible with the notion that electronic communication tools are artifacts developed to solve specific problems, but that also add new problems of their own (Ellis, Gibbs, & Rein, 1991; Nunamaker, Dennis, Valacich, Vogel, & George, 1991; Nunamaker, Briggs, Mittleman, Vogel, & Balthazard, 1997; Walther, 1996). There seems to be a general pattern of gains due to the use of electronic communication tools to relate to group *efficiency*, for example, higher number of ideas generated per unit of time (Dennis, Haley, & Vanderberg, 1996;

Nagasundaram & Bostrom, 1995) and lower costs associated with running groups (Kock, 2000); even though sometimes losses occur in connection with obstacles to group *effectiveness*, for example, less commitment toward group decisions due to lower group cohesiveness and satisfaction (Ellis et al., 1991; Nunamaker et al., 1991; Walther, 1996).

While it is intuitive to think that obstacles to high group effectiveness invariably lead to lower quality of group outcomes, there is a wealth of evidence from fields as diverse as biological anthropology (Dobzhansky, 1971) and analytical psychology (Jung, 1968) suggesting that human beings voluntarily and involuntarily compensate for obstacles posed to them, in some cases overcompensating for those obstacles and achieving even better outcomes than if the obstacles were not present (Kock, 1998). This compensatory adaptation phenomenon has the potential to contradict deterministic predictions linking negative communication media influences on group effectiveness with low group outcome quality. Kock (1998, 1999, 2005) obtained empirical evidence of this compensatory adaptation phenomenon in the context of electronic communication in a study that compared groups performing complex and knowledge-intensive tasks over e-mail and face-to-face. The e-mail medium was consistently seen by group members as less appropriate than the face-to-face medium to accomplish the tasks. Yet, the tasks accomplished through e-mail yielded outcomes that were perceived as being of slightly better quality than those produced by the face-to-face groups.

The Compensatory Adaptation Principle

Compensatory adaptation theory argues that users of electronic communication tools present two common patterns of reaction toward those tools. First, users of electronic communication tools in general perceive those tools as creating communication media that pose cognitive obstacles to communication when compared with the face-to-face medium (Kock, 2001a, b), as proposed by the media naturalness principle, discussed above. That is, even though electronic communication tools may reduce or eliminate physical obstacles to face-to-face communication—for example, e-mail and instant messaging allow people to communicate instantly over long distances—they also increase the cognitive effort required to communicate information and knowledge. The second common pattern of reaction is one of compensation for the obstacles posed by the media (Kock, 1998, 1999, 2005), which is embodied in the theory's *compensatory adaptation principle*. The principle states that individuals who choose to use electronic communication media tend to *compensate* for the cognitive obstacles they perceive as associated with the lack of naturalness of those media, which leads those individuals to generate, when engaged in collaborative tasks, outcomes of the same or better quality than if they had interacted solely face-to-face.

Copyright © 2007, Idea Group Inc. Copying or distributing in print or electronic forms without written permission of Idea Group Inc. is prohibited.

So, in summary, compensatory adaptation theory argues, in an apparently paradoxical way, that obstacles posed by electronic communication media will have no negative effect on the quality of group outcomes as individuals engaged in collaborative tasks attempt to (often involuntarily) and often succeed in compensating for them. Since electronic communication media offer some advantages over the face-to-face medium, such as the possibility of asynchronous and noncollocated interaction, the compensatory adaptation theory argument based on the two complementary theoretical principles of *media naturalness* and *compensatory adaptation* just discussed seems to support the paradoxical notion that "less can be more," so to speak.

Hypotheses

As it can be inferred from the review of compensatory adaptation theory presented in the previous section, the theory takes a somewhat general view of collaborative tasks, and does not refer to any collaborative task in particular. This places compensatory adaptation theory in a good position to be tested, and potentially falsified, according to Stinchcombe's (1968) principle of empirical testing variety. That epistemological principle maintains that a theory's validity can be best tested when a variety of predictions regarding related empirical results can be derived from the theory. In other words, the more independent corroborations are made of the theory's basic propositions under different circumstances, the more likely it is that those propositions are generally correct.

The application of Stinchcombe's (1968) principle of empirical testing variety is illustrated in this study by the choice of two related collaborative tasks as the bases for an empirical test of compensatory adaptation theory, which should be seen as an initial step in testing the theory, and one of many (future) empirical tests of the theory. The related tasks are those of process modeling and redesign, whereby individuals respectively: (a) create a model of a particular organizational process; and (b) based on the model created, conceptually redesign the process so that improvements in quality and productivity can be achieved. For the sake of simplicity in formulating testable hypotheses, the two related tasks are referred in this section as one main "process redesign" task. This is consistent with current organizational practices, where process modeling is usually seen as part of the larger task of process redesign.

Compensatory adaptation theory's media naturalness principle states that electronic communication media in general, which are assumed to suppress some of the elements of face-to-face communication, cause higher cognitive effort in connection with communication interactions than the face-to-face medium. The reason for this increase in cognitive effort is, according to compensatory adaptation theory, that evolutionary forces shaped our biological communication apparatus so that we excel in face-to-face communication. Because of the suppression of elements that are found in typical face-to-face communication interactions electronic communication, our brain cannot make use of certain hardwired communication circuits (e.g., those aimed at speech generation and recognition), and thus must rely on other, less efficient learned brain circuits (e.g., those developed through use-induced learning of electronic communication tools). This argument, which is explored in more detail by Kock (2002) and is only summarized here, leads us to hypothesis H1.

H1: *The use of an electronic communication medium by process redesign dyads will increase the level of cognitive effort experienced by the members of the dyads.*

When individuals are brought up in different cultural environments, they invariably develop different information processing schemas over their life times. Different schemas make individuals interpret information in different ways, especially when information they expect to receive is not actually provided. This phenomenon has been originally demonstrated by Bartlett (1932) through a series of experiments he conducted involving the American Indian folk tale, "The War of The Ghosts," which is well-known among experimental psychologists for its strange gaps and bizarre causal sequences. The experiments yielded evidence that subjects who held different information processing schemas interpreted the tale in substantially different ways, and according to their specific cultural schemas. Individuals were expecting certain pieces of information to be provided to them in Bartlett's (1932) experiments. When they were not provided with the information they expected to receive, those individuals "filled in the gaps" based on their existing information processing schemas and the limited information that they were given (see also Gardner, 1985). This conclusion provided a solid foundation on which to explain key differences in the way different individuals interpreted the tale.

Several generic problems have occurred recurrently during the millions of years that led to the evolution of the human species (e.g., how to identify a fruit that is rich in certain minerals), and the human brain possesses a series of hardwired information processing schemas that are designed to solve those problems (Cosmides & Tooby, 1992; Tooby & Cosmides, 1992). Several of those problems have been addressed by evolutionary adaptations that are associated with the communication process (Pinker & Bloom, 1992). Those adaptations have led to the development of hardwired schemas tied to the communication process that make us search for enough information to effectively interpret the message being communicated, and that information comes to use through several of the stimuli that are present in actual face-to-face communication (Lieberman, 2000), such as contextual cues (available in collocated communication), and immediate feedback (available in synchronous communication) in the form of facial expressions and body language, and voice intonations. When many of those stimuli are absent, which may be caused by their selective suppression through e-communication technologies, one would expect that e-communication technology users will "fill in the gaps" in manner similar what the subjects in Bartlett's (1932) experiments did.

However, in the absence of information-giving stimuli, "filling in the gaps" is likely to lead to a higher proportion of misinterpretations, and thus ambiguity, than if the stimuli were not suppressed—as Bartlett's (1932) and other studies show (see, e.g., Gardner, 1985; Pinker, 1997). Given the general similarity of the biological apparatus shared by different individuals, it is likely that they will look for the same types of communicative stimuli. Yet, given their different information process schemas, their interpretation of the message being communicated in the absence of those stimuli is likely to differ from the interpretations reached at by other individuals. This leads to the conclusion that a decrease in medium naturalness, caused by the selective suppression of media naturalness elements in a communication medium, is likely to lead to an increase in the probability of misinterpretations of communicative cues, and thus an increase in *communication ambiguity*. This leads us to hypothesis H2 below.

H2: *The use of an electronic communication medium by process redesign dyads will increase the level of communication ambiguity experienced by the members of the dyads.*

The compensatory adaptation principle of compensatory adaptation theory argues that individuals that choose to use electronic communication media for communication try to compensate for the cognitive obstacles they perceive as associated with the lack of naturalness of those media. This behavior is posited by the theory to be a natural and often involuntary reaction to the perception of cognitive obstacles posed by electronic communication tools in general, as stated in the media naturalness principle. Previous exploratory research (Kock, 1998, 1999, 2001c) suggests that this compensatory adaptation behavior is indicated by at least two behavioral patterns—more careful preparation of communication messages, and decreased communication fluency (which is defined as the number of words per unit of time conveyed through the medium). This takes us to hypotheses H3 and H4.

H3: *The use of an electronic communication medium by process redesign dyads will lead to increased preparation of communication messages by the members of the dyads.*

H4: *The use of an electronic communication medium by process redesign dyads will decrease the fluency displayed by the members of the dyads.*

Finally, compensatory adaptation theory argues that compensatory behavior usually leads individuals to compensate for the obstacles posed by electronic communication media of low naturalness, which often leads to outcomes of the same or better quality than those achieved through more natural media. This provides the basis for hypothesis H5.

H5: *The use of an electronic communication medium by process redesign dyads will have no negative effect on the quality of the outcomes produced by the members of the dyads.*

In summary, we could say that the set of hypotheses above comprises the essence of compensatory adaptation theory and thus provides the basis for a valid test of the theory. Underlying the theory is the notion that communication media that suppress key face-to-face communication elements pose obstacles to communication, leading to increased cognitive effort (H1) and communication ambiguity (H2). Nevertheless, the theory also argues that these obstacles will trigger compensatory adaptation mechanisms, indicated by increased preparation of communication messages (H3) and decreased fluency (H4). This will, according to the theory, lead to compensation and, in what appears to be a counterintuitive twist, no negative effect on the quality of outcomes in connection with a process redesign task (which arguably requires intense communication) performed electronically (H5).

Research Method

The hypotheses were tested through a field experiment employing a repeated measures design where the communication medium used varied according to two experimental conditions: face-to-face and electronic. The impact of changes in the communication medium factor on a set of dependent variables was assessed by means of multiple ANOVA tests (Green, Salkind, & Akey, 1997; Rosenthal & Rosnow, 1991).

Participants and Treatment Conditions

The research study involved subjects with substantial hands-on experience in process redesign in the defense sector, recruited from management and engineering ranks of a large defense contractor. All of the subjects were college-educated, and most held undergraduate degrees in business, computer science, or engineering. The subjects were familiar with each other and with the electronic communication medium used prior to their participation in this field experiment. However, they had no prior experience using the electronic communication medium for the collaborative completion of tasks of the same type as or even similar complexity to the experimental task. Their ages ranged from 23 to 60, with a mean age of 35. Fifty-nine percent of the subjects were male.

The subjects were randomly assigned to dyads and to communication media conditions. Each dyad completed two similar process redesign-related tasks using different communication media for each task. Half of the dyads (i.e., 10 dyads) completed one of the tasks face-to-face while the other half completed the same task electronically. After this, all dyads moved on to the next task, using different media than they had used in the previous task—that is, the dyads previously interacting face-to-face now interacted electronically and vice-versa. This led to the collection of research data in connection with 40 cases of dyads performing the same type of collaborative task.

Electronic Communication Medium

A set of Web-based threaded online discussion boards created the electronic communication media employed in the experiment. The online discussion boards were developed using Microsoft FrontPage 2000 and Active Server Pages. They were used in a quasisynchronous manner—that is, they were "refreshed" at short time intervals, creating an online chat-like environment where the discussions were threaded. One Web-based online discussion board was created for each dyad. All online discussion boards were identical.

Tasks

Two experimental tasks were used, which can be seen as being of the same general type, and also as subtasks of a larger process redesign task. Both tasks were developed based on a "real" process redesign project previously reported by Kock and Murphy (2001) that targeted the process whereby the U.S. Department of Defense procured and purchased complex software development services. Since that real project was a successful process redesign project and experts evaluated its outcomes and found them to be optimal, it was assumed that those outcomes should serve as a basis for comparison with the outcomes produced by the participants in our field experiment. In other words, we employed two hidden-profile tasks in our field experiment (see, e.g., Dennis, Kinney, & Hung, 1999).

In the first task, which involved process modeling, participants were given different pieces of information about a defense acquisition process and were asked to develop a full graphical model of the process using a set of predefined symbols (see Appendix A for a more detailed description of the process modeling task). Both pieces of information initially received by each of the members of the dyad were necessary for the generation of the full graphical model of the process (see Appendix C for the expected outcome).

In the second task, which involved process redesign, participants were given different sets of guidelines about how to redesign the process modeled in the previous task and were asked to develop a graphical model of the process after the application of all the redesign guidelines, using the same set of symbols employed in the previous task (see Appendix B for a more detailed description of the process redesign task). Both sets of guidelines initially received by each of the members of the dyad were necessary for the generation of the graphical model of the redesigned process (see Appendix D for the expected outcome).

Procedure

After the participants were randomly assigned to dyads and each dyad was randomly assigned to one of the two communication media conditions, the participants received a general orientation about the tasks and went through a 15-minute "refresh" session on process modeling and redesign.

The dyads were then given 40 minutes to complete the process modeling task, after which each member of the dyads handed in their initial process model (sketch) to an experiment facilitator and completed a questionnaire. After a short break, the dyads (now interacting through different communication media) were given 40 minutes to complete the second process redesign task, after which each member of the dyads handed in their redesigned process model (sketch) to an experiment facilitator and completed a questionnaire (the same questionnaire completed at the end of the process modeling task). No dyad was able to complete its task in less than the time allocated (i.e., 40 minutes)—a few dyads appeared to have completed their work in slightly less than 40 minutes, but nevertheless decided to use the remaining time to perfect their sketches.

Measures

The dependent variables were cognitive effort (H1), communication ambiguity (H2), message preparation (H3), fluency (H4), and task outcome quality (H5). The following variables were measured at the individual level of analysis (thus based on 40 data points) through one-item, perception-related questions (see Appendix F): cognitive effort, communication ambiguity, message preparation, and task outcome quality. The remaining variable, fluency, was measured at the dyadic level of analysis (based on 20 data points).

The question-statement and scale for the cognitive effort variable was based on NASA's task load index (or NASA-TLX) developed by Hart and colleagues (Hart & Staveland, 1988). The question-statements for communication ambiguity and message preparation were based on a focus group discussion with the participants, conducted prior to the experiment, in which the meaning of the constructs communication ambiguity and message preparation and the proper wording of related questions (to be answered on a 1 to 7 Likert-type scale) were agreed upon. Rosenthal and Rosnow (1991) suggest the test-retest method as an alternative method for reliability assessment, which is a convenient alternative when single-item measures are used since component reliability cannot be computed. Following that suggestion, the instrument comprising the single question-statements for each variable was assessed through the test-retest method with two similar "dummy" process redesign projects conducted two weeks apart. That assessment yielded acceptable results (alpha = 0.88).

As proposed by Kock (1998), fluency was measured by counting the number of words exchanged by the members of the dyads and dividing it by the number of minutes each dyad took to complete the task (40 minutes for all dyads), yielding a measure of the number of words per minute exchanged by the dyads. These measures were obtained based on 4 videotaped face-to-face dyad sessions (2 for the process modeling and 2 for the process redesign task) and 10 electronic dyad sessions (5 for the process modeling and 5 for the process redesign task).

Task outcome quality was measured by comparing the process sketches generated by the dyad members with the "correct" models (see appendices C and D)—that is, the models generated based on the successful process redesign project team studied by Kock and Murphy (2001). Two different coders generated these "similarity scores" used to assess task outcome quality independently. The scores were generated based on criteria addressing syntactic as well as semantic correctness of the sketches. Intercoder reliability was high (alpha = 0.91).

Table 1a. Descriptive statistics and one-way ANOVA results for all variables but fluency

Variable	Mean face-to-face	St. dev. face-to-face	Mean electronic	St. dev. electronic	F	p
Cognitive effort	55.01	20.23	77.76	25.12	9.94	< .01
	2.47	1.55	4.44	2.00	12.11	< .01
Message preparation	2.99	1.78	4.41	1.79	6.34	< .05
Task outcome quality	4.06	1.69	3.91	1.61	.09	.77

Table 1b. Descriptive statistics and Mann-Whitney U test results in connection with fluency

Variable	Mean face-to-face	St. dev. face-to-face	Mean electronic	St. dev. electronic	Z	p
Fluency	71.01	15.75	16.58	5.93	-2.83	< .01

Analysis Results

Table 1a summarizes one-way ANOVA statistics as well as means and standard deviations in connection with all variables but fluency. Since fluency data did not conform to assumptions underlying ANOVA (e.g., the number of data points was different for each treatment condition), a Mann-Whitney U test (a nonparametric technique—see, for example, Siegel & Castellan, 1998) was employed and its results are summarized in Table 1b.

The analyses of variance yielded statistically significant results in connection with cognitive effort; $F(1, 38) = 9.94$, $p < .01$; communication ambiguity; $F(1, 38) = 12.10$, $p < .01$; and message preparation; $F(1, 38) = 6.34$, $p < .05$. Participants generally perceived cognitive effort, communication ambiguity, and message preparation to be higher in the electronic communication than in the face-to-face condition, which provides general support for H1, H2, and H3.

The Mann-Whitney U test yielded statistically significant results in connection with fluency; $Z = -2.83$, $p < .01$. Fluency was significantly lower in the electronic communication than in the face-to-face condition, falling below what the "typing-vs.-speaking effect" would allow us to expect (i.e., typing is inherently slower than speaking; see McQueen, Payner, and Kock (1999) for a review of studies that addressed this effect). Given that the participants used computers for preparation of written documents on a daily basis, the "typing-vs.-speaking effect" would allow us to expect the fluency over the electronic communication medium to be, on average, no less than half the fluency face-to-face (or about 36 words per minute; see McQueen et al., 1999). Thus, the actual fluency in the electronic communication medium (16.58 words per minute) provides general support for H4.

The analyses of variance yielded statistically insignificant results in connection with task outcome quality; $F(1, 38) = 0.08$, $p = 0.77$. That is, there was no significant difference in the quality of the outcomes generated by the members of the dyads across different communication media conditions, which provides general support for H5.

Discussion

This study suggests that the use of a Web-based threaded online discussion board by dyads redesigning a defense acquisition process, when compared with the face-to-face medium, increased perceived cognitive effort by about 41%, perceived communication ambiguity by about 80%, and perceived message preparation by about 47%, while at the same time reducing actual fluency by approximately 77%. The study also suggests that the use of the Web-based threaded online discussion board had no significant impact on the quality of the outcomes generated by the dyads.

Since the hypotheses tested through this study were derived from compensatory adaptation theory, and were generally supported by the evidence, we can conclude that the study overall supports compensatory adaptation theory. In particular, the marked increases in perceived cognitive effort and communication ambiguity provide support for the theory's media naturalness principle. At the same time, the significant increase in perceived message preparation, and the drastic reduction in "fluency," coupled with the neutral impact on the quality of the outcomes generated by the dyads, provide strong support for the compensatory adaptation principle.

As previously discussed, many doubts have been raised by researchers (e.g., Fulk et al., 1990; Lee, 1994; Markus, 1994; Ngwenyama & Lee, 1997) in connection with media richness theory. Given those doubts, it seems plausible to explore the possibility that compensatory adaptation theory can replace media richness theory, perhaps with some advantages. This would probably require an expansion of compensatory adaptation theory so that specific predictions could be made in connection with particular types of tasks (Zigurs & Buckland, 1998), and could prove to become a fertile line of theoretical research given the influence that media richness theory has continually exerted on electronic communication research (Allen & Griffeth,

1997; Carlson & Zmud, 1999; Dennis & Kinney, 1998; Dennis & Valacich, 1999; Jackson & Purcell, 1997).

The potential for compensatory adaptation theory to replace media richness theory is highlighted by the fact that it explains findings of this study, which arguably supports one of the notions seen by researchers (Carlson & Zmud, 1999; Jackson & Purcell, 1997; Rice, 1992) as validating in part media richness theory (i.e., that the face-to-face medium is perceived by users as generally "richer" than electronic communication media) while, at the same time, enables compensatory adaptation theory to be used as a basis on which to explain findings that generally contradict one of the key predictions of media richness theory—that is, that groups interacting through a relatively "lean" medium invariably produce outcomes of lower quality than groups interacting through "richer" media.

Some researchers may argue that the findings of this study may be interpreted differently, and be seen as supporting in part media richness theory and pointing at ways in which that theory could be revised to incorporate such notions as that of social influence (Fulk et al., 1990) and common ground (Clark & Brennan, 1991). Fulk et al.'s (1990) social influence model provides the basis on which to predict that social influences, such as peer pressure, can lead to the use of a "lean" medium even though media that are perceived as richer (e.g., face-to-face, telephone) may be available. That could lead individuals to develop common ground (Clark & Brennan, 1991) elements (e.g., mutual knowledge, shared beliefs, goals and attitudes etc.) in connection with the use of "lean" medium to support a particular collaboration task or types of tasks. This could, in turn, lead to a "channel expansion" phenomenon (Carlson & Zmud, 1999), where both the perceived and actual richness of the medium would be increased by the development of common ground elements. Such plausible alternative interpretation is analogous to that proposed by Carlson and Zmud (1999) in connection with their channel expansion theory. Therefore, future research should consider the possibility that compensatory adaptation theory is not the best theoretical framework to explain this study's findings; even though there are some indications that this may be the case. Such skepticism and theoretical neutralism is likely to lead to greater progress than the narrower view of compensatory adaptation as a sort of "grand theory" (which it is unlikely to be).

Much of the past research on behavior toward electronic communication tools has focused on individual choice of communication media and, to some extent, the outcomes produced by individuals engaged in collaborative tasks. While that research has led to mixed findings, it nevertheless suggests that behavior toward electronic communication tools is both complex and, notwithstanding much research done in the area, somewhat unpredictable (DeSanctis, Poole, Dickson, & Jackson, 1993; Postmes, Spears, & Lea, 1998; Sallnas et al., 2000). Research findings that appear to be somewhat contradictory have supported predictions based on theories that emphasize characteristics of the communication medium (Daft & Lengel, 1986;

Short et al., 1976), as well as theories that emphasize social influences (Fulk et al., 1990; Lee, 1994; Markus, 1994; Ngwenyama & Lee, 1997), which have often been seen as competing types of theories (Trevino et al., 2000; Webster & Trevino, 1995). Underlying this debate between advocates of communication media and social influence theories is a set of puzzling findings, which can be summarized into two main groups of findings: (a) that the face-to-face medium is consistently perceived by individuals as a very appropriate communication medium for a variety of collaborative tasks (Daft et al., 1987; Markus, 1994; Rice, 1992; Rice & Shook, 1990; Walther, 1996); and (b) that this perception has often been contradicted by the choice of communication media different from face-to-face by individuals conducting collaborative tasks (Lee, 1994; Markus, 1994; Ngwenyama & Lee, 1997) and by those individuals sometimes producing the same or better quality task outcomes than individuals interacting primarily face-to-face (Kock, 1998).

The study described in this chapter makes an important theoretical contribution that can be used as a basis for reconciling the competing findings above. It does so by providing evidence that generally supports a new theory, compensatory adaptation theory, which builds on the contemporary version of Darwin's (1859) evolution theory. In spite of the caveat presented above regarding the possibility of alternative theoretical explanations that are different from those of compensatory adaptation theory, it is not unreasonable to argue that this chapter shows beyond much doubt that compensatory adaptation theory has the potential to explain the puzzling and contradictory findings discussed above, and provide a new basis for future research on electronic communication.

Conclusion

Much of the past research on electronic communication media suggests that those media pose obstacles to communication when compared with the face-to-face medium. Yet, past research also points at mixed findings in connection with the quality of the outcomes of tasks, suggesting that the use of electronic communication media has no negative effect on them. A new theoretical framework, called compensatory adaptation theory, has been proposed to explain these contradictory findings. This study provides a test of compensatory adaptation theory by investigating the impact of the use of an electronic communication medium on 20 business process redesign dyads involving managers and professionals at a large defense contractor, with a focus on cognitive effort, communication ambiguity, message preparation, fluency, and task outcome quality.

This study suggests that even though electronic communication media use in process redesign dyads involving managers and professionals seemed to increase cognitive effort and communication ambiguity, that use had a neutral impact on task outcome quality. These results appear to be an outcome of compensatory adaptation, whereby the members of the dyads interacting through the electronic communication medium modified their behavior in order to compensate for the obstacles posed by the medium, which finds confirmatory support from a marked decrease in fluency and an increase in message preparation. The results generally support predictions based on compensatory adaptation theory.

The findings above provide a new basis on which users of electronic communication tools can understand why tools that seem to make communication more difficult can still lead to no impact on the effective use of those tools for communication about complex issues. It is important for electronic communication tool users to understand the phenomenon of compensatory adaptation, particularly because its paradoxical nature may lead those users to believe that outcomes of collaboration tasks are not negatively affected by the use of electronic communication tools because of the tools' effectiveness in supporting communication interactions. This will probably lead to frustration when those users realize that "good [electronic] communication requires hard work" (see Bartlett, 2001, p. 1).

Nevertheless, one implication of this study for practice is that individuals collaborating electronic to accomplish complex and knowledge-intensive tasks such as process redesign can expect to be successful, even when the tasks are conducted entirely electronically. In light of the emergence of the Internet as a key enabler of communication in organizational processes, and the consequent multiplication of organizational forms characterized by their low dependence on physical structures for employee interaction, such as the so-called "virtual organizations" (Barnatt, 1995; Davidow & Malone, 1992), this is not only good news for organizations but also provides the basis on which to call for increasing use of electronic communication media to support a variety of types of group tasks, ranging from routine group tasks, where the use of electronic communication media is already relatively common, to more ad-hoc (or project-based) ones, where the use of electronic communication media is still rare.

However, the extra "cost" imposed on individuals who wish to communicate electronically, rather than face-to-face, about complex issues is an important issue that must be addressed in further research. As posited by the media naturalness principle, and indicated by this study, compensatory adaptation is associated with "working hard" to compensate for increases in cognitive effort and communication ambiguity. That is, compensatory adaptation has "a price." One possible negative consequence of this, which was not addressed by this study, could be avoidance by group members to participate in future electronic groups after their initial experience, as they would become increasingly aware of the extra cognitive effort required from them. This could have an overall negative impact on the use of electronic media by organizations to support organization-wide initiatives, such as process redesign programs aimed at enabling organizations to obtain quality or productivity certifications. Perhaps the education about users of electronic communication technologies about compensatory adaptation would allow them to understand the extra "cognitive price" that they have to pay, and thus mitigate their negative perceptions about the use of those technologies to accomplish complex and knowledge-intensive collaborative tasks.

Another alternative to address the issue above is to break down complex tasks such as process redesign into subtasks, and use different communication media to support those subtasks. Prior research has shown that the amount of knowledge transfer involved in a communication interaction correlates the perceived difficulty in interacting through non-face-to-face media (Kock, 1998). Therefore, subtasks could be classified according to the amount of knowledge transfer involved, and assigned different communication media, where the degree of similarity of each medium to the face-to-face medium should be matched with the amount of knowledge transfer needed for effectively completion of each subtask. That is, for high knowledge transfer subtasks, media that is very face-to-face-like (e.g., video-conferencing) should be used; whereas for low knowledge transfer subtasks, media that incorporate few of the elements found in face-to-face communication (e.g., e-mail) could be used. Following Kock and Davison's (2003) conceptual formulation, high knowledge transfer subtasks are defined here as those that involve process-related explanations and related associative assertions (e.g., explanations of why a certain car assembly process is designed the way it is), rather than only descriptions of process attributes (e.g., the current production capacity of a car assembly process). This matching of subtasks and media is likely to become increasingly common in industry, as new electronic communication tools are developed to support specific types of tasks. In fact, from a long-term perspective, this may become one of the most common approaches to effectively employ electronic communication tools in organizations in general.

Acknowledgments

The research reported here has been funded in part by grants from the U.S. Department of Defense and Temple University, for which the author is most grateful. The author would also like to thank the subjects of the research study reported in this chapter for their participation and candid answers. An earlier version of this chapter was published in 2005 in the *Information Resources Management Journal* (volume 18, number 29).

References

Allen, D.G., & Griffeth, R.W. (1997). Vertical and lateral information processing: The effects of gender, employee classification level, and media richness on communication and work outcomes. *Human Relations, 50*(10), 1239-1260.

Baker, G. (2002). The effects of synchronous collaborative technologies on decision making: A study of virtual teams. *Information Resources Management Journal, 15*(4), 79-94.

Barnatt, C. (1995). Office space, cyberspace and virtual organization. *Journal of General Management, 20*(4), 78-92.

Bartlett, F. (1932). *Remembering: A study in experimental and social psychology.* Cambridge, MA: Cambridge University Press.

Bartlett, M. (2001). Good e-mail communication requires hard work. Retrieved July 10, 2006, from the *Washington Post* (washingtonpost.com), http://www.newsbytes.com/news/01/168549.html

Basdogan, C., Ho, C.H., Srinivasan, M.A., & Slater, M. (2000). An experimental study on the role of touch in shared virtual environments. *ACM Transactions on Computer-Human Interaction, 7*(4), 443-460.

Bates, B., & Cleese, J. (2001). *The human face.* New York: DK Publishing.

Boaz, N.T., & Almquist, A.J. (1997). *Biological anthropology: A synthetic approach to human evolution.* Upper Saddle River, NJ: Prentice Hall.

Carlson, J.R., & Zmud, R.W. (1999). Channel expansion theory and the experiential nature of media richness perceptions. *Academy of Management Journal, 42*(2), 153-170.

Cartwright, J. (2000). *Evolution and human behavior: Darwinian perspectives on human nature.* Cambridge, MA: MIT Press.

Clark, H.H., & Brennan, S.E. (1991), Grounding in communication. In L.B. Resnick, J. Levine, & S. D. Teasley (Eds.), *Perspectives on socially shared cognition* (pp. 127-149). Washington, DC: American Psychological Association.

Cosmides, L., & Tooby, J. (1992). Cognitive Adaptations for Social Exchange. In J.H. Barkow, L. Cosmides, & J. Tooby (Eds.), *The adapted mind: Evolutionary psychology and the generation of culture* (pp. 163-228). New York: Oxford University Press.

Daft, R.L., & Lengel, R.H. (1986). Organizational information requirements, media richness and structural design. *Management Science, 32*(5), 554-571.

Daft, R.L., Lengel, R.H., & Trevino, L.K. (1987). Message equivocality, media selection, and manager performance: Implications for information systems. *MIS Quarterly, 11*(3), 355-366.

Davenport, T.H., (2000), *Mission Critical: Realizing the promise of enterprise systems*. Boston: Harvard Business School Press.

Davidow, W.H., & Malone, M.S. (1992). *The virtual corporation*. New York: HarperCollins.

Darwin, C. (1859), *On the origin of species by means of natural selection*. Cambridge, MA: Harvard University Press.

Dennis, A.R., Carte, T.A., & Kelly, G.G. (2003). Breaking the rules: Success and failure in groupware-supported business process reengineering. *Decision Support Systems, 36*(1), 31-47.

Dennis, A.R., Haley, B.J., & Vanderberg, R.J. (1996). A meta-analysis of effectiveness, efficiency, and participant satisfaction in group support systems research. In J.I. DeGross, S. Jarvenpaa, & A. Srinivasan (Eds.), *Proceedings of the 17th International Conference on Information Systems* (pp. 278-289). New York: The Association for Computing Machinery.

Dennis, A.R., & Kinney, S.T. (1998). Testing media richness theory in the new media: The effects of cues, feedback, and task equivocality. *Information Systems Research, 9*(3), 256-274.

Dennis, A.R., Kinney, S.T., & Hung, Y.C. (1999). Gender differences and the effects of media richness. *Small Group Research, 30*(4), 405-437.

Dennis, A.R., & Valacich, J.S. (1999). *Rethinking media richness: Towards a theory of media synchronicity*. Athens, GA: Terry College of Business, University of Georgia.

DeSanctis, G., Poole, M.S., Dickson, G.W., & Jackson, B.M. (1993). Interpretive analysis of team use of group technologies. *Journal of Organizational Computing, 3*(1), 1-29.

Dobzhansky, T. (1971). *Mankind evolving: The evolution of the human species*. New Haven, CN: Yale University Press.

Ellis, C.A., Gibbs, S.J., & Rein, G.L. (1991). Groupware: Some issues and experiences. *Communications of ACM, 34*(1), 38-58.

El-Shinnawy, M., & Markus, L. (1998). Acceptance of communication media in organizations: Richness or features? *IEEE Transactions on Professional Communication, 41*(4), 242-253.

Fingar, P., Aronica, R., & Maizlish, B. (2001). *The death of "e" and the birth of the real new economy*. Tampa, FL: Meghan-Kiffer Press.

Fulk, J., Schmitz, J., & Steinfield, C.W. (1990). A social influence model of technology use. In J. Fulk & C. Steinfield (Eds.), *Organizations and communication technology* (pp. 117-140). Newbury Park, CA: Sage.

Gardner, H. (1985). *The mind's new science*. New York: Basic Books.

Graetz, K.A., Boyle, E.S., Kimble, C.E., Thompson, P., & Garloch, J.L. (1998). Information sharing in face-to-face, teleconferencing, and electronic chat groups. *Small Group Research, 29*(6), 714-743.

Green, S.B., Salkind, N.J., & Akey, T.M. (1997). *Using SPSS for Windows: Analyzing and understanding data.* Upper Saddle River, NJ: Prentice Hall.

Grudin, J. (1994). Groupware and social dynamics: Eight challenges for developers. *Communications of the ACM, 37*(1), 93-105.

Hart, S.G., & Staveland, L.E. (1988). Development of NASA-TLX (Task Load Index): Results of empirical and theoretical research. In P. Hancock & N. Meshkati (Eds.), *Advances in psychology* (pp. 139-184). Amsterdam: North Holland.

Jackson, M.H., & Purcell, D. (1997). Politics and media richness in World Wide Web representations of the former Yoguslavia. *Geographical Review, 87*(2), 219-239.

Jung, C.G. (1968). *Analytical psychology: Its theory and practice.* New York: Vintage Books.

Kinney, S.T., & Watson, R.T. (1992). Dyadic communication: The effect of medium and task equivocality on task-related and interactional outcomes. In J.I. De-Gross, J.D. Becker, & J.J. Elam (Eds.), *Proceedings of the 13th International Conference on Information Systems* (pp. 107-117). Dallas: The Association for Computing Machinery.

Kock, N. (1998). Can communication medium limitations foster better group outcomes? An action research study. *Information & Management, 34*(5), 295-305.

Kock, N. (1999). *Process improvement and organizational learning: The role of collaboration technologies.* Hershey, PA: Idea Group Publishing.

Kock, N. (2000). Benefits for virtual organizations from distributed groups. *Communications of the ACM, 43*(11), 107-113.

Kock, N. (2001a). The ape that used email: Understanding e-communication behavior through evolution theory. *Communications of the AIS, 5*(3), 1-29.

Kock, N. (2001b). Behavior toward e-communication tools: A new theoretical model based on evolution theory. In E. Cohen & A.J. Zaliwski (Eds.), *Proceedings of the 2001 Informing Science Conference* (pp. 310-317). Crakow, Poland: Cracow University of Economics.

Kock, N. (2001c). Compensatory adaptation to a lean medium: An action research investigation of electronic communication in process improvement groups. *IEEE Transactions on Professional Communication, 44*(4), 267-285.

Kock, N. (2002). Evolution and media naturalness: A look at e-communication through a Darwinian theoretical lens. In L. Applegate, R. Galliers, & J.L. De-

Gross (Eds.), *Proceedings of the 23rd International Conference on Information Systems* (pp. 373-382). Atlanta: The Association for Information Systems.

Kock, N. (2005a). *Business process improvement through e-collaboration: Knowledge sharing through the use of virtual groups*. Hershey, PA: Idea Group Publishing.

Kock, N. (2005b). Media richness or media naturalness? The evolution of our biological communication apparatus and its influence on our behavior toward e-communication tools. *IEEE Transactions on Professional Communication, 48*(2), 117-130.

Kock, N., & Davison, R. (2003). Can lean media support knowledge sharing? Investigating a hidden advantage of process improvement. *IEEE Transactions on Engineering Management, 50*(2), 151-163.

Kock, N., Davison, R., Ocker, R., & Wazlawick, R. (2001). E-collaboration: A look at past research and future challenges. *Journal of Systems and Information Technology (Special Issue on E-Collaboration), 5*(1), 1-9.

Kock, N., Hassell, L., & Wazlawick, R.S. (2002, April 4-5). Tacit knowledge sharing and human evolution: A framework for developing "natural" collaboration technologies. In G.M. Hunter & K.K. Dhanda (Eds.), *Proceedings of the 1st ISOneWorld Conference*. Las Vegas, NV: ISOneWorld, (pp. 1-12).

Kock, N., Hilmer, K., Standing, C., & Clark, S. (2000). Supporting learning processes with collaboration technologies: A brief look at past research and challenges that lie ahead. *Journal of Systems and Information Technology, 4*(4), 1-8.

Kock, N., Jenkins, A., & Wellington, R. (1999). A field study of success and failure factors in asynchronous groupware-supported process improvement groups. *Business Process Management, 5*(3), 238-253.

Kock, N., & Murphy, F. (2001). *Redesigning acquisition processes: A new methodology based on the flow of knowledge and information*. Fort Belvoir, VA: Defense Acquisition University Press.

Laitman, J.T. (1984). The anatomy of human speech. *Natural History, 20*(7), 20-27.

Laitman, J.T. (1993). The anatomy of human speech. In R.L. Ciochon & J.G. Fleagle (Eds.), *The human evolution source book* (pp. 56-60). Englewood Cliffs, NJ: Prentice Hall.

Lee, A.S. (1994). Electronic mail as a medium for rich communication: An empirical investigation using hermeneutic interpretation. *MIS Quarterly, 18*(2), 143-157.

Lengel, R.H., & Daft, R.L. (1988). The selection of communication media as an executive skill. *Academy of Management Executive, 2*(3), 225-232.

Lieberman, P. (1998). *Eve spoke: Human language and human evolution*. New York: W.W. Norton & Company.

Lieberman, P. (2000). *Human language and our reptilian brain: The subcortical bases of speech, syntax, and thought.* Cambridge, MA: Harvard University Press.

Markus, M.L. (1994). Electronic mail as the medium of managerial choice. *Organization Science, 5*(4), 502-527.

McNeill, D. (1998). *The face: A natural history*. Boston: Little, Brown & Company.

McQueen, R.J., Payner, K., & Kock, N. (1999). Contribution by participants in face-to-face business meetings: Implications for collaborative technology. *Journal of Systems and Information Technology, 3*(1), 15-33.

Nagasundaram, M., & Bostrom, R.P. (1995). The structuring of creative processes using GSS: A framework for research. *Journal of Management Information Systems, 11*(3), 87-114.

Nardi, B.A., Schwarz, H., Kuchinsky, A., Leichner, R., Whittaker, S., & Sclabassi, R. (1993). Turning away from talking heads: The use of video-as-data in neurosurgery. In *Proceedings of the Conference on Human Factors in Computing Systems* (pp. 327-334). New York: The Association for Computing Machinery.

Ngwenyama, O.K., & Lee, A.S. (1997). Communication richness in electronic mail: Critical social theory and the contextuality of meaning. *MIS Quarterly, 21*(2), 145-167.

Nunamaker, J.F., Briggs, R.O., Mittleman, D.D., Vogel, D.R., & Balthazard, P.A. (1997). Lessons from a dozen years of group support systems research: A discussion of lab and field. *Journal of Management Information Systems, 13*(3), 163-207.

Nunamaker, J.F., Dennis, A.R., Valacich, J.S., Vogel, D.R., & George, J.F. (1991). Electronic meeting systems to support group work. *Communications of ACM, 34*(7), 40-61.

Pinker, S. (1994). *The language instinct*. New York: William Morrow & Co.

Pinker, S. (1997). *How the mind works*. New York: W.W. Norton & Co.

Pinker, S., & Bloom, P. (1992). Natural language and natural selection. In J.H. Barkow, L. Cosmides, & J. Tooby (Eds.), *The adapted mind: Evolutionary psychology and the generation of culture* (pp. 451-493). New York: Oxford University Press.

Postmes, T., Spears, R., & Lea, M. (1998). Breaching or building social boundaries? Side-effects of computer-mediated communications. *Communication Research, 25*(6), 689-715.

Rice, R.E. (1992). Task analyzability, use of new media, and effectiveness: A multi-site exploration of media richness. *Organization Science, 3*(4), 475-500.

Rice, R.E. (1993). Media appropriateness: Using social presence theory to compare traditional and new organizational media. *Human Communication Research, 19*(4), 451-484.

Rice, R.E., & Shook, D.E. (1990). Relationship of job categories and organizational levels to use of communication channels, including electronic mail: A meta-analysis and extension. *Journal of Management Studies, 27*(2), 195-230.

Rosenthal, R., & Rosnow, R.L. (1991). *Essentials of behavioral research: Methods and data analysis.* Boston: McGraw-Hill.

Sallnas, E.L., Rassmus-Grohn, K., & Sjostrom, C. (2000). Supporting presence in collaborative environments by Haptic Force Feedback. *ACM Transactions on Computer-Human Interaction, 7*(4), 461-476.

Short, J., Williams, E., & Christie, B. (1976). *The social psychology of telecommunications.* London: John Wiley.

Siegel, S., & Castellan, N.J. (1998). *Nonparametric statistics for the behavioral sciences.* Boston: McGraw-Hill.

Standing, C., & Benson, S. (2000). An effective framework for evaluating policy and infrastructure issues for e-commerce. *Information Infrastructure & Policy, 6*(4), 227-237.

Stinchcombe, A.L. (1968). *Constructing social theories.* New York: Harcourt Brace.

Tooby, J., & Cosmides, L. (1992). The psychological foundation of culture. In J.H. Barkow, L. Cosmides, & J. Tooby (Eds.), *The adapted mind: Evolutionary psychology and the generation of culture* (pp. 19-136). New York: Oxford University Press.

Trevino, L.K., Webster, J., & Stein, E.W. (2000). Making connections: Complementary influences on communication media choices, attitudes, and use. *Organization Science, 11*(2), 163-182.

Walther, J.B. (1996). Computer-mediated communication: Impersonal, interpersonal, and hyperpersonal interaction. *Communication Research, 23*(1), 3-43.

Warkentin, M.E., Sayeed, L., & Hightower, R. (1997). Virtual teams versus face-to-face teams: An exploratory study of a Web-based conferencing system. *Decision Sciences, 28*(4), 975-996.

Webster, J., & Trevino, L.K. (1995). Rational and social theories as complementary explanations of communication media choices: Two policy-capturing studies. *Academy of Management Journal, 38*(6), 1544-1573.

Wills, C. (1989). *The wisdom of the genes: New pathways in evolution.* New York: Basic Books.

Wills, C. (1993). *The runaway brain: The evolution of human uniqueness.* New York: Basic Books.

Zigurs, I., & Buckland, B.K. (1998). A theory of task/technology fit and group support systems effectiveness. *MIS Quarterly, 22*(3), 313-334.

Appendix A: Process Modeling Task

The U.S. Department of Defense (DoD) routinely acquires software development services from several companies, including Lockheed Martin and Computer Sciences Corporation. Our task involves the redesign of a hypothetical business process, called the software services acquisition process (SSAP), through which a branch of the DoD contracts the development of computer-based defense systems. For the sake of illustration, one such computer-based defense system contracted in the past is the Amphibious Tank Radar Manager (ATRM—a fictitious name), which automates the operation of the radar of an amphibious tank.

You and your partner are receiving different pieces of information about the SSAP process (listed in bullet items below), which starts with the DoD issuing a request for proposals (RFP) and ends with the DoD receiving a proposal (or several proposals) from a bidder (or a group of bidders). You will now first discuss these different pieces of information with each other and develop each a sketch of the entire process. **Please bear in mind that each of you will develop a separate sketch based on your discussion. You may discuss the sketch as much as you want, but you must not show your sketch to each other.**

Information Provided to the First Member of the Dyad

•   The SSAP process starts with DoD's program manager e-mailing a request for proposals (RFP) document to the bid consultant of a company called Webmasters.

- The DoD program manager then calls Webmasters' bid consultant over the phone to provide him with extra information about the RFP, including the deadline for receipt of proposals and types of organizations eligible to bid.

- Webmasters' bid consultant uploads the RFP from his e-mail inbox onto DoD's RFP's Web site using a system called SecureWorkflow, which automatically notifies potential bidders by e-mail about the RFP.

- The contracts manager of a bidder receives the RFP notification in his e-mail's inbox folder, downloads the RFP from DoD's RFP Web site using Secure-Workflow, and places it in his personal folder.

- As soon as he has some time, the bidder's contracts manager e-mails the RFP to the bidder's technical lead.

Information Provided to the Second Member of the Dyad

- Once a day, the bidder's technical lead checks her e-mail's inbox folder for RFP's. Once an RFP is found, she enters the cover page information about the RFP into a control spreadsheet and saves the RFP document in her RFP's folder.

- As soon as she has some time, the bidder's technical lead e-mails the RFP to the bidder's project manager.

- Once a week, the bidder's project manager checks his e-mail inbox for new RFP's and, once he finds one, prepares a related proposal in consultation with his team.

- The bidder's project manager e-mails the prepared proposal to the bidder's technical lead.

- The bidder's technical lead enters the cover page information about the proposal into the same control spreadsheet in which she previously entered information about the RFP, and uploads the proposal onto DoD's proposals Web site using the SecureWorkflow system, which automatically notifies DoD's program manager of the receipt of a new proposal.

Appendix B: Process Redesign Task

You will now apply the process redesign techniques discussed below to the SSAP process, which should lead to a simplification of the process. You and your partner are receiving only half of the redesign techniques each, so you will have to discuss the other techniques with each other in order to be able to apply all of the process redesign techniques. Finally, you will each develop a sketch of the simplified process. **Please bear in mind that each of you will develop a separate sketch based on your discussion. You may discuss the sketch as much as you want, but you must not show your sketch to each other.**

Redesign Guidelines Provided to the First Member of the Dyad

- *Foster asynchronous communication.* When people exchange information they can do it synchronously, that is, interacting at the same time, or asynchronously, that is, interacting at different times. One example of synchronous communication is a telephone conversation. If the conversation takes place via e-mail, it then becomes an example of asynchronous communication. It has been observed, especially in formal business interaction, that in the vast majority of cases asynchronous communication is more efficient than synchronous communication. For example, synchronous communication often leads to time waste (e.g., waiting for the other person to be found) and communication tends to be less objective. Asynchronous communication can be implemented with simple artifacts such as in-boxes and out-boxes, fax machines, and billboards. Asynchronous communication can also be implemented with more complex artifacts such as computer files. These artifacts work as dynamic information repositories.

- *Reduce information flow.* Excessive information flow is often caused by an overcommitment to efficiency to the detriment of effectiveness. Information is perceived as an important component of processes, which drives people to an unhealthy information hunger. This causes information overload and the creation of unnecessary information processing functions within the organization. Information overload leads to stress and, often, the creation of information filtering roles. These roles are normally those of aides or middle managers, who are responsible for filtering in the important bit from the information coming from the bottom of, and from outside, the organization. Conversely, excessive information flowing top-down forces middle managers to become messengers, to the damage of more important roles. Information flow can be reduced by selecting the information that is important in processes and eliminating the rest, and by effectively using group support and database management systems.

Redesign Guidelines Provided to the Second Member of the Dyad

- *Reduce control*. Control activities do not normally add value to customers. They are often designed to prevent problems from happening as a result of human mistakes. In several cases, however, control itself fosters neglect, with a negative impact on productivity. For example, a worker may not be careful enough when performing a process activity because he knows that there will be some kind of control to catch his mistakes. Additionally, some types of control, such as those aimed at preventing fraud, may prove to be more costly than no control at all. Some car insurance companies, for example, have found out that the cost of accident inspections, for a large group of customers, was much more expensive than the average cost of frauds that that group committed.

- *Reduce the number of contact points*. Contact points can be defined as points where there is interaction between two or more people, both within the process and outside. This involves contacts between functions, and between functions and customers. Contact points generate delays and inconsistencies and, when in excess, lead to customer perplexity and dissatisfaction. In self-service restaurants and warehouses, for example, the points of contact were successfully reduced to a minimum. Additionally, it is much easier to monitor customer perceptions in situations where there are a small number of contact points. This makes it easier to improve process quality.

Appendix C: Correct Answer for Process Modeling Task

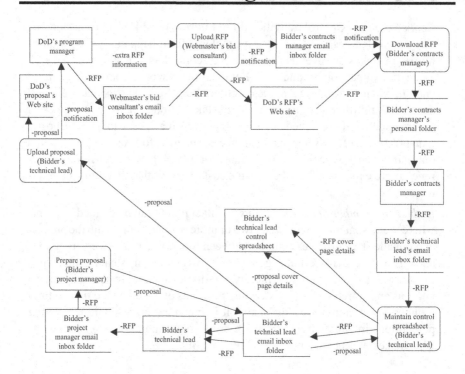

Appendix D: Correct Answer for Process Redesign Task

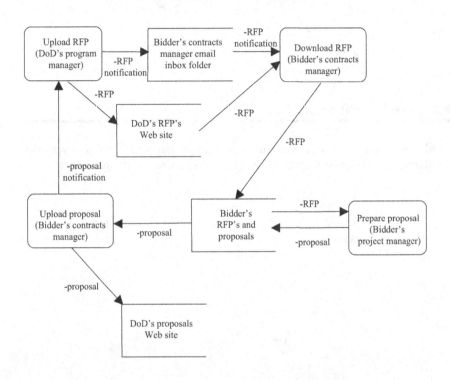

Appendix E: Questionnaire Measures

Cognitive Effort

Indicate how much effort it took for you to complete the process redesign task by marking anywhere on the continuous scale below with an "X".

0 ----- 25 ----- 50 ----- 75 ----- 100 ----- 125 ----- 150

Absolutely   Extreme
no effort   effort

Communication Ambiguity

Communication between my partner and myself was ambiguous.

1 ------- 2 ------- 3 ------- 4 ------- 5 ------- 6 ------- 7
Strongly   Strongly
Disagree   Agree

Message Preparation

I had to spend a lot of time preparing my contributions (e.g., group of sentences summarizing facts or conveying ideas) in my discussions with my partner.

1 ------- 2 ------- 3 ------- 4 ------- 5 ------- 6 ------- 7
Strongly   Strongly
Disagree   Agree

Chapter VII

Information Technology as a Target, Shield, and Weapon in the Post-9/11 Environment

Laura Lally, Hofstra University, USA

Abstract

This chapter draws upon normal accident theory and the theory of high reliability organizations to examine the potential impacts of information technology being used as a target in terrorist and other malicious attacks. The chapter also argues that information technology can be used as a shield to prevent further attacks and mitigate their impact if they should occur. A target and shield model is developed, which extends normal accident theory to encompass secondary effects, change, and feedback loops to prevent future accidents. The target and shield model is applied to the Y2K problem and the emerging threats and initiatives in the post-9/11 environment. The model is then extended to encompass the use of IT as a weapon against terrorism.

Introduction: IT Initiatives in the Post-9/11 Environment

In the post-9/11 environment, information technology (IT) security has become a growing issue. Even though computer budgets are being cut, spending on security has increased. Funding for IT based initiatives has increased dramatically since 9/11. New government regulations require that organizations keep their systems more secure and keep better track of their documents. As a result, an increasing number of IT based initiatives have been developed to solve these problems.

MIT's Magazine of Innovation: Technology Review reports that the budget for the 2005 Department of Homeland Security was $30 billion dollars (MIT Editors, 2005). For Customs, Immigration, and Border Protection, it included $2.9 billion for container security and $340 million for U.S.-VISIT, an automated entry and exit system for frequent international travelers. For the Coast Guard, it included $724 million to upgrade the technology and communications division. For the Transportation Security Administration, it included $475 million for explosives detection systems, baggage screening equipment, and their installation. For state and local assistance programs, it included $150 million in port security grants, $150 million in rail/transit security grants, and $715 million in grants to fire departments. For the Emergency Preparedness and Response Directorate, it included $2 billion for an emergency relief fund. For the Science and Technology Directorate, it included $593 million to develop technologies that counter threats from chemical, biological, nuclear and radiological weapons, and high explosives, and $61 million to continue the development of innovative countermeasures to protect commercial aircraft against possible missile systems. For Information Analysis and Infrastucture Protection Directorate, it included $2 billion to assess and protect critical infrastructures including cyberspace.

This chapter proposes a theory based model for creating a taxonomy of these initiatives. The goals of the taxonomy will be (1) to increase interoperability among the initiatives, (2) to identify areas of basic IT research which support these new applications, and which may need to be developed further for the applications to be successful, (3) to identify additional applications of these initiatives, and (4) to identify potential privacy and civil rights violations that could result from the inappropriate use of these initiatives.

Developing a Theory Based Model to Address these Initiatives

Yourdon (2002) categorized post-9/11 challenges in three categories:

1.   More organizations are dependent on the Internet for day-to-day operations.
2.   An increasing number of computer systems, networks, and databases make up a global IT infrastructure. Individuals, organizations, and nations arc "increasingly 'wired,' increasingly automated, and increasingly dependent on highly reliable computer systems" (Yourdon, 2002, p. 96).
3.   IT managers face more sophisticated and malevolent forms of attacks on these systems. Unlike the Y2K problem, which was the result of an innocent bad judgment, "the disruptive shocks to our organizations are no longer accidental, benign, or acts of nature; now they are deliberate and malevolent" (Yourdon, 2002, p. 205).

Furthermore, IT based systems may not only be the targets themselves, they may be used as a weapon in attacks against other key infrastructure systems (National Research Council, 2002, p. 136). Designing secure, resilient systems in the face of these new threats will be a major challenge for IT managers in the next decade. Robust methodologies will be needed to identify the sources of these threats, eliminate them if possible, contain their impact if they do materialize, and prevent damage they cause from propagating further.

As the events 9/11 illustrated, IT based threats are not the only source of disasters and IT based systems not the only target of malevolent individuals. However, on 9/11, IT based systems were used to mitigate the impacts of the damage and, as this analysis will indicate, could have done so to an even greater extent with proper design, implementation, and training. This analysis will argue, therefore, that IT based systems are not only a target, a source of vulnerability, but that they can also be a shield, a means of combating the threats and mitigating the damage malicious individuals are able to accomplish.

IT developers, managers, and educators, therefore, must face two new challenges:

1.   how to design more secure, resilient IT based systems in the future, and
2.   how to use IT to combat threats to IT based systems, as well as physical threats.

To address these two issues, this research will first develop a "target and shield" conceptual model of the sources, propagation and potential impacts of IT related threats, as well as the means by which IT can be used to identify, eliminate, and mitigate the damages caused by other sources of threats. The model will focus on:

1.   how the current IT infrastructure allows for the propagation of IT based threats,

2.   means by which available IT tools can help identify potential IT based threats and to mitigate their impacts, and

3.   means by which IT can be used to counter physical attacks.

The Y2K problem and the information technology implications of 9/11 will be used to illustrate the analysis. Implications for developers of new initiatives, managers planning future IT based systems, as well as for educators preparing new generations of IT specialists, will emerge from the analysis.

The conceptual model will draw on two theoretical perspectives, an extended version of Perrow's normal accident theory, and the theory of high reliability organizations.

Normal Accident Theory and the Theory of High Reliability Organizations

Normal accident theory argues that characteristics of a system's design make it more or less prone to accidents. Accidents are defined as "a failure in a subsystem, or the system as a whole, that damages more than one unit and in doing so disrupts the ongoing or future output of the system" (Perrow, 1984, p. 66). Perrow distinguishes between disastrous "accidents," which are system-wide and seriously impact the system's overall functioning and "incidents," which involve single failures that can be contained within a limited area and which do not compromise the system's overall functioning. Perrow argues that no system can be designed to completely avoid incidents, but that inherent qualities of the system determine how far and how fast the damage will spread. Systems that are not designed to contain the negative impact of incidents will, therefore, *be subject to accidents in the course of their normal functioning.*

The first key characteristic of accident prone systems is their complexity. Normal accident theory argues that as systems become more complex, they become more accident prone. Normal accident theory distinguishes a second characteristic of systems that exacerbate potential problems brought about as a result of complexity—tight coupling. Tight coupling means there is no slack time or buffering of resources be-

Figure 1. Perrow's normal accident theory model

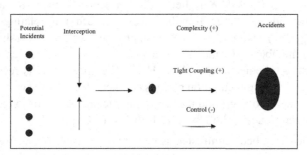

tween tasks; interactions happen immediately. Both complexity and tight coupling are often more efficient from a productivity standpoint. However, incidents tend to propagate faster and their impact becomes more severe because there is no lag time during which human intervention can occur. Figure 1 illustrates Perrow's normal accident theory model.

Perrow developed his theory while studying complex technologies such as nuclear power plants and petrochemical plants to determine the conditions under which incidents such as valve failures could lead to accidents such as meltdowns and the release of poisonous gases into populated areas. Normal accident theory argues that incidents need to be anticipated and controls built into the system to contain their propagation.

Researchers in high reliability organizations have examined organizations in which complex, tightly coupled, technologically based systems appeared to be coping successfully with the potential for disaster. High reliability theorists' studies of the Federal Aviation Administration's air traffic control system, the Pacific Gas and Electric's electric power system, including the Diablo Canyon nuclear power plant, and the peacetime flight operations of three United States Navy aircraft carriers indicate that organizations can achieve nearly error free operation (Klein, Bigley, & Roberts, 1995; La Porte & Consolini, 1991; Sagan, 1993).

High reliability organization theorists identify four critical causal factors for achieving reliability:

1. Political elites and organizational leaders put safety and reliability first as a goal.
2. High levels of redundancy in personnel and technical safety measures.
3. The development of a "high reliability culture" in decentralized and continually practiced operations, and
4. Sophisticated forms of trial and error organizational learning.

The key element in high reliability organizations "is their effective and varied communications" (Grabowski & Roberts, 1997, p. 156). Risk is mitigated by communications methods that range from the intense "heedful interrelating" (Weick & Roberts, 1993, p. 357) on flight decks to "enhancing the development of shared mental models among members" (Grabowski & Roberts, 1997, p. 156) when individuals are not physically together in one place. High reliability theorists recognize that many disasters have long incubation periods (Turner, 1976). Good communication should "keep issues above ground thus reducing the possibility of long incubation periods for unseen issues" (Grabowski & Roberts, 1997, p. 157).

The two theories have been contrasted as "pessimistic"—Perrow's contention that disaster is inevitable in badly designed systems, vs. "optimistic"—high reliability theory's pragmatic approach to achieving greater reliability. The theories, however, are in agreement as to which characteristics of systems make them more or less accident prone.

Applying Normal Accident Theory to Information Technology

Lally (1996) argued that normal accident theory was a sound theoretical perspective for understanding the risks of information technology, because IT is:

1. **Complex:** The hardware that makes up IT infrastructures of most organizations is complex, containing a wide range of technologies. Software often contains thousands of lines of code written by dozens of programmers. Incidents such as bugs can, therefore, propagate in unexpected ways, causing the "unknowability" problem.

2. **Tightly Coupled:** Both hardware and software are designed to increase the speed and efficiency of operations. Incidents such as operator errors can quickly have real world impacts.

3. **Poorly Controlled:** Security features are often not built into systems. Testing of software is often inadequate in the rush to meet release deadlines.

As a result, Lally (1996) predicted that IT based systems were likely to be subject to serious system crashes as the result of relatively minor incidents and that real world accidents could occur before the incidents could be identified and contained.

Two Extensions of Normal Accident Theory: Second Order Effects and the Problem of Change

In her study of reengineering, Lally (1996, 1997) distinguished two types of complexity and tight coupling in reengineered organizations:

1.   the complexity and tight coupling of the underlying IT infrastructure needed to enable reengineered processes, and

2.   the increased complexity and tight coupling of organizational processes enabled by the IT infrastructures.

She argued that incidents arising from first order IT based systems could propagate through second order organizational systems to create more serious, businesswide accidents.

Lally (2002) argued that the rapid pace of change in information technology is a further exacerbating factor increasing the likelihood of disasters.

1.   **Changes in Hardware:** Computer hardware continues to evolve rapidly. Furthermore, entirely new kinds of hardware are continually developed and must be integrated into existing systems.

2.   **Changes in Software:** New software releases fuel revenue streams in the software industry, resulting in mandatory "upgrades" every two years. The changes create an additional learning burden on users. Programmers are again under time pressure that can result in poor testing and debugging (Austin, 2001; Halfhill, 1998; Westland, 2000).

In addition to these first order effects, Lally also argued that changes in IT create second order effects by enabling changes in organizational processes such as reengineering and enterprise resource planning. The resulting processes are even more complex, tightly coupled, and poorly controlled, further increasing the potential for serious accidents. As a result, IT managers and users are faced with complex, tightly coupled, poorly controlled systems that undergo radical changes on a regular basis, making these systems even more prone to normal accidents. Figure 2 illustrates Lally's extensions to Perrow's normal accident theory; her contributions are in bold.

In time period A on the timeline, a number of potentially threatening incidents exist. Some are intercepted and neutralized, but others materialize in time period B. The complexity, tight coupling, and rapid rates of change of IT help propagate the

Figure 2. An IT-based extension to Perrow's model

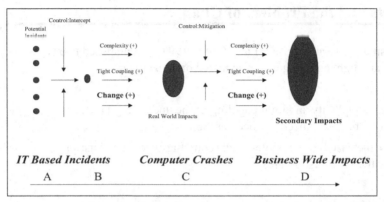

incident by making it harder to control and contain. If the incident is not contained and eliminated, it will result in an accident, a significant failure with serious real world repercussions, in time period C. If the damage of the original accident is not mitigated, it will continue to propagate and have further serious impacts in time period D. In today's tightly coupled, IT dependent society, the actual time passed between time periods A and D may be a matter of seconds.

We will now apply this extended model to the Y2K problem and the events of 9/11 and a *third extension to the model will result*. We argue that:

IT based systems are not only a target used as a weapon of destruction to cause serious accidents, but that IT based systems can be a shield used to prevent damage from future incidents, whether they be IT based or physical.

This "Target and Shield" conceptual model draws on insights from the theory of high reliability organizations and suggests that IT designers and managers, as well as government and law enforcement agencies learn from past experiences and embody this knowledge in the design and implementation of future IT based systems. The resulting systems should not only be more secure and resilient, they should aid in preventing future IT based or physical attacks, or mitigating their impact should they occur.

A Third Extension to Normal Accident Theory: The Target and Shield Model

Figure 3 illustrates the target and shield conceptual model for analyzing the source, propagation, and impacts of IT based threats, as well as ways in which IT can be used to identify and mitigate the impact of future threats.

The target and shield model incorporates Lally's previous extensions to normal accident theory. The model also contains *three significant feedback loops*, which allow IT to play a positive role in preventing future incidents from materializing, having real world impacts, and mitigating their impacts when they do occur. In Feedback Loop #1, when incidents are identified, controls can be built into the system to prevent future incidents from materializing. In Feedback Loop #2, controls can be built into the system to prevent future incidents that have materialized from turning into accidents. In Feedback Loop #3, IT based systems can be developed to prevent accidents resulting from IT based or physical attacks from propagating even further. Therefore, the model permits the system to learn from past mistakes and exploits the ability of IT systems to evolve over time to create more secure, resilient systems in the future.

Figure 3. The target and shield model

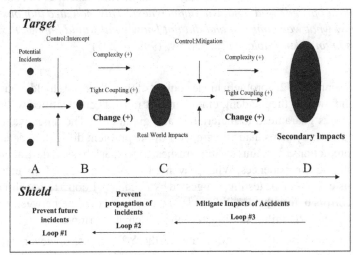

Lessons from Y2K

By the late 1990s, a significant number of researchers and IT professionals were highly concerned about the Y2K problem causing catastrophic IT failures (Anson, 1999; Golter & Hawry, 1998; Kirsner, 1998; Ullman, 1999). Although the Y2K problem had been recognized by the professional programming community as early as 1984, the problem incubated for years before action was taken to mitigate the potential impact. Computer systems had become increasingly integrated and spanned organizational, and even global, boundaries. Y2K failures in one organization, therefore, were believed to be likely to propagate to other organizations and to the economy as a whole. Y2K practitioners referred to this as the "ripple effect": "One patched together, wrapped up system exchanges data with another patched together wrapped up system—layer upon layer of software involved in a single transaction until the possibility of failure increases exponentially" (Ullman, 1999, p. 7).

Ed Yardeni, Chief Economist at Deutsche Morgan Grenfell predicted a 60% chance that Y2K would lead to a global recession (Golter & Hawry, 1998).

Perrow emphasized that Y2K made him more keenly aware of the problem of "unknowability":

One of the key themes of the theory, but not one formalized as much as it could have been, was the notion of incomprehensibility—What has happened? How could such a thing have happened? And What will happen next? This indicated that observers did not know what was going on and did not know what would happen next. The system was in an unknowable state. (Perrow, 1999, p. 293)

Figure 4 presents the Y2K problem in the context of the target and shield model. The Y2K design flaw was the incident, unique in that it had been identified well ahead of time and was guaranteed to materialize at a given date. The unknowability of existing computer systems made the impacts of the problem difficult to determine, leading to predictions of serious system crashes, as well as physical destruction and severe economic consequences. What prevented the Y2K problem from creating a serious disaster was (1) the testing, suggested by Feedback Loop #1, that eliminated many Y2K errors before the deadline and (2) the lack of coupling between systems that experienced Y2K failures, mitigating the anticipated "ripple effect."

The learning processes that occurred during the Y2K crisis, however, provided managers with methodologies for dealing with future disasters. Better programming practices can make new design flaws and bugs less likely to happen, as suggested by Feedback Loop #1. A better understanding of systems as a result of Y2K efforts, suggested by Feedback Loop #2, make it more likely other bugs and design flaws will be intercepted. Finally, Feedback Loop #3 suggests that an enhanced aware-

Figure 4. The target and shield model applied to Y2K

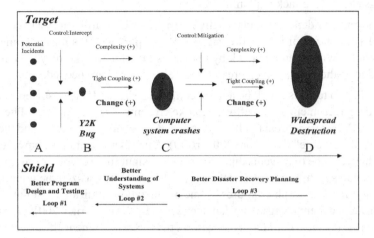

ness of disaster recovery techniques on the part of managers would prepare them for accidents that did materialize.

9/11/2001: What Has Happened? How Could Such a Thing Happen? What Will Happen Next?

On September 11, 2001, surprise terrorist attacks left the world wondering, "What has happened? How could such a thing happen? What will happen next?" The damage caused by the initial impact of the planes hitting the World Trade Center towers quickly spread causing massive destruction and loss of life in lower Manhattan. The Y2K problem was an innocent error, recognized ahead of time, and prevented from causing catastrophic failures. 9/11 was a deliberate, well organized, surprise attack that caused catastrophic damage before the military, the police, or the thousands of individuals who lost their lives could do anything to circumvent it. The prediction of the Y2K bug causing a worldwide recession did not come true. 9/11, however, will have serious global economic ramifications for years to come. One common feature of both Y2K and 9/11, however, was their long incubation periods. The

9/11 congressional report indicated that the intelligence community had received warnings about the attack beginning in 1998.

From a normal accident theory perspective the most striking difference between Y2K and 9/11 is the issue of intent. If designers of complex systems must assume that these systems will be under attack by malicious individuals who may have inside knowledge of the system, even greater degrees of control are needed.

"Responding to terrorism will be a more complex task," as John Koskinen, former head of the government's Y2K effort, remarked recently, "Unlike the Y2K Phenomenon, today's terrorist threat to IT is undefined, the response is difficult, and there is no known time frame" (Yourdon, 2002, p. 29). A number of parallels, however, do emerge between the two events that can provide insight for preventing and mitigating the impacts of future terrorist attacks. Both events emphasized the importance of planning for catastrophic failures. Some organizations indicated that their Y2K planning helped them mitigate the damage caused by 9/11 (Merian, 2001). Pressure is on from the business community to recreate the U.S. government effort in combating the Y2K problem as a means of combating terrorism (Thibodeau, 2001).

Figure 5 illustrates the events of 9/11 in terms of the target and shield model. Feedback Loop #1 would involve the use of IT to help reveal the existence of future terror plots. High reliability theory suggests the creation of a decentralized culture where individuals are encouraged to report information they consider threatening. "We need to make it easier for front line observers to communicate their warnings quickly and effectively, without worrying about being criticized as alarmists" (Yourdon, 2002, p. 199). More sophisticated IT based methods are also available. Customer relationship management software, such as that used by Amazon books

Figure 5. The target and shield model applied to 9/11

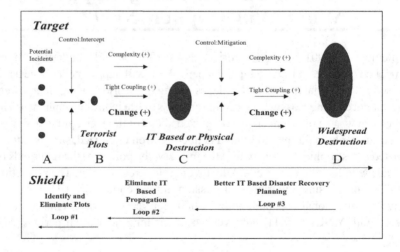

to detect patterns in buyer behavior, can also be used to detect patterns of suspicious behavior (Bowman, 2002; Perera, 2001; Popp, 2003).

However, recognizing a potential terrorist and uncovering a terrorist plot is a challenging intelligence task, which is likely to result in many "false positives" with serious implications for individual privacy. Surveys have begun to emerge addressing privacy issues in the post-9/11 environment that focus on individuals concerns with government agencies and law enforcement collecting data on individuals. Preliminary results indicate that the attitude of many individuals has shifted from privacy concerns to security concerns (*Economist*, 2002). Privacy rights activists, however, have begun to express alarm at the extent to which government and law enforcement agencies are extending their powers. Rigorous, theory based, studies are needed in the area to explore ways government agencies and law enforcement can collect information necessary to prevent further attacks while addressing individual privacy concerns.

Another serious source of IT based threats is the use by terrorists of the Internet and other IT based systems to develop their plots, receive funding, and disseminate information. Feedback Loop #2 indicates that once genuine threats are identified, IT based solutions could be applied to shut these communication and funding channels down. For example, reconstructed data from hard drives found in the ruins of the World Trade Center are being used to identify investors who may have profited by the impending attack (Perera, 2001). Building systems to support an integrated coordinated response to genuine threats, however, is likely to be a challenge. "The number of responding agencies, including those from the local, regional, state and federal levels—with possibly conflicting and overlapping areas of responsibility—increases the level of complexity" (National Research Council, 2002, p. 146).

Modeling the Unthinkable: Mitigating the Impacts of Terrorist Attacks

On 9/11, many lives were lost after the initial impact of the two planes because bad judgments based on incomplete information were made by individuals working in the towers, as well as by firemen and police. This was particularly true in the North Tower. Individuals remained in the upper portion of the North Tower hoping to be rescued despite the fact that they were unreachable and that one stairway was still passable. Firemen continued climbing up into the lower portion of the North Tower despite the fact that the South Tower had collapsed and they were in imminent danger. Incompatible communication devices prevented critical information from reaching the firefighters (Dwyer, 2002). However, wireless communication devices, e-mails, and other Internet communication did increase social coherence during the disaster. Victims said goodbye to loved ones, and the passengers on Flight 93 were able to mitigate the impact of the disaster they had become a part of. Regular business communication took place over employee cell phones and personal Internet accounts (Disabatino, 2001; Kontzer, 2001).

In terms of the target and shield model, Feedback Loop #3 provides insight into how we can learn from 9/11 to mitigate the impact of physical attacks. High reliability theorists emphasis on good communication and shared mental models appears critical. First, better communication through improved communication devices could aid police, firemen, and medical workers to reduce unknowability and improve social coherence. Second, simulation models of the building, such as those designed afterward (see Nova, 2002, *Why the Towers Fell*) could be used to minimize the problem of "unknowability" that resulted in so many deaths. Office workers in all large complex buildings could use these models to develop optimal evacuation plans during an emergency. Firemen could train by simulating rescue missions in all large complex buildings in their area. Finally good communication between structural engineers, who are best able to determine the condition of the building, and the workers and firemen inside could also save hundreds of lives. Post-9/11 disaster training has already mitigated the damage done in a recent nightclub fire by preparing emergency workers for handling a large number of individuals with burns (Wielawski, 2003).

Lally (2004) applied the target and shield model to terrorist attacks in urban environments, in contrast to innocent mistakes in organizational settings in which the theory was originally developed. She argued that two key issues must be addressed when applying the model to 9/11 type attacks. First the model must be extended to *address the possibility of deliberate attacks rather than innocent mistakes.* Second, the model must be extended to *address the challenges of applying the principles of these theories to large diverse urban environments, rather than organizational settings.* Large urban areas add additional layers of complexity and tight coupling when compared to organizational settings. In organizational settings, the shared mental models recommended by high reliability theory are easier to enforce. Organizations can appoint professionals who are educated in preventing disasters and involve all employees in disaster training. Terrorist attacks in urban areas are likely to involve "a spectrum of trained professionals, cognitively and physically fatigued individuals, motivated volunteers, and frightened victims" (Murphy, 2004, p. 68), making shared mental models harder to achieve and appropriate social interaction harder to achieve. The complex, tightly coupled infrastructure of large urban areas makes fault isolation more difficult and system restoration more difficult to achieve, the blackout of 8/14/2003 the most striking recent example. IT based initiatives for combating terrorism must address these new challenges as well.

Lally and Nolan (2005) applied the target and shield model to map developments in emerging wireless technologies. Their analysis indicated that wireless technologies are a target because of their vulnerabilities to air interface denial of service attacks, snooping attacks that threaten data integrity, and the limitations of standards in applications that use unlicensed spectrum. Their analysis also indicated that wireless technology could be used as a shield because the distributed architecture of these networks can provide robustness and redundancy to prevent catastrophic failures. Finally, they indicated that location aware devices could be used for tracking suspected cyber attackers.

Extending the Model: IT as a Weapon

In the target and shield model, Feedback Loop #1 addresses the challenge of preventing future incidents. In a learning environment, once incidents occur, knowledge should be gained about the nature of the incident to prevent future incidents from occurring. The proactive prevention of future incidents involves more than waiting for new incidents to occur and developing defensive techniques when they do. IT based tools are emerging for tracing incidents to their source and eliminating them. When IT is used as a weapon to fight back against potential attackers, the dynamics of the "target and shield" model is reversed. Instead of responding to a single negative event and its propagation through a large and complex system, the emphasis is

Figure 6. IT as a weapon against potential threats

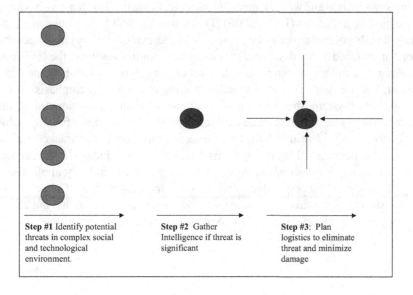

Step #1 Identify potential threats in complex social and technological environment.

Step #2 Gather Intelligence if threat is significant

Step #3: Plan logistics to eliminate threat and minimize damage

on identifying potential threats in a complex technological and social environment, gathering intelligence on those threats, and if the threats are confirmed, planning the logistics to eliminate the threat with a minimum of damage to innocent people and their property. With use, the model should also provide insight into which threats are the most serious and need to be eliminated.

Figure 6 illustrates the use of IT as a weapon.

In Step #1, IT can be used to identify anomalous behavior, such as a group of people who have never contacted one another suddenly being in frequent contact. Artificial intelligence based systems for identifying anomalous patterns in telecommunication behavior can identify unusual patterns. The challenge in Step #1 is identifying potential threats in an environment that consists primarily of innocent people, whether corporate employees or civilians. In Step #2, IT based intelligence gathering can then reveal whether the members of the new group are on a "watch list" —indicating that they may be a terrorist cell becoming active, or perhaps members of a new computer class, corporate subcommittee, or scout troop. In Step #3, if the threat is real, IT can then be used to monitor the activities of the group and eliminate the threat in a manner that will cause the least collateral damage.

Directions for Future Research

The target and shield and weapon model is currently being used to create a taxonomy of emerging IT initiatives (Lally, 2006). This taxonomy will be used to categorize the functionality of initiatives as they emerge and address several key challenges and opportunities faced by the developers of new security initiatives. First, the challenge of making new initiatives *interoperable* with existing systems will become more apparent. Second, with venture capitalists putting an increased emphasis on the development of systems that can be made operational within a short time frame, the need for *basic research* that must be explored to make the initiatives fully operable will be more easily identified. This basic research can then be fast tracked and its cost allocated between all the applications that depend on it. Finally, opportunities for *additional applications of emerging technology*, such as military applications being used to help first responders, will be more apparent as well. The results of the analysis will be useful to IT researchers and educators as well as having global implications for designing systems to combat terrorism and other threats.

This research was sponsored by a Summer Research Grant from the Frank G. Zarb School of Business at Hofstra University.

References

Anson, R.S. (1999, January). 12.31.99. *Vanity Fair*, 80-84.

Austin, R. (2001, June). The effects of time pressure on quality in software development. *Information Systems Research*, 195-207.

Bowman, L. (2002, June 6). *FBI digs deeper into the Web*. Retrieved July 12, 2006, from http://www.news.news.com

Disabatino, J. (2001, September 17). Internet messaging keeps businesses, employees, in touch. *Computerworld*.

Dwyer, J. (2002, September). Radio problem could last years. *New York Times*.

Economist. (2002, August 17). Go on, watch me (p. 12).

Golter, J., & Hawry, P. (1998). *Circles of risk*. Retrieved July 12, 2006, from http://year2000.com/archive/circlesrisk.html

Grabowski, M., & Roberts, K. (1997, Summer). Risk mitigation in large scale systems: Lessons from high reliability organizations. *California Management Review*, 152-162.

Halfhill, T. (1998). *Crash-proof computing*. Retrieved July 12, 2006, from BYTE, http://www.byte.com/art/9804/sec5/art1.html

Kirsner, S. (1998). *The ripple effect*. Retrieved July 12, 2006, from http://www.cio.archive/y2k_ripple_content.html

Klein, R.L., Bigley, G.A., & Roberts, K.H. (1995). Organizational culture in high reliability organizations. *Human Relations, 48*(7), 771-792.

Kontzer, T. (2001, September 12). With phone lines bottlenecked, Internet messaging became lifeline. *Information Week*.

Lally, L. (1996). Enumerating the risks of reengineered processes. In *Proceedings of the 1996 ACM Computer Science Conference* (pp. 18-23).

Lally, L. (1997). Are reengineered organizations disaster prone? In *Proceedings of the National Decision Sciences Conference* (pp. 178-182).

Lally, L. (2002). Complexity, coupling, control and change: An IT based extension to normal accident theory. In *Proceedings of the International Information Resources Management Conference* (pp. 1089-1095).

Lally, L. (2004). Information technology as a target and shield in urban environments. In *Proceedings of the AMCIS Conference*.

Lally, L. (2006). Target, shield and weapon: A taxonomy of IT security initiatives. In *Proceedings of the International Information Resources Conference*.

Lally, L., & Nolan, J. (2005). Applying the target and shield model to wireless technology. In *Proceedings of the International Information Resources Conference* (pp. 436-441).

LaPorte, T.R., & Consolini, P. (1991). Working in practice but not in theory: Theoretical challenges of high reliability organizations. *Journal of Public Administration, 1*, 19-47.

Merian, L. (2001, September 19). Y2K plans aided in recovery, but more planning needed. *Computerworld*.

MIT Editors. (2005, March). Technology and finance: 2005. *MIT's Magazine of Innovation*, 36-44.

National Research Council. (2002). *Making the nation safer: The role of science and technology in countering terrorism*. Washington, DC: National Academies Press.

Nova. (2002). *Why the towers fell*. PBS Video.

Perera, R. (2001, December 19). Recovered data in N.Y. could explain preatttack financial dealings. *Computerworld*.

Perrow, C. (1984). *Normal accidents: Living with high risk technologies*. New York: Basic Books.

Perrow, C. (1999). *Normal accidents: Living with high risk technologies* (2nd ed.). New York: Basic Books.

Popp, R. (2003, July/August). Total information overload. *MIT Technology Review*, 68-71.

Sagan, S. (1993). *The limits of safety*. Princeton, NJ: Princeton University Press.

Ullman, E. (1999). The myth of order. Retrieved July 12, 2006, from *Wired*, http://wired.com/archive/7.04/y2k_pr.html

Thibodeau, P. (2001, October 2). Businesses eye Y2K effort as model for terrorism fight. *Computerworld*.

Turner, B.M. (1976). The organizational and interorganizational development of disasters. *Administrative Science Quarterly, 21*, 378-397.

Weick, K.E., & Roberts, K. (1993). Collective mind in organizations: Heedful interrelating on flight decks. *Administrative Science Quarterly, 38*, 357-381.

Westland, J.C. (2000, September). Modeling the incidence of postrelease errors in software. *Information Systems Research*, pp. 320-324.

Wielawski, I. (2003, March 23). Post 9/11 drills aid club fire rescue. *New York Times*.

Yourdon, E. (2002). *Byte wars: The impact of September 11 on information technology*. Upper Saddle River, NJ: Prentice Hall.

Chapter VIII

An Extended Trust Building Model:
Comparing Experiential and Non-Experiential Factors

D. Harrison McKnight, Michigan State University, USA

Norman L. Chervany, University of Minnesota, USA

Abstract

This study examines a model of factors influencing system troubleshooter trust in their supervisors, contrasting experiential and nonexperiential factors. System troubleshooters keep important organizational systems operating. Traditional research suggests that trust forms through interactional experience. Recent research indicates that initial interpersonal trust develops through nonexperiential factors that are dispositional (individual differences-related) or institutional (structural/situational). This chapter combines initial and experiential factors to see which remain effective over time. We found that both institutional and dispositional factors affected troubleshooter trust in the supervisor even after parties gained experience with each other. Quality of experience with the supervisor affected interpersonal trust, while quantity of experience did not. Surprisingly, institutional trust, an initial trust factor, predicted trusting beliefs as strongly as did quality of experience. The study shows that both experiential and nonexperiential factors are important to troubleshooter trust even after parties know each other well.

Introduction

Trust is defined as the willingness to depend upon another with a feeling of relative security, even though negative consequences are possible and one cannot control the other (Mayer, Davis & Schoorman, 1995). Researchers have found trust to affect performance in many information systems (IS) tasks (Hart & Saunders, 1993; Jarvenpaa, Knoll, & Leidner, 1998; Nelson & Cooprider, 1996). This chapter investigates the factors that lead to the development of trust in one IS environment—troubleshooting—that is increasingly important to the ongoing performance of mission-critical information systems. The organization of the chapter is as follows. The remainder of the introduction overviews two general theories of trust building, defines the troubleshooting task, and introduces the research questions. The second section presents two versions of a trust-building model. In the next two sections, the methods and results are presented and discussed.

Two General Theories of Trust Building

While there is widespread agreement on the importance of trust in the workplace (Kramer, 1999; Zand, 1972), less agreement exists about the factors upon which trust is built. Two general theories of trust-building factors compete at the center of the trust-building debate today.

Experiential Trust Building

The most dominant general theory posits that trust grows through positive interaction and experience with the trustee (Blau, 1964; Gefen, Karahanna, & Straub, 2003a; Jarvenpaa & Leidner, 1998; Kramer, 1999; Ring & Van de Ven, 1994). This makes sense, because people build a mental image of the other's trustworthiness via interactions over time. The more one interacts with another, the more information one gains about their attributes and the more confidence one has about predicting their actions, which translates into trust. What are the managerial implications of this theory? The supervisor controls the interactional relationship with the employee. Supervisors can develop a positive relationship with the employee over time through interactive steps that reveal the supervisor's trustworthiness.

Nonexperiential Trust Building
___

The second general theory, which we call nonexperiential trust building, posits that nonexperiential factors like institutional context or personality traits are important in building trust, especially when parties are so new to each other that they have no experiential basis for trusting (McKnight, Cummings, & Chervany, 1998; Meyerson, Weick, & Kramer, 1996). Institutional context factors are perceived situational/ structural features that provide confidence in the organizational and work context, thus encouraging trust among parties in that context. One institutional construct is structural assurance, defined as a belief that structures make the workplace safe or secure. Institutional factors are important, because they can be managed. For example, developing a work environment that employees feel is structurally secure and fair should increase employee trust in management. Some have also shown that in e-commerce, trust building factors differ over time (Gefen, Karahanna, & Straub, 2003b; McKnight, Choudhury, & Kacmar, 2004).

Managers also need to be cognizant of the effects of dispositional (personality) issues on trust. One personality factor is disposition to trust, defined as how much one generally trusts others. Although personality issues cannot be managed, per se, the manager who is aware of their effects can take action. For example, the manager of an employee with low disposition to trust can spend more time winning this skeptical employee's trust. Since trust and influence are highly correlated concepts (Nelson & Cooprider, 1996; Zand, 1972), trust is key to managerial success, because employee trust will determine how amenable the employee is to supervisory influence and coaching. The above two general theories of trust building form the basis of the research models presented in the Trust and Trust Building section.

The IS Troubleshooting Task
___

Information systems troubleshooting is an important task. It involves reacting, often under extreme time pressure, to find and fix both software and hardware problems that have caused a system to crash. The research reported in this chapter studied troubleshooters in two *Fortune 500* companies in the computer services industry. In one of the companies, troubleshooters maintained a large computer reservation system for a major airline. In the other company, the troubleshooters maintained computer software that the company marketed to various customers. In both firms, successful, quick-response troubleshooting was a key customer service issue. If done well, it led to customer loyalty; if done poorly, it led to loss of customers.

To be successful, the troubleshooters and their supervisors needed to cooperate through an on-the-job coaching process. Troubleshooters said they liked coaching and related supervisor confidence in them, but disliked being micromanaged. Because of this interdependence, the relationship issues among the troubleshooters and their supervisors constituted a key to managing the performance of these critical systems. Because trust is essential in interdependent relationships (Kramer, 1999), it is clear that troubleshooter-supervisor trust is key in this setting.

The Research Questions

Two questions intrigued us, combining experiential and nonexperiential trust theory.

Research Question #1: *How well (if at all) do nonexperiential constructs predict troubleshooter trust in the supervisor after these parties gain experience with each other? Nonexperiential trust-building theory (McKnight et al., 1998), which proposes that dispositional/institutional factors build trust before parties become familiar, implicitly suggests that these factors erode in strength post-familiarity.*

Research Question #2: *When a troubleshooter has experience with the supervisor, does that experience replace the effects of dispositional and institutional factors on troubleshooter trust in the supervisor? That is, do experiential factors erode the effect of nonexperiential factors on trust?*

By examining research question #1, this study tests whether or not the nonexperiential trust-building factors are still relevant beyond the initial relationship timeframe. If so, this synthesizes the two extant theories of trust building. By examining research question #2, the research begins to identify the trade-offs among experiential and nonexperiential trust building factors.

Trust and Trust Building

Basic Trust Concepts

This section defines the individual constructs that are at work and presents two versions of a detailed model incorporating these constructs. Definitions of three main types of trust, each from a different academic discipline, are found in the literature. First, psychologist Rotter (1971) defined trust as a generalized tendency to assume that others would fulfill expectations. This is the disposition to trust already defined (Gefen, 2000) (see Figure 1, column 1). Second, sociologists Lewis and Weigert

Figure 1. Trust building model (TBM)

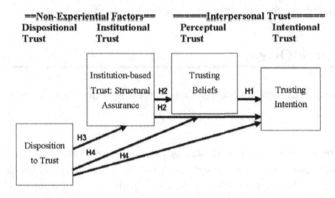

Scope of the McKnight, Cummings, and Chervany (1998) model

(1985a, b) proposed that trust is not a personal trait but a function of social or institutional structures that makes one feel confident of success in that context. One subset of institutional trust—structural assurance—was previously defined (see Figure 1, column 2). Third, organizational researchers and social psychologists have defined trust as an interpersonal construct (Rousseau, Sitkin, Burt, & Camerer, 1998; Scanzoni, 1979). This chapter employs two such constructs: trusting beliefs (belief that the trustee has beneficial attributes, such as integrity, competence, benevolence [Rempel, Holmes & Zanna, 1985]) and trusting intention (willingness to depend on the trustee in a risky situation [Currall & Judge, 1995]) (see Figure 1, columns 3 and 4). We use the terms *interpersonal trust* and *trust* to refer to trusting beliefs and trusting intention.

A Trust-Building Model

This chapter builds on a model of unfamiliar relations (McKnight et al., 1998) to focus on how trust builds in familiar relations. Familiar relationships are defined as those in which parties have sound information about each other (Bigley & Pearce, 1998) through interaction.

- **A trust-building model for an unfamiliar setting:** McKnight et al. (1998) suggested that when parties first meet, disposition to trust and institution-based trust affect interpersonal trust, because one is forced to rely on individual ten-

Figure 2. Extended trust building model (ETBM)

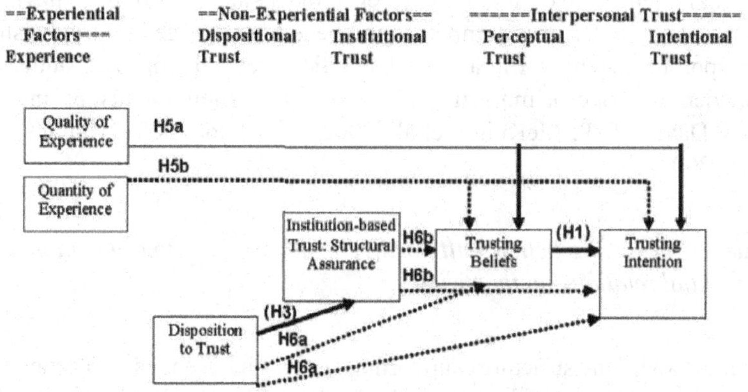

Dotted lines indicate relationships proposed to be nonsignificant. Solid lines indicate relationships proposed to be significant.

dencies and contextual beliefs when one has no information about the trusted party (see Figure 1). Their model excluded experience with the trusted party, because, in the initial timeframe, the parties have little or no experience with each other. In the only full test of this model of which we are aware, McKnight, Choudhury, and Kacmar (2002a) found that disposition to trust was a factor of trusting beliefs and trusting intention, but institution-based trust was not. Subsets or variants of the model also have been tested in Gefen (2000), Gefen et al. (2003a), Pavlou (2002), and McKnight, Choudhury, and Kacmar (2002b), each of which found either dispositional or institutional trust to be factors of one or more interpersonal trust variables in e-commerce domains. This chapter reports the first test of the model in employee-supervisor relationships within IS organizations. We also extend the original model (see Figure 2) by adding experiential factors.

Research Hypotheses

Research Question #1 (Effects of Original Model Constructs under Familiarity)

Hypotheses 1 through 4 (Figure 1) propose that the initial relationship trust constructs continue to affect trust after technical troubleshooters become familiar with their supervisors. The link between trusting beliefs and trusting intention should prevail over time, because having favorable beliefs about the other tends to make one willing to depend upon them, the essence of trusting intention. Believing, for example, that a supervisor is competent and benevolent suggests a troubleshooter can rely upon the supervisor in a crucial situation. Several empirical studies have found evidence of one or more links from trusting beliefs to trusting intentions (Mayer & Davis, 1999; McKnight et al., 2002a, b; Pavlou, 2003; Ridings, Gefen & Arinze, 2002).

Hypothesis 1: *Trusting beliefs will positively influence trusting intention beyond the initial relationship timeframe.*

One's beliefs about the structures supporting success in an endeavor (structural assurance) will continue to influence one's beliefs about the people who operate within those institutional structures. For example, a troubleshooter who feels the setting is safe and fair should form trust in the supervisor in the setting. Even though interpersonal events may intervene that cause one to reduce reliance on institutional beliefs and to infer interpersonal trust directly from experience, it is likely that structural perceptions will continue to affect trusting beliefs and trusting intention. This is because they provide a success-favoring background in which to trust. Structural assurance provides safeguards or safety nets (Shapiro, 1987) for the troubleshooter that reduce the risk of the negative effects from supervisor deficiencies. Empirical researchers found that institution-based (or system) trust influenced trust in e-commerce vendors or in the community of sellers (Pavlou & Gefen, 2004; Pennington, Wilcox, & Grover, 2003). Pavlou and Gefen (2004) found that institutional structures (similar to structural assurance) predicted trust in the community of sellers.

Hypothesis 2: *institution-based trust: structural assurance will positively influence trusting beliefs and trusting intention beyond the initial relationship timeframe.*

Disposition to trust will relate positively to institution-based trust after the initial timeframe. Those with low disposition to trust will continue to evaluate institutional structures more negatively (McKnight et al., 2002a) and will be more watchful or attentive to problems, greeting them with an I-thought-so attitude, because they expect the worst. In contrast, those with a high disposition to trust will continue to view institutional structures with optimism.

Hypothesis 3: *Disposition to trust will positively influence structural assurance beyond the initial relationship timeframe.*

Since disposition to trust colors one's perceptions of others generally, it will continue to predict trusting beliefs and trusting intention. Here's why. First, people with low disposition to trust are more critical of others (Holmes, 1991), so their trust-related judgments tend to be harsher. Second, one who does not trust others generally is more attentive to the other's behavior, per Holmes. This makes it more likely that they will find behavior they perceive negatively, which will produce lower trusting beliefs and trusting intention. Over time, one's trust in others generally will be reflected in the level of trust for most individuals within one's acquaintance. Several studies have found evidence of this link (Gefen, 2000; Jarvenpaa et al., 1998; Ridings et al., 2002).

Hypothesis 4: *Disposition to trust will positively influence trusting beliefs and trusting intention beyond the initial relationship timeframe.*

Research Question #2 (Decrease in Construct Predictive Strength vis-à-vis Experience)

Hypotheses 5 and 6 add two experience constructs to the model and then propose the relative strength of model constructs. Experience will affect trusting beliefs and trusting intention, per the experience-based trust literature (Bhattacherjee, 2002; Ratnasingham & Phan, 2003). Gefen (2000) found that familiarity (similar to experience) predicted trust. Experience with the trustee will build both trusting beliefs and intention (Blau, 1964; Ring & Van de Ven, 1994).

We believe quantity and quality of experience will have differential effects. Quantity of experience means the amount of interaction one has had with the trustee over time. Quality of experience means the degree of perceived positive nature of those interactions. The raw quantity of experience is not a good predictor of trust, because those interactions may either be positive or negative. For example, a trouble-shooter may have some interactions with the supervisor that build trust, some that decrease trust, and some that have no effect. Thus, on balance, the quantity of experience is not likely to influence trust. However, the quality of experience will. Positive troubleshooter interactions with the supervisor should increase troubleshooter trust. The more positive the quality of the interactions, the higher the trust should be.

Hypothesis 5a: *Quality of experience with the trustee will positively influence trusting beliefs and trusting intention.*

Hypothesis 5b: *Quantity of experience with the trustee will not positively influence trusting beliefs and trusting intention.*

Disposition to trust should be replaced as a predictor of trusting beliefs and trusting intentions by quality of experience after the parties become familiar. This is because people rely on experience-based information more readily than disposition, which is based on assumptions (McKnight et al., 1998). The quality of one's experience with the trustee provides important firsthand trustworthiness information that should be preferred over a general disposition to trust others. Trust researchers support this idea (Mayer et al., 1995; Rotter, 1971).

Hypothesis 6a: *The effects of disposition to trust on trusting beliefs and trusting intention will become nonsignificant in the presence of quality and quantity of experience.*

Institution-based trust is based on assumptions about people's motivation to act, as shaped by situational cues. Experience with the trustee can provide detailed and solid information (Lewicki, McAllister, & Bies, 1998) about the trustee (detailed schemas) (Berscheid, 1994). Over time, the effects of institution-based trust should be replaced by experiential knowledge about the trustee. This means that the trouble-shooter will come to feel confident enough about interactions with the supervisor that structural assurance no longer affects troubleshooter trust.

Hypothesis 6b: *The effects of institution-based trust—structural assurance on trusting beliefs and trusting intention—will become nonsignificant in the presence of quality and quantity of experience.*

Methodology and Results

Scale Item Development

We first interviewed 17 troubleshooters and their managers to identify issues important to their success. Then, we did the questionnaire study reported here. In order to develop and test survey items, a pilot study was conducted with undergraduate introductory IS students at a large midwestern U.S. university, who answered paper questionnaires during class. The trusting beliefs measures were adapted from various scales discussed in Wrightsman (1991). Trusting intention measures were adapted from Dobing (1993). Disposition to trust measures were taken from Rosenberg (1957). The institution-based trust measures were developed new. The pilot results, analyzed through factor analysis, showed that the items needed significant rework, especially the disposition to trust items, which formed three factors from five items. The institution-based trust items formed three scales. The trusting beliefs and trusting intention items formed two distinct scales, one for trusting beliefs and one for trusting intentions. The researchers used pretest methods similar to those used by Davis (1989) to refine the scales.

Final Measures Used

The Appendix shows the final measures used. Because of item problems in the pilot, all dispositional items were created new and represent the benevolence of others. The structural assurance factor from McKnight et al. (1998) represented institution-based trust and used items adapted from the pilot study. We developed the quantity of experience measure to take into account both the length and intensity of experience. One item measured each component. The quality of experience measures tap into the effects of interactions with the supervisor on troubleshooter self-esteem, which is one important positive impact of interaction. This concept was derived from interviews. We found that when a troubleshooter did a good job of solving a system problem, it had a positive impact on self-esteem. For example, when asked how he felt when he solved a difficult system problem, one troubleshooter flexed his muscles and said, "Like Superman! You feel like there's nothing this computer can present me that I can't solve."

Study Respondents

Study respondents were technical software or hardware troubleshooters in two *Fortune 500* companies in the computer services industry; 101 out of 115 troubleshooters (88%) agreed to participate in the study, providing an adequate sample. Each respondent answered every question during a telephone interview (Dillman, 1978) conducted during work hours. On average, workers were 41 years old and had worked with their supervisor for three and a half years. 30% were female. From prequestionnaire discussions at the company, we learned that supervisors played an active role in the teams, often giving advice, training tidbits, feedback, and encouragement to team members. The most critical task of these IS professionals was system problem troubleshooting (i.e., getting the system running again when it crashed), which was done in team fashion, involving workers at all levels, including supervisors. Supervisors were considered team members, organizational learning repositories, and team morale tonesetters. When systems are "up," troubleshooters look for potential system problems by contacting help desk personnel. They research and provide technical fixes to software about which users log complaints. Some hardware problem troubleshooters were also part of the sample.

The respondents answered questions about the relationship with their supervisor. To increase the likelihood that the respondents fell in the very-familiar relationship category, we removed those 14 cases in which the respondent had less than six months of interaction with the supervisor (new relationship duration mean = 4.0 years). Partial Least Squares (PLS) was used to analyze the data because of the relatively small final sample size (n = 87) (Chin, 1998). Means and standard deviations of the variables are found in Table 1.

Measurement Model Results

PLS standards were used to test the reliability and validity of the measurement model (Chin, 1998; Fornell & Larcker, 1982). Inspecting the outer model loadings, all but one were 0.89 or above, supplying initial evidence of construct unidimensionality (Chin, 1998). The loading under 0.89 was for the fourth trusting belief-competence item, which was 0.67. This item was retained, because the overall average variance extracted (AVE) of the construct was acceptable (Chin, 1998). Next, we assessed convergent validity using internal composite reliability (ICR) and AVE measures. Table 1 shows that the ICR figures for all constructs were adequate (>0.80), and the AVE measures all exceed the standard of 0.50, indicating convergent validity (Chin,

Table 1. Correlation of latent variables and other statistics

Latent Variable Correlation Matrix	Mean	S. D.	AVE	ICR	1	2	3	4	5	6	7
1 Disposition to Trust	5.4	1.3	.85	0.95	.92						
2 Structural Assurance	4.5	1.7	.84	0.95	.21	.91					
3 Trusting Belief-Benevolence	6.0	1.4	.91	0.96	.14	.57	.95				
4 Trusting Belief-Competence	6.2	1.1	.75	0.87	.14	.42	.77	.87			
5 Trusting Intention	5.5	1.8	.96	0.98	.27	.52	.86	.77	.98		
6 Quantity of Experience	13.6	13.2	1.00	1.00	.23	.32	.30	.24	.31	1.00	
7 Quality of Experience	5.7	1.6	.97	0.99	.24	.40	.53	.44	.57	.25	.99

The diagonal is the square root of the average variance extracted (AVE).
Notes: 1. S. D. = Standard Deviation; 2. ICR = Internal Composite Reliability

1998). To assess discriminant validity, the PLS standard is that each latent variable correlation should be lower than the square roots of the AVEs of the two variables correlated (Fornell & Larcker, 1981). Discriminant validity is shown, since all correlations are lower than the square root of their associated AVEs (see figures along Table 1 diagonal). Thus, the measurement model has acceptable psychometrics, based on PLS standards (Chin, 1998).

In addition to the variables shown in the model, we inserted these control variables to predict trusting intention: age, gender, and education.

Structural Model Results

Research Question #1 (Effects of Trust Building Constructs under Familiarity)

Hypothesis 1 was supported (Figure 3) in that both trusting beliefs predicted trusting intention (0.28** and 0.62***). In partial support of Hypothesis 2, structural assur-

Figure 3. Structural model results: Trust building model (TBM)

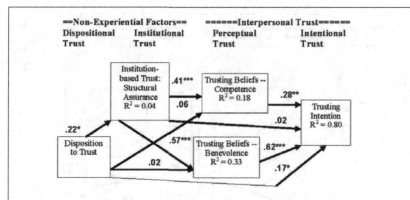

*** p< .001 ** p< .01 * p< .05

Effects of Control Variables:

Dependent Variable	Age	Gender (1=M 2=F)	Education
Trusting Intention	-.09*	-.08	.01

ance predicted both trusting beliefs (0.41*** and 0.57***). Structural assurance did not predict trusting intention (0.02), although they were correlated at 0.52 (Table 1). As support for Hypothesis 3, disposition to trust predicted structural assurance (0.22*). Disposition to trust did not predict either trusting belief but did significantly predict trusting intention (0.17*), partially supporting Hypothesis 4.

In response to Research Question #1, the results indicate that most factors in the McKnight et al. (1998) model were still effective predictors, even after parties became familiar. That is, trusting beliefs were strong predictors of trusting intention, structural assurance was a strong factor of trusting beliefs, and disposition to trust was still a significant predictor of structural assurance and trusting intention. Six of the nine links were supported, including all direct links.

Research Question #2 (Does Experience Replace Nonexperiential Factors?)

Figure 4 shows that Hypothesis 5a was supported, in that quality of experience was predictive of both trusting beliefs and trusting intention. Hypothesis 5b was

Figure 4. Structural model results: Extended trust building model (ETBM)

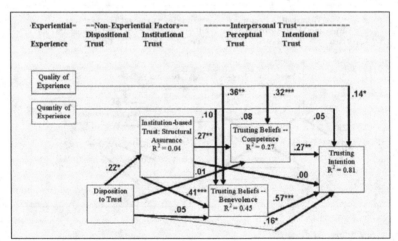

*** p< .001 ** p< .01 * p< .05

Effects of Control Variables:

Dependent Variable	Age	Gender (1=M2=F)	Education
Trusting Intention	-.11*	-.10*	.01

supported, in that quantity of experience did not predict trusting intention or trusting beliefs. Hypothesis 6a was either inconclusive or not supported. The effect of disposition to trust on trusting beliefs was still not significant, which is inconclusive. Contrary to H6a, however, the effect of disposition to trust on trusting intention did not become nonsignificant in the presence of the experience variables. Hypothesis 6b was also either inconclusive or not supported. Structural assurance still did not predict trusting intention, which is inconclusive. Although quality of experience significantly affected both trusting beliefs, structural assurance was still a significant factor of both beliefs, contradicting Hypothesis 6b. Note that the coefficients for the links from structural assurance decreased, however.

Research Question #2 asks whether nonexperiential factors become nonsignificant as factors of interpersonal trust in the presence of quality and quantity of experience. This study fails to show that they do. In the presence of quality and quantity of experience, disposition to trust continued to be a significant factor of trusting intention. Structural assurance continued to be a significant factor of both trusting beliefs, revealing an unexpected longevity of effect.

Discussion

Overall, the results provide mixed support for both the trust building model (TBM) and the extended trust building model (ETBM). When parties had become familiar, TBM was effective, but mainly in terms of the direct links. The most general type of trust (disposition to trust) influenced the context-oriented institutional trust, which influenced perceptual trust (trusting beliefs), which influenced trusting intention. ETBM was not supported in terms of the full erosion of institutional and dispositional factors. The results show that both experiential and nonexperiential factors were important among troubleshooters familiar with the supervisor. As predicted, the quantity of experience did not affect troubleshooter trust, but quality did.

Implications for Research

Research Question #1 Implications

The results indicate that the original TBM factors continue to be effective predictors of troubleshooter trust in the supervisor after parties have experience. This suggests the model is useful for more than the initial relationship. Because nonexperiential factors (especially institution-based trust) affect interpersonal trust among troubleshooters familiar with supervisors, this research casts doubt upon the primacy of experience for ongoing trust building. The context in which trust operates (institution-based trust) and the trustor's personal tendencies (disposition to trust) influence interpersonal trust even during the familiar stage of the relationship. Researchers should test the extent to which disposition to trust and institution-based trust help build ongoing interpersonal trust in different settings and relationships.

- **Temporal Model Boundary Condition:** The continued strength of both institutional and dispositional trust constructs casts doubt upon the temporal boundary condition set by McKnight et al. (1998) for their model. However, additional work is needed to affirm this finding. We speculate that institution-based trust and disposition to trust are consistent predictors no matter the relationship stage. Our finding agrees with and complements the e-commerce/virtual work research findings that disposition to trust affects trusting beliefs (Gefen, 2000; Kimery & McCord, 2002; McKnight et al., 2002a; Ridings et al., 2002; Stewart, 2003). However, Lee and Turban (2001) found disposition to trust to moderate in only one of three cases. Note that earlier trust work predicted disposition to trust would not predict trust beyond the initial timeframe (Mayer et al., 1995).

Research Question #2 Implications

- **Structural Assurance Salience:** The study provides evidence that quality of experience predicts trusting intention better than does structural assurance. Surprisingly, however, structural assurance predicted trusting beliefs as well as did quality of experience. Overall, this suggests that although quality of experience matters in trust building, so does structural assurance. The implication for researchers is that models of trust building that omit institutional trust (Kimery & McCord, 2001; Mayer et al., 1995) are missing a key trust factor. Institution-based trust is key not only because it is highly predictive, but also because it forms a mediating link between disposition to trust and interpersonal trust. The absence of the institution-based trust link may explain why the dispositional trust variable did not figure in the Mayer and Davis (1999) model, even though it was well justified conceptually in Mayer et al. (1995).

- **Disposition to Trust Salience:** The results for disposition to trust are interesting. Disposition to trust did not predict trusting beliefs, but it did predict trusting intention, the opposite of what McKnight et al. (2002a) found in the initial e-commerce setting. It is possible that the troubleshooter, through experience quality, may come to think highly of the supervisor in terms of trusting beliefs, whether or not they have high or low disposition to trust. On the other hand, the risk inherent in trusting intention in the supervisor may be such that a high disposition to trust helps prepare a troubleshooter to take that extra leap of faith beyond trusting beliefs to trusting intention. This is a leap of faith because it is riskier to be willing to depend on the supervisor when it counts than it is to simply believe the supervisor is trustworthy. Even after experience, one cannot rule out disposition to trust as a viable trust factor of trusting intention.

- **Quality and Quantity of Experience Salience:** Quality of experience was the only variable that affected both types of interpersonal trust. Self-esteem has been used as a way to describe how one's job motivates (Lawler & Hall, 1970). Other measures should be examined. Here's an interview example of a supervisor dealing with outages related to a mistake.

[M]ost of the time when I talk to operators they're very contrite about it, you know, "Gee, I really feel bad, I don't know what happened, I don't know why I did that." And I think that to a large degree there's a lot of sincerity in that. And I think they're prideful of the systems that they run...[I] think that goes a long way in trying to prevent more of that.

The fact that quantity of experience did not predict trust, while quality of experience did help sort out contradictory findings about familiarity. While Gefen (2000) and Bhattacherjee (2002) found that familiarity influenced trust, Pavlou (2002) and Gefen et al. (2003a) did not. Our results suggest a need to split familiarity or experience into quality and quantity components in order to determine what builds trust and what does not.

Our findings suggest that the ETBM (Figure 2) be modified in two ways. First, a solid line should be drawn from structural assurance to trusting beliefs. Second, a solid line link is needed from disposition to trust to trusting intention. These links should be further tested. In order to see if another test would make a difference, we gathered a second dataset (sample size 169) and tested both the TBM and ETBM models. For the TBM, all relationships were significant at $p < .05$ or better. When quantity and quality of experience were added for the ETBM, the links from disposition to trust to trusting beliefs became nonsignificant, while its link to trusting intention stayed significant ($p < .05$). The links from structural assurance to trusting beliefs became less significant (from $p < .001$ to $p < .01$), while the link from structural assurance to trusting intention stayed at $p < .001$. The links from trusting belief-benevolence and trusting belief-competence to trusting intention stayed at the same levels of significance ($p < .001$ and $p < .01$, respectively). Quality of experience was a strong factor of trusting beliefs ($p < .001$), but not of trusting intention (ns), while quantity of experience was only significant as a predictor of trusting belief-benevolence ($p < .05$). Overall, then, this second sample confirms: (a) that structural assurance is a strong predictor of trust, (b) that experience does not completely erode the effects of structural assurance and disposition to trust, and (c) that quality of experience is a stronger predictor than is quantity of experience. Both solid line additions were confirmed with this second sample.

- **Rationality of the Trust-Building Process:** Traditional researchers posit that trust is built through an interaction history (Blau, 1964) that secures direct, firsthand information. This rational view assumes that trust is built on firsthand information and gradually increases in validity. While this rational approach to trust building is intuitively appealing, it does not account for the dispositional and institutional factors that continue to influence trust. These factors are not rational in terms of being based on personal interaction. While this study shows that trust is affected by a rational variable, quality of the relationship, the study also shows that trust continues to be affected over time by impersonal (institutional) and assumptional (dispositional) information, indicating that trust building is not as rational or experiential a process as some have argued.

Implications for Practice

The systems organization should pay attention to work environment institutional structures by improving perceptions of structural assurance. Per our interviews, this can be done by providing better job security and by helping employees understand why the company is headed in a successful direction. IS managers also can ensure safety nets and proper procedures (e.g., grievance procedures) to protect employees. Employees with low dispositional trust will tend to think more negatively about the work environment, doubting structural assurances, than will those with high dispositional trust. Dedicating time for personal communication on equivocal issues with employees who have low dispositional trust may help.

Given that quality of experience with the supervisor helps to build trust, managers and supervisors should provide feedback and interact with employees in a way that positively impacts employee self-esteem. IS managers should cultivate a positive relationship with key employees (e.g., troubleshooters) in order to have a positive effect on employee self-esteem. This study contributes to practice by introducing the important IS category of troubleshooters and how their supervisors can build their trust. By developing a relationship that builds up the employee's self-esteem, managers will assure that the employee will develop appropriate trusting beliefs and intentions about them. Managers should express confidence or trust in the employee as part of that expression. One manager said, "I make it a conscious effort to let my people know I trust them. Because I remember when I sat in those seats out there, and what it was that my management did that made me feel that they didn't trust me."

Study Limitations

One limitation is external validity. These results may be unique to the trouble-shooter-supervisor relationships in these two firms and may not generalize. A second limitation is the data collection method. The study primarily used one method, the questionnaire, which could introduce self-report bias. This limitation is mitigated, however, by the fact that with trust, perception is much more important than objective fact. Further, self-report bias would be indicated by systematic inflation of constructs correlations (James, Gent, Hater & Corey, 1979), which was not found. Third, the study was not longitudinal; hence, causality is not proven.

Conclusion

This chapter makes several contributions, although these are tentative, given that the results may not be generalizable. First, the findings demonstrate the important influence of quality of experience with the supervisor on troubleshooter trust in the supervisor. Second, the findings show that institutional trust-structural assurance is key in predicting troubleshooter trusting beliefs. Structural assurance remained an important predictor in the presence of experience variables. This finding is very significant, because it demonstrates how contextually embedded (Granovetter, 1985) trusting relationships are. Neither researchers nor practitioners can afford to ignore the effects of structural assurance on building interpersonal trust. Third, the findings demonstrate that disposition to trust matters to trusting intention development even after the initial relationship phase is over.

The fact that both institutional and dispositional trust continued to be significant factors implies that although quality of experience mattered, it mattered less than expected. Rather than relegating nonexperiential (institutional and dispositional) factors to the initial trust relationship, as McKnight et al. (1998) implies, this study extends their usefulness to the time period after the trustor becomes familiar with the trustee.

Finally, if these findings prove generalizable, and we have presented one study's evidence that they are, the chapter suggests extensions to existing trust models. To the Mayer et al. (1995) model, it suggests that institution-based trust be used as a mediator of the effects of propensity to trust on trustworthiness factors. To the McKnight et al. (1998) model, it suggests that its timeframe boundary be extended past the initial stage and that quality of experience be included. Testing the useful temporal boundaries of theories is an important scientific endeavor, because it clarifies a theory's practical range (Bacharach, 1989). Overall, these extensions to the trust-building model should prove fruitful as a way to better understand trust development within information systems support settings.

Acknowledgments

For helpful insights and suggestions on an earlier version of this chapter, we would like to thank Roger Calantone, Severin Grabski, Nancy Gustafson, Brian Pentland, V. Sambamurthy, and Cheri Speier. We would also like to thank the two organizations that enabled us to gather data for this study and the reviewers and editors of *IRMJ* for their helpful suggestions.

References

Bacharach, S.B. (1989). Organizational theories: Some criteria for evaluation. *Academy of Management Review, 14*, 496-515.

Berscheid, E. (1994). Interpersonal relationships. *Annual Review of Psychology, 45*, 79-129.

Bhattacherjee, A. (2002). Individual trust in online firms: Scale development and initial test. *Journal of Management Information Systems, 19*, 211-242.

Bigley, G.A., & Pearce, J.L. (1998). Straining for shared meaning in organization science: Problems of trust and distrust. *Academy of Management Review, 23*, 405-421.

Blau, P.M. (1964). *Exchange and power in social life*. New York: John Wiley & Sons.

Chin, W.W. (1998). The partial least squares approach to structural equation modeling. In G.A. Marcoulides (Ed.), *Modern methods for business research* (pp. 295-336). Mahwah, NJ: Lawrence Erlbaum.

Currall, S.C., & Judge, T.A. (1995). Measuring trust between organizational boundary role persons. *Organization Behavior and Human Decision Processes, 64*, 151-170.

Davis, F.D. (1989). Perceived usefulness, perceived ease of use, and user acceptance of information technology. *MIS Quarterly, 13*, 319-340.

Dillman, D.A. (1978). *Mail and telephone surveys: The total design method.* New York: Wiley.

Dobing, B. (1993). *Building trust in user-analyst relationships.* Doctoral Dissertation, University of Minnesota, Information and Decision Sciences Department, Minneapolis.

Fornell, C., & Larcker, D. (1981). Evaluating structural equation models with unobservable variables and measurement error. *Journal of Marketing Research, 18*, 39-50.

Gambetta, D. (1988). Can we trust trust? In D. Gambetta (Ed.), *Trust: Making and breaking cooperative relations* (pp. 213-237). New York: Blackwell.

Gefen, D. (2000). E-commerce: The role of familiarity and trust. *Omega: The International Journal of Management Science, 28*, 725-737.

Gefen, D., Karahanna, E., & Straub, D.W. (2003a). Trust and TAM in online shopping: An integrated model. *MIS Quarterly, 27*, 51-90.

Gefen, D., Karahanna, E., & Straub, D.W. (2003b). Potential and repeat e-consumers: The role of trust vis-à-vis TAM. *IEEE Transactions on Engineering Management, 50*, 307-321.

Granovetter, M. (1985). Economic action and social structure: The problem of embeddedness. *American Journal of Sociology, 91*, 481-510.

Hart, P.J., & Saunders, C.S. (1993). Themes of power and trust in EDI relationships. In *Proceedings of the Fourteenth International Conference on Information Systems.*

Holmes, J.G. (1991). Trust and the appraisal process in close relationships. In W.H. Jones & D. Perlman (Eds.), *Advances in personal relationships* (pp. 57-104). London: Jessica Kingsley.

James, L.R., Gent, M.J., Hater, J.J., & Corey, K.E. (1979). Correlates of psychological influence: An illustration of the psychological climate approach to work environment perceptions. *Personnel Psychology, 32*, 563-588.

Jarvenpaa, S.L., Knoll, K., & Leidner, D.E. (1998). Is anybody out there? Antecedents of trust in global virtual teams. *Journal of Management Information Systems, 14*, 29-64.

Jarvenpaa, S.L., & Leidner, D.E. (1998). Communication and trust in global virtual teams. *Journal of Computer-Mediated Communication.* Retrieved July 12, 2006, from http://jcmc.mscc.huji.ac.il/vol3/issue4/ jarvenpaa.html

Kee, H.W., & Knox, R.E. (1970). Conceptual and methodological considerations in the study of trust and suspicion. *Journal of Conflict Resolution, 14*, 357-366.

Kimery, K.M., & McCord, M. (2002). Third-party assurances: Mapping the road to trust in e-retailing. *Journal of Information Technology Theory and Application, 4*, 63-82.

Kramer, R.M. (1999). Trust and distrust in organizations: Emerging perspectives, enduring questions. *Annual Review of Psychology, 50*, 569-598.

Lawler, E.E., & Hall, D.T. (1970). Relationship of job characteristics to job involvement, satisfaction, and intrinsic motivation. *Journal of Applied Psychology, 54*, 305-312.

Lee, M.K.O., & Turban, E. (2001). A trust model for consumer Internet shopping. *International Journal of Electronic Commerce, 6*, 75-91.

Lewicki, R.J., McAllister, D.J., & Bies, R.J. (1998). Trust and distrust: New relationships and realities. *Academy of Management Review, 23*, 438-458.

Lewis, J.D., & Weigert, A.J. (1985a). Trust as a social reality. *Social Forces, 63*, 967-985.

Lewis, J.D., & Weigert, A.J. (1985b). Social atomism, holism, and trust. *The Sociological Quarterly, 216*, 455-471.

Mayer, R.C., & Davis, J.H. (1999). The effect of the performance appraisal system on trust for management: A field quasi-experiment. *Journal of Applied* Psychology, *84*, 123-136.

Mayer, R.C., Davis, J.H., & Schoorman, F.D. (1995). An integrative model of organizational trust. *Academy of Management Review, 20*, 709-734.

McKnight, D.H. (1997). *Motivating critical computer systems operators: Job characteristics, controls, and relationships.* Unpublished doctoral dissertation, University of Minnesota.

McKnight, D.H., Choudhury, V., & Kacmar, C. (2002a). Developing and validating trust measures for e-commerce: An integrative typology. *Information Systems Research, 13*, 334-359.

McKnight, D.H., Choudhury, V., & Kacmar, C. (2002b). The impact of initial consumer trust on intentions to transact with a Web site: A trust building model. *Journal of Strategic Information Systems, 11*, 297-323.

McKnight, D.H., Choudhury, V., & Kacmar, C. (2004). Shifting factors and the ineffectiveness of third party assurance seals: A two-stage model of initial trust in an e-vendor. *Electronic Markets, 14*(3), 252-266.

McKnight, D.H., Cummings, L.L., & Chervany, N.L. (1998). Initial trust formation in new organizational relationships. *Academy of Management Review, 23*, 473-490.

Meyerson, D., Weick, K.E., & Kramer, R.M. (1996). Swift trust and temporary groups. In R.M. Kramer & T.R. Tyler (Eds.), *Trust in organizations: Frontiers of theory and research* (pp. 166-195). Thousand Oaks, CA: Sage.

Nelson, K.M., & Cooprider, J.G. (1996). The contribution of shared knowledge to IS group performance. *MIS Quarterly, 20*, 409-434.

Pavlou, P.A. (2002). Institution-based trust in interorganizational exchange relationships: The role of online B2B marketplaces on trust formation. *Journal of Strategic Information Systems, 11*, 215-243.

Pavlou, P.A. (2003). Consumer acceptance of electronic commerce: Integrating trust and risk with the technology acceptance model. *International Journal of Electronic Commerce, 7*, 101-134.

Pavlou, P.A., & Gefen, D. (2004). Building effective online marketplaces with institution-based trust. *Information Systems Research, 15*, 37-59.

Pennington, R., Wilcox, H.D., & Grover, V. (2003). The role of system trust in business-to-consumer transactions. *Journal of Management Information Systems, 20*, 197-226.

Ratnasingham, P., & Phan, D.D. (2003). Trading partner trust in B2B e-commerce: A case study. *Information Systems Management, 20*, 39-50.

Rempel, J.K., Holmes, J.G., & Zanna, M.P. (1985). Trust in close relationships. *Journal of Personality and Social Psychology, 49*, 95-112.

Ridings, C.M., Gefen, D., & Arinze, B. (2002). Some antecedents and effects of trust in virtual communities. *Journal of Strategic Information Systems, 11*, 271-295.

Ring, P.S., & Van de Ven, A.H. (1994). Developmental processes of cooperative interorganizational relationships. *Academy of Management Review, 19*, 90-118.

Rosenberg, M.J. (1957). *Occupations and values*. Glencoe, IL: Free Press.

Rotter, J.B. (1971). Generalized expectancies for interpersonal trust. *American Psychologist, 26*, 443-452.

Rousseau, D.M., Sitkin, S.B., Burt, R.S., & Camerer, C. (1998). Not so different after all: A cross-discipline view of trust. *Academy of Management Review, 23*, 393-404.

Scanzoni, J. (1979). Social exchange and behavioralinterdependence. In R.L. Burgess & T.L. Huston (Eds.), *Social exchange in developing relationships* (pp. 61-98). New York: Academic Press.

Shapiro, S.P. (1987). The social control of impersonal trust. *American Journal of Sociology, 93*, 623-658.

Stewart, K.J. (2003). Trust transfer on the World Wide Web. *Organization Science, 14*, 5-17.

Wrightsman, L.S. (1991). Interpersonal trust and attitudes toward human nature. In J.P. Robison, P.R. Shaver, & L.S. Wrightsman (Eds.), *Measures of personality and social psychological attitudes: Volume 1: Measures of social psychological attitudes* (pp. 373-412). San Diego, CA: Academic Press.

Zand, D.E. (1972). Trust and managerial problem solving. *Administrative Science Quarterly, 17,* 229-239.

Zucker, L.G. (1986). Production of trust: Institutional sources of economic structure, 1840-1920. In B.M. Straw & L.L. Cummings (Eds.), *Research in organizational behavior* (pp. 53-111). Greenwich, CT: JAI Press.

Appendix: Study Measures

Construct	Measures
Dispositional Trust (Disposition to trust)* [all scales were 7-point Likert]	1. In general, people really do care about the well being of others.
	2. The typical person is sincerely concerned about the problems of others.
	3. Most of the time, people care enough to try to be helpful, rather than just looking out for themselves.
Institutional Trust (Structural Assurance)*	1. Our workplace has processes that assure that we will be treated fairly and equitably.
	2. I work in an environment in which good procedures make things fair and impartial.
	3. Fairness to employees is built into how issues are handled in our work environment.
	4. In this workplace, sound practices exist that help ensure fair and unbiased treatment of employees.
Interpersonal Trust (Trusting Belief-Benevolence)*	1. When it comes to my well being, my lead/supervisor really cares.
	2. If I required help, my lead/supervisor would care enough to help me.
	3. I believe that my lead/supervisor cares enough to act in my personal best interest
	4. When you get right down to it, my lead/supervisor cares about what happens to me.
Interpersonal Trust (Trusting Belief Competence)*	1. My lead/supervisor is skillful and effective in his/her work.
	2. My lead/supervisor performs his/her job very well.
	3. Overall, I have a capable and proficient lead/supervisor
	4. Overall, my lead/ supervisor is competent technically.
Interpersonal Trust (Trusting Intention)*	1. When an issue that is critical to my career arises, I feel I can depend on my lead/supervisor.
	2. I can always rely on my lead/supervisor in a career-related issue.
	3. My lead/supervisor is a person on whom I feel I can rely when the issue is important to my career.
	4. I feel I can depend on my lead/supervisor on a career-sensitive issue.

Quantity of Experience	Multiplicative variable: (Years worked with supervisor) X (Frequency of interaction with supervisor)
Quality of Experience	1. My work-related interactions with my lead/supervisor usually have a positive effect on my self-esteem.
	2. Interacting with my lead/supervisor on the job generally reinforces my feelings of self-esteem.

Several rounds of pretesting were conducted before these items were finalized (McKnight, 1997). The pretests used student raters.

Chapter IX

A Question of Timing:
Information Acquisition and Group Decision Making Performance[1]

Souren Paul, North Carolina A&T State University, USA

Carol Stoak Saunders, University of Central Florida, USA

William David Haseman, University of Wisconsin – Milwaukee, USA

Abstract

Information acquisition and its use are frequently considered critical to the deci-sion-making process, yet related research, especially about the timing of information acquisition, is limited. This study explores the impact of information acquisition on decision time and perceived decision quality for groups that used group support systems (GSS) to work on a fuzzy task. We found that more information was accessed from a Web-based system in the first part of the group decision-making process, when the decision environment was searched and possible courses of action were analyzed. We also found that the proportion of information accessed in the first part of the meeting was significantly related to the decision time. More specifically, when most information was accessed in the first part of the decision-making session, the relationship between decision time and amount of information accessed in the early part of the meeting was positive and linear. However, a curvilinear relationship was found between decision time and amount of information accessed in the latter part of the decision-making session. Unlike the findings of a previous study, this earlier access of information is not associated with improved perceived decision quality.

Introduction

As organizations rely increasingly on groups, it is not surprising that managers are more concerned than ever with improving the quality of group decisions and the time required to make them. To this end, they would like to improve the decision-making process itself. A possible area for improvement in the decision-making process is information acquisition since better decisions can be made when based on higher quality information.

While information acquisition and use seems critical to the decision-making process (Janis, 1989), related research, especially about the timing of information acquisition, is limited. In the popular linear (rational) model of decision making, information acquisition is greatest in early stages of the process: to define the problem correctly, focus on relevant issues, search for a good solution, and develop or explore alternatives that otherwise might not be considered. Acquisition of critical information early in the decision-making process streamlines the process by reducing or eliminating unnecessary time spent in analyzing inappropriate solutions. However, in actuality it may be difficult to acquire information in a prescribed sequence or to process it when it is acquired. Decision makers may be plagued by information overload.

Saunders and Jones (1990) proposed a model that synthesizes the decision-making literature and explains the timing of information access during the decision-making process. Their model has three major components: decisional, information acquisition, and contextual. The decisional component focuses on decision processes. The information acquisition component focuses on source and medium and their links to decision-making phases and routines. The contextual component considers how contextual elements such as task type, decision arrival time, and time pressures affect source and media selection.

In this research, the Saunders and Jones (1990) model serves as the theoretical basis for exploring how the timing of information acquisition influences group decision making performance in complex tasks. In particular, we seek to answer two questions: (1) How do group decision makers engaged in fuzzy tasks acquire information over time? and (2) How does information acquired early in the decision-making process impact decision time and quality?

Exploring Information Acquisition

Decisional Component

A popular and frequently cited model of the decision-making process is Simon's (1965) three-stage model of intelligence, design, and choice. In Simon's linear model, information is accessed primarily at the first stage, when the problem is studied and identified. Both Simon (1965) and Janis (1989) imply that decision makers begin the decision-making process with a search for information related to the problem at hand. Janis further concludes from anecdotal evidence that decision-making groups have a tendency to accept only information that supports their preferred position. Information that fails to support the solution preferred by the majority of group members is discarded or refuted. This indicates that decision-making groups examine and assimilate relevant information early in the decision-making process before forming a strong preference for a solution.

At the other end of the spectrum from Simon is a decision-making model that is based on organized anarchy—the garbage can model (Cohen, March, & Olsen, 1972; Cyert & March, 1963; Olsen, 1976). The garbage can model focuses on decision making as a social-interaction process rather than a sequential series of decision-making activities. Decision making is characterized by an element of chance. In this model, information may be acquired any time throughout the decision-making process.

In actuality, the decision-making process is probably a blend of Simon's (1965) linear, rational decision-making model and the anarchistic garbage can model. Mintzberg, Raisinghani, and Theoret (1976) synthesize these two perspectives by introducing interruptions, delays, and deviations into the rational, linear decision-making model. As decision makers loop back and forth among decision-making activities, they acquire information to support these activities. Thus, jointly considering the linear and garbage can models of decision making is important when studying information acquisition because it reflects the decision maker's need to gather information throughout the process (Saunders & Jones, 1990).

Information Acquisition Component: Group Support Systems

An important aspect of the information acquisition component is the medium. We focus on a particular medium, the group support system (GSS), and the manner in which this medium's computer support and information processing features impact information acquisition. At the basic level (Level 1), GSS offer communication support features such as anonymous messaging or voting. At an enhanced level (Level

2), information processing support includes modeling or mathematical techniques (DeSanctis & Gallupe, 1987). Information processing support features also include immediate access to electronic databases, relevant Web sites, and information systems outside the meeting room (Huber, 1990), as well as electronic links to individuals outside the group. The information processing capabilities of GSS affect the extent and patterns of information acquisition in decision-making groups. For example, in their study of information acquisition across traditional face-to-face and GSS environments for two different task types, Saunders and Miranda (1998) found that individuals in GSS groups accessed information significantly more often and later in the decision process than the face-to-face groups.

GSS communication support provides numerous features to enhance communication, including simultaneity and anonymity. GSS use allows individual group members to obtain information simultaneously without impinging on the ability of other group members to concurrently retrieve information from the same source. In contrast, in traditional face-to-face group discussions, individuals take turns and complete the discussion on one issue before moving on to another issue (Miranda & Saunders, 2003). This need in face-to-face groups to wait to speak until others finish has been associated with poor performance in brainstorming and poor information sharing in decision making (Dennis, Wixom & Vandenberg, 2001). Anonymity likewise encourages group members, especially those with relatively low status, to contribute to group discussions since their comments cannot be attributed to them.

However, because anonymity generates more information needing to be shared and simultaneity increases the "floor time," group members may experience information overload (Dennis et al., 2001; Thorngate, 1997). As the number of ideas conveyed in the group discussion balloons, the additional information competes for the attention of those receiving it and challenges their ability to process it (Gopal & Prasad, 2000). The individual team members may cope with the resulting overload by selectively attending to only certain information (Dennis et al., 2001; Schultze & Vandenbosch, 1998). Thus, while facilitating information acquisition, GSS use also may create situations where more information is acquired than can be processed (Davenport & Beck, 2001).

Contextual Component: Group Task Types

An important contextual component element in the Saunders and Jones (1990) model is problem or task type. Group task type plays an important role in information needed (Poole, 1978) and accessed over time. Complex tasks demand higher levels of information acquisition than simple tasks. Zigurs and Buckland (1998) define five types of group tasks (i.e., simple, problem, decision, judgment, and fuzzy) which vary in terms of the complexity resulting from increased levels of information load, diversity, or rate of change.

The focus of our research is on tasks described by Zigurs and Buckland as fuzzy. Fuzzy tasks are relatively hard to define. Those who execute the tasks must access more information during the early stage of decision making to analyze the multiple desired outcomes and multiple ways to reach these outcomes (solution schemes). To complete fuzzy tasks, it is frequently necessary to uncover members' conflicting opinions, even though the members are not fully cognizant of societal values, other reasons for their opinions, or subtleties differentiating their opinions from those held by other group members. Further, group members bolster their own position by soliciting information from sources outside the group. Thus, problem identification and analysis of various courses of action are often difficult in fuzzy tasks. They require considerable information access in identifying the problem. Consistent with this reasoning, Saunders and Miranda (1998) found that groups completing a cognitive conflict (fuzzy) task sought information earlier in the decision-making process than for an intellective, or problem, task. When information was accessed late in the decision-making process for the fuzzy task, decision quality suffered. Saunders and Miranda (1998) also found that when both face-to face and GSS groups completed an intellective task, they accessed significantly more information in the last stage (selection) rather than in the first stage (intelligence) of decision making. They argued that when the problem is defined with relative ease, as is the case with intellective tasks, more emphasis is placed on gathering information for developing and choosing alternatives than on defining the problem. Thus, more information may be acquired later in the decision-making process.

Information Acquisition and Group Performance

Groups engaged in complex tasks, such as fuzzy tasks, often consider vast amount of diverse information. This creates input information load, which may impact group decision-making performance in two ways. First, acquiring information earlier in the process means that there is more time to deal effectively with the input information load. Second, the input complexity of a task environment depends on the input information load and influences how individuals or group decision makers process information.

Information processing by individuals or groups involves the cognitive processes of differentiation and integration (Schroder, Driver, & Streufert, 1967). Individuals or groups sort stimulus information into different dimensions or points of view. *Differentiation* is the number of different dimensions or points of view, and *integration* is the interconnection among these dimensions. The amount of integration among different dimensions, known as integrative complexity, reflects the level of information processing complexity. Schroder, Driver, and Streufert (1967) hypothesize an inverted U-shaped relationship between environmental input complexity and the level of information processing (Figure 1). The level of information processing is the maximum (IP_M) when the environmental input complexity is optimal (I_{TH}) (i.e., neither too high nor too low). Driver and Streufert (1969) suggest that the inverted U-shaped relationship also holds for the behavior, perception, and decision making of the individuals or groups engaged in information processing.

Although the relationship between environmental input complexity and level of information processing has been studied in the context of individual decision making (Chewning & Harrell, 1990; Hwang & Lin, 1999), there is a paucity of research on information processing in GSS-based groups. Grise and Gallupe (1999-2000) found that information load in groups was positively related to participants' mental workload and negatively related to complexity. Miranda and Saunders (2003) suggested that computer-mediated communication media led to information overload and, subsequently, reduced information sharing in groups. Groups that acquire information early in their sessions have more time to process it than groups that acquire it late in the decision-making process. Acquiring a large amount of information late in the decision-making process subjects group members to time pressure and hence experience information overload. Hahn, Lawson, and Lee (1992) reported an inverted U-shaped relationship between decision quality and information load under time pressure conditions. The timing of information acquisition seems to be critical in group performance.

In this research we examine the impact of temporal information acquisition patterns on decision quality and decision time, which are the two most widely used measures of group performance in GSS literature (Fjermestad & Hiltz, 1998-1999). An underlying assumption of our research is that the level of GSS technology support matches the requirements of the fuzzy task that we use in our study.

Figure 1. Relationship between environmental input complexity and level of information processing (Schroeder et al., 1967)

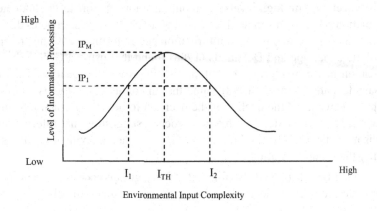

Statement of Hypotheses

Decision makers engaged in a fuzzy task turn to less accessible sources outside the group for information to bolster their own opinion or to understand reasons for the opinions of the other group members (Saunders & Miranda, 1998). The critical role of opinions and views in completing fuzzy tasks is supported by research on normative influence in GSS environments (Huang, Raman, & Wei, 1993; Kaplan & Miller, 1987), which suggests that decision makers actively seek the opinions and views of group members engaged in a task.

In the context of fuzzy task, acquiring information to understand and appropriately channel normative influences is especially critical in the early stages of decision making when the task problem is defined. When issues are uncertain in the early stages of decision making, soliciting a large number of viewpoints may aid in defining issues comprehensively (Mohammed & Ringseis, 2001). Levin, Huneke, and Jasper (2000) found that college students making decisions about which computer to purchase accessed about three times as many separate pieces of information in the first stage of decision making than in the second stage.

However, not all information is acquired in the early stages of decision making for fuzzy tasks. Even though decision makers seek opinions and views heavily in the early stages, a more limited amount of information, either for confirmation or further problem definition, still may be needed as the decision-making session progresses. Since the decision-making process is highly iterative, the group acquires additional information as it loops back to problem definition later in the decision-making session (Mintzberg et al., 1976; Saunders & Jones, 1990). Hence, we propose:

Hypothesis H1: *In GSS meetings for fuzzy tasks, more information is accessed in the first half of the meeting than in the second half of the meeting.*

In a GSS meeting with high levels of communication support to facilitate access to information sources, information gathered early in the process enables decision-making groups to consider relevant information before forming a strong preference for a solution. Gallupe and DeSanctis (1988) found that using a GSS early in the identification phase of a problem finding task improved the quality of the decision. Saunders and Miranda (1998) found that in cognitive conflict (fuzzy) tasks, participants considered the quality of the decision to be poorer when information was accessed late in the decision-making process, suggesting that information accessed is more likely to be used detrimentally to bolster individual positions than to modify the group's solution.

Saunders and Miranda (1998) also found that when groups access a high proportion of information early in the decision-making process, the group members experience at least some information overload in the beginning of the process. However, since early access provides more time to process information, this input information can be analyzed throughout the decision-making process. The subjects in the Levin et al. (2000) study were able to make better decisions by successfully screening out weaker options during the first, or formation, stage of decision making. Reducing the number of options allowed them to consider each remaining option more thoroughly in the second, or final choice stage.

Finally, in GSS meetings with high levels of information processing support, participants can analyze the input information more thoroughly and efficiently (Zigurs & Buckland, 1998). They are likely to perceive decision quality as high. Hence, for these reasons, we hypothesize:

Hypothesis H2: *In GSS meetings for fuzzy tasks, perceived decision quality is linearly associated with the proportion of information accessed early in the meeting in such a way that higher perceived decision quality is associated with accessing a high proportion of information early in the meeting.*

When only a small amount of information is needed for a decision, relatively little time is spent processing it, irregardless of decision type. However, when decisions require sizeable amounts of information, the input information load increases, and this influences decision time. The relationship between amount of information acquired and decision time is not as easy to describe as the input information load increases.

We propose that temporal arrangements of information acquisition can lengthen or shorten the decision time for a fuzzy task. Performing detailed analyses of the acquired information adds to the time required for groups to reach their final decision. Groups that acquire information earlier in the meeting have more time to process and analyze that information thoroughly and require less time to process the low level of information acquired later in the meeting (Saunders & Jones, 1990). Thus, the relationship between decision time and amount of information acquired early in the meeting is a linear one (Levin et al., 2000) (see Figure 2a).

In contrast, groups that acquire a large volume of information in the later part of their meetings are more likely to perceive that the available time to complete the task is not sufficient to process the information. This perception time pressure can cause stress and result in information overload (Allen & Wilson, 2003). However, the overload does not occur until the group members perceive that the acquired information can not be managed effectively (Schick & Gordon, 1990). As such, initially the decision time increases linearly the acquired information up to a certain point beyond which groups experience information overload. To cope with the overload, the group members start cutting back on information processing (Grise & Gallupe, 1999-2000) which shortens the time to reach a decision. Thus, the decision time is less when the amount of information acquired later in the process is either very low or so high that group members experience information overload. This implies that the relationship between the amount of information accessed later in the meeting and the decision time is curvilinear (Figure 2b). We therefore hypothesize:

Hypothesis H3: *In GSS meetings for fuzzy tasks:*

    3a: *decision time is linearly and positively associated with the amount of information accessed in the early part of the meeting.*

    3b: *decision time is ∩ curvilinearly associated with the amount of information accessed late in the meeting in such a way that decision time is lower when either a low or a high amount of information is accessed late in the meeting.*

Figure 2. Information acquisition and decision time [Proposed]

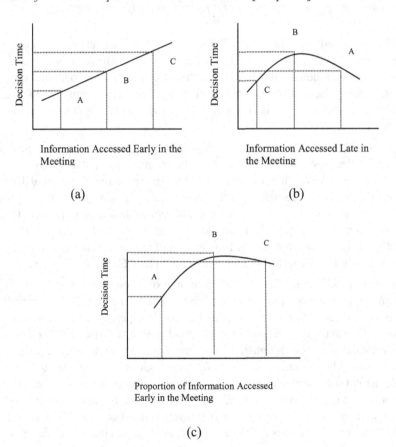

(a)   (b)

(c)

We now synthesize the effects of accessing information early and late in the meetings to work on a fuzzy task. When a group acquires a low proportion of information early in the meeting, the information accessed later in the meeting is high (Point A in Figures 2a and 2b) which generates overload. Under overload condition, groups cut back information processing, and decision time shortens. When a higher proportion of information is acquired in the first part of the meeting (i.e., a movement from point A to point B in Figures 2a and 2b), the information processing time and decision time increases. This increasing trend continues until a group acquires an optimal level of information in the later part of the meeting (point B). However, when a group moves beyond this optimum level—that is, acquires even higher proportion of information early in the meeting (Point C in Figures 2a and 2b)—the greater amount of time needed to process the high level of information acquired early in the meeting is counterbalanced by the relatively lower time required to process the low level of information acquired late in the meeting. The overall effect is a reduction in the information processing and decision time (from the optimum level at B). The proportion of information acquired early in the meeting is, thus, curvilinearly related to decision time (Figure 2c). Hence:

Hypothesis H3c: *In GSS meetings for fuzzy tasks, decision time is ∩ curvilinearly associated with the proportion of information accessed early in the meeting in such a way that decision time is lower when either a low or a high proportion of information is accessed early in the meeting.*

Research Methodology

Data collected from a controlled experiment were used to test these hypotheses. The study sample consisted of 54 five-member groups drawn from undergraduate business students in introductory information system classes at a large public university in the midwestern U.S. The experimental setup included a group decision support system integrated with a Web-based intranet application that presented the information on the decision situation to the subjects.

The Group Decision and GSS Application

The decision situation considered in this research is the development of a group level preference structure for the attributes for MBA programs so that a rank-ordered list of the programs could be formed. Undergraduate business students, who have a natural interest in evaluating MBA programs, were selected as the appropriate decision makers in this experiment. The students were randomly assigned to five-member groups and were engaged in a group task that involved assigning weights to a preselected list of MBA program attributes (Appendix 1) by allocating 100 points among them, generating a rank-ordered list of MBA programs based on the group level weights of the attributes and voting on the decision of attribute weights assigned by the group. The task was completed when group members agreed upon the attribute weights and the associated rank-ordered list of programs.

This task was classified as a fuzzy task because multiple rank-ordered lists could be generated depending upon the solution scheme (i.e., group weights) that was employed. A high weighting on one attribute resulted in a lower weighting of other attributes, thereby leading to a condition of conflicting interdependence.

A hypermedia-based application for MBA programs and attributes selection was developed and placed on an intranet Web server. This Web-based application was integrated with a GSS tool, VisionQuest. A typical GSS may offer support along three dimensions: communication, process structure, and information processing (Zigurs & Buckland, 1998). All groups had high levels of communication support including the ability to simultaneously input attribute weights, anonymity when inputting weights and votes, displays of group weights on each workstation, and synchronous communication of changes in allocation of a weight by any participant. The process structure was at the medium level and was applied in its simplest form: a meeting agenda specifying how the group should use the GSS to perform the task (Dennis et al., 2001). Although group members could not set the agenda (which was predetermined), the system enabled them to enforce the agenda and allow a coordinator in each group to provide partial facilitation for the task. All 54 groups also had high levels of information processing support that included the Web-based information displays, a hypermedia-based system for gathering information, and GSS-based weighting models. Thus, the level of GSS support theoretically fit the fuzzy task requirements. Information available from the Web sites of the Graduate Management Admissions Council, Princeton Review, and Peterson's Guide was used to design the MBA admissions information system. A small sample of 24 schools offering MBA programs was considered for this prototype. Data were collected on a set of 18 attributes (Appendix 1) for each school.

Next, the schools were rated on the attributes by following predetermined algorithms. For example, if the minimum and maximum values for tuition fees of schools are T_{min} and T_{max} respectively, the rating of a school with a tuition fee of T is given by $[1 - (T-T_{min})/(T_{max}-T_{min})]$. This results in ratings in the range of 0 and 1. Based on the principles of simple additive weighting method (Churchman & Ackoff, 1954; Hwang & Yoon, 1981), a score for each school is computed by multiplying the weight on each attribute by the predetermined normalized rating of the school on that attribute.

The Experiment

A total of 270 undergraduate business students of a core course in information systems participated in the experiment. Participation was voluntary; each study participant received a waiver for one assignment in the course. To heighten student motivation in the group work, it was announced before each experimental session that experts would assess the quality and performance of the group work, and this evaluation would be used to determine each student's grade on this assignment.

The experiments were conducted in a group decision room equipped with Vision-Quest. Each experiment session could continue for two hours. The two-hour time limit is well within the norms followed in GSS research, where the majority of the controlled experiments had session lengths less than one hour (Fjermestad & Hiltz, 1998-1999) and was found to be adequate in our pilot sessions. A systems specialist was present to clarify any question about the system and the task and to address any malfunctioning of the system. However, no major system malfunction occurred during any session.

The experimental procedure was as follows:

1.   Each participant was assigned a workstation in the decision room. Each group had five workstations, one of which was configured to function as a coordinating workstation. This workstation was used to submit some special instructions (such as computation of total score for schools) to the system.

2.   Participants completed a consent form.

3.   All participants were shown the same video presentation about the experiment.

4.   Each participant browsed the hypermedia-based information system on the decision situation. As the system was placed on an intranet server, the group members could browse only the pages on this system. Access to other pages on the World Wide Web was restricted.

5.   With the help of the allocating tool of VisionQuest, each participant assigned 100 points among one or more attributes. Once all team members had allocated weights, the coordinator instructed the system to display group results. Each member could view both individual and group weights on the workstation screen. At this stage, each participant could change his/her weight allocation scheme.

6.   Once all participants finalized their allocation of weights, the coordinator exported the group weights to a database and instructed the database to compute rankings of the schools. Finally, the rank-ordered list of schools was imported from the database to VisionQuest.

7.   Participants viewed the rank-ordered list of the schools on the screen.

8. Participants used the voting tool of VisionQuest to evaluate the school ranking that resulted from the weight allocation of group members.

9. If four or more group members voted in favor of the decision scheme, step 10 was performed; otherwise, the group repeated steps 4 through 8. A maximum of seven iterations were allowed in a decision-making session. When a group took multiple iterations to reach the final decision, it revisited information pages and revised individual preferences regarding MBA program attributes. Thus, information acquisition was not restricted to the beginning of the session but could spread throughout the decision-making session.

10. Each participant browsed a Web page titled "End of Experiment" and completed a questionnaire about his/her assessment of the decision outcome. Moreover, the questionnaire collected demographic data, such as age, gender, GPA, and computer skill.

Operationalization of Variables

The dependent variables in this research are the meeting performance variables: perceived decision quality and decision time. The independent variables are information

Table 1. Variables and their measurements

Variable	Measured By	Type and Source of Data
Perceived decision quality	Average of scores on four items about understandability, reliability, comprehensiveness, and user's confidence in the decision. The items were derived from Bailey and Pearson (1983) and Ives, Olson, and Baroudi (1983) and measured using a Likert-scale (Appendix 2).	Self-reported data collected from questionnaire
Decision time	Elapsed time between the start and end of the decision-making session. The initial time stamp was recorded when participants started browsing Web pages on school MBA programs and attributes. The ending time stamp was recorded when participants accessed the "End of Experiment" page.	Objective data collected from intranet server log file
Information accessed in each half of the meeting	Total number of attribute pages and school pages accessed by the group members in each half of the meeting.	Objective data collected from intranet server log file
Proportion of information accessed earlier in the meeting	Calculated as: (No. of attribute and school pages browsed in the 1st half of the meeting) / (Total no. of attribute and school pages browsed during the entire meeting)	Objective data collected from intranet server log file

accessed in each half of the meeting and also the proportion of information accessed earlier in the meeting. The dependent and independent variables and their measures are shown in Table 1. The control variables in this research include decision task (i.e., only fuzzy tasks), motivation of subjects (i.e., similar motivation), and familiarity with the system (i.e., common training). We collected data on gender, Internet skill, college GPA, and age of the participants. Our statistical analyses (ANOVA and χ^2) revealed that these variables (i.e., age, college GPA, gender, and Internet skill) did not vary significantly across the 54 groups.

Results

Reliability and Validity

As evident from Table 1, the measures of the variables fall into two categories: objective and self-reported perceptions. Three experts on group decision making and attitude measurement established the face validities of the perceived decision quality self-report instrument through the initial review process. The Cronbach's alpha for the instrument is 0.785.

Content validity was established by examining the correlation matrix of the indicator variables for the construct (Nunnally, 1978). All inter-item correlation coefficients for perceived decision quality scale are 0.381 or better (p values are 0.0001 or better). Factor analysis with VARIMAX orthogonal rotation demonstrated convergent validity of the instrument with factor loadings ranging between 0.656 and 0.800.

Hypotheses Testing

A paired comparison t-test and regression analyses were employed to test the hypotheses presented in this chapter. SAS software was used to develop the General Linear Models (GLM) for the regression analyses.

H1: Information Accessed During Each Half of the Meeting

A paired comparison t-test was carried out using the PROC MEANS of SAS. The result demonstrates significant difference in the number of pages browsed in two halves of the meeting sessions ($\bar{x}_{first\_half} = 72.65$ and $\bar{x}_{second\_half} = 25.33$, Mean difference in pages browsed = 47.31, t = 9.628, p < 0.0001), thereby supporting Hypothesis 1.

Table 2. Regression results for perceived decision quality and decision time

Variable	Perceived Decision Quality	Decision Time		
Proportion of Information Accessed Earlier in the Meeting	0.0010 (0.0024)			1.1640* (0.5763)
Proportion of Information Accessed Earlier in the Meeting^2 – Quadratic Term				-0.0099* (0.0042)
Information Accessed Early in the Meeting		0.1909*** (0.0533)		
Information Accessed Late in the Meeting			0.5726** (0.1817)	
Information Accessed Late in the Meeting^2 – Quadratic Term			-0.0046* (0.0019)	
R^2	0.0029	0.1979	0.2201	0.1562
F	0.16	12.83	7.20	4.72
N	54	54	54	54
Hypothesis Supported?	*H2: No*	*H3a: Yes*	*H3b: Yes*	*H3c: Yes*

* $p<0.05$ ** $p<0.01$ *** $p<0.001$
Standard errors in parentheses

H2: Perceived Decision Quality

A regression analysis assessed if perceived decision quality is positively related to the proportion of information accessed earlier in the meeting. The results of the regression analysis, presented in Table 2, do not indicate any statistical significance in favor of Hypothesis 2.

H3: Decision Time

As hypothesized in Hypothesis 3a, the information acquired in the early part of the meeting has a linear relationship with decision time (see Figure 3a). In contrast, as hypothesized in Hypothesis 3b, the information acquired later in the meeting has a curvilinear relationship with the decision time (see Figure 3b). The analysis also demonstrates a statistically significant curvilinear relationship between decision time and proportion of information accessed earlier in the meeting (see Figure 3c). Table 3 presents the results of testing hypotheses 3a, 3b, and 3c.

Figure 3a. Plot of the predicted decision time and early access of information

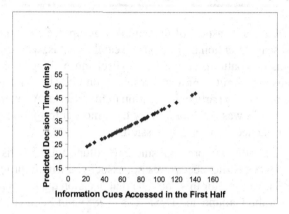

Figure 3b. Plot of the predicted decision time and late access of information

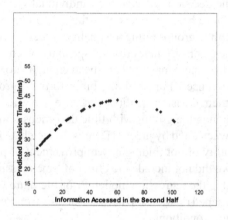

Figure 3c. Plot of the predicted decision time and proportion of information accessed early in the meeting

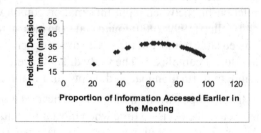

Discussion

This research addresses an aspect of the complex group decision-making process that has received scant attention in previous research. That is, we explore temporal information acquisition patterns during a group decision-making process supported by a GSS. Because the limited previous research on GSS has yielded seemingly conflicting findings, we pay particular attention to fuzzy tasks. As hypothesized, we found that when a GSS was used for a fuzzy task, more information was accessed in the first half of the decision-making session.

However, unlike the findings of previous studies (Gallupe & DeSanctis, 1988; Saunders & Miranda, 1998), earlier access was not associated with improved perceived decision quality. The reason for this could be that decision quality was assessed by the participants. In the Gallupe and DeSanctis (1988) and Saunders and Miranda (1998) studies, experts evaluated the quality of the groups' decisions. But when participants evaluate decision quality, their assessments may be biased depending upon whether or not the decision reflected their individual views and opinions. In fact, these views may have been incorrect and, thus, could have detrimentally affected the decision. Further, groups rating the quality of their own decisions may be more positive about the results of their efforts, especially when there was a reward tied to performance. Thus, there may not have been enough variance to adequately test for significant differences. For example, brainstorming groups without time decomposition rated their decision quality about the same as groups with time decomposition even though the groups with time decomposition had significantly more and better ideas when rated by judges (Dennis, Valacich, Connolly, & Wynne, 1996). Another possibility of not finding any improvement of perceived decision quality could be that we did not include the effect of time pressure (that the group members experienced) in the regression model. Prior literature (Hahn et al., 1992) reports an inverted U-shaped relationship between decision quality and information load under time pressure conditions.

This study also relies on the information processing model proposed by Schroder et al. (1967). Although the model has been tested in the context of individual decision making, very few GSS studies (with the exception of Grise & Gallup, 1999-2000) have examined the relationship between input information complexity and group performance. Grise and Gallup (1999-2000) found that in an idea-organization task, GSS groups that organized large number of ideas perceived higher mental workload and generated output of lower complexity. The study did not reveal any curvilinear relationship between input information load and output information complexity.

Our study is unique in that it proposes (and finds) a curvilinear relationship between the access of information and the decision time when most information is accessed later in the decision. When more information was acquired late in the meeting, group members had less time to process the input information. As the late acquisition of information exceeded an optimum level, group members experienced information overload, filtered input information, processed fewer information cues, and took less time to make the decision. In contrast, we found that when groups acquired more information in the early part of the meeting, they took more time to process the information, and their decision time increased linearly. This finding signals the importance of timing in information acquisition.

Implications for Managers

Encouraging computer-assisted groups solving fuzzy problems to access information earlier in the decision-making process may improve their task completion times and, consequently, enhance their efficiency. To gain this increased efficiency, GSSs could be designed and developed to provide (1) decisional guidance by prompting managers to access more information earlier rather than later in a meeting, (2) improved GSS features including user-friendly interfaces such as icon-based interfaces to minimize the cognitive load of users and facilitate learning, and (3) problem modeling tools. In addition, managers may provide for trainings, allow sufficient time for performing the task, and install process enablers that support cognitive activities (Eppler & Mengis, 2004; Grise & Gallupe, 2000). Providing these tools and aids earlier, rather than later, in the decision-making process could also improve group decision-making effectiveness.

Implications for Researchers

This study suggests several other avenues for future research. Obviously, we only tested the impact of GSS for a fuzzy task. How does the timing of information acquisition affect other types of GSS-based tasks? Zigurs and Buckland's (1998) task/technology fit model suggests that information acquisition patterns may be different for other types of tasks. For example, simple tasks with only one outcome and one solution scheme may not require additional information acquisition. Thus, limited information acquisition, if any, may be evenly distributed throughout the decision-making process, and less communication support may be needed. Future research should address the difference in information acquisition patterns across different task types and suggest how the information overload can be avoided by providing appropriate technology to enhance the capacity of information processing, by controlling information characteristics and task parameters (Eppler & Mengis, 2004). Lurie (2004) demonstrates how information structure impacts information processing, especially during the acquisition of information. In tasks that involve multiple outcomes (such as decision making), the information structure includes the number of alternatives, the number of attributes of each alternative, the number of different attribute levels associated with each attribute, and the distribution of attribute levels across alternatives. Information structure is clearly a variable that should be included in future studies on the timing of information acquisition in GSS-based group work.

Another important issue relates to the information search pattern of the decision makers. Two search strategies that have been discussed in the literature are *breadth-first* and *depth-first* (Montgomery & Svenson, 1976). Research has shown that the proportion of depth-first to breadth-first search strategies varies strongly over different individuals (Levin et al., 2000; Payne, 1976). Can the group members follow a consistent search strategy? What influence does the information search strategy have on information acquisition and the performance of a group decision-making process? Some of these issues may be addressed in future research.

Limitations

Fjermestad and Hiltz (1998-1999), based on their survey of 200 GSS studies, report that undergraduates were used as subjects in 73% of the experiments. Our study, like the preponderance of other GSS studies, used a student sample. Although the problem (the ranking of MBA program attributes) presented to the participants is most appropriate for a student sample, future research could be undertaken in business settings to study problems that managers commonly face in-group decision making. Further, since information overload, as well as integrative complexity, cannot be measured directly, these qualities must be inferred from performance or experimental design in future studies (Grise & Gallupe, 1999-2000).

Conclusion

Leading GSS researchers are concerned that GSS studies across task types have not fully explored temporal impacts on decision making (Dennis et al., 2001; Hollingshead & McGrath, 1995). Using a model of information access during the decision-making process (Saunders & Jones, 1990), this chapter introduces specific ways in which temporal patterns play an important role in information acquisition during the decision-making process. The experiment described in this study addresses only one aspect of information acquisition in group decision making. Yet, the findings are a start, and they are striking enough to warrant further studies to clarify the role of GSS in the information acquisition and decision-making process over time.

Acknowledgments

The authors would like to thank Laku Chidambaram for his valuable comments and suggestions on an earlier draft.

References

Allen, D., & Wilson, T.D. (2003). Information overload: Context and causes. *The New Review of Information Behavior Research*, 31-44.

Bailey, J.E., & Pearson, S.W. (1983). Development of a tool for measuring and analyzing computer user satisfaction. *Management Science, 29*(5), 530-545.

Chewning, E., Jr., & Harrell, A. (1990). The effect of information load on decision makers' cue utilization levels and decision quality in a financial distress decision task. *Accounting, Organizations and Society, 15*, 527-542.

Churchman, C.W., & Ackoff, R.L. (1954). An approximate measure of value. *Journal of Operations Research Society of America, 2*(2), 172-187.

Cohen, M.D., March, J.G., & Olsen, J.P. (1972). A garbage can model of organizational choice. *Administrative Science Quarterly, 17*(1), 1-25.

Cyert, R.M., & March, J.G. (1963). *A behavior theory of the firm*. Englewood Cliffs, NJ: Prentice Hall.

Davenport, T., & Beck, J.C. (2001). *The attention economy: Understanding the new currency of business*. Boston: Harvard Business School Press.

Dennis, A.R., Valacich, J., Connolly, T., & Wynne, B.E. (1996). Process structuring in electronic brainstorming. *Information Systems Research, 7*(2), 268-277.

Dennis, A.R., Wixom, B.H., & Vandenberg, R.J. (2001). Understanding fit and appropriation effects in group support systems via meta-analysis. *MIS Quarterly, 25*(2), 167-193.

DeSanctis, G., & Gallupe, R.B. (1987). A foundation for the study of group decision support systems. *Management Science, 33*(5), 589-609.

Driver, M.J., & Streufert, S. (1969). Integrative complexity: An approach to individuals and groups as information-processing systems. *Administrative Science Quarterly, 14*(2), 272-285.

Eppler, M.J., & Mengis, J. (2004). The concept of information overload: A review of literature from organization science, accounting, marketing, MIS, and related disciplines. *The Information Society, 20*, 325-344.

Fjermestad, J., & Hiltz, S.R. (1998-1999). An assessment of group support systems experimental research: Methodology and results. *Journal of Management Information Systems, 15*(3), 7-149.

Gallupe, B., & DeSanctis, G. (1988). Computer-based support for group problem-finding: An experimental investigation. *MIS Quarterly, 12*(2), 277-296.

Gopal, A., & Prasad, P. (2000). Understanding GSS in symbolic context: Shifting the focus from technology to interaction. *MIS Quarterly, 24*(3), 509-549.

Grise, M.L., & Gallupe, R.B. (1999-2000). Information overload: Addressing the productivity paradox in face-to-face electronic meetings. *Journal of Management Information Systems, 16*(3), 157-185.

Hahn, M., Lawson, R., & Lee, Y.G. (1992). The effects of time pressure and information load on decision quality. *Psychology and Marketing, 9*(5), 365-378.

Hollingshead, A.B., & McGrath, J.E. (1995). Computer-assisted groups: A critical review of the empirical research. In R.A. Guzzo & E. Salas (Eds.), *Team effectiveness and decision making in organizations* (pp. 46-78). San Francisco: Jossey-Bass.

Huang, W., Raman, K.S., & Wei, K.K. (1993). A process study of effects of GSS and task type on informational and normative influence in small groups. In J. DeGross, B. Bostrom, & D. Robey (Eds.), *Proceedings of the Fourteenth International Conference on Information Systems* (pp. 91-101). Orlando, Florida.

Huber, G.P. (1990). A theory of the effects of advanced information technologies on organizational design, intelligence, and decision making. *Academy of Management Review, 15*(1), 47-71.

Hwang, M.I., & Lin, J.W. (1999). Information dimension, information overload and decision quality. *Journal of Information Science, 25*(3), 213-218.

Hwang, C., & Yoon, K. (1981). *Multiple attribute decision-making.* New York: Springer-Verlag.

Ives, B., Olson, M.H., & Baroudi, J.J. (1983). An empirical study of the impact of user involvement on system usage and information satisfaction. *Communications of the ACM, 29*(3), 232-238.

Janis, I.L. (1989). *Crucial decisions: Leadership in policymaking and crisis management.* New York: Free Press.

Kaplan, M.F., & Miller, C.E. (1987). Group decision making and normative versus informational influence effects of type of issue and assigned decision rule. *Journal of Personality and Social Psychology, 53*(2), 306-313.

Levin, I., Huneke, M., & Jasper, J. (2000). Information processing at successive stages of decision making: Need for cognition and inclusion-exclusion effects. *Organization Behavior and Human Decision Performance, 82*(2), 171-193.

Lurie, N.H. (2004). Decision making in information-rich environments: The role of information structure. *The Journal of Consumer Research, 30*, 473-486.

Mintzberg, H., Raisinghani, D., & Theoret, A. (1976). The structure of "unstructured" decision processes. *Administrative Science Quarterly, 12*(2), 246-275.

Miranda, S., & Saunders, C. (2003). The social construction of meaning: An alternative perspective on information sharing. *Information Systems Research, 14*(1), 87-106.

Mohammed, S., & Ringseis, E. (2001). Cognitive diversity and consensus in group decision making: The role of inputs, processes and outcomes. *Organization Behavior and Human Decision Processes, 85*(2), 310-335.

Montgomery, H., & Svenson, O. (1976). On decision rules and information processing strategies for choices among multiattribute alternatives. *Scandinavian Journal of Psychology, 17*, 283-291.

Nunnally, J.C. (1978). *Psychometric theory.* New York: McGraw-Hill.

Olsen, J.P. (1976). Choice in an organized anarchy. In J.G. March & J.P. Olsen (Eds.), *Ambiguity and choice in organizations.* Bergen, Norway: Universitetsforlaget.

Payne, J.W. (1976). Task complexity and contingent processing in decision making: An information search and protocol analysis. *Organizational Behavior and Human Performance, 16*, 366-387.

Poole, M.S. (1978). An information-task approach to organizational communications. *Academy of Management Review, 3*(3), 493-504.

Saunders, C.S., & Jones, J.W. (1990). Temporal sequences in information acquisition for decision making: A focus on source and medium. *Academy of Management Review, 15*(1), 29-46.

Saunders, C.S., & Miranda, S. (1998). Information acquisition in group decision making. *Information and Management, 34*(2), 55-74.

Schick, A.G., & Gordon, L.A. (1990). Information overload: A temporal approach. *Accounting, Organizations and Society, 15*(3), 199-220.

Schroder, H.M., Driver, M.J., & Streufert, S. (1967). *Human information processing.* New York: Holt, Rinehart and Winston.

Schultze, U., & Vandenbosch, B. (1998). Information overload in a groupware environment: Now you see IT, now you don't. *Journal of Organizational Computing Electronic Commerce, 8*(2), 127-148.

Simon, H.A. (1965). *The shape of automation.* New York: Harper and Row.

Thorngate, W. (1997). More than we can know: The attentional economics of Internet use. In S. Kiesler (Ed.), *Culture of the Internet* (pp. 296-287). Mahwah, NJ: Lawrence Earlbaum Associates.

Zigurs, I., & Buckland, B. (1998). A theory of task/technology fit and group support systems effectiveness. *MIS Quarterly, 22*(3), 313-334.

Endnote

[1] An earlier version of this paper was published as:

Paul, S., Saunders, C.S., & Haseman, W.D. (2005). A question of timing: The impact of information aquisition on group decision making. *Information resources management journal, 18*(4), 81-100.

Appendix 1: List of Attributes for MBA Admission (as Used in the Prototype)

1. AACSB accreditation
2. Average age
3. Average starting salary
4. Closeness to Milwaukee
5. Executive MBA program
6. Minimum months to degree
7. Nontuition fees
8. Part-time MBA program
9. PhD program
10. Percentage of applicants admitted to the program
11. Percentage of international students
12. Percentage of minority students

13. Percentage of students receiving aid
14. Percentage of women students
15. Tuition fees
16. Typical GMAT score
17. Typical undergraduate GPA
18. Typical work experience

Appendix 2: Indicator Items
for Perceived Decision Quality

[derived from the prior instruments on computer user satisfaction (Bailey & Pearson, 1983) and user information satisfaction (Ives et al., 1983)]

1. The output was easy to understand.
2. The output generated was reliable.
3. The output was comprehensive.
4. I have confidence in the accuracy of the output.

Chapter X

Progress in Internet Privacy Policies:
A Review and Survey of U.S. Companies from 1998 through 2006

Alan R. Peslak, Penn State University – Worthington Scranton, USA

Abstract

Privacy on the Internet has been of increasing concern with the explosive growth of electronic commerce. A series of past surveys by the Federal Trade Commission and other organizations measured the implementation of fair information practices and industry self-regulation of privacy. This report includes two important additional factors in the review—enforcement and simplicity. Using historical studies and this more comprehensive analysis, this article reviews the current Internet privacy polices of the 50 largest U.S. companies in 2003 and updates this review for 2006.

Introduction

Privacy in modern times is a difficult proposition. Due to our ever increasing reliance on computers and information technology, it is challenging to maintain privacy in our business and personal activities. Banks keep track of our purchases through detailed credit card transactions. Grocery stores monitor our cash food purchases through "discount" cards and register scanner databases. Even our Internet activities are monitored by ISP and government officials. Given that privacy is a basic need and that there is a human tendency to invade other's privacy, the government has begun to become more actively involved in studying and legislating information privacy.

This report is a review and analysis of privacy and privacy policies of commercial Web sites as represented by the Fortune 50. First, this report examines the concept of privacy from both historical and recent perspectives. Next privacy regulation (both legislated and self-regulation) as it has evolved for commercial Web sites is briefly reviewed. This includes an analysis of factors used to analyze Web site privacy. Following this is a review of a series of studies by the government and other organizations to determine compliance with and conformance to these privacy factors. The top Fortune 50 Web sites are analyzed to determine current conformance to privacy factors, including several additional factors not previously measured. After the analysis, the implications for privacy are noted.

The goals of this study are as follows:

- Provide a background on Internet privacy.
- Summarize prior Internet privacy studies.
- Update and expand on Internet privacy studies.
- Propose the expanded analysis as a guide for future studies.

Privacy Concept

Warren and Brandeis (1890) described the right to privacy in their seminal Harvard Law Review article as the right to be left alone. Westin (1967) lists four features of privacy that appear in nearly all societies:

- The need for seclusion and isolation at certain times.
- The concept that we are never alone even in solitude.
- The tendency to invade the privacy of others.
- The need for freedom, due to social and technical advancements.

As noted, the concept of a "right to privacy" called for the right to be left alone. Publication and dissemination of personal information extends from this right to be left alone. Warren and Brandeis (1890) also suggest that the right to privacy stops when the individual consents to give up the right. Consent has been rendered ambiguous in the Internet realm with the concept of requiring a specific opting-out. Opting-out requires an individual to give specific notice that they do not want information they provided to organizations over the Internet sold or used for other purposes; otherwise it may be used. This suggests that, as a default, a person gives up the right to freedom. This is a troubling premise for Internet users.

Review of Recent Literature

Ackerman, Cranor, and Reagle (1999) studied user concerns over privacy and security in electronic commerce transactions over the Internet. Specifically the authors found that 87% of the respondents were concerned about privacy on the Internet. About 97% of Internet users did not wish to share credit card information on the Internet. More than 80% of respondents were not comfortable with sharing their phone number, income, and medical information over the Internet. These figures suggest a very high concern with Internet privacy.

Milne and Culnan (2002) developed a review of past online privacy notices and noted three areas of concern with studies conducted thus far. First, they suggested that the studies have been more effective in determining the existence of policies than in assessing content and inclusion of intended fair information practices. Given that there is no template or checklist of required elements to achieve fair information practice goals, there is necessarily variability in measurement and satisfaction of these goals. The second element mentioned is that the surveys have not measured compliance with standards. This suggests enforcement has not specifically been measured in past surveys. Finally, there is the issue of understanding by consumers. There must be some element of comprehension for these policies to achieve their objective of fair play between vendors and consumers.

A *Business Week* study by Green, France, Stepanek, and Borrus (2000) suggests a four point plan for dealing with privacy online. Their key four points are display, choice, access, and enforcement. Policies without some type of enforcement and penalty provisions are meaningless. Security is a key element of a successful Internet privacy program according to Cranor (1999). This includes both transmission security, when the data are received or distributed, as well as storage security when the information is stored at a company site.

Individuals should have a right to view information held about them and to correct this information if it is erroneous. A series of laws from Congress related to credit, telecommunications, health insurance, and education have codified consumers' rights to access information in these areas. No such legislation currently exists with regard to general marketing data or personal information (Hoofnagle, 2003). By providing this access, there is, however, an issue of insecurity. By providing access to individuals, the information is potentially more available to unscrupulous individuals. This problem must be dealt with through stronger security measures (Hadley, 2003).

In December 2001, Harris Interactive published a report on privacy notices. They surveyed adults and found that only 3% carefully read privacy policies of Web sites visited. The number one reason given for not reading notices was "lack of time/do not want to take time." The second most important was that policies were too lengthy. All fair information practices are useless unless people read the policies. Generally, people do not currently read policies because they are too lengthy. The study showed that 77% of people surveyed preferred a short privacy policy because a longer policy was "too confusing to understand." Also, an important factor in a privacy policy according to the Harris survey (Harris Interactive, 2001) was "if and how personal information is shared or sold to other companies." Fully 86% of those surveyed viewed this as important or very important.

The review of current literature thus suggests the following:

- Internet privacy is a major concern for users.
- The length of a privacy policy is significant with longer policies confusing.
- Ability to view personal information held by Internet providers is desirable.
- Security of information provided is important.
- Important issues for Internet privacy are display, choice, access, and enforcement.

Modern Privacy Regulation

There have been some instances of regulation of Internet privacy. One of the early countries to adopt legislation was New Zealand. They enacted a Privacy Act in 1993 that requires electronic commerce providers in the country to abide by certain information privacy rules. Generally their legislation focuses on notice, purpose, disclose of dissemination, access, and enforcement (Chung & Paynter, 2002).

The United Kingdom (UK) passed the Data Protection Act of 1998 to deal with data privacy in both written and electronic form. Bath and North East Somerset Council (2002) note some of the important principles that underlie the act:

- Personal data should only be collected for a specific purpose and not used for other purposes.

- Personal data should be accurate and current but disposed of when no longer needed.

- Appropriate security measures to protect data should be adopted.

- Data cannot be transferred out of the European Economic Area unless the transferring country has proper data privacy policies and security.

- Personal data can only be collected and processed under certain set conditions.

But even in the UK, where there is a specific law dealing with information privacy; implementation and enforcement are still uneven. The UK Office of Information contracted with the University of Manchester Institute of Science and Technology (UMIST) to determine whether UK company Web sites were implementing and complying with Provisions of the Data Protection Act of 1998. The result was a comprehensive study which sampled UK Web sites and found generally disappointing compliance with the Act (UMIST and the Office of the Information Commissioner, 2002).

The UMIST study found some startling statistics. First, only 58% of the sites had a privacy statement of some form, yet 75% of sites did collect personal information. The study found incomprehensible statements in 95% of cases based on the average Internet users' reading levels. About 50% of the sites placed cookies. Access to personal information stored about individuals was provided by only 43% of sites, but much lesser percentages would be achieved if considerations of how to question the data or correct the data were considered. Though specifically required in the act, 25% of sites do not include a retention policy and only 37% have a security policy. Thus, even though specific legislated Internet data privacy policies exist in the UK, the lack of aggressive enforcement renders these laws relatively ineffective (UMIST and the Office of the Information Commissioner, 2002).

Recent U.S. Privacy Reports

The United States has only limited Internet privacy regulation, focused primarily on specific groups such as children or special information such as medical records. Most other Internet privacy issues rely on self-regulation. Due to the large amount of information that is now being solicited and captured online, the Federal Trade Commission began a review of privacy policies adopted by online Internet firms. Their first report was prepared in 1998 and was titled "Privacy Online: A Report to

Congress." The report surveyed 1,400 online firms to determine the extent of their privacy self-regulation and assess its effectiveness (Federal Trade Commission, 1998). The conclusion of the report was that most firms did not do an effective job of self-regulation and failed to establish and follow basic concepts of privacy. Their approach began in 1995 with public workshops, continued in 1996 with a staff report, and in 1997 continued with in-depth workshops. Their overall approach at that time was to encourage self-regulation, identify privacy issues, and provide a forum to exchange ideas.

With increased Internet traffic and resulting online business, the Federal Trade Commission became more active, and prepared their first study. The Federal Trade Commission developed five basic "core principles" for its privacy policy: notice, choice, access, security, and enforcement. They called these concepts fair information practices (Federal Trade Commission, 1998).

- Notice, also known as awareness, is the concept that before any information is collected online, the individual must be made aware of what will be done with the information. Notice, as defined in the Federal Trade Commission 2000 survey, requires posting of a Privacy Policy, notice of what information is collected, how the information is used internally, and whether the information is distributed to third parties (Federal Trade Commission, 2000).

- Choice, or consent, is the ability of a consumer or visitor to a Web site to determine if and how information that is provided will be used after the reason for the specific visit is over. The Federal Trade Commission 2000 report requires a choice on using personal data to send information back to consumers, and disclosure to third parties or statements that these are not done (Federal Trade Commission, 2000).

- Access, or participation, is the ability and process to find out what information a company has collected about a person and to verify or change information if necessary. Access, according to the Federal Trade Commission, allows review, correction, and deletion of personal information (Federal Trade Commission, 2000).

- Security, or integrity, is the protection of the data a person submits to an online site. Security (Federal Trade Commission, 2000) requires a statement that steps are taken to "provide security."

- Enforcement is the process or steps to uphold the policy or to enact redress if the policy has been violated. There are three methods of enforcement possible according to the Federal Trade Commission—self-regulation (or regulation by the site itself), private remedies (such as certification companies), or government enforcement of existing or future regulations (Federal Trade Commission, 2000).

Table 1. Percentage of companies whose Web sites contained each online privacy characteristic (FTC, 1998); (RS = random sample, PG = popular group); Source: Federal Trade Commission, 1998

	FTC 1998 RS	FTC 1998 PG
Post Privacy Disclosure/ Information Practice Disclosure	15%	73%
How information used	14%	61%
Notice	54%	71%
Collect	92%	97%
Choice	33%	39%
Access	9%	10%
Security	15%	16%
Sell to Third Parties	33%	14%

The results of a survey performed in 1998 by the FTC are presented in Table 1. Several groups of Web sites were measured, including a group of most popular U.S. commercial Web sites and a random sample of commercial Web sites "likely to be of interest to consumers." The survey measured key online privacy characteristics. Overall, the results showed poor participation by online sites for most of the five fair information practices. The Federal Trade Commission 1998 report chided firms for poor self-regulation and noted that further recommendations on actions were forthcoming (Federal Trade Commission, 1998). As a result of the survey, a majority of the Federal Trade Commission issued a report in 1999 calling for the allowance of more time for self-regulation by Internet sites; however it did also recommend adoption of the fair information principles (Federal Trade Commission, 1999).

The next major study of Internet privacy policies was a "progress report" to the Federal Trade Commission coordinated by Mary Culnan at Georgetown University (Table 2). The study was an update that was patterned after the 1998 Federal Trade Commission study and included random sample companies of the top 7,500 URLs. The 1998 study by the Federal Trade Commission came from a larger population base. Because this study came from a much smaller database, direct comparisons may not be fully appropriate; however the study found much improved results from 1998. Some type of privacy disclosure was found in 66% of random sites compared to 15% in 1998 (though less than the 73% most popular group sample). Notice increased from 54% and 71% in the Federal Trade Commission random and popu-

Table 2. Percentage of companies whose Web sites contained each online privacy characteristic (Georgetown, 1999 vs. FTC, 1998); (RS = random sample, PG = popular group); Sources: Culnan, 1999; Federal Trade Commission, 1998

	FTC 1998 RS	FTC 1998 PG	Georgetown 1999
Post Privacy Disclosure/ Information Practice Disclosure	15%	73%	66%
How information used	14%	61%	
Notice	54%	71%	90%
Collect	92%	97%	
Choice	33%	39%	62%
Access	9%	10%	40%
Security	15%	16%	46%

lar samples, respectively, to 90% in GIPPS (Georgetown Internet Privacy Policy Survey). In both the Federal Trade Commission and GIPPS surveys, the concept of enforcement, the fifth fair information practice, was not specifically measured or studied (Culnan, 1999).

The Federal Trade Commission followed up their 1998 survey with a second report issued in May 2000 (Table 3). The survey included similar group samples, random and most popular, as in the 1998 survey. They reviewed four fair information practices of notice, choice, access, and security, and began to measure enforcement through the review of adoption of third party "seal," or certification programs such as TrustE. The study consisted of a random survey including e-commerce, information, and entertainment sites. The most popular site sample included of 91 of the 100 busiest sites on the Internet. The results of the survey showed continued progress in meeting the goals of adoption of fair information practices, but the progress was deemed too slow for the Federal Trade Commission. Their recommendation in the report was the enactment of legislation that would require consumer and commercial Web sites to implement four fair information practices of notice, choice, access, and security. This recommendation came despite growth in all categories from both the 1998 Federal Trade Commission report and the Georgetown 1999 survey. Overall, just 20% of the busiest sites implemented the four fair information practices.

In March of 2002, a private organization, The Progress and Freedom Foundation, prepared yet a fourth survey. They studied three types of sites: one based on a random

Table 3. Percentage of companies whose Web sites contained each online privacy characteristic (FTC, 2000 vs. FTC, 1998); (RS = random sample, PG = popular group); Sources: Federal Trade Commission, 1998, 2000

	FTC 1998 RS	FTC 1998 PG	FTC 2000 RS	FTC 2000 PG
Post Privacy Disclosure/ Information Practice Disclosure	15%	73%	88%	100%
How information used	14%	61%	82%	100%
Notice	54%	71%	55%	89%
Collect	92%	97%	97%	99%
Choice	33%	39%	71%	88%
Opt-out			71%	75%
Cookies			44%	87%
Access	9%	10%	43%	83%
Security	15%	16%	55%	74%
Seal			8%	45%
Sell to Third Parties	33%	14%	52%	80%

Table 4. Percentage of companies whose Web sites contained each online privacy characteristic; (MP = most popular, RS = random sample, PG = popular group, PFF = Progress and Freedom Foundation); Sources: Adkinson, Eisenrach & Lenard, 2002; Federal Trade Commission, 2000

	FTC 2000 RS	FTC 2000 PG	PFF 02 RS	PFF 02 MP
Post Privacy Disclosure/ Information Practice Disclosure	88%	100%	88%	98%
Choice	71%	88%	71%	89%
Security	55%	74%	33%	72%
Seal	8%	45%	12%	44%
Mention P3P			5%	23%

sample, one based on a subset of the random sample, and another based on popular Web sites. In general, the subset of the random sample yielded similar results as the random sample. Table 4 shows a comparison of their results from the most popular and random sample to the FTC 2000 results. Their study reportedly measured their results based on the instructions in the Federal Trade Commission 2000 survey to make their report comparable. Overall, the results of this survey were very similar to the Federal Trade Commission 2000 report. For example, posting privacy policy was 98% vs. 100% in the FTC most popular group. Likewise security was mentioned in 74% of FTC 2000 vs. 72% in PFF02 (Adkinson, Eisenrach, & Lenard, 2002).

Methodology of This Survey

This study is an extension of the past studies as well as a review of a new subset of Web sites. For the first time, the issue of enforcement has been reviewed directly. Enforcement is the fifth fair information practice listed by the Federal Trade Commission. The issue of enforcement includes the concept of recourse to a user if there is some question as to whether stated information practices have been followed. Also, this study attempts to measure accessibility of the fair information practices to the user. This is accomplished through a review of the length of the company privacy statement as well as the number of links to obtain all information. Finally, this study addresses the Web sites of the largest companies in the U.S., the Fortune 50, as measured by the annual survey of *Fortune* magazine. This is to determine fair information practice adoption by the biggest companies in the U.S. today, and to compare to other studies of random and popular Web sites as measured by other surveys.

All studies have focused on popular commercial Web sites. This study specifically looked at the top 50 corporations in the U.S. according to *Fortune* magazine. The sites surveyed were the top 50 of the Fortune 500. The sites were reviewed over a two-week period in June 2003; and an attempt was made to review the sites according to rules consistent with the past Federal Trade Commission surveys so that comparisons of results could be made. Specifically, there was a determination of the top companies' compliance with the five information practices that were promulgated by the Federal Trade Commission. In addition, a measure of the simplicity of the notice was attempted by performing a simple word count of the privacy disclosures. According to Culnan, privacy notices in order to be effective and read by individuals need to be "concise, clearly written, and comprehensive" (Culnan, 2003). The measure of conciseness was developed as "total number of words." This is an area that deserves further research.

These same top 50 corporations were then again reviewed in January of 2006 to view changes in the intervening two and a half years. The same corporations were studied from 2003 to 2006 to eliminate changes that have taken place in ranking. The approach was to just view how these large companies changed their policies over this time frame.

Results of Survey

Overall, the 2003 survey showed that the Fortune 50 Web sites were similar to popular Web sites surveyed over time. Complete results are shown (last column) and compared in Table 5. First, 94% of the Web sites had some type of privacy policy posted. This rate compares to a rate of 100% of the most popular Web sites

Table 5. Percentage of companies whose Web sites contained each online privacy characteristic (MP = most popular, RS = random sample, PG = popular group, ARP = this survey); Sources: Adkinson, Eisenrach, and Lenard, 2002; Culnan, 1999; Federal Trade Commission, 1998, 2000

	FTC 1998 RS	FTC 1998 PG	FTC 2000 RS	FTC 2000 PG	Gtown 1999	PFF 2002 RS	PFF 2002 MP	ARP June 2003
Post Privacy Disclosure/ Information Practice Disclosure	15%	73%	88%	100%	66%	88%	98%	94%
How information used	14%	61%	82%	100%				94%
Notice	54%	71%	55%	89%	90%			91%
Collect	92%	97%	97%	99%				96%
Choice	33%	39%	71%	88%	62%	71%	89%	62%
Opt-out			71%	75%				86%
Cookies			44%	87%				79%
Access	9%	10%	43%	83%	40%			57%
Security	15%	16%	55%	74%	46%	33%	72%	74%
Enforcement								23%
Words (number)								1581
Links (number)								1.19
Seal			8%	45%		12%	44%	26%
Sell to Third Parties	33%	14%	52%	80%				23%
Mention P3P						5%	23%	4%

in the Federal Trade Commission year 2000 survey and 98% in the most popular PFF survey. None of the top Fortune 25 companies failed to have a privacy policy but three in the second 25 lacked such a policy.

Information has and continues to be collected by nearly all Web sites. Of the Fortune 50, 96% of the sites that have a privacy policy that explicitly states that they collect personal information. This is a consistent trend with all prior samples and surveys, ranging between 92 and 99%.

The Federal Trade Commission samples in 2000 included a review of whether the privacy policy disclosed how information was used by the company. The George-town and PFF likewise collected similar information. This survey of the Fortune 50 found that of the companies that have privacy policies, 94% disclose how infor-mation collected is used. This compares to 93% in the Georgetown survey, 100% in the Federal Trade Commission 2000 survey, and 100% in the PFF survey (most popular). Three organizations of the 47 who had privacy policies did not mention how the information collected was used. One of these firms was in the top 25.

The first fair information practice as detailed in the 1998 Federal Trade Commission report is notice. 43 of the 47 companies in the Fortune 50 that have privacy policies meet the notice standard equating to 91%. This is consistent with the Georgetown most popular group at 90% and the Federal Trade Commission 2000 most popular study at 89%. Notice has grown from the 71% in the most popular group reported in 1998.

Choice on how information is used has had a slow beginning. The 1998 Federal Trade Commission sample reported that only 33% of the random sample and 39% of the popular group sample allowed consumer choice. This factor has shown significant growth, however. The 1999 Georgetown study recorded 62% of sites having choice. The Federal Trade Commission 2000 report found 71% of the random sample and 88% of the popular group sample had choice. The PFF study likewise achieved 71 and 89%, respectively. These sites were mainly consumer sites, however. Only 62% of the Fortune 50 sites had privacy policies allowing choice on the use of personal information. This is due perhaps to the inclusion of many nonconsumer sites in the top Fortune 50.

In the sites where choice is offered, the top Fortune 50 showed a clear preference for opt-out choice. Opt-out choice allows a company to use the information it col-lects for specified or nonspecified purposes unless a user specifically informs the company that it does not want this use. This differs from an opt-in choice in which a user must specifically agree to the use prior to a company utilizing the information. The Fortune 50 had an opt-out policy of choice for 86% of the sites where choice was offered. The Federal Trade Commission 2000 report ranged from 71% to 75%. Lawler and Cooper (2003) argue for an opt-in approach rather than an opt-out ap-proach. The opt-in approach is not in place in any of the Fortune 50. The authors argue that such an approach would be in companies' best interests by fostering trust and confidence which would subsequently improve consumer acceptance and participation in e-commerce and e-transactions. They suggest that better quality data would also result from this choice.

The use of cookies is explicitly denoted in 79% of the privacy policies of the Fortune 50. Cookies are small pieces of code left on users' systems in order for a Web site to provide a customized experience the next time the site is visited. The 79% is consistent with the 87% of the most popular sites noted in the Federal Trade Commission 2000 survey.

Access to a user's information that is being kept by a company Web site is a key fair information practice. The Federal Trade Commission reports showed a significant increase in access between 1998 and 2000. The most popular group sample only had 10% of sites providing access in 1998. In the Georgetown 1999 study, access increased to 40%. In the FTC 2000 study, this percentage had increased to 83%. For the Fortune 50 sites, however, in 2003, only 57% of sites provided a means of access.

Security, as noted, is an area that has gained increasing attention over the years. The Fortune 50 companies note security measures to protect user information in 74% of the Web sites that have privacy policies. This percentage is the same as the most popular group in Federal Trade Commission 2000. This percentage has risen from 16% in 1998 and 46% in 1999. The 2002 PFF study in the most popular group showed a 72% rate.

A fair information practice that is noted in the Federal Trade Commission report (1998), but not specifically measured, is enforcement. In reviewing the Fortune 50 Web sites, only 32% provide some type of enforcement or procedure to follow if a user believes that privacy policies are not being enforced. Most of these sites use a third party certification or seal to provide this dispute resolution. The use of a privacy seal has been measured in this study as well as past studies. In the Fortune 50, 26% of sites have privacy seals. This compares to 45% in the most popular sample in the Federal Trade Commission 2000, and 44% in the most popular group 2002 PFF report.

One of the factors not generally recognized as a fair information practice, but which is essential to practical understanding of privacy policy, is complexity. In the top 50 Fortune companies, the average length of the privacy policy is 1,581 words. This is clearly too long to be comprehended by the average user. Only 2 of the 47, or 4%, had reasonable privacy policy lengths of less than 300 words. Also 8 of the 47 sites, or 17%, had privacy policies that required additional links to get to all the privacy policy pages.

Two other additional factors were studied in the Fortune 50 analysis: notice that information could be sold to third parties and mention of the P3P (platform for privacy preference) standard, XML enabled privacy policy. For the Fortune 50, nearly one quarter or 23% specifically mentioned that they may share information to third

Table 6. Percentage of companies whose Web sites contained each online privacy characteristic (MP = most popular, RS = random sample, PG = popular group; ARP 2003 survey, ARP, 2006); Sources: Adkinson, Eisenrach & Lenard, 2002; Culnan, 1999; Federal Trade Commission, 1998, 2000

	FTC 1998 RS	FTC 1998 PG	FTC 2000 RS	FTC 2000 PG	Gtown 1999	PFF 2002 RS	PFF 2002 MP	ARP June 2003	ARP Jan 2006
Post Privacy	15%	73%	88%	100%	66%	88%	98%	94%	98%
How information used	14%	61%	82%	100%				94%	92%
Notice	54%	71%	55%	89%	90%			91%	92%
Collect	92%	97%	97%	99%				96%	98%
Choice	33%	39%	71%	88%	62%	71%	89%	62%	63%
Opt-out			71%	75%				86%	94%
Cookies			44%	87%				79%	86%
Access	9%	10%	43%	83%	40%			57%	55%
Security	15%	16%	55%	74%	46%	33%	72%	74%	78%
Enforcement								23%	20%
Seal			8%	45%		12%	44%	26%	22%
Sell to Third Parties	33%	14%	52%	80%				23%	18%
Mention P3P						5%	23%	4%	4%
Mention Children									53%

parties. The major initiative of providing an XML file that conforms to P3P specification was only mentioned on 4% of the Fortune 50 sites. A similar examination of Web sites by the PFF in 2002 found that 5% of the random sample and 23% of the most popular sites identified with a P3P policy.

As noted, significant progress was made between the years 1998 and 2000 but since that time, progress has slowed considerably. The little gains were noted between 2000 and 2003. In January of 2006, the same Fortune 50 companies were revisited to see what progress if any had been made in the intervening two and a half years. As can be seen in Table 6, there has been little progress at all in the last two and a half years by the largest companies in the U.S. In fact, in some cases, notably the use of a privacy seal and inclusion of enforcements provisions actually declined from 2003 to 2006. Also fewer companies that allow choice on use of information implemented an opt-in choice vs. an explicit opt-out. There were small decreases in detail on how information is used, access to information being held by companies, and the use of a privacy seal. On the favorable side of the ledger, there were small

Figure 1. Inclusion of FTC FIP 1998-2006

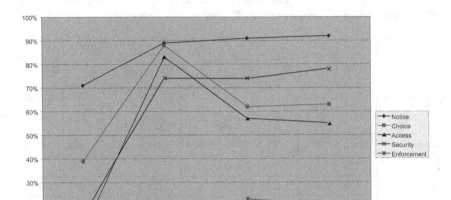

increases in posting a privacy policy (only one now does not post), choice of what is done with your information, notice, and inclusion of a security provision. First measured in this survey was a study of whether mention was made in the privacy policy of special provisions with regard to children. Only 53% of the companies mention children in their privacy policies.

The progress made in each of the five fair information practices is graphically presented in Figure 1. Though the groups studied are different between the FTC and the author's studies, the chart suggests the slow progress that has been made since 2000. Major strides were made between 1998 and 2000 but since that time most of the indicators show little or flat activity with minor gains or losses. There appears to be little impetus on the part of major corporations to change their policies to include more or all of the fair information practices.

Summary, Discussion, and Implications

The goals stated in the introduction have been addressed in this study. First, the report reviewed the historical background for privacy. This was followed by a review of the literature, which noted key factors dealing with privacy and the importance of privacy in the context of Internet use. A review of prior Internet privacy studies revealed limited insight, but some progress, in key privacy issue areas. A study was then undertaken to review Internet privacy in three new ways:

- New and current information was used.
- Top 50 Fortune companies in 2003 rather than popular Web sites were analyzed.
- Additional factors were included.
- Both 2003 and 2006 were studied in a similar manner. The same companies from 2003 were used in the 2006 survey.

For the most part the findings of the study of the Fortune 50 are similar to and consistent with prior reports. Some of the initial findings could be rated positive to neutral.

- In 2003, 94% of the top Fortune 50 Web sites posted a privacy disclosure or information practice disclosure. This is consistent with recent past surveys of popular Web sites and dramatically increased from the 1998 FTC survey. In 2006, this figure rose to 98%. Only one firm in the Fortune 50 did not have privacy policy in 2006.
- Notice (per FTC definition) was provided in 91% of the top Fortune 50 Web sites in 2003 and 92% in 2006.
- Choice percentages of 62% and 63% for 2003 and 2006 respectively, were somewhat lower than prior studies of random and most popular Web sites.
- Specific mention of collection of information was seen in 96% to 98% of top 50 Web sites vs. much lower percentages in prior studies.

Unfortunately, Internet privacy issues of concern to Internet users remain significant. The survey of the top Fortune 50 U.S. publicly held companies reveal some unfavorable findings:

- In 2003, only 16% of the Fortune 50 Web sites had all five fair information practices suggested by the FTC. This percentage has only grown to 18% in 2006. The details on inclusion of at least each number of FIP are shown in Figure 2.
- Only 42% of the Fortune 50 Web sites had four of the five fair information practices of the FTC in 2003 and only 46% in 2006.

- The average length of an Internet privacy notice was too long at 1,581 words. This is neither concise enough nor accessible to most users.
- In 2006, only 22% used a third party independent privacy group for certification of their security policies.
- Only 55% specified ability to access information held by the company.
- 94% of sites had an opt-out choice for use of information.
- Only 63% of Fortune 50 Web sites allowed choice in use of information.
- Only 78% of Fortune 50 Web sites addressed security in their privacy policy.
- In 2003, 16% required more than one link to get to a privacy policy.
- In 2006, specific mention of whether information was sold to third parties was only mentioned in 18% of Web sites vs. 80% in the most popular group in the FTC 2000 survey.
- Children were specifically mentioned in only 53% of the privacy policies.

Though this was a study of only the largest U.S. corporations, one can assume that a survey of smaller companies would yield even less attractive results. Self-regulation is not proceeding fast enough to satisfy consumer concerns. Legislation

Figure 2. Inclusion of at least each number of FIP (2003 vs. 2006)

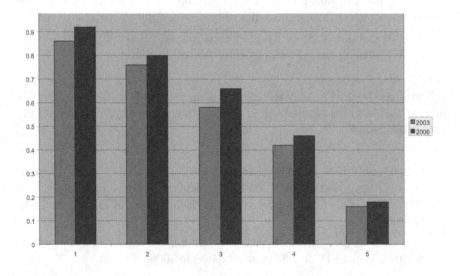

and regulation are required if we are to achieve our right of Internet privacy. The overall results of this survey of the top Fortune 50 U.S. are poor. Nearly eight years after the initial promulgation by the Federal Trade Commission of fair information practices, self-regulation as measured by the top companies in the United States has failed to produce a majority of companies implementing the four prominent factors. A recent study of 500 interactive company sites also suggests that self-regulation is ineffective (Ashrafi & Kuilboer, 2005). Legislation is winding its way through Congress to require these four fair information practices and is currently in a Senate subcommittee. Much more work remains to be done to assure consumer protection and the fundamental right to privacy on the Internet. The extended factor list used in this survey can be used to analyze the Internet policy of a broader cross section of commercial Web sites to determine the progress of industry regulation. Assuming similar results to those found in the Fortune 50, governmental regulation will be required to address privacy concerns since industry self-regulation has proven ineffective.

References

Ackerman, M., Cranor, L., & Reagle, J. (1999). Privacy in e-commerce: Examining user scenarios and privacy preferences. In *Proceedings of the 1ˢᵗ ACM Conference on Electronic Commerce* (pp. 1-8).

Adkinson, W., Eisenrach, J., & Lenard, T. (2002). *Privacy online: A report of the information practices and policies of commercial Web sites.* Retrieved July 13, 2006, from http://www.pff.org/publications/privacyonlinefinalael.pdf

Ashrafi, N., & Kuilboer, J. (2005). Online privacy policies: An empirical perspective on self-regulatory practices. *Journal of Electronic Commerce in Organizations, 3*(4), 61-75.

Bath and North East Somerset Council. (2002). *Data protection code of practice.* Retrieved July 13, 2006, from http://www.bathnes.gov.uk/dataprotection/data14.htm

Chung, W., & Paynter, J. (2002). Privacy issues on the Internet. In *Proceedings of the 35ᵗʰ Annual Hawaii International Conference on System Sciences* (pp. 2501-2509).

Cranor, L. (1999). Internet privacy. *Communications of the ACM, 42*(2), 29-31.

Culnan, M. (2003). How privacy notices promote informed choice. In *Considering consumer privacy: A resource for policy makers and practitioners—Center for Democracy and Technology* (pp. 12-16). Retrieved July 13, 2006, from http://www.cdt.org/privacy/ccp/ccp.pdf

Culnan, M. (1999). *Georgetown Internet privacy policy survey: Report to the Federal Trade Commission.* Retrieved July 13, 2006, from http://www.msb.edu/faculty/culnanm/glpps/glpps1.pdf

Federal Trade Commission. (1998). *Privacy online: A report to Congress.* Retrieved July 13, 2006, from http://www.Federal Trade Commission.gov/reports/privacy3/priv-23a.pdf

Federal Trade Commission. (1999). *Prepared statement of the Federal Trade Commission on "Self-Regulation and Privacy Online."* Retrieved July 13, 2006, from http://www3.Federal Trade Commission.gov/os/1999/07/privacyonlinetestimony.pdf

Federal Trade Commission. (2000). *Privacy online: Fair information practices in the electronic marketplace: A report to Congress.* Retrieved July 13, 2006, from http://www.Federal Trade Commission.gov/reports/privacy2000/privacy2000.pdf

Green, H., France, M., Stepanek, M., & Borrus, A. (2000, March 20). Our four point plan. *Business Week, 3673,* 86.

Hadley, T. (2003). Consumer access to marketing data: Let's look before we leap. In *Considering consumer privacy: A resource for policy makers and practitioners—Center for Democracy and Technology* (pp. 12-16). Retrieved July 13, 2006, from http://www.cdt.org/privacy/ccp/ccp.pdf

Harris Interactive. (2001). *Privacy leadership initiative (PLI) privacy notices research final results.* Retrieved July 13, 2006, from http://www.Federal Trade Commission.gov/bcp/workshops/glb/supporting/harrris%20results.pdf

Hoofnagle, C. (2003). Access enhances openness and accountability. In *Considering consumer privacy: A resource for policy makers and practitioners—Center for Democracy and Technology* (pp. 40-42). Retrieved July 13, 2006, from http://www.cdt.org/privacy/ccp/ccp.pdf

Lawler, B., & Cooper, S. (2003). The opt-in approach to choice. In *Considering consumer privacy: A resource for policy makers and practitioners—Center for Democracy and Technology* (pp. 22-23). Retrieved July 13, 2006, from http://www.cdt.org/privacy/ccp/ccp.pdf

Milne, G., & Culnan, M. (2002). Using the content of online privacy notices to inform public policy: A longitudinal analysis of the 1998-2001 U.S. Web surveys. *The Information Society, 18*(5), 345-359.

UMIST and the Office of the Information Commissioner. (2002). *Study of compliance with the Data Protection Act of 1998 by UK based Websites.* Retrieved July 13, 2006, from http://www.co.umist.ac.uk/research/tech_reports/trs_2002_008_lam.pdf

Warren, S., & Brandeis, L. (1890). The right to privacy. Originally published in *Harvard Law Review, 4*(5). Retrieved July 13, 2006, from http://www.louis-ville.edu/library/law/brandies/privacy.html

Westin, A. (1967). *Privacy and freedom*. New York: Antheneum.

Chapter XI

The Relationship of Strategic Intent to the Enablers and Inhibitors of E-Business Adoption in SMEs

Margi Levy, University of Warwick, UK

Philip Powell, University of Bath, UK

Les Worrall, University of Wolverhampton, UK

Abstract

Small firms' use of e-business is limited and little is known about what drives them to embrace e-business. Using survey data from 354 small and medium-sized enterprises (SMEs) in the UK West Midlands, this chapter investigates e-business use and drivers. It first discusses different growth strategies adopted by SMEs and reviews Internet adoption in SMEs. Drivers and inhibitors of e-business are identified. Three research questions are derived—does strategic intent drive e-business adoption and is it a factor of market position or product innovation? Is this consistent across sectors? And how is strategic intent and industry adoption influenced by the enablers and inhibitors of e-business adoption? This research demonstrates that strategic intent influences decisions to invest in e-business. Those SMEs remaining in their existing markets are the least likely to invest, primarily due to the Internet not being seen as necessary for growth. Product innovation rather than market penetration drives e-business and e-business drivers and inhibitors provide insights into this.

Introduction

Small and medium sized enterprises (SMEs) (firms with 10-249 employees under the EU definition) are a vital and growing part of most economies. Internet technologies are recognised by governments across the world as critical to the development of this sector. Many governments offer financial incentives through intervention projects to encourage SMEs to adopt the Internet, particularly e-mail and Web sites, and subsequently to develop e-business systems that enable them to trade more effectively with business partners (Evans, 2002; Zhu, Kramer, & Xu 2003). Despite this effort, penetration of e-business in SMEs is slow (Kendall, Tung, Chua, Ng, & Tan, 2001).

The limited research into Internet adoption and e-business in SMEs reveals a perceived benefit as the major driver (Brown & Lockett, 2004; Mehrtens, Cragg, & Mills 2001; Poon & Swatman, 1999). Other factors, however, may influence SMEs' decisions to invest in e-business. For example, SMEs' approach to adoption of information and communication technologies (ICT) to manage and grow depends largely on the firm's strategic intent: either cost or valued-adding (Levy, Powell, & Yetton, 2001). This chapter discusses whether, and in what way, strategic intent affects SMEs attitudes to Internet adoption. Here, strategic intent encompasses two dimensions: markets and products. Most SMEs plan growth through some combination of these (Storey, 1994). The chapter also considers drivers and inhibitors of e-business adoption to determine any relationship between these and strategic intent.

The chapter first discusses different growth strategies and then reviews Internet adoption in SMEs. Drivers and inhibitors of e-business are identified. Three research questions are derived—does strategic intent drive e-business adoption and is it a factor of market position or product innovation? Is this consistent across industry sectors? How is strategic intent and industry adoption influenced by the enablers and inhibitors of e-business adoption? The research approach taken to investigate these issues is through a survey of SMEs in the UK West Midlands. The implications from the survey analysis are discussed leading to recommendations and proposals for further research.

SMEs and Strategic Intent

Strategy for SMEs is "action taken by the firm once in business" (Storey, 1994). Storey suggests it is the relationship between the entrepreneur, the SME's strategy, and its context that is important for growth. Key drivers for SMEs are usually market positioning, new product introduction, and technological sophistication. Their strategies are often based round niche differentiation, although they may well have a "hybrid strategy" which reflects their adaptability and flexibility (Karagozoglu & Lindell, 2004). Strategic intent in SMEs may be usefully understood using Ansoff's (1965) framework which considers these issues. Ansoff identifies four strategies for growing businesses (Figure 1).

Market penetration is defined as continuing to sell current products into current markets. Market development is selling current products into new markets. Product development is selling new products into current markets. Diversification is selling new products into new markets.

This model is relevant to SMEs' strategic intent as it focuses on growth. The model uses the current growth strategies of the firm to consider the direction it is taking in relation to the current mix of product and market development. Understanding the growth direction enables business strategy to be better directed towards achieving growth. The strategic focus may either be towards product development or towards market development. The fourth strategy, diversification, is more difficult as firms are moving into uncharted territories in both product and market development (Ansoff, 1965).

Defining E-Business

E-business has grown rapidly over the last few years. The Internet and the development of the World Wide Web have opened up the potential of the global information society. Growth is driven by accessibility of the Internet; firms using the Internet for electronic transaction; digital delivery of informational goods and services such as music and finally retail sale of tangible goods (Currie, 2000). E-business is a generic

Figure 1. Strategic Intent framework (Adapted from Ansoff, 1965)

	Current Product	**New Product**
Present Market	Market Penetration	Product Development
Future Market	Market Development	Diversification

term for the development of strategies for firms to use the Internet (Fillis & Wagner, 2005; Sauer, 2000). There are three main aspects to e-business: intraorganisational (internal to the firm); interorganisational (between firms in supply chain), and e-commerce (customer to firm). Both intraorganisational and interorganisational e-business are usually undertaken to improve productivity through better internal communication and processes. E-commerce is seen as providing an alternative route to market for both tangible and intangible goods.

Precise Internet benefits remain unclear, but speculation suggests the greatest benefits occur under full supply chain integration (Currie, 2000). Value arises once businesses use the knowledge and experience to produce outputs accessible through the Internet. The potential for transformation is thought to emerge once businesses recognise the need to reorganise processes and focus on core competencies (Willcocks & Sauer, 2000).

Opportunities for e-business transformation require visionary changes in four aspects of the business: communication, information, transaction, and distribution. Communication includes relationship building between strategic partners through new channels offered by the Internet. Information distribution is defined as accessibility of knowledge within and between firms and market enabled by the Internet. Transactions are considered electronic order processing and tracking. Distribution is the ability to use the Internet for delivery and support of goods and products (Angehrn, 1997). These need to be seen within the context of an "e-vision" (Feeny, 2000) that identifies new business opportunities within a dynamic market that focuses on customer needs.

E-Business and SMEs

SMEs believe that the Internet will enable them to reach wider geographical markets and increase customers (Lunati, 2000). For these firms e-business adoption is often reactive and opportunistic rather than strategic (Quayle, 2002; Sadowski, Maitland, & van Dongen, 2002). E-business and e-commerce is not recognised as appropriate to the way some SMEs compete (McGregor & Vrazalic, 2005).

There is little evidence of business strategy driving Internet adoption among SMEs; however, strategic commitment is found to be critical in Singaporean SMEs (Kowtha & Choon, 2001). Indeed, Internet adoption is faster when SMEs recognise a business need (Kendall et al., 2001).

In common with most large businesses, SMEs have embraced the use of e-mail (Poon & Swatman, 1999), with 90% of SMEs using it regularly a year after its introduction to the business (Chapman, James-Moore, Szczygiel, & Thompson, 2000). There is evidence that many have also developed "brochureware" Web sites. Few

SMEs have taken the next step to integrate their Web sites with their back-office systems. While many see value in e-mail and Web sites, there is scant evidence of decisions to invest in internal networks or e-business systems (Brown & Lockett, 2004; Keindl, 2000; Santarelli & D'Alti, 2003).

Influencing Factors

One Internet adoption model (Mehrtens et al., 2001) suggests that three main factors influence SMEs' decisions: perceived benefits, organisational readiness, and external pressures. There are three aspects to perceived benefit. First, efficiency benefits arise from improved communication using e-mail; this is also identified by Poon (2000) and Sadowski et al. (2002). Second, effectiveness benefits obtain from the ability to gather research and competitor information, identified by Poon too. Third, use of the Internet presents a modern image and improves SME promotion.

Organisational readiness for Internet adoption is personified in the SME owner. SMEs do not see Internet adoption as an IT issue, but as a business one. SMEs that are attracted to Internet-based commerce tend to be more entrepreneurial, risk takers, innovative, and, invariably, creative (Poon & Swatman, 1999). A second organisational readiness factor is the requirement for SMEs to have adequate IS in place to access the Internet (Mehrtens et al., 2001).

The final factor, external pressure, is primarily from customers, though suppliers and employees are also influencing factors. While Poon (2000) recognises that customer pressure is influential, there is evidence that a lack of customer use is an inhibitor, particularly of e-mail (Sillence, MacDonald, Lefang, & Frost, 1998). Additionally, some customers actively discourage SMEs from adopting e-business (Fillis & Wagner, 2005; McGregor & Vrazalic, 2005).

A study of e-business adopters and nonadopters in Chile finds organisational readiness the most important factor in the decision to adopt. Organisational readiness implies adequate technological and financial resources to enable e-business adoption. The effectiveness perceived benefit of managerial productivity is of second importance, with external pressure third (Grandon & Pearson, 2004).

Drivers and Inhibitors of E-Business in SMEs

Perceived benefit is identified above as a key driver for SME e-business adoption. Efficiency benefits include reducing operating costs including transaction costs involved in sales and purchasing. Effectiveness benefits include improved market intelligence and ability to identify suppliers for product development purposes through the Internet. Additionally, e-business is seen as improving trading relationships. Image is important for two reasons. First, it helps maintain market share and second, increases it. Improved customer service is identified as a key driver by most researchers, not merely as an external pressure, but also in improved effectiveness,

Table 1. Drivers for Internet adoption in SMEs

Driver	Source
Reduced operating costs	Standing, Sims, & Stockdale, 2003; Quayle & Christiansen, 2004; Quayle, 2002; Kendall et al., 2001; Riemenschneider, Harrison, & Mykytyn, 2003
Sales and purchasing cost reduction	Quayle & Christiansen, 2004; Jeffcoate, Chappell, & Feindt, 2004; Tse & Soufani, 2003; Riemenschneider et al., 2003; Simpson & Docherty, 2004
Improved range and quality of services to customers	Quayle & Christiansen, 2004; Jeffcoate et al., 2004; Tse & Soufani, 2003; Mehrtens et al., 2001; Teo & Pian, 2003; Sadowski et al., 2002; Santarelli & D'Altri, 2003; Ramsey et al.; Quayle, 2002; Daniel & Grimshaw, 2002; Riemenschneider et al., 2003; Karagozoglu & Lindell, 2004; Simpson & Docherty, 2004
Increased speed in dispatch of goods	Tse & Soufani, 2003
Finding suppliers	Dendridge & Levenburg, 2000; Teo & Pian, 2003; Santarelli & D'Altri, 2003
Avoiding loss of market share	Santarelli & D'Altri, 2003; Kendall et al., 2001; Riemenschneider et al., 2003
Increase market share	Standing et al., 2003; Quayle & Christiansen, 2004; Ramsey et al, 2003; Daniel & Grimshaw, 2002; Kendall et al., 2001; Karagozoglu & Lindell, 2004; Simpson & Docherty, 2004
Market intelligence	Quayle & Christiansen, 2004; Jeffcoate et al., 2004; Ramsey et al.; Mehrtens et al., 2001
Improved trading relationships	Quayle & Christiansen, 2004; Mehrtens et al., 2001; Simpson & Docherty, 2004; Fillis & Wagner, 2005

Table 2. E-business inhibitors

Inhibitor		Source
Cost	Implementation costs	Santarelli & D'Altri, 2003; Kendall et al., 2001; Grandon & Pearson, 2004; Van Akkeren & Cavaye, 2000; Lawson, Alcock, Cooper, & Burgess, 2003; Simpson & Docherty, 2004; Fillis & Wagner, 2005; McGregor & Vrazalic, 2005
	Limited financial resources	Sharma, Wichramasinghe, & Gupta, 2004; Chapman et al., 2000; Ramsey et al., 2003; Riemenschneider et al., 2003; Simpson & Docherty, 2004; Fillis & Wagner, 2005
	Need for immediate return on investment	Van Akkeren & Cavaye, 2000
Security	Concerns about confidentiality	Santarelli & D'Altri, 2003; Kendall et al., 2001; Lawson et al., 2003; Fillis & Wagner, 2005; McGregor & Vrazalic, 2005
	Fear of fraud	Van Akkeren & Cavaye, 2000
Management	Insufficient time spent on planning	Bianchi & Bivona, 2002; Grandon & Pearson, 2004
	Insufficient knowledge or experience of IS	Klein & Quelch, 1997; Premkumar & Roberts, 1999; Zhu et al., 2003; Sharma et al., 2004; Kowtha & Choon, 2001; Ramsey et al., 2003; Simpson & Docherty, 2004
	Inexperienced owner	Van Akkeren & Cavaye, 2000; Klein & Quelch, 1997; Premkumar & Roberts, 1999; Fillis & Wagner, 2005
Technology	Complexity requiring new skills	Kowtha & Choon, 2001; Van Akkeren & Cavaye, 2000; Riemenschneider et al., 2003; Fillis & Wagner, 2005; McGregor & Vrazalic, 2005
	Existing IS limiting future development	Van Akkeren & Cavaye, 2000; Zhu et al., 2003
	Lack of trust in external IS suppliers	Chapman et al., 2000; McGregor & Vrazalic, 2005
	Limited in-house IS skills	Santarelli & D'Altri, 2003; Kendall et al., 2001; Poon & Swatman, 1999; Sharma et al., 2004; Chapman et al., 2000; Ramsey et al., 2003; Lawson et al., 2003; Riemenschneider et al., 2003; Simpson & Docherty, 2004; Fillis & Wagner, 2005; McGregor & Vrazalic, 2005

for example, in increased service delivery such as dispatch of goods and online support. Table 1 summarises the drivers of e-business adoption in SMEs.

For many SMEs, failure to plan the introduction and exploitation of new technology stems from management limitations (Klein & Quelch, 1997; Premkumar & Roberts, 1999). One issue for many SMEs is that they have already invested heavily in communication and data exchange systems with their major customers. For example, many SMEs have invested in EDI and their current dilemma is whether to fulfill customer demands to move to Internet-based systems. This is in part due to SMEs' concerns about e-commerce that inhibit future development (Van Akkeren & Cavaye, 2000). Table 2 summarises the factors inhibiting e-business adoption in SMEs.

Thus, a range of issues may affect SMEs decisions to invest in e-business and to take advantage of future opportunities. This chapter considers whether these factors affect all SMEs, or if strategic intent acts as a moderator of the drivers and inhibitors.

Influence of Industry Sector

There is little evidence of sector affecting Internet adoption or the development of e-business in SMEs. In earlier research on IS adoption in SMEs, industrial sector is not identified as an influence (Levy & Powell, 2000). However, there is some evidence to support industry specific factors influencing e-business adoption, although it appears to be closely tied into customers' service expectations (Fillis & Wagner, 2005; Karagozoglu & Lindell, 2004). The research described here adds to the limited research in this area.

Research Questions

This research centres on three questions:

- Does strategic intent drive e-business adoption in SMEs, and is it a factor of market position or product innovation?
- Is this consistent across sectors, given research suggesting that sector is not a determining factor in ICT adoption (Levy et al., 2001)?
- How is strategic intent and industry adoption influenced by the enablers and inhibitors of e-business adoption?

Research Approach

This research is designed to capture data about the strategic intent of SMEs, as defined by the Ansoff framework. Additionally, data about the current and future use of the Internet are collected. The survey asks SMEs about the importance of e-business and what they consider to be the drivers and inhibitors.

The survey is part of a major study into e-business undertaken throughout the UK West Midlands, a region regarded by the European Union as in need of development. The data were collected by telephone with the respondent being the SME owner who is knowledgeable about strategic intent.

A total of 1,403 firms responded. This was reduced to 354 usable responses here for a number of reasons. Some responses were obtained from firms that could not be considered to be SMEs. They were often small business units operating within larger organisations (the 136 responses from the Education and Health Sectors were examples of this). Microfirms that had no intention of using technology to grow their business were also excluded—those that did not use PCs, and those sectors that displayed little evidence of strategic intent. For example, the construction industry was removed from the sample as 80% of the firms aimed to stay within existing markets and existing products. This contrasted with other sectors that had over 50% of SMEs moving towards new products and new markets.

For some of the more detailed analyses on drivers and inhibitors for e-business, firms that did not answer all questions were excluded. This is reflected in the lower number of firms shown in Tables 6a and 6b.

Dimensions of Analysis

The two dimensions used in the analysis are shown in Table 3.

Industry sector differences are investigated through manufacturing, wholesale/retail, and business services sectors which represent the main categories within the survey dataset. The differences in the sectors also demonstrate key differences, as manufacturing SMEs are often dependent upon major customers, while the other two sectors are more likely to have a broader range of customers.

Strategic intent characteristics are as defined by Ansoff (1965) and discussed earlier. SMEs that are content to stay with existing markets and products are likely to take a more conservative strategic stance than those who are either selling new products into existing markets or selling existing products into new markets. The most radical strategic stance is seen in those SMEs aiming to diversify, by selling new products into new markets.

Table 3. Dimensions of analysis for assessing strategic intent and e-business

Dimension	Characteristics	Description
Industry Sector	Manufacturing	
	Wholesale/Retail	
	Business Services	
Strategic Intent	Market Penetration	Selling existing products into existing markets
	Product Development	Selling new products into existing markets
	Market Development	Selling existing products into new markets
	Diversification	Selling new products into new markets

Strategic Intent Patterns

Respondents are asked where they expected most growth—in current or new products/services—and whether the growth would be in new or existing markets in order to assess strategic intent. The market penetration category accounts for 172 (49%) of firms, product development for 82 (23%), market development for 43 (12%), while diversification accounts for 56 firms (16%). Figure 2 presents the strategic intent by industry of the case firms.

Many SMEs start as a result of identifying a market niche for one or two products with which the owner is familiar, has knowledge to develop, and possible initial contracts. Many stay within the comfort zone of their knowledge and experience,

Figure 2. Strategic intent by industry

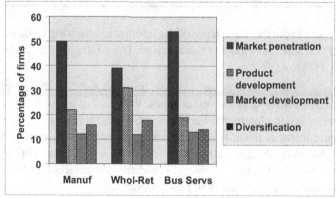

preferring not to grow beyond a certain size. Hence market penetration is their strategy of choice.

The wholesale/retail sector provides a slightly different pattern of strategic intent to the other sectors (Figure 2) perhaps reflecting market volatility, as this market requires new products more frequently. A further reason may relate to the SME-customers relationship. As many manufacturers are tied in with customers, their products are more clearly defined by a preferred supplier relationship. Given the strategic intent of most firms is limited, it is likely that the main focus of ICT will be on systems that reduce costs. Owners are less likely to invest for future growth.

Current Use of the Internet

Eighty-six percent of survey SMEs have Internet access, with little industry variation; all use e-mail. 40% of these firms use e-mail internally and externally, suggesting there is some recognition of Internet value in managing internal efficiencies as well as external communication. Fifty-three percent of the SMEs have a marketing Web site, with 56% of these updating it at least once a quarter. While there is little cross-sector difference, strategic intent does appear to drive development with over 63% of firms that are looking to introduce new products to existing markets having marketing Web sites.

Importance of the Internet in Achieving Business Growth

SMEs were asked about the importance of the Internet in achieving business growth over the next year and the responses were analysed by strategic intent and business sector jointly (Table 4).

Some important distinctions emerge: firms in business services show a clear and marked gradation across strategic intent types. While 27% of market penetration business services see the Internet as very important, this increases to 35% for those whose strategic intent is towards product development; 47% in market development; and to 59% in the diversification category. This may reflect new opportunities emerging because of the Internet. Delivery of products and services and development of new services may be more likely in business services.

Somewhat counter-intuitively, the reverse is found for manufacturers: while 25% of market penetration manufacturers view the Internet as very important, this declines

Table 4. Importance of the Internet for growth by sector and strategic intent

Strategic Intent	Sector	Unimportant (%)	Marginally Important (%)	Moderately Important (%)	Very Important (%)
Market Penetration	Manufacturing	25	28	21	25
	Wholesale-retail	21	29	21	29
	Business services	6	24	43	27
	Average	**17**	**27**	**30**	**27**
Product Development	Manufacturing	7	28	41	24
	Wholesale-retail	13	23	43	20
	Business services	4	17	39	35
	Average	**8**	**23**	**41**	**26**
Market Development	Manufacturing	19	44	19	19
	Wholesale-retail	0	58	33	8
	Business services	20	13	20	47
	Average	**14**	**37**	**23**	**26**
Diversification	Manufacturing	24	38	29	9
	Wholesale-retail	22	28	28	22
	Business services	6	18	18	59
	Average	**18**	**29**	**25**	**30**

to 24% in the product development category; to 19% in market development; and to 9% in diversification. This might reflect the well-developed relationships with customers driving Internet adoption for market penetration, while new markets are found in other ways.

The wholesale and retail sector shows more market penetration firms consider the Internet as important for strategic growth. Market development firms show little interest in the Internet. It is surprising that the Internet is not seen as a distribution method for products, although it may reflect the type of products for which the Internet is not a suitable distribution mechanism. Alternatively, it may reflect a desire not to trade outside a limited geographic area.

What is striking is that firms with a product development focus see the Internet as much more important than any of the other strategic intent categories.

Importance of E-Business

SMEs are then asked about their attitude towards e-business and its importance in three years. Fify-one percent of survey SMEs regard e-business as essential or very important. The cross-sector patterns are similar. E-business is less important for manufacturers than for the other sectors, with only 45% of SMEs considering it either essential or very important. One explanation may be the perception that e-business is about consumer trading rather than supporting customer requirements through business-to-business exchanges. This is somewhat surprising, given the emphasis placed on the importance of Electronic Data Interchange (EDI) by many major manufacturers. The other sectors, however, are only slightly more optimistic suggesting that there is still a need to educate owners about future Internet potential (Figure 3).

Table 5 shows analysis by strategic intent of firms that see e-business as essential or very important.

Clearly, firms that are most strategically conservative are less likely to see e-business as essential or very important. For example, manufacturers in the market penetration category are least likely to see it as essential or very important (34%). Interestingly, firms that intend to develop new products are more likely to see the future importance of e-business. This suggests that, contrary to current thinking, the use of technology is triggered more by a new product orientation in firms than by a new market orientation. For example, business services firms in the diversification category are most likely to see e-business as essential or very important (65%). Thus, while many SMEs can be criticised for having a too one-sided perspective on strategic development, there is a need to encourage SMEs to take a more simultaneous view of new product development *and* new market development.

Figure 3. Importance of e-business by sector

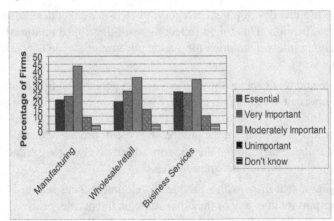

Table 5. Importance of e-business by strategic intent

Strategic Intent	Essential (%)	V. Important (%)	Both (%)
Market Penetration	23	17	40
Product Development	17	38	55
Market Development	23	28	51
Diversification	29	25	54

Drivers for E-Business

SMEs were asked to indicate the importance of nine "drivers" in encouraging them to use e-business. The respondents were asked to indicate the importance of each of the drivers on a five point scale ranging from unimportant (score 1) to very important (score 5). The drivers are:

D1: Customer demand

D2: Reduced operating costs

D3: Reduction in costs associated with sales and purchasing

D4: Improve the range and quality of services that can be offered to customers online

D5: Increase in speed of dispatch of goods

D6: Increase in speed by which supplies are obtained

D7: Avoiding loss of market share to competitors already using e-business

D8: Increase market share

Table 6a shows the mean score of firms in each strategic intent category on each of the nine drivers. The data are shown graphically in Figure 4.

The analysis reveals that there are systematic differences between the four strategic intent categories. Firms that are categorised as "market development" and "market penetration" tend to record lower importance scores on all of the drivers compared to firms that are contained in the "diversification" and "product development" categories. While firms that are contained in the market development category score lowest on all but one of our driver measures (D8: As a means to gain new customers or increase market share), firms in the product development category scored highest on five of the eight measures (D4 to D8 in Figure 4). Yet, the differences between

Figure 4. Mean scores by strategic intent of e-business drivers

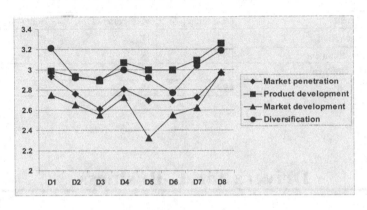

the mean scores on the driver measures, following an analysis of variance with appropriate post hoc tests, are not statistically significant at the 5% level. Consequently, while systematic differences between the four strategic intent categories are found, further research is needed to be able to confirm the findings here.

Table 6b shows the mean score of firms on each of the nine drivers by industry

Table 6a. Mean score by strategic intent for e-business drivers

Strategic intentions		E-Business Drivers							
		D1	D2	D3	D4	D5	D6	D7	D8
Market penetration	Mean	2.93	2.76	2.61	2.81	2.69	2.69	2.73	2.97
	N	153	153	153	153	153	153	153	153
Product development	Mean	2.99	2.93	2.89	3.07	3.00	3.00	3.10	3.26
	N	72	72	72	72	72	72	72	72
Market development	Mean	2.75	2.65	2.55	2.73	2.33	2.55	2.63	2.98
	N	40	40	40	40	40	40	40	40
Diversification	Mean	3.21	2.92	2.90	3.00	2.92	2.77	3.04	3.19
	N	52	52	52	52	52	52	52	52
All	Mean	2.97	2.81	2.71	2.89	2.75	2.76	2.85	3.07
	N	317	317	317	317	317	317	317	317

Table 6b. Mean score by industry for e-business drivers

Sector		D1	D2	D3	D4	D5	D6	D7	D8
Manufacturing	Mean	3.09	2.75	2.68	2.79	2.56	2.74	2.74	3.05
	N	122	122	122	122	122	122	122	122
Wholesale-retail	Mean	2.90	2.82	2.77	2.83	2.94	2.85	3.0	3.11
	N	87	87	87	87	87	87	87	87
Business services	Mean	2.90	2.88	2.71	3.06	2.83	2.71	2.86	3.06
	N	109	109	109	109	109	109	109	109
Total	Mean	2.97	2.81	2.71	2.89	2.75	2.76	2.85	3.07
	N	318	318	318	318	318	318	318	318

sector. The difference in responses between Table 6a and Table 6b is due to missing values in one firm.

The analysis by industry sector does not reveal any significant differences between the impacts of the set of drivers. This confirms earlier research that industry sector is not a factor in e-business adoption decisions.

Table 7 shows an analysis by both industry sector and strategic intent.

An analysis of Table 8 reveals that the different drivers have differing effects on the categories of firm. Customer push/demand is highest for manufacturers in the market penetration, product development, and market development categories but particularly pronounced for wholesale/retailers that are looking to diversify.

Reducing purchasing cost and operating costs are most prevalent for firms in the product development category, perhaps indicating a heightened need to reduce the cost-base of products to win market share for new products in existing markets. The need to use e-business to reduce purchasing and operating costs is particularly prevalent among market penetration wholesale/retailers—again there may be a strong emphasis on the need to reduce costs to continue to survive with existing products in existing markets. Firms looking to develop new markets seem less concerned about the use of e-business to reduce costs—perhaps this might arise after new markets are penetrated and firms need to compete more on cost than on "novelty" and innovation.

Improving the range and quality of services delivered online item is most pronounced in business services across all strategic intent categories and in wholesale/retailers looking to diversify.

The speed of dispatch driver is strongest for business services in the product development category and for diversifying wholesalers. The increased speed of supply

Table 7. Mean score for e-business drivers by industry and strategic intent

Sector	Strategic intentions		1	2	3	4	5	6	7	8
Manufacturing	Market penetration	Mean	3.21	2.66	2.57	2.70	2.61	2.75	2.61	2.93
		N	61	61	61	61	61	61	61	61
	Product development	Mean	2.85	2.88	2.88	2.73	2.58	2.65	2.96	3.12
		N	26	26	26	26	26	26	26	26
	Market development	Mean	2.87	2.60	2.40	2.87	2.27	2.60	2.53	3.07
		N	15	15	15	15	15	15	15	15
	Diversification	Mean	3.16	2.95	2.95	3.05	2.58	2.89	2.95	3.32
		N	19	19	19	19	19	19	19	19
	Total	Mean	3.08	2.74	2.68	2.79	2.55	2.74	2.73	3.05
		N	121	121	121	121	121	121	121	121
Wholesale-retail	Market penetration	Mean	2.75	2.78	2.66	2.75	2.88	2.75	2.97	3.06
		N	32	32	32	32	32	32	32	32
	Product development	Mean	3.00	2.92	2.88	3.08	3.27	3.35	3.12	3.27
		N	26	26	26	26	26	26	26	26
	Market development	Mean	2.33	2.17	2.50	2.17	2.17	2.25	2.33	2.50
		N	12	12	12	12	12	12	12	12
	Diversification	Mean	3.41	3.18	3.00	3.06	3.12	2.71	3.35	3.41
		N	17	17	17	17	17	17	17	17
	Total	Mean	2.90	2.82	2.77	2.83	2.94	2.85	3.00	3.11
		N	87	87	87	87	87	87	87	87
Business services	Market penetration	Mean	2.75	2.85	2.62	2.95	2.68	2.60	2.72	2.95
		N	60	60	60	60	60	60	60	60
	Product development	Mean	3.15	3.00	2.90	3.50	3.20	3.00	3.25	3.45
		N	20	20	20	20	20	20	20	20
	Market development	Mean	3.00	3.15	2.77	3.08	2.54	2.77	3.00	3.31
		N	13	13	13	13	13	13	13	13
	Diversification	Mean	3.06	2.62	2.75	2.88	3.13	2.69	2.81	2.81
		N	16	16	16	16	16	16	16	16
	Total	Mean	2.90	2.88	2.71	3.06	2.83	2.71	2.86	3.06
		N	109	109	109	109	109	109	109	109
		N	317	317	317	317	317	317	317	317

items is most prevalent in the product development strategic intent category as is concern about the loss of market share and winning new customers. Clearly, the product development category emerges as a class of business with a specific and pronounced set of needs and concerns about the move to e-business. Firms in this category have a great interest in e-business given their need to:

- Reduce operating costs and costs associated with sales and purchasing;
- Increase speed in doing business (important in generating customer satisfaction/lock-in);
- Win new customers; and
- Avoid losing their existing customer base.

Inhibitors of E-Business Adoption

Respondents are asked whether, and to what degree, they agree with nine statements that may discourage them from adopting e-business. The statements involve:

I1: Concerns abut confidentiality

I2: Concerns about the risk of fraud

I3: Technology costs associated with e-business development being too high

I4: Poor public telecommunications infrastructure inhibiting technological development

I5: Obtaining authorisation for credit card clearance

I6: IT skills shortages among the workforce

I7: Lack of management willingness to adopt IT as an obstacle to further e-business development

I8: Further e-business development offers no tangible benefits

I9: Further e-business development is not relevant

The overall rating of the nine inhibitors is shown in Table 8.

This confirms findings in the literature that concerns about confidentiality, fraud, and technology costs are inhibitors to investing in e-business. Additionally, the process of obtaining authorisation to clear cards is a major inhibitor. Lack of IT skills and lack of management willingness to adopt are not seen as inhibitors. This

Table 8. Mean scores for inhibitors for e-business

Inhibitor	Mean score
Concerns about confidentiality	3.62
Obtaining authorisation to clear cards	3.59
Concern about the risk of fraud	3.56
Technology costs	3.26
Poor public telecommunications infrastructure	3.08
E-commerce development offers no tangible benefits	2.92
E-commerce development is not relevant	2.82
IT skills shortages amongst workforce	2.79
Lack of management willingness to adopt it	2.70

Table 9. E-business inhibitors by sector and strategic intent

Strategic intentions		I1 Net agree	I2 Net agree	I3 Net agree	I4 Net agree	I5 Net agree	I6 Net agree	I7 Net agree	I8 Net agree	I9 Net agree
Market Penetration	Manufacturing	29	33	0.	-13	-1	-51	-33	-16	-28
	Wholesale-retail	3	-3	-31	-22	-19	-19	-44	-16	-31
	Business services	37	25	13	-13	-20	-28	-33	-25	-20
	Average	**27**	**22**	**-1**	**-15**	**-19**	**-35**	**-35**	**-20**	**-25**
Product Development	Manufacturing	35	31	4	-15	-31	-12	-35	-19	-19
	Wholesale-retail	-8	4	0	-4	-31	-23	-42	-23	-35
	Business services	-10	-5	-4	-20	-30	-15	-40	-15	10
	Average	**7**	**11**	**-10**	**-12**	**-31**	**-17**	**-39**	**-19**	**-17**
Market Development	Manufacturing	-7	-13	0	-13	-13	-33	-33	-27	-20
	Wholesale-retail	58	0	-8	-50	-42	-58	-58	-50	-33
	Business services	62	54	38	8	15	-38	-54	-61	-54
	Average	**35**	**12**	**10**	**-17**	**-12**	**-42**	**-47**	**-45**	**-35**
Diversification	Manufacturing	37	58	-11	-5	-11	-5	0	-5	-5
	Wholesale-retail	29	29	23	-24	-6	-41	-35	-23	-24
	Business services	44	37	12	12	19	-19	-19	-25	-12
	Average	**36**	**42**	**8**	**-6**	**0.1**	**-21**	**-17**	**-17**	**-13**
	Overall	**25**	**22**	**0**	**-13**	**-15**	**-29**	**-34**	**-23**	**-23**

suggests that SME managers are aware of the potential from e-business, but need to be convinced of its benefits to their firms.

Table 9 enables differences between industry sectors and strategic intentions to be explored for potential inhibitors to e-business. Respondents are offered five categories of response ranging from totally agree (score 5) to totally disagree (score 1) for each of the nine inhibitors. A "net agree" score is calculated for each category of firm on each factor. The net score adds together those agreeing or strongly agreeing and subtracts those disagreeing or strongly disagreeing. Thus, the higher the number, the more respondents agree with the statement.

There is a net positive view that firms are concerned about confidentiality and fraud over the Internet, and these views are most pronounced among diversifying SMEs. The net agree score for confidentiality and fraud in firms in the market development category is 36 and 42 respectively and these are higher than any other strategic intent category. There are particular concerns about confidentiality and fraud among business service SMEs in the market development, diversify, and market penetration categories, together with wholesale/retailers in market development (confidentiality only). Business service firms in the product development category seem less concerned about confidentiality and fraud than business service firms in other strategic intent categories.

As to technology costs being excessive, the "jury is still out." Although there are concerns about technology costs in the business services market development and the wholesale/retail diversify categories, this is countered by low scores in the wholesale/retail market penetration and the business services product development categories. Concerns about credit card clearance do not seem to be an issue except in the business services diversify and market development categories—the only two categories to record a positive net agree score.

A skill shortage measure gets a strong negative score across the board. Skill shortages are more evident in firms that wish to develop new products for existing markets or develop new markets and new products, suggesting that skills may be more of an issue where the objective is to develop new products. Manufacturers in the diversify category are more likely to experience skills shortages than all other classes of firm, followed by manufacturers in the product development category.

Management unwillingness achieves a high negative net agree score. The diversify manufacturers are radically different as it is the only sector to reveal any significant negativity among managers. Both the "not relevant" and "no benefits" measures have negative scores across the board, but negativity is less pronounced in manufacturing diversification.

Discussion

Three research questions are posed here. The first question focused on whether strategic intent drives e-business adoption and whether it is a function of market position or product innovation. This research shows that those SMEs remaining in their existing markets are the least likely to invest, primarily due to the Internet not being seen as necessary for growth and less interest in winning new customers. This supports research by McGregor and Vrazalic (2005) in a study of SMEs in Sweden and Australia which indicates that nonadoption is due to the unsuitability of e-business for the the delivery of product or services; the way the SME does business, its customers approach to business and lack of benefits. The main finding from the analysis in this chapter is that product innovation rather than market penetration drives e-business in SMEs. This counters current thinking that market penetration is the more critical.

The second research question is whether industry sector is a determining factor in e-business adoption. Only just over half of the SMEs in all sectors believe that e-business is very important or essential. There is some sectoral difference when firms are asked the importance of the Internet for growth. Over 35% of business service firms see the Internet as very important. This compares with just over 20% for manufacturing and wholesale/retail. More research is required to confirm whether there is industry differentiation and the nature of that differentiation.

The final research question asked whether the enablers and inhibitors of e-business adoption varied by strategic intent or industry. There is little differentiation between industry sectors or strategic intent perspectives with customer demand, increasing market share, avoiding loss of market share, and improving online services to customers are seen as vital to most firms. These findings concur with existing research. This suggests that SMEs believe that their market niches are their strengths and these are where they should continue to compete. The main difference is in the wholesale/retail sector where being able to dispatch goods more quickly is seen as the main driver. This may indicate that this is a more highly competitive market and that firms need to be efficient to survive. Other efficiency factors are generally seen as less important. The key difference in strategic intent is that those firms pushing new products into existing markets perceive the need to improve online services to customers as of lesser importance that reducing operating costs.

Turning to the inhibitors concerns about confidentiality, fraud, and the high cost of e-business are the main deterrents across all sectors and strategic intent groups. This is similar to findings in the literature. In contrast to the literature, most SMEs here do not believe that limited IT skills in the workforce nor management unwillingness are issues except in more innovative firms looking to develop new products in new markets. This might be due to firm age and existing skills bases. SMEs also believe to a lesser degree that e-business is both relevant and may offer some benefit to the firm.

Thus, it appears that the pressure to adopt is likely to be driven by external factors rather than internal ones. This may go some way to explain the cautious approach of SMEs to Internet adoption; given their resource constraints, they may be waiting for signs from the market that the investment is required.

Management Perspective

There is evidence here that strategic intent affects Internet adoption and decisions to invest in e-business in SMEs. This may be better understood by not considering SMEs as a homogeneous group which much of the literature does. There are various ways in which SMEs may be classified but a useful starting point is to consider SME attitude to ICT investment. Levy et al. (2001) identify four different scenarios followed by SMEs towards ICT investment. These scenarios are demonstrated in the Focus-Dominance model (Figure 5).

The different scenarios clearly suggest separate strategic intents. The efficiency scenario is found when SMEs are starting up. There are some SMEs that are in business for the "lifestyle advantages" for their owners (Hay & Kamshad, 1994). They are, thus, only interested in selling their current products into existing markets and market penetration is the espoused strategic intent. Their use of ICT mirrors this. These organisations usually have simple, stand-alone systems possibly with a simple Web site (Levy et al., 2001). This research shows that the main driver for e-business for these firms is customer demand. While customer demand and improving online services are also important, they are considerably less so. The lack of resources in most SMEs is likely to be more prevalent in this group and limits e-business adoption. Inhibitors are similar to other categories with confidentiality and fraud being most important. Thus, it is the drivers that are likely to be the main factors in decisions to invest. The market is clearly not yet demanding such investment.

Figure 5. Focus-dominance model (Levy et al., 2001)

Customer Dominance	Low	Coordination	Repositioning
	High	Efficiency	Collaboration
		Cost	Value Added

Strategic Focus

The coordination scenario is found as businesses grow. The businesses here are increasingly looking to sell their products into new markets, in other words, market development. They are looking for steady growth for their existing products. They utilise more sophisticated information systems to allow them to do this including the development of intranets and often externally focused e-mail to work with customers (Levy & Powell, 2003). The e-business driver and inhibitor profile is similar to market penetration. The main difference is that these firms are often larger and have more structure, hence the stronger feeling that management unwillingness, skill shortages, and lack of benefits are more strongly disputed. There is, again, little evidence of market demand for investment in e-business.

Product development is the focus of the collaboration scenario. This group of SMEs is usually closely allied to a few major customers and develops new products to support their requirements. These SMEs are looking for growth, but through the development of the customer relationship. The information systems here include the use of electronic data interchange and often extranets. Winning new customers is seen as critical for this group with customer demand and avoiding loss of market share as important. Many of these firms work closely with a small group of customers where the loss of one can be catastrophic. The search for a replacement occupies a lot of time. Thus, customer demand is taken very seriously and is often a requirement to maintain preferred supplier status. Reduced operating costs are important to this group of firms to a far greater degree than others, as most of their customers are large firms that can exert a lot of pressure. For this group the inhibitors are less of an issue.

While the SMEs in the coordination and collaboration quadrants are often looking for steady growth, the final group in the repositioning scenario sees diversification as the way forward as they are looking for rapid growth. This often means different delivery means of products but also developing new product to satisfy their markets. This group is likely to put ICT at the centre of the business growth strategy. Interestingly customer demand is high in this group, while winning new customers is lower. This is surprising as it might be expected that diversification is about gaining a broader customer base. It might be that these firms are responding to what they see as customer demand by changing their business. Again, confidentiality and fraud are seen as important inhibitors that may not be surprising as these firms are taking a risk in diversification.

Conclusion

Using survey data from SMEs, this chapter investigates e-business use and drivers by posing three questions—does strategic intent drive e-business adoption and is it a factor of market position or product innovation? Is this consistent across sectors?

And how is strategic intent and industry adoption influenced by the enablers and inhibitors of e-business adoption? The research demonstrates that strategic intent influences decisions to invest in e-business. Those SMEs remaining in their existing markets are the least likely to invest, primarily due to the Internet not being seen as necessary for growth. Product innovation rather than market penetration drives e-business. This is explored through e-business drivers and inhibitors that provide insights into uses. Finally, a model of SME information communication technologies investment that does not treat SMEs as a homogeneous group is used to further understand the processes involved here.

References

Angehrn, A. (1997). Designing mature Internet business strateiges: The ICDT model. *European Management Journal, 15*(4), 361-369.

Ansoff, I. (1965). *Corporate strategy.* McGraw-Hill.

Bianchi, C., & Bivona, E. (2002). Opportunities and pitfalls related to e-commerce strategies in small-medium firms: A systems dynamics approach. *Systems Dynamics Review, 18*(3), 403-429.

Brown, D., & Lockett, N. (2004). Potential of critical e-applications for engaging SMEs in e-business: A provider perspective. *European Journal of Information Systems, 13*, 21-34.

Chapman, P., James-Moore, M., Szczygiel, M., & Thompson, D. (2000). Building Internet capabilities in SMEs. *Logistics Information Management, 13*(6), 353-360.

Currie, W. (2000). *The global information society.* Chichester, UK: John Wiley & Sons.

Dendridge, T., & Levenburg, N. (2000). Hi-tech potential: An exploratory study of very small firms usage of the Internet. *International Small Business Journal, 18*(2), 81-121.

Daniel, E., & Grimshaw, D. (2002). An exploratory comparison of electronic commerce adoption in large and small enterprises. *Journal of Information Technology, 17*, 133-147.

Evans, R. (2002). E-commerce, competitivenss and local and regional governance in greater Manchester and Merseyside: A preliminary assessment. *Urban Studies, 39*(5-6), 947-975.

Feeny, D. (2000). E-opportunity: The strategic marketing perspective. In L. Willcocks, C. Sauer, & Associates (Eds.), *Moving to e-business,* pp. 143-167. Random House.

Fillis, I., & Wagner, B. (2005). E-business development: An exploratory investigation of the small firm. *International Small Business Journal, 23*(6), 604-634.

Grandon, E., & Pearson, J. (2004). E-commerce adoption: Perceptions of manager/ owners of small and medium sized firms in Chile. *Communications of the Association for Information Systems, 13,* 81-102.

Hay, M., & Kamshad, K. (1994). Small firm growth: Intentions, implementation and impediments. *Business Strategy Review, 5*(3), 49-68.

Jeffcoate, J., Chappell, C., & Feindt, S. (2004). Assessing the impact of e-commerce on SMEs in value chains: A qualitative approach. In N. Al-Qirim (Ed.), *Electronic commerce in small to medium-sized enterprises: Frameworks, issues and implications,* pp. 180-198. Hershey, PA: Idea Group Publishing.

Karagozoglu, N., & Lindell, M. (2004). Electronic commerce strategy, operations and performance in small and medium-sized enterprises. *Journal of Small Business and Enterprise Development, 11*(3), 290-301.

Keindl, B. (2000). Competitive dynamics and new business models for SMEs in the virtual marketplace. *Journal of Developmental Entrepreneurship, 5*(1), 73-85.

Kendall, J., Tung, L., Chua, K., Ng, D., & Tan, S. (2001). Receptivity of Singapore's SMEs to electronic commerce adoption. *Journal of Strategic Information Systems, 10,* 223-242.

Klein, L.R., & Quelch, J.A. (1997). Business-to-business market making on the Internet. *International Marketing Review, 14*(5), 345-361.

Kowtha, N., & Choon, T. (2001). Determinants of Website development: A study of electronic commerce in Singapore. *Information and Management, 39,* 227-242.

Lawson, R., Alcock, C., Cooper, J., & Burgess, L. (2003). Factors affecting adoption of electronic commerce technologies by SMEs: An Australian study. *Journal of Small Business and Enterprise Development, 10*(3), 265-276.

Levy, M., & Powell, P. (2000). Information systems strategy in SMEs: An organizational perspective. *Journal of Strategic Information Systems, 9*(1), 63-84.

Levy, M., & Powell, P. (2003). SME Internet adoption: Towards a contingent model. *Electronic Markets, 13*(2), 173-181.

Levy, M., Powell, P., & Yetton, P. (2001). SMEs: Aligning IS and the strategic context. *Journal of Information Technology, 16,* 133-144.

Lunati, M. (2000). *SMEs & electronic commerce: An overview* (Tech Rep. No. DST/IND/PME(2000)11). OECD, Directorate for Science, Technology and Industry Committee.

McGregor, R., & Vrazalic, L. (2005). A basic model of electronic commerce adoption barriers. *Journal of Small Business and Enterprise Development, 12*(4), 510-527.

Mehrtens, J., Cragg, P., & Mills, A. (2001). A model of Internet adoption by SMEs. *Information and Management, 39*, 165-176.

Poon, S. (2000). Business environment and Internet commerce benefit: Small business perspective. *European Journal of Information Systems, 9*, 72-81.

Poon, S., & Swatman, P. (1999). An exploratory study of small business Internet commerce issues. *Information and Management, 35*, 9-18.

Premkumar, G., & Roberts, M. (1999). Adoption of new information technologies in rural small businesses. *Omega, International Journal of Management Science, 27*, 467-484.

Quayle, M. (2002). E-commerce: The challenge for UK SMEs in the twenty-first century. *International Journal of Operations and Production Management, 22*(10), 1148-1161.

Quayle, M., & Christiansen, J. (2004). Business issues in the 21st century: An empirical study of e-commerce adoption in UK and Denmark SMEs. In N. Al-Qirim (Ed.), *Electronic commerce in small to medium-sized enterprises: Frameworks, issues and implications,* pp. 53-68. Hershey, PA: Idea Group Publishing.

Ramsey, E., Ibbotson, P., Bell J., & Gray, B. (2003), E-opportunities of service sector SMEs: an irish cross-border study, *Journal of small business and enterprise development, 10*(3), 250-264.

Riemenschneider, C., Harrison, D., & Mykytyn, P. (2003). Understanding IT adoption decisions in small business: Integrating current theories. *Information and Management, 40*, 269-285.

Sadowski, B., Maitland, C., & van Dongen, J. (2002). Strategic use of the Internet by small and medium-sized companies: An exploratory study. *Information Economics and Policy, 14*, 75-93.

Santarelli, E., & D'Altri, S. (2003). The diffusion of e-commerce among SMEs: Theoretical implications and empirical evidence. *Small Business Economics, 21*, 272-283.

Sauer, C. (2000). Managing the infrastructure challenge. In L. Willcocks, C. Sauer, & Associates (Eds.), *Moving to e-business,* pp. 57-79. Random House.

Sharma, S., Wichramasinghe, N., & Gupta, J. (2004). What should SMEs do to succeed in todays knowledge-based economy? In N. Al Qirim (Ed.), *Electronic commerce in small to medium-sized enterprises: Frameworks, issues and implications,* pp.289-303. Hershey, PA: Idea Group Publishing.

Sillence, J., MacDonald, S., Lefang, B., & Frost, B. (1998). Email adoption, diffusion, use and impact with small firms. *International Journal of Information Management, 18*(4), 231-242.

Simpson, M., & Docherty, A. (2004). E-commerce adoption support and advice for UK SMEs. *Journal of Small Business and Enterprise Development, 11*(3), 315-328.

Standing, C., Sims, I., & Stockdale, R. (2003, June 15-17). Can e-marketplaces bridge the digital divide? In *Proceedings of the Working Conference on Information Systems Perspectives and Challenges in the Context of Globalization* (pp. 339-353).

Storey, D.J. (1994). *Understanding the small business sector.* London: Routledge.

Teo, T., & Pian, Y. (2003). A contingency perspective on Internet adoption and competitive advantage. *European Journal of Information Systems, 12*, 78-92.

Tse, T., & Soufani, K. (2003). Business strategies for small firms in the new economy. *Journal of Small Business and Enterprise Development, 10*(3), 306-319.

Van Akkeren, J., & Cavaye, A. (2000). Factors affecting entry-level Internet technology adoption by small firms in Australia. *Journal of Systems and Information Technology, 3*(2), 33-47.

Willcocks, L., & Sauer, C. (2000). Moving to e-business: An introduction. In L. Willcocks, C. Sauer, & Associates (Eds.), *Moving to e-business,* pp. 1-18. Random House.

Zhu, K., Kramer, K., & Xu, S. (2003). Electronic business adoption by European firms: A cross-country assessment of the facilitators and inhibitors. *European Journal of Information Systems, 12*, 251-268.

Chapter XII

Understanding Web Site Usability:
The Influence of Web Site Design Parameters

Monideepa Tarafdar, University of Toledo, USA

Jie (Jennifer) Zhang, University of Toledo, USA

Abstract

Web site usability is concerned with how easy and intuitive it is for individuals to learn to use and interact with a Web site. It is a measure of the quality of a Web site's presence, as perceived by users. The usability of Web sites is important because high usability is associated with a positive attitude and greater trust towards the Web site. Poorly designed Web sites with low usability lead to negative financial impacts. Existing approaches to Web site usability include measurement and tracking of parameters such as response time and task completion time, and software engineering approaches that specify general usability guidelines and common practices during software development. This chapter analyzes usability from the point of view of Web site design parameters. An analysis of usability and other design characteristics of 200 Web sites of different kinds revealed that design aspects such as information content, ease of navigation, download delay, and Web site availability positively influence usability. Web site security and customization were not found to influence usability. The chapter explains these results and suggests design strategies for increasing Web site usability.

Introduction

Web site usability is concerned with how easy and intuitive it is for individuals to learn to use and interact with a Web site, in order to quickly and easily accomplish their tasks on it (Preece, 2001). It is typically a measure of the quality of a Web site's presence, as perceived by users (Agarwal & Venkatesh, 2002; John & Bass, 2001). That is, Web sites which are highly usable are easy to learn, remember, and use. Web site usability is derived from a broader framework of system usability, as described in concepts from the literature on human computer interaction (HCI) (Schneiderman, 1998). The primary premise of HCI studies is that the design of information systems should include features and characteristics that make it easy for users to interact with and use the system.

The usability of Web sites is important for a number of reasons (Huang, 2002). First, the World Wide Web (WWW) is an open and connected environment and switching Web sites is easy. To ensure that people actually stay with a Web site until the transaction is completed, the Web site needs to be usable. In this context, Ellis and Kurniawan (2000) state that browsers often do not wait to complete their transactions on Web sites that are not user friendly, do not facilitate the retrieval of information, and do not present the information in a well organized and relevant form. Second, the WWW provides access to an increasing range of information, products, and services. Its users range from experts to novices, and have dramatically different expectations and skills. Hence it is important to understand the factors that increase Web site usability, for different kinds of browsers. Third, prior research suggests that high usability is associated with user-related positive outcomes such as a reduction in the number of user errors (Siau, 2003-2004) and a more positive attitude towards the Web site (Lecerof & Paterno, 1998; Nielsen, 2000). Fourth, greater Web site usability leads to greater user trust and loyalty for the Web site. Carlos, Guinalíu, and Gurrea (2006) performed a study to determine the influence of perceived usability on the user's loyalty to Web sites. The results showed that greater Web site usability was associated with increased loyalty towards the Web site and greater satisfaction from it.

Finally, the Web site is the interface through which employees and customers interact with the organization. In that sense, it is analogous to a brick and mortar store. High Web site usability is therefore akin to a user-friendly and pleasant store environment and influences the Web site traffic. It gives an impression of a strong customer orientation and services mindedness (Heldal, Sjovold, & Heldal, 2004). Likewise, low usability portrays the opposite of these sentiments.

Financial and economic impacts of poor usability have also been documented. Landauer (1996), for example, found that inadequate use of usability engineering methods in software and Web site development projects costs the U.S. economy $30 billion per year in lost productivity. According to the consulting firm A.T. Kearney, poor Web site usability costs e-tailers almost $4 billion in potential revenue, as many prospective purchasers do not actually complete the transactions they start. In a similar vein, Forrester research (see Manning, McCarthy, & Souza, 1998) estimated that 50% of potential sales from a Web site are lost when visitors to a Web site cannot find the relevant product, services, or information. They also found that almost 40% of visitors do not return to a site when their first visit results in a negative experience. Taken together, these two factors can result in potential losses of millions of dollars annually due to poor usability, for a reasonably large Web site. At the same time, in a longitudinal study of 98 commercial Web sites, Yeung and Lu (2004) showed that while the sampled Web sites generally grew larger in content, their usability characteristics were only marginally enhanced over time.

Considering all of the above, it is clear that usability is one of the most important characteristics of Web sites. This has been described succinctly by Nielsen (2000), who suggests that "usability rules the Web." If the user cannot conveniently use a Web site to find a product or service, that user would not buy it.

Different approaches have been adopted in order to study usability (Huang, 2002). System designers have taken a software engineering approach and have specified general usability guidelines, principles, and common practices that would ensure that the system is found "usable" by its users (Nielsen, 2000; Pearrow, 2000; Schneiderman, 1998). Practitioners have stressed specific Web site usability features such as response time, task completion time, and error rates (Huang, 2002). Beliefs about the task value and user friendliness form the basis of present theories about user acceptance of technologies. Technology acceptance model (Venkatesh & Davis, 2000) related characteristics such as "ease of use," "user friendliness," "perceived usefulness," and "self reported user satisfaction" have also been found to correlate with and explain Web site usability (Karhanna & Straub, 1999). In a recent article, Agerfalk and Eriksson (2004) have described the concepts of "action oriented modeling" and "actability." They suggest that systems should be designed so that they are "actable"; that is, they enable users to perform the desired actions. Hence they should be designed, keeping in mind the specific information processing requirements, in terms of content and storage.

It has been suggested (Nielsen, 2000; Palmer, 2002; Schneiderman, 1998) that Web site usability can be increased by incorporating appropriate elements and features in the design, and poor Web site design has been a key element in many Web site failures (see, for example, the case of Boo.com, described in Turban & Laudon, 2004). Therefore it is important to explore the effects of design parameters such as network delays, navigation strategies, and layout and information content, on the usability of Web sites and Web-based systems (Sears, 2000). In this study, we look at usability from the point of view of Web site design parameters. The chapter is based on an analysis of usability and other design characteristics of 200 Web sites of different kinds. The objective was to identify the antecedent influence of various

Web site design parameters on usability, with the aim of suggesting strategies for increasing the usability.

Literature Survey and Hypothesis Formulation

The definition of usability has been a problem and a well defined set of usability criteria is not available (Agarwal & Venkatesh, 2002; Gray & Salzman, 1998; Huang, 2002). Indeed Sears (2000) suggests that usability is an elusive, comprehensive, and complex concept. It is difficult to analyze because it is contingent upon the system and its users and since Web users are highly diverse in terms of their computing experiences, it is not easy to design a system to fit everyone's needs (Huang, 2002).

There are different frameworks within which usability can be investigated. According to Palmer (2002), prior to the widespread use of the WWW, usability of information systems, in general, was equivalent to a set of design principles that articulated elements such as the consistency of the interface, system response time, semantics and metaphors, interaction styles, and the use of multimedia. As the WWW became an increasingly essential interface, usability research focused on extending existing principles to the domain of the Web site. Nielsen (2000) and Schneiderman (1998) extended these design principles for the Web and suggested four parameters for usability: navigation, response time, credibility, and content.

Microsoft Usability Guidelines, analyzed with respect to Web sites in Agarwal and Venkatesh (2002), suggest that the Web site content, ease of use, promotion, and emotional content are important aspects of usability. In another framework, Rosen and Lloyd (2004) suggest that Web site usability should address users' needs of understanding and exploration. Accordingly, they describe three dimensions of usability. The coherence dimension includes a logical and friendly environment, ease of navigation, and clarity of design. Complexity implies that the Web site should contain a variety of information and images which can be explored by the user. Legibility refers to the creation of a consistent and distinct design for the Web site. Muylle, Moenaert, and Despontin (2004) conceptualized and empirically validated a Web site user satisfaction construct having four dimensions: layout, information (relevancy, accuracy, comprehensibility, and comprehensiveness), connection (ease of use, entry guidance, structure, hyperlink connotation, and speed), and language customization.

Other measures of usability include task completion time at the Web site, and throughput, or number of tasks performed per unit time (Huang, 2002). Subjective measures include enjoyment, playfulness, intention to use, familiarity, aesthetic, and perceived systems quality (Lecerof & Paterno, 1998).

Broadly speaking, therefore, factors which affect Web site usability are related to the content and layout of information, navigation properties, and technical parameters such as download time. Based on these discussions, we now frame the hypotheses for the study.

Information Content

From actability principles, Agerfalk et al. (2004) suggest that information processed and stored in any system should be such that it enables users to perform desired tasks through the system. From basic usability principles, authors suggest that users like information systems that provide comprehensive information. This was reported in a study of the "INFO" system, the computer system at the Sydney Olympic Games, designed by IBM (Healy & Herder, 2002). Information content is therefore an important characteristic of Web sites (Gehrke & Turban, 1999; Palmer, 2002) and is a predictor of online sales (Bellman & Lohse, 1999; Venkatesh, Ramesh, & Massey, 2003). Content includes the variety, amount (Evans & Wuster, 2000), quality (Katteranukul & Siau, 1999; Schneiderman, 1998; Shapiro & Varian, 1999), and usefulness of information (Eighmey & McCord, 1998).

Hence we frame the first hypothesis.

Hypothesis 1: *The information content of the Web site positively influences Web site usability.*

Ease of Navigation

The ease of navigation depends on the way in which information is organized on the Web site. Good links, navigation mechanisms, graphical design, and layout are prime components in making the page easier to use.

Users often have navigation-related difficulties in using the WWW (Preece, 2001). For example, they often cannot identify where they are and cannot return to previously visited locations. This is known as *disorientation* (Park & Kim, 2000). Disoriented users do not know how they arrived at a particular page, where to go next, where the information is, and how to get there. In a related concept, *cognitive overhead* is the effort and concentration necessary to maintain several tasks at one time. Web site users have to perform many tasks (browsing, remembering sequences, moving from item to item, and comparing items) simultaneously and this causes them to experience cognitive overload, because of which, they may get lost (Kim & Hirtle, 1995).

All of this leads to problems of navigability (Park & Kim, 2000). Navigability denotes the ease that users can navigate the Web site. It is determined by the number and nature of hyperlinks (Machlis, 1998) and their sequence and layout (Nielsen, 2000; Randall, 1997). Effective links help make the page easier to use. For instance, hyperlinks should be at places where they are easy to see, are fairly large and surrounded by dead spaces (Ellis & Kurniawan, 2000). Further, contextual information such as a hierarchical structure of hyperlinks helps to provide context to the information and eases the navigability of the Web site. Effective use of hypermedia (Schubert & Selz, 1997; Siau, 2003-2004) and graphical content (Belkin, 2000; Huang, 2002) also increases navigability.

The previous arguments lead us to the second hypothesis.

Hypothesis 2: *The navigation properties of the Web site positively influence Web site usability.*

Download Speed

In the context of information systems in general, the response time of a system affects system usability (McLaughlin & Skinner, 2000). Analogously, the download time of a Web site influences its usability. The download time is crucial because the WWW being an open system, it is easy to switch from one Web site to another (Gehrke & Turban, 1999; Pitkow & Kehoe, 1996; Rose, Khoo, & Straub, 1999). Heldal et al. (2004) suggest that users will tolerate only 10 seconds of inactivity before switching to a different Web site.

Hence we frame the third hypothesis.

Hypothesis 3: *The download speed associated with a Web site positively influences Web site usability.*

Customization and Personalization

As customers buy more and more goods from different "stores" on the Web, there is an increase in the number of different Web sites they use and have to remember the details of. Customization and personalization determine the extent to which a Web site fits the needs of specific users. Customization enhances users' comfort and hence increases the usability of the system (Huang, 2002; Siau, 2003-2004). Customization also provides flexibility and control regarding the content and organization of the information they want (Huang, 2002) and facilitates interactivity (Schubert & Selz,

1997). The ability to customize and personalize Web pages therefore is a critical element and can considerably influence the usability of the Web site. Customization is also referred to as "made-for-the-medium" (Agarwal & Venkatesh, 2002).

This leads us to the fourth hypothesis.

Hypothesis 4: *The customization and personalization properties associated with a Web site positively influence Web site usability.*

Security

Security is one of the most critical characteristics of Web sites engaged in e-commerce transactions and is an important predictor of users' trust in a Web site (Torkzadeh & Dhillon, 2002). This is because of the rise in the amount of sensitive information exchanged over the Internet as a result of increasing B2B e-commerce, and also because of the increasing amounts of personal information, such as social security numbers and credit card numbers being stored on Web servers and database servers, as a result of B2C e-commerce (Gehrke & Turban, 1999; Huang, 2002). Users may simply not use a system that they perceive as insecure.

Hence we state the fifth hypothesis.

Hypothesis 5: *Web site security positively influences Web site usability.*

Availability and Accessibility

Perceived accessibility of technology has been found to be related to technology use in general (El Sawy, 1985; Swanson, 1985). The more accessible an information system is, the less effort it takes to use it (Karhanna & Straub, 1999). In the context of Web sites, too, accessibility and availability are important, especially because customers cannot use a Web site that is not regularly and consistently available.

Therefore our sixth hypothesis states:

Hypothesis 6: *Web site accessibility positively influences Web site usability.*

We summarize all of the hypotheses in the research in Table 1.

Table 1. Summary of hypotheses

Hypothesized Factors Influencing Usability	Hypothesis
Information Content	1: The information content of the Web site positively influences Web site usability
Ease of Navigation	2: The navigation properties of the Web site positively influence Web site usability
Download Speed	3: The download speed associated with a Web site (that is, the time that it takes to download pages) positively influences Web site usability
Customization and Personalization	4: The customization and personalization properties associated with a Web site positively influence Web site usability
Security	5: Web site security positively influences Web site usability
Availability and Accessibility	6: Web site accessibility positively influences Web site usability

Research Method

The research was conducted in several steps, as depicted in Figure 1.

The different Web site characteristics described in the second section were summarized and incorporated into a survey questionnaire. A set of 46 questions was formulated to measure and evaluate characteristics of Web sites. Each item was designed as a five-point Likert Scale, and described an aspect of a specific Web site characteristic. The questionnaire was pretested for general correctness and content validity (Kerlinger, 2002; Venkataraman & Grant, 1986), by administering it to six e-commerce researchers and academics. The questionnaire was subsequently refined on the basis of their feedback and suggestions.

Next, we used the Nielsen NetRatings database to select Web sites for this study. NetRatings has a widely used Internet measurement database that provides online data about Web site traffic patterns. It also ranks Web sites based on specific parameters related to Web site traffic such as the number of times a Web site has been viewed. We wanted our sample of Web sites to be as representative as possible, so we chose Web sites from different categories or different domains, based on their

Figure 1. Research framework

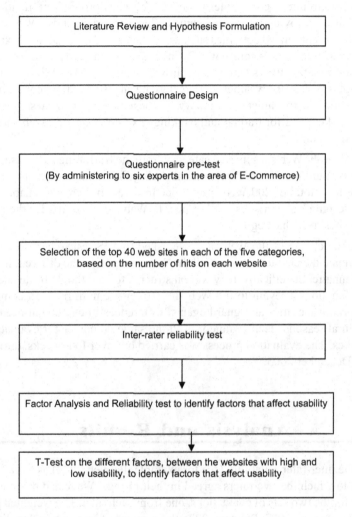

functions. The categories include portals and search engines, retail, entertainment, news and information, and financial services. Portals and search engines include Web sites whose primary purpose is to provide varied and wide-ranging information over a wide variety of sources (www.yahoo.com), or detailed information over a narrow range of topics (www.iboats.com), which is a portal dedicated to resources on boats. This category also includes Web sites that have search facilities, such as www.google.com. The primary purpose of retail Web sites is selling to customers using a B2C (business-to-customer) model. These include general retail Web sites such as www.amazon.com and www.target.com, as well as category retail Web sites such as www.circuitcity.com. Entertainment Web sites provide information and content regarding movies, music, and games. This category includes Web sites that offer entertainment related activities such as casinos and online gaming. Examples include www.Gamewinners.com, www.Casinoonthenet.com, and www.movies.com. News and information Web sites describe current events and provide information on specific topics such as the weather, jobs, real estate, and so forth. Examples include www.cnn.com, www.weather.com, and www.monster.com. Financial services Web sites provide facilities for trading and banking. Examples include Web sites such as www.etrade.com.

We selected the 40 Web sites in each category from the NetRatings database, which had the maximum number of hits on them during the month of December 2003. This made for a total of 200 Web sites. Selecting the top Web sites enabled us to study the design characteristics with respect to Web site usability, for the leading edge Web sites in each category.

Following the choice of the Web sites, we asked two IS researchers to independently evaluate the characteristics of all the Web sites, using the different items on the questionnaire. Specifically, they were instructed to load the Web site and carry out some functions relevant to the Web site. To ensure uniformity in computing and networking facilities and guard against differences in evaluation because of infrastructural reasons, each evaluator used the same computer for evaluating all the Web sites. The evaluation process was carried out over four weeks, during the month of December 2003.

Analysis and Results

We used the inter-rater reliability (see for example, Palmer, 2002) as a measure of the extent to which the two raters agreed in their ratings. We tested the inter-rater reliability for the two sets of evaluations, one from each rater. The weighted Kappa (Cohen, 1960; Gwet, 2002; Palmer, 2002), the measure of inter-rater reliability, was 0.63, with the upper and lower 95% confidence limits being 0.617 and 0.644. We also tested how significantly different the Kappa statistic was, from zero. The one-sided and two-sided p-values for both tests were less than 0.0001. Hence we had significant agreement and a good inter-rater reliability between the two raters. We therefore considered the mean values of the two sets of evaluations for each Web site, as the values of the evaluation items for that Web site.

Factor Analysis

Next, we identified different Web site characteristics by conducting a factor analysis (with Varimax Rotation) test across the 200 Web sites. This process presented us with six interpretable factors: information content, ease of navigation, customization and personalization, download speed, security, and availability. To further ensure that the factors were distinct and not significantly correlated among one another, we carried out reliability analysis through Cronbach's alpha. For all but one of the factors, the reliability was greater than 0.7. For Factor 6, the reliability was 0.61. All the reliability values are greater than that suggested by Nunnally (1967), which is 0.6. The high value of Cronbach's alpha indicates that the individual items for each of the factors are highly related among each other; in other words, the reliability of these factors is high. The factor analysis results have been described in Table 2.

Web site usability (USAB) was measured through a set of five Likert-scale questions that included aspects of the usability parameters described in the literature survey. The questions included characteristics such as how exciting, attractive, and entertaining the Web site was, the use of multimedia, and to what extent it was easy to learn and use the Web site. The reliability value of USAB was 0.88.

The six factors conform to existing descriptions of Web site characteristics. For example, Factor 1 (INFOCON) describes the content of information on the Web site, how easy it is to understand, its quality, its variety, and other similar characteristics. It also includes parameters such as "relevance" and "timelines" described by McKinney, Yoon, and Zahedi (2002) and Palmer (2002). INFOCON, therefore agrees well with the literature. In addition, it also includes other information-related parameters such as the adequacy and depth of information, how easily the information can be located, and how well organized and well arranged it is. Similarly, Factor 2 (ENAV) represents those characteristics that help users navigate the Web site better. These include the broad layout of the different components and the way in which elements such as hyperlinks and tabs are arranged. It describes characteristics that enhance the navigability of the Web site. It is similar to other constructs described in Palmer (2002). Factor 3 describes the extent to which a Web site can be customized to user needs, and has been named CUSTOMIZATION. It is similar to the characteristics of response, interactiveness, and personalization described in Palmer (2002) and McKinney et al. (2002). Factor 4 (DSPEED) refers to the download speed of the Web site and is a measure if the delay in loading the Web pages from the Web site. Factor 5 (SECURITY) consists of items that describe the extent to which the Web site can be perceived and characterized as "safe" and has provisions for executing secure transactions. Factor 6 (AVAILABILITY) describes the extent to which the Web site is available. SECURITY, AVAILABILITY, and DSPEED are dependent on the underlying IT infrastructure on which the Web site is hosted.

Table 2. Factor descriptions

Factor	Definition	Measurement (Number and brief description of items that represent the factor)	Factor Loadings of Individual Items	Reliability (Cronbach's Alpha)
1. Information Content (INFOCON)	The content, nature, and	10 items Questions included aspects such as range, relevance, clarity, and usefulness of the information	.777 .755 .710 .689 .688 .637 .624 .593 .582 .545	.91
2. Ease of Navigation (ENAV)	The ease with which users can navigate the Web site	5 items Questions included aspects such as the appropriate arrangement of hyperlinks, their meaningfulness, and consistency	.778 .714 .705 .645 .612	.83
3. Customization and Personalization	The extent to which the Web site can be customized to the needs of individual customers	3 items Questions included aspects such as provisions for personalized information and customized products	.839 .802 .742	.87
4. Download Speed (DSPEED)	The technical superiority of the Web site in terms of download speed	3 items Questions included aspects such as the speed of display between pages and the rate of information display	.808 .786 .745	.82

Table 2. continued

Factor	Definition	Measurement (Number and brief description of items that represent the factor)	Factor Loadings of Individual Items	Reliability (Cronbach's Alpha)
5. Security (SECURITY)	The extent to which the Web site is perceived and	4 items Questions included aspects such as the presence of an information policy and provisions for authentication and secure transactions	.820 .759 .750 .830	.79
6. Availability (AVAILABILITY)	The extent to which the Web site makes its contents available to users in a form that is easy to acquire and understand	3 items Questions included aspects such as the availability of the Web site and how well it is maintained	.718 .545 .512	.61

T-Test for Analyzing Factors That Affect Usability

We used the T-test for analyzing the influence of the six factors on Web site usability, and hence to test the six hypotheses. This analysis was carried out in four steps. First, we calculated the mean of USAB for all the 200 Web sites. Second, we divided the Web sites into two groups. Group 1 consisted of those Web sites whose USAB values were lower than the mean value and Group 2 included those Web sites whose usability values were higher than the mean value. Hence, Group 1 consisted of those Web sites which had "low" values of USAB, and Group 2 consisted of those Web sites which had "high" values of USAB. Next, we calculated the mean values of Factors 1 through 6, for all Web sites belonging to each group. Finally,

Table 3. T-test analysis of factors affecting usability

Factor	Group	Mean	*t*-Value	Significance	Hypothesis
1. Information Content	1. 2.	3.9 4.2	-5.29 ***	Significant	Hypothesis 1 supported
2. Ease of Navigation	1. 2.	3.9 4.1	-4.031***	Significant	Hypothesis 2 supported
3. Customization and Personalization	1. 2.	3.3 3.3	-.292	Not Significant	Hypothesis 3 not supported
4. Download Speed	1. 2.	3.9 4.1	-2.185*	Significant	Hypothesis 4 supported
5. Security	1. 2.	2.7 2.4	1.224	Not Significant	Hypothesis 5 not supported
6. Availability	1. 2.	4.2 4.4	-2.785***	Significant	Hypothesis 6 supported

*** *significance level = 0.0001, * significance level = 0.05*

we performed the T-test on these mean values, between the Web sites belonging to Groups 1 and 2. Those factors for which the means differed significantly between the two groups (as given by the value of the corresponding T-statistic) influenced the value of USAB. The results are shown in Table 3.

Discussions

Interpretation of Results

Our results show that INFOCON, ENAV, DSPEED, and AVAILABILITY influence Web site usability. This has implications for the design of Web sites, as discussed below.

Navigability has emerged as an important factor influencing usability. This is not surprising, given that the WWW is a hyperlink based nonlinear medium and has a wide variety of users with varying levels of comfort with the technology. Although the hypertext features of the WWW can produce complex and richly interconnected structures of information (Fillion & Boyle, 1991), complicated and disorganized Web sites do not have any consistent links within themselves or to other Web sites. Hence it is important to provide for aids and cues, in the form of appropriate links and graphics, which make it easy for users to navigate around different parts of the Web site. In this regard, context information (Park & Kim, 2000), that helps users understand where they have previously been and where they can go from their present positions, aids in making the navigation convenient and reduces the number of links that users needs to click on, in order to accomplish their task at the Web site (Park & Kim, 2000). Without context information, users tend to experience cognitive overload.

Information content and organization are two other important characteristics that determine usability. Web site designers should keep in mind that the information should be current, of high quality, and make sense to the users of the particular Web site. Sears, Jacko, and Dubach (2000) suggest that given increasing multimedia capabilities, excessive and unnecessary use of graphics, for example, actually makes users confused and hence decreases Web site usability. The absence of dead links is also an important criterion for increasing usability (Laudon & Travers, 2004)

Existing literature supports our findings that *download speed* and *Web site availability* affect usability. Preece (2001) states that users are very concerned with whether or not all the features available on a Web site can be downloaded and used, within reasonable response times. Download speed is linked to user satisfaction: a low download speed can lead to a state of anxiety for users. Download delay and Web site availability are primarily dependent on the underlying technical infrastructure of the Web site, which includes database design, Web design, database connectivity, wide area network speeds, and the overall distributed computing infrastructure of the WWW (Huang, 2002). The growing complexity of application software and business logic in Web application development has meant that information retrieval mechanisms of Web sites are becoming increasingly dependent on back-end data processing capabilities such as database access and application logic execution. This can increase the download delay. Hence multimedia elements such as Flash should be carefully used because they increase the complexity and the download time for Web sites (Heldal et al., 2004).

Our analysis did not support Hypotheses 3 and 5. That is, our results show that Web site *security* and *customization* do not influence usability. The requirements for providing Web site security include authentication, authorization, encryption, and password protection. All of these activities require additional processing, either at the server end or at the client end, and hence increase the complexity of the Web site. They also result in extra processing and extra tasks to be performed by users. For instance, complicated passwords and multiple levels of authentication can increase security, but they are also harder to remember and make the Web site more difficult to use. Hence, they decrease the usability. Also, most e-commerce Web sites are built from components supplied by third-party vendors. The focus is on ease of use and time to market, and not on security features. Hence security often takes a back seat to customer requirements of quick and easy implementation and use. Indeed the requirements of security and usability are "often antithetical to one another" (Turban, King, Lee, et al., 2002, p. 545). We think that this finding is significant for Web site designers, given that as a result of increasing usability of e-commerce systems, the skills, and knowledge required by novice hackers to copy and execute known methods of attack have decreased considerably.

Customization also did not emerge as a factor that affects usability. One reason for this could be that in order to customize and personalize Web pages, users may have to enter significant information about themselves and navigate additional elements such as forms and questionnaires, that may be present on the Web site. This can actually lead to more efforts being expended on part of the user to create and maintain their profiles (Turban et al., 2002, p. 133). Hence usability may decrease with increasing customization, in that increasing customization capabilities may lead to more complexity as far as the user's experience with the Web site is concerned. In a related context, Ellis and Kurniawan (2000) found in a study of Web site usage of senior citizens, that older people, because of lower levels of experience and declining problem solving skills, do not prefer flexibility and customization features in Web sites. Instead they like the information to be presented in a structured and consistent format.

Implications for Web Site Design: Guidelines for Designers

The above findings provide guidelines for developers and users for articulating their requirements and for frame appropriating design principles, in order to improve Web site usability. To improve Web site usability so as to increase the value and attraction of the Web site to viewers, Web site designers should pay attention to the *Ease of Navigation*, *Information Content*, *Download Speed*, and the *Availability*.

To increase the *Ease of Navigation*, the following aspects are important.

- Provide meaningful hyperlinks, which make it easy for users to navigate around different parts of the Web site.

- Provide contextual links, for example, back and forward arrows that help users understand where they have previously been and where they can go from their present positions.

- Provide a summary of the Web site structure, in terms of the various Web pages and their linkages so that users can get an idea of the overall organization of the Web site.

To make sure that the ***Information Content*** is meaningful and contributes to the usability, the following are important.

- Ensure that the information is current and relevant: implement an appropriate Web site content update strategy.
- Use graphics and multimedia elements appropriately, so as to add to the meaningfulness of the information, not distract the browser.
- Eliminate dead links.

To make sure that the ***Download Speed*** is reasonably fast and the Web site is ***available,*** the following strategies are useful.

- Have appropriate infrastructure design and upgrades including database connectivity, adequate wide area network capabilities, and an efficient overall distributed computing infrastructure. Use Web caching, server imaging, and other technology and algorithms to improve the rate at which the Web site pages download and the rate of information display between pages.
- Appropriately design the application logic so as to interface efficiently with back end databases.
- Efficiently design the database and information retrieval activities.
- Use multimedia elements such as Flash carefully.

Our findings indicate that Web site ***security*** and ***customization*** do not necessarily increase Web site usability. Designers and end users, therefore, need to take a close look at requirements for security and customization. On the one hand, Web sites that are more secure and have significant customization capabilities do provide important functionalities. At the same time, the benefits from these two design parameters must be carefully weighed against any effects they may have, in making the Web site less usable, as perceived by the users. The following strategies are useful in this context.

- Minimize the information elements that need to be collected, in order to personalize Web pages.
- Provide different levels of personalization and customization, that is, provide advanced customization capabilities on some Web pages and provide standard information on others, so that browsers can choose appropriately.
- Minimize the extra tasks that browsers may have to perform as a result of increased security; for instance, avoid users having to go through multiple

levels of authentication and to remember different passwords. Identify ways of automating some of these tasks within the processing capabilities of the Web site.

Scope for Further Research

McLaughlin and Skinner (2000) suggest that usability is highly contextual and greatly dependent on the specific interaction between the user and Web site. While on the one hand it is necessary that all users find the Web site easy to use (Heldal et al., 2004; Nielsen, 2000), concepts from HCI theory state, on the other hand, that users have needs specific to the kind of information they seek, their expertise level, and even the culture they come from (Heldal et al., 2004). In this context, there are a number of interesting ways in which this study can be further expanded.

First, even though the WWW is internationally used, few studies have investigated Web site usability from the point of view of different countries and cultures. For instance, when text is translated from English to other languages, it often becomes bigger and longer. Moreover, common images, symbols, and icons such as the trash-can are not universally known and recognized. Hence there is a need to study Web site usability from the point of view of different cultural and societal contexts (Sears, 2000).

Second, Web sites are used by a variety of people, from power users such as early adopters of Internet technologies, to people in hospices, assisted living and librar-ies. Notions of usability differ, for different kinds of users. For instance, in a study of Web site usage of senior citizens, Ellis and Kurniawan (2000) found that even though it is expected that most people would find that flexibility and customization are desirable, older people prefer to have a consistent look and feel of the pages, to enable them to find out where they are. They also do not like complexity on the Web site. They prefer simple and secure Web pages. The issues of download delay and latency are also of much less concern than they are for younger users. Hence Ellis and Kurniawan (2000) recommend that design elements such as the font and color, for example, should be consistent and that the links should be large and easy to see. Analyzing usability from the point of view of user demographics would be an interesting extension to this study.

Third, the concept of "actable" systems (Agerfalk et al., 2004), that is, systems that enable desired functions to be performed by users, has also emerged as an important criterion in system design. As this study has shown, some aspects of actability such as the content of information have similarities with aspects of usability. It would be interesting to analyze the two concepts in greater detail, identify similarities and differences, and to find out implications for Web site design.

Fourth, it is possible that usability criteria might differ according to the kind of Web site. In this context there are studies that analyze usability of Web sites from different categories. Zviran, Glezer, and Avni (2006) empirically investigated the effect of user-based design and Web site usability on user satisfaction across four types of commercial Web sites: online shopping, customer self-service, trading, and content providers. They found for example that trading sites were the lowest rated and online shopping and customer self-service sites the highest rated, on usability. It would be worthwhile to study different usability criterion contributing to these differences.

Finally, there are now many different kinds of devices that customers use to access the World Wide Web, such as desktops, laptops, handheld PDAs, and cell phones. Conventional Web sites are now being adapted to these smaller devices. Aspects such as the use of multimedia, font size, screen layout, and navigational aids, therefore have to be changed. Hence the concept of usability also differs significantly across the devices (Jones, Marsden, Mohd-Nasir, Boone, & Buchanan, 1999). For instance, users of handheld devices tend to search more and scroll less, so there are implications of presenting the information in a more structured form, such that all search navigation links can be accessed without scrolling down.

Conclusion

Historically, system designers have concentrated on the technical (memory and processor speed related) aspects of system design. Over the past decade and a half, the requirements from information systems have changed, from fulfilling focused technical requirements for expert users, to enabling end users to carry out operational tasks. Hence usability, and a need to make the system easy and effective for end users (John & Bass, 2001; McLaughlin & Skinner, 2000) have emerged as important system characteristics. Web sites are highly interactive systems, used by many different kinds of end users. High usability is therefore an essential characteristic of Web sites. However, as a recent review (Kasper, 2006) on measuring current practice in usability suggests, measures for usability are varied and far from reliable.

In this chapter we have analyzed Web site usability from the point of view of other design characteristics, and have identified design parameters that influence usability. We have found that Web site navigability, information content and organization, download speed, and Web site availability positively influence Web site usability. These results can be expected to aid designers in incorporating appropriate usability criteria in their Web sites. Two interesting findings of this study have been the results that security and customization may actually decrease rather than enhance Web site usability. Although this seems contrary to current Web site design practices, we feel that given the ever increasing complexity of Web sites in terms of both form and function, it is worthwhile to consider and address the dual effects of these two design parameters.

The results, however, must be analyzed in the light of the fact that the Web sites were evaluated by two users of Web sites. A similar study conducted on a larger number of users could possibly yield more robust results. On the whole, however, the results are significant reinforcements of the fact that the design of Web sites is a complex activity and that there are various trade-offs involved in arriving at an appropriate set of design characteristics.

References

Agarwal, R., & Karahanna, E. (2000, December). Time flies when you're having fun: Cognitive absorption and beliefs about information technology usage. *MIS Quarterly, 24*(4), 665-694.

Agarwal, R., & Venkatesh, V. (2002, June). Assessing a firm's Web presence: A heuristic evaluation procedure for the measurement of usability. *Information Systems Research, 13*(2), 168-186.

Agerfalk, P.J., & Eriksson, O. (2004). Action-oriented conceptual modelling. *European Journal of Information Systems, 13*, 80-92.

Bellman, S., & Lohse, G.L. (1999, December). Predictors of online buying behavior. *Communications of the ACM, 45*(12), 32-38.

Flavián, C., Guinalíu, M., & Gurrea, R. (2006, January). The role played by perceived usability, satisfaction and consumer trust on Website loyalty. *Information & Management, 43*(1), 1-14.

Cohen, J.B. (1960). A coefficient of agreement for nominal scales. *Educational and Psychology Measurement, 20*, 37-46.

Eighmey, J., & McCord, L. (1998). Adding value in the information age: Uses and gratifications of sites on the World Wide Web. *Journal of Business Research, 41*(3), 187–194.

Ellis, R.D., & Kurniawan, S.H. (2000). Increasing the usability of online information for older users: A case study in participatory design. *International Journal of Human-Computer Interaction, 12*(2), 263-276.

El Sawy, O.A. (1985). Implementation by cultural infusion: An approach for managing the introduction of information technologies. *MIS Quarterly, 9*(2), 131-140.

Evans, P., & Wurster, T. (2000). *Blown to bits*. Boston: Harvard Business School Press.

Fillion, F.M., & Boyle, C.D.B. (1991). Important issues in hypertext documentation usability. In *Proceedings of the 9ᵗʰ ACM Annual International Conference on Systems Documentation SIGDOC'91* (pp. 59-66). New York: ACM.

Gefen, D., & Straub, D. (2000). The relative important of perceived ease of use in IS adoption: A study of e-commerce adoption. *Journal of the Association for Information Systems, 1*(8), 1-30.

Gehrke, D., & Turban, E. (1999). *Determinants of successful Website design: Relative importance and recommendations for effectiveness.* In Proceedings of the 31ˢᵗ Hawaii International Conference on Information Systems.

Gray, W.M., & Salzman, M.C. (1998). Damaged merchandise? A review of experiments that compare usability evaluation methods. *International Journal of Human-Computer Interaction, 13*, 203-261.

Gwet, K. (2002, October). *Computing inter-rater reliability with the SAS System* (Statistical Methods for Inter-Rater Reliability Assessment Series No. 3).

Healy, V., & Herder, R. (2002). A walk-up-and-use information system for the Sydney Olympics: A case study in user-centered design. *International Journal of Human-Computer Interaction, 14*(3-4), 335-347.

Heldal, F., Sjovold, E., & Heldal, A.F. (2004). Success on the Internet: Optimizing relationship through the corporate site. *International Journal of Information Management, 24*, 115-129.

Huang, A.H. (2002). A research taxonomy for e-commerce system usability. In *Proceedings of the Eighth Americas Conference on Information Systems* (pp. 638-642).

John, B.E., & Bass, L. (2001). Usability and software architecture. *Behaviour & Information Technology, 20*(5), 329-338.

Jones, M., Marsden, G., Mohd-Nasir, N., Boone, K., & Buchanan, G. (1999). Improving Web interaction on small displays. *Computer Networks, 31*, 1129-1137.

Karahanna, E., & Straub, D.W. (1999). The psychological origins of perceived usefulness and ease-of-use. *Information & Management, 35*, 237-250.

Kasper, H. (2006, February). Current practice in measuring usability: Challenges to usability studies and research. *International Journal of Human-Computer Studies, 64*(2), 79-102.

Katerattanukul, P., & Siau, K. (1999). Measuring information quality of Web sites: Development of an instrument. In P. De & J. DeGross (Eds.), *Proceedings of the 20ᵗʰ International Conference of Information Systems* (pp. 279-285). Charlotte, North Carolina.

Kim, H., & Hirtle, S. (1995). Spatial metaphors and disorientation in hypertext browsing. *Behavior and Information Technology, 14*, 239-250.

Kim, S., & Stoel, L. (2004). Dimensional hierarchy of retail Website quality. *Information and Management, 11*, 619-633.

Kerlinger, F.N., & Lee, H.B. (2000). *Foundations of behavioral research* (4th ed.). FL: Harcourt Publishers.

Landauer, T.K. (1996). *The trouble with computers: Usefulness, usability, and productivity.* MIT Press.

Laudon, K.C., & Travers, G.C. (2004). *E-commerce: Business, technology and society* (2nd ed.). Addison-Wesley.

Lecerof, A., & Paterno, F. (1998). Automatic support for usability evaluation. *IEEE Transactions on Software Engineering, 24*, 863-887.

Machlis, S. (1998). Site redesign keeps it simple. *Computerworld, 32*(28), 25.

Maclaughlin, J., & Skinner, D. (2000). Developing usability and utility: A comparative study of the users of new IT. *Technology Analysis & Strategic Management, 12*(3), 413-423.

Manning, H., McCarthy, J.C., & Souza, R.K. (1998, September). *Why most Web sites fail. Interactive Technology Series, 3*(7). Forrester Research.

McKinney, V., Yoon, K., & Zahedi, F.M. (2002, September). The measurement of Web-customer satisfaction: An expectation and disconfirmation approach. *Information Systems Research, 13*(3), 296-315.

Muylle, S., Moenaert, R., & Despontin, M. (2004). The conceptualization and empirical validation of Web site user satisfaction. *Information & Management, 41*(5), 543-560.

Nielsen, J. (2000). *Designing Web usability.* IN: New Riders.

Nielsen, J. (1999, January). User interfaces directions for the Web. *Communications of the ACM, 42*(1), 65-72.

Nunnally, J. (1967). *Psychometric theory.* McGraw-Hill.

Palmer, J.W. (2002, June). Web site usability, design, and performance metrics. *Information Systems Research, 13*(2), 151-167.

Pearrow, M. (2000). *Web site usability.* Rockland, MA: Charles River Media.

Pitkow, J., & Kehoe, C. (1996). Emerging trends in the WWW user population. *Communications of the ACM, 39*(6), 106-108.

Preece, J. (2001). Sociability and usability in online communities: Determining and measuring success. *Behaviour & Information Technology, 20*(5), 347-356.

Randall, D. (1997). Consumer strategies for the Internet: Four scenarios. *Long Range Planning, 30*(2), 157-168.

Rose, G., Khoo, H., & Straub, D. Current technological impediments to business-to-consumer electronic commerce. *Communications of the AIS, 1*(16), 1-74.

Rosen, D.E., & Lloyd, S.J. (2004, January-March). Web site design: Building a cognitive framework. *Journal of Electronic Commerce in Organizations, 2*(1), 15-28.

Schubert, P., & Selz, D. (1998). *Web assessment: A model for the evaluation and assessment of successful electronic commerce applications.* In Proceedings of the 31st Hawaii International Conference of Information Systems.

Sears, A. (2000). Introduction: Empirical studies of WWW usability. *International Journal of Human-Computer Interaction, 12*(2), 167-171.

Sears, A., Jacko, J.A., & Dubach, E.M. (2006). International aspects of World Wide Web usability and the role of high-end graphical enhancements. *Journal of Human-Computer Interaction, 12*(2), 241-161.

Shapiro, C., & Varian, H. (1999). *Information rules.* MA: Harvard Business School Press.

Shneiderman, B. (1998). *Designing the user interface: Strategies for effective human-computer interaction.* Reading, MA: Addison-Wesley.

Siau, K. (2003-2004). Evaluating the usability of a group support system using co-discovery. *Journal of Computer Information Systems, Winter*, 17-28.

Swanson, E.B. (1982). Measuring user attitudes in MIS research: A review. *Omega, 10*(2), 157-165

Torkzadeh, G., & Dhillon, G. (2002, June). Measuring factors that influence the success of Internet commerce. *Information Systems Research, 13*(2), 187-204.

Turban, E., King, D., Lee, J., et al. (2002). *Electronic commerce: A managerial perspective* (2nd ed.). Prentice Hall.

Venkatesh, V., Ramesh, V., & Massey, A.P. (2003, December). Understanding usability in mobile commerce. *Communications of the ACM, 46*(12), 53-56.

Venkatraman, N., & Grant, J.H. (1986). Construct measurement in organizational strategy research: A critique and proposal. *Academy of Management Review, 11*, 71-87.

Yeung, W.L., & Lu, M. (2004). Functional characteristics of commercial Web sites: A longitudinal study in Hong Kong. *Information & Management, 41*(4), 483-495.

Zviran, M., Glezer, C., & Avni, I. (2006). User satisfaction from commercial Web sites: The effect of design and use. *Information & Management, 43*, 157-178

Chapter XIII

Breaking Out of Lock-In:
Insights from Case Studies into Ways to Up the Value Ladder for Indian Software SMEs

Abhishek Nirjar, Indian Institute of Management, Lucknow, India

Andrew Tylecote, University of Sheffield Management School, UK

Abstract

Small and medium enterprises in the Indian software development industry, like their larger counterparts, are mostly low on the value ladder. This chapter examines the difficulties confronting them in moving up the ladder, and the strategies and circumstances conducive to success, drawing on three case studies. Human resource development emerges as central. Though SMEs have meager resources for moving up, compared to large firms, they have a greater incentive to do so—and this organizational interest accords with the interests and motivations of their employees for career development. It is found that the keys to success are to treat employees as co-investors in their own human capital, to form an effective "community of practice" across the firm, and to find market opportunities which "stretch" the firm in the right direction and to the right extent. For the last of these the main contri-

bution is made by existing clients, but an important role may be played by venture capitalists, particularly those which are U.S.-based.

Introduction

The Indian software industry today has over 7,000 firms operating domestically, of which about 90% are small and medium sized (i.e., less than 250 employees). It has seen dramatic growth during the last decade. The industry grew at a compound annual growth rate of over 50% from 1994-1999 and from 1999-2002 at over 26%. Its output has been forecast to exceed US$50 billion by 2008 (NASSCOM, 2002, 2003). While in 2003 SMEs accounted only for 10-15% of revenues, this share was forecast to grow to 50-60% by 2008 (NASSCOM, 2004). The growth of the industry has been heavily dependent on exports, particularly to the United States: total software and services exports rose from US$489 million in 1994-1995 to US$9.6 billion in 2002-2003. Indian firms have been operating mostly at the lower end of the software value ladder—programming/maintenance services—but even these have seen a switch from over 95% "body-shopping" in the early 1990s (NASSCOM, 1999)—work undertaken for clients at their site of operations—to "offshore" software development, where India has become dominant. A survey by Merrill Lynch (NASSCOM, 2002) predicted that the proportion of IT spending outsourced to India would increase from below 5% to over 15% in 2002-2004. The software exports increasingly include the output of the Indian operations of large consulting firms like IBM, Accenture, EDS, and CSC.

Indian firms have been trying to move up the software development value ladder (Figure 1). The activities that Indian firms are undertaking now vary from high value consulting, system integration, packaged software integration, and custom application development to low value legacy application management, maintenance,

Figure 1. The software value ladder (Adopted from Presentation by Nilekani (2001), Managing Director, Infosys Technologies, India, at the NASSCOM-IT Conference, 2001)

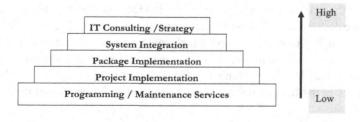

and migrations. One indication of this is the number of firms with a SEI-CMM level rating. This system of ratings was developed by the Software Engineering Institute (SEI) of Carnegie Mellon University and represents the level of maturity of the development processes used by a software development firm. There are five levels, from 1 (Fair) to 5 (very good) of the Capability Maturity Model (CMM). An SEI-CMM rating brings credibility to the process of software development being used by the firm. India has the highest number of firms with such a rating—out of 58 firms with a SEI-CMM level 5 there are 36 from India (NASSCOM, 2002). As firms grew in size, spin-offs began from large companies, some of which have been the nursery to some of the most dynamic software and services start-ups in the Indian industry.

The strength of the software producing industry in India has been by no means matched by local demand for its services. This has been hindered by lack of PC penetration within Indian industry, among other factors. Although it has seen growth from US$298 million in 1994-1995 to US$2.6 billion in 2001-2002 (NASSCOM, 2002), the domestic market is still small relative to exports, and it is moreover deficient qualitatively, in the sense that few software users are advanced by world standards. It seems that if Indian software development is going to make a general move up the value ladder, it will be exports that lead the way. However D'Costa (2002) argues that it is precisely the profitability of producing on the basis of existing, successful routines that may reinforce the desire of Indian software exporters to specialize in low-end activities such as systems maintenance projects. They learn, but only within limited, path-dependent "learning trajectories" (Maskell & Malmberg, 1999, p. 180). D'Costa (2000) predicts that they:

... will attempt to capture whatever projects come by since the strategy is to maximize absolute revenues rather than revenues per unit of labor. ... It is evident that without some specific domain expertise such businesses run the risk of spreading expertise thinly over a wide variety of projects. For large firms this is a feasible strategy but for small firms it could lead to a rudderless trajectory. (p. 10)

It is a classic problem for less developed countries that their exporting industries tend to be locked into a low-end innovation trajectory (Balasubramanyam & Balasubramanyam, 1997). They establish a presence in developed countries' markets on the basis of low labor costs, but these are only a crucial advantage at the bottom end of the market. Further up the "value ladder," there is a virtuous circle of competence development and market development (in the sense of winning orders which demand higher competences) which moves much more easily where the producer is physically or culturally close to the market and face-to-face interaction is possible (Cohendet, Kern, Mehmanpazir, & Muneir, 1999, pp. 227, 231-232). The tendency of multinational firms to centralize core functions makes them reluctant to give contracts for relatively complex assignments at long range. If they are going to outsource them at all, they prefer to do so to local firms. No firm, in fact, wants to collocate critical projects overseas, due to coordination and communication problems (Mariani, 2002; Narula, 2001). Tacit knowledge, which is a key element of learning in software as elsewhere, is mostly generated inside firms, but this process depends very much on the local context. Tacit knowledge is experiential and heavily influenced by user needs; it is converted into core competencies through repeated problem solving of a similar kind—which develops routines for solving those problems. This yields increasing returns (Arthur, 1994)—and thus no doubt increasing profits—but it may well be at the cost of lock-in to technological inertia (Coombs & Hull, 1998, p. 242). This is the more likely when distance from users means that new tacit knowledge is hard to come by.

There are some relatively optimistic views about the prospects of Indian software development. Krishnan (2003) agrees with D'Costa that the evolution of the software services sector "has been based on a distinct role in the global production system that involves relatively low value-added work, 'locked-in' to the global division of labor"; but he makes some points about the industry that suggest that the "lock-in" may not be impossible to escape from: notably that software—the services side at least—does not require irreversible commitments on specialized resources, since its main resources are human capital using generic skills. (See also Krishnan, Gupta, & Matta, 2003.) So long as the large Indian cost advantage persists, Indian firms will have comfortable profit margins, giving them scope for experimentation to find the right business model (Athreye, 2002) and—we might add—to invest in building expertise in new domains. That cost advantage gives a matching incentive to experimentation by overseas customers. The fact that these customers are still concentrated in one geographical area, the USA, which is seen by some (e.g., Balasubramanyam & Balasubramanyam, 1997) as compounding the lock-in problem, may help in their learning. In the same way, shortage of highly skilled manpower in the parent country is forcing multinational firms to establish R&D centers in countries which have highly skilled manpower—for example, India (Reddy, 1997). Such centers may offer excellent bridges between Indian producers and overseas markets.

Our concern in this chapter is to explore the means that SMEs in the Indian software development industry may be able to use in order to go "up-market." In certain respects the problems described are the more severe for SMEs, for they lack resources to promote themselves in new market areas or to invest in developing competences. We examine the difficulties confronting Indian SMEs in moving up the software development value ladder, and the strategies and circumstances conducive to success, drawing on three case studies. Given the key role of human resources in software development, we give considerable attention to human resource management issues. The chapter has been divided into four sections: the next section explains the factors that make a firm dynamic in this industry, the third section sketches the case studies conducted and draws out some relevant insights, and the fourth section concludes.

Factors Making SMEs Dynamic

The main challenge for a software firm, as we have seen, is to move up the value ladder by taking on increasingly complex tasks technologically. At the bottom of the ladder are the routine tasks of programming and maintenance services, requiring only technical skills. The first step towards complexity is project implementation, which involves implementation of small-scale projects addressing specific narrow functionalities defined by the client (whether a software developer or user). Some expertise in project management and software design is required at this level. The next step is package implementation, which is the set of procedures which a software firm conducts in order to establish and implement a commercial off-the-shelf product (e.g., Lotus 1-2-3, ERP packages, etc.) for a client firm. Although the source code of the package remains with the software firm, the precise requirements of the client have to be understood and the package has to be customized accordingly. Thus, package implementation requires software professionals to have functional understanding and higher-level project management skills. System integration requires the software firms to be able to create an integrated, enterprise-wide IT platform to suit the business needs of the vendor. The level of understanding of business processes and IT architecture development has to be of a very high order. The software firm has to execute from conceptualization to implementation of enterprise-wide systems. Clearly the topmost step of the software development value ladder, IT consulting, requires software firms to have high-end expertise in how IT-based systems can benefit the firm by driving the performance of the vendor: this involves business modeling and process reengineering. So as the firm moves from lower level of the software development value ladder to the higher end, the level of technological complexity (whether an existing technology or a new or improved version is being used) increases and requires software firms to ensure they have the requisite domain expertise and competence to perform the required tasks. (See Figure 3.)

However, together with this vertical dimension, it may well gain by developing horizontally, that is, serving new markets geographically or sectorally—which may allow it to exploit competences in which it has already invested, and even customize software it has already written. For both purposes it needs an *innovation capability,* which we take to have both internal and external determinants (see Figure 2). We look at internal and external determinants, in turn.

Figure 2. Innovation capability of firm (Bold lines indicate definite predictions of direction of effect; dotted line is speculative.)

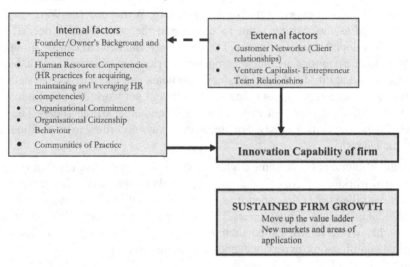

Internal Determinants of Innovation Capability

The resource-based view of the firm states that the internal resources and capabilities of a firm are the basis for creating sustainable competitive advantage (Barney, 1991; Amit & Schoemaker, 1993; Mahoney & Pandian, 1992). The internal factors of innovation capability that are considered here are based on the fact that software development is a knowledge-intensive task and technological advancement is characterized as a learning process.

Founder/Owner's Background and Experience

Almost all studies on start-ups and in particular on software start-ups (Romijn & Albaladejo, 2002; Romijn & Albu, 2001) have considered the founder/owner background and experience as a strategic factor for innovation and growth. Nambisan (2002) in his study of innovation-orientation and software firm evolution found that the innovation-orientation of founder and top managers plays an important role in growth and in generating innovations. It is people with substantial experience in software development activities in a large firm who may start a new firm based on their strengths and expertise.

Competencies and Human Resources

The study of traits of expert software developers by Wynekoop and Walz (2000) may be taken as the starting point to understand the competencies needed by software development professionals. The traits they enumerated can be grouped into two major categories, technical competencies (level of technical and business knowledge and ability to abstract business problems and translate into systems), and management competencies (needed to work and get work done through and with teams, effectively interact with clients, users and other stakeholders). The set of individual competencies that a firm needs must vary according to its position on the value ladder.

Software development is, to some degree, an *inherently* innovative activity. It is an intellectual workforce (also called knowledge workers) that undertakes this activity. Sommerville (1982) described it as "a craft task that relies on the capabilities of individual, creative, programmers." These capabilities of individual programmers—what we have just called their technical competencies—are a blend of technical qualifications, experience, and continuous learning.

Development and growth needs of software professionals are very high compared to people in other professions. Given the speed of technological change in the industry, if they do not upgrade their competence levels on a regular basis they are bound to become redundant. Firms in this sector have created cultures and systems that support autonomy and involvement in decision making, because software professionals are motivated by challenging work (Van Slyke, 1996).

Figure 3. Software development value ladder and competence levels (Presentation by Nandan Nilekani at NASSCOM- IT Conference, 2001, Mumbai)

Business Strategy	In-depth domain knowledge	Level
IT Consulting/ Strategy	Business modelling Process re-engineering	V
System integration	IT architecture development	IV
Package implementation	Project management Functional understanding	III
Project implementation	Software project management Software design	II
Programming / maintenance services	Technical skills	I

Technological complexity increases   Competence

Pare, Tremblay, and Lalonde (2001) concluded from a study of Canadian software firms that (if retention is to be maximized):

IT specialists should not be managed as disposable productive resources but considered as humans with specific needs and interests such as equity and justice, opportunity to learn and innovate, recognition of peers and managers, attainment of new levels of responsibility, and empowerment. Therefore, managers have to bolster IT professionals' sense of self-worth by treating them as intellectual assets, not operating expenses, and by helping them shape and direct their careers, so they can gain experience within the enterprise rather than outside it. (p. 6)

Innovativeness and Commitment to the Organization

In small and medium enterprises, the managers with the responsibility outlined above for nurturing and empowering professionals, will normally be line managers, not human resource management specialists. Clearly a firm in which such a style of management is normal belongs, in the terms of Burns and Stalker's classic "The Management of Innovation" (1961), very much in the organic (rather than mechanistic) category—and as Burns and Stalker argue, an organic firm is decidedly more innovative. It is an essential feature of an organic firm that even junior employees should not be prevented by rules or authority from taking initiative in the interests of the firm. If they are not to abuse this latitude, they need to display what Organ (1988) calls "organizational citizenship behaviour":

... individual behaviour that is discretionary, not directly or explicitly recognized by the formal reward system, and that in the aggregate promotes the effective functioning of the organization. By discretionary, we mean that the behaviour is not an enforceable requirement of the role or job description, that is, the clearly specifiable terms of the person's employment contract with the organization; the behaviour is rather a matter of personal choice, such that its omission is not generally understood as punishable. (p. 4)

Why should employees display organizational citizenship behaviour? Coyle-Shapiro, Kessler, and Purcell (2004) conducted a study to explore the underlying mechanism used to explain why individuals engage in such behaviour. The study revealed that organisational citizenship behaviour can be explained as a form of reciprocation where employees engage in such behaviour to reciprocate fair or good treatment. This is well complemented by an individual's perception of the commitment that exists in their relationship with the organisation and is related to broadening of job boundaries to include citizenship behaviours. According to Meyer and Allen

(1997), organizational citizenship behaviour may arise from any of three types of *organizational commitment*:

1. **Affective Commitment:** An employee's attachment and identification to the organization resulting in a strong belief in an acceptance of an organization's goals and values.

2. **Continuance Commitment:** A tendency to engage in consistent lines of activity based on the individual's recognition of the costs associated with discontinuing the activity.

3. **Normative Commitment:** Employees exhibit behaviours solely because they believe it is a right and moral thing to do.

Zannad and Rouet (2003) studied the types of organizational commitment prevalent in high technology innovating companies. Affective commitment was found to be the dominant type. Pare, Tremblay, and Lalonde (2001) treat normative as practically equivalent to affective commitment, which seems a helpful simplification, and they find that high affective and continuance commitment makes employees less inclined to leave the organization—a great advantage for a firm seeking to upgrade its capability by upgrading its employees' individual competences. Even more to the present point, we would predict that, by encouraging the sort of behaviour required in an organic firm, such commitment—particularly the affective type—will enhance the firm's innovation capability.

We predict that Organizational Citizen Behavior (OCB) would positively impact the innovation capability of the firm.

Communities of Practice

Wenger, McDermott, and Snyder (2002) define communities of practice (CoP) as "groups of people who share a concern, a set of problems, or a passion about a topic and who deepen their knowledge and expertise in this area by interacting on a ongoing basis" (p. 4). In Nonaka and Kono (1998) "ba" is a similar concept. A CoP can exist within a firm – an "organizational community" —or among firms—an "occupational community" (Lam, 2002). In either case, varying degrees of formalization are possible. Thus a CoP within a firm could be, in the terms of Wenger et al. (2002).

•   **Unrecognized:** Invisible to the organization, sometimes even to its members.

•   **Bootlegged:** Only visible informally to a circle of people "in the know."

- **Legitimized:** Officially sanctioned as a valuable entity.
- **Supported:** Provided with direct resources from the organization.
- **Institutionalized:** Given an official status and function in the organization (p. 28).

Even in the case of institutionalization the essence of a CoP remains that people participate because they want to do so (Brown & Duguid, 1991; Wenger, 1998): it is characteristic of an organic firm, and hard to imagine working in a mechanistic one. The organizational culture and the way in which work is organized are crucial in determining whether individuals can and will create and participate in a CoP. As a CoP provides substantial inputs to learning through sharing of experiences, problem solving, and discussions on a regular basis it should make a substantial contribution to enhancing the individual competencies and collective capabilities of a software development firm. We posit that a mechanism for informal learning in the form of CoP would positively influence the innovation capability of the firm.

External Determinants of Innovation Capability of Firms

There are two important external stakeholders to any software entrepreneurial firm. The first is the client. The second is the venture capitalist who not only funds the start-up but acts like a partner in business by providing other assistance and support in managing risk that is associated with a start-up in a high-tech sector. The relationship the firm has with its clients and the VC has an enduring impact not only on the efforts to enhance competence through learning but also on the effort to develop new and improved products and services.

Client Relationship

Software development is either customer-driven or customer-focused. It cannot take place in isolation from a requirement. Even if there is a ready-made software product (commercial off-the shelf software), it may require some amount of customization in order to suit the precise requirements of the customer (Blum, 1994; Torrisi, 1998). In various studies on innovation and new product development, it has been found that interaction with customers and suppliers is highly beneficial (Lundvall, 1988; Panda & Ramanathan, 1996; Von Hippel, 1988). Various studies on high-tech firms (Jassawala & Sashittal, 1998; Vagasi, 2001) have shown the value of customer participation in new product development. A study by Nambisan (2000) on software firms has also supported the need for firms to utilize customer networks for purpose of developing new and improved products and solving problems associated with existing products. Firms have been organizing "user meets" and other events that help in bridging the gap between user and developer. We therefore posit that client relationship would have an impact on the innovation capability of the software firm.

Venture Capitalist: Entrepreneur Team Relationship

Higashide and Birley (2000) and Gustafsson and Metzner (2002) studied the effect of the frequency of interaction between the venture capitalist and entrepreneurial team in start-ups and suggest that the level of VC involvement had a positive impact on firm performance. We posit the same for Indian software SMEs. Moreover we suggest that (given the range of guidance which VCs sometimes give and the importance of human resources in software) this may well work partly via the HR practices of the firm.

We conclude this section by summarizing the propositions for this research and by presenting the sources of learning for software professionals in Figure 4.

Summary of Propositions for this Research

- The innovation capability of a firm has a positive impact on its sustainable growth.
- Organizational commitment would positively impact the innovation capability of the firm.
- Organizational citizenship behavior would positively impact the innovation capability of the firm.

Figure 4. Sources of learning for software professionals

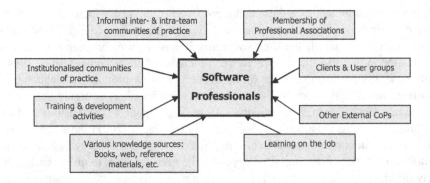

- A mechanism for informal learning in the form of one or more communities of practice (internal or external) would positively influence the innovation capability of the firm.

- The human resource practices of a firm have a positive impact on the innovation capability of a firm, largely by fostering organizational commitment, OCB, and CoP.

- The quality of the relationship with clients and (where applicable) venture capitalists would have an impact on the innovation capability of a firm.

The Case Studies

Methodology Used

Three case studies were conducted using semistructured interviews. The general approach to the case studies was very much that of Yin (1994), who argued that a case study "benefits from the prior development of theoretical propositions to guide data collection and analysis" (p. 13). This was done (as set out above) on the basis of the literature and the authors' own experience of the industry. The aim in the studies was to generate insights that would allow the further development—rather than any sort of testing—of these theoretical propositions. As in Visintin, Ozgen, Tylecote, and Handscombe (2004), the case studies were "not exactly undertaken with an open mind. We were, however, open to the possibility of surprise. ... semi-structured interviews ... allowed our informants to tell us things that we did not expect to hear; and to use categories which were not those we had in mind" (p. 2 of print-out). The firms were chosen on the basis that they illustrated a variety of types or modes of success: all three firms had moved up the value ladder or into a new area of application and their financial performance ranged from above average to very good; one firm had funding from a U.S. venture capitalist. Initially six firms had been selected (from the NASSCOM, 2002 directory) and were approached for the study; three agreed. The CEO/director was directly approached in two of the cases while in the third the approach was made to the head of HR; these then arranged the other interviews. (The initial approaches were made by e-mail and followed up with telephone calls, with further requests and references provided by senior academic people from reputed institutes in India who are known to one of the authors.)

Since the research was intended to get and compare perspectives of different stakeholders, interviews were conducted for a range of categories of employee. For each firm, interviews were conducted with the chief executive officer/director of the firm and the head of the human resource function, and one middle level manager—variously GM projects, project manager, and business manager. Two software professionals from each firm were also interviewed, each with less than five years of work experience. Interviews with top managers lasted between 60 to 90 minutes while in the case of head of HR, middle level managers, and software professionals, they ranged between 50 minutes to 120 minutes. There was a core of general questions asked in all interviews, with another set of questions specific to the level and function of the interviewee. All interviews were recorded and transcripts prepared. The transcripts were then analyzed by one of the authors over a three month period, and a detailed interpretation was prepared. Given the limited aims of the work, it was not thought appropriate to conduct content or discourse analysis. However, a senior social scientist not otherwise involved in the work read all the transcripts and the interpretation and concurred with it. (For details of the instrument see the Appendix.)

Company Details

Brief descriptions of the three firms are followed by the findings of the case studies on various dimensions of the study.

Company A

Based in North India, at Jaipur, this firm was established in 1999. It has a very strong export orientation. Initially started by doing low-value services like maintenance and programming, after two years it moved up one step on the software value ladder, and has now successfully completed project implementation assignments. It has a number of products: its main expertise lies in project implementation, legacy system upgrading, and software solution development. Company A has obtained ISO 9001 certification for its design and development activities, and has recently begun working with the latest Microsoft .net technology.

Company B

B was established in 1999 by two ex-Tata Consultancy Services employees out of the savings they had made from 12-15 years of employment, at Coimbatore in the state of Tamil Nadu. The firm has an ISO 9001 certification and strategic relationship with firms in Switzerland and Italy and one large Indian firm; it has clients across the globe from India, U.S., Canada, Europe, and Australia. The workforce numbers about 80 people of whom 75% are certified Sun/IBM/Microsoft professionals. About 90% have experience working abroad; qualifications range from graduate in engineering to postgraduates in engineering and computer science. Having started as a financial system and banking specialist, now it is involved also in embedded software systems for cameras and automotive parts, Internet technology, and tele-coms. B has been growing at a steady pace. It has major links in Europe and gives this as the reason for its survival after the slowdown in U.S. occurred.

Company C

C was established in 2000 with the help of US$5 million venture capital funding from two U.S.-based VC firms, Global Internet Ventures and Westbridge Partners. Led by two ex-Wipro and one ex-Hughes Software employees, the firm has been expanding and moving up from the beginning. It has over a dozen partners across the globe, and its clients range from HP to HDFC Bank (an Indian bank with a global and domestic presence). The firm was the first to come up with account aggregation software. At present it has three products. Besides these, C is involved in consulting and system integration—both high value activities, as we have seen.

Case Study Findings

Growth: The Preference for Going Up-Market

We cited D'Costa (2002) in the Introduction as arguing that the profitability of producing on the basis of existing routines might reinforce the desire of Indian software exporters to remain specialized in low-end activities—in which they could grow extensively, so to speak, without going up-market. Our respondents however regarded this option as much easier for large firms to follow than for SMEs:

Software firms do not have the option of growing in number of employees, as it calls for a firm to have deep pockets and plenty of leads to engage the workforce. The only option SMEs have is to remain focused in a niche area and move up the value ladder by developing high levels of expertise. (Director of Company B)

Software SMEs cannot grow through number of employees with ease, it has a lot of risk associated with it. The best option is to identify a niche area, develop competence in that and grow by moving up the value ladder. (CEO of Company A)

Top Managers and External Relationships

The top managers of our SMEs are those who have the experience and strategic thinking about the way in which a start-up should and can grow. Their competences play a major role in deciding the direction and growth of the firm. The top managers also handle the marketing of the product and services offered by the firm, though the marketing effort also involves certain senior technical people involved in managing at the operations level. These people play the role of interface between the top management's discussions with prospective clients and the operations team of the firm.

The manner in which the client and software firm interact has a bearing on the efforts of the firm to move up the value ladder or approach new geographic markets and application areas. Software SMEs look forward to having a long-standing relationship with their clients. If they are able to build such a relationship it not only helps in serving the client for a longer duration but also helps in getting more assignments as the reputation of the firm is enhanced and other firms are attracted to become the clients of the software firm. All three companies have evidence that good client relationships fetch repeat orders and that at times the client would recommend the firm to other prospective clients. But the new clients are not the ones to help in the move up-market. In case the order comes from a referred prospective client it would certainly be for a task of which the existing client has experience. Orders from an existing client, on the other hand, may be for a task at a higher value level.

A problem that software SMEs have with their clients is that they can usually only approach similar-sized firms. Resource constraints prevent them taking on the multimillion-dollar projects typical for large firms—these will have smaller projects too, but their large software suppliers will tend to get these too. But here the SMEs' relationships with large Indian software companies are key. The latter have chosen to hold their costs down by focusing their workforces on core competences. Further, in any large project there could be parts that can be handled by SMEs. For this purpose some SMEs have established strategic relations with large companies so that work in a particular domain is something the large firm would ask them to do. All these subcontracting relationships have a significant impact on the competence building of a firm. All our three firms have strategic partnerships with software companies across the globe. Further, Company C has a strategic partnership with a large Indian software firm for handling competence-based work.

Assistance for export marketing in higher-value areas is also provided by venture capitalists, where they are based in the U.S. —as is the case with Company C. The funding from their two U.S.-based VCs was possible because the top three people in the firm have extensive experience in the software industry at the very highest of levels. In the words of head of HR of Company C, "to get funding from US VCs is truly an illustration of the faith they have in the competence and dedication of the top team of the company. They are certain that the people at the top will build this organization on strong foundations of values, competence and sincerity." On this basis, in addition to their classic roles of providing funding and guidance, they are prepared to recommend the firm to prospective clients.

Extending markets geographically is a useful way of consolidating progress up the value ladder and into new areas of application. In all three cases we found that while initially the focus had been the U.S. or other developed country markets, in recent times there are plenty of activities being undertaken for domestic markets. The expertise developed as a consequence of serving foreign markets had helped the companies in serving the domestic market better.

Having stayed afloat during the global software slowdown we realized we needed to shift some of the focus to other markets. Having served German clients of embedded software, we were able to get work from domestic players who required embedded software for parts of automotive vehicles. That opportunity helped us to realize that one should not neglect opportunities, which are available here in our own markets. (Director of Company B)

If we have a product, it does not mean it is for US clients only. If we are able to sell it here in India then that also is beneficial to us. Our products are 80% ready and the remaining we customize according to the requirements of the clients. (Business Manager for Company C)

Internal Relationships and HR Practices

Middle Management Initiative

Moving up the value ladder is normally linked to the willingness and efforts of the top management, but at times, it has been seen that this willingness can emanate from the middle level of the firm. There are examples of managers who are confident they can deliver at a higher level of the value ladder and they demand that type of assignment.

Certain key people in the firm demonstrated the confidence and strong desire that they can handle project implementation work. (The firm at that stage was doing routine maintenance work.) They were able to get an assignment of that nature. Although the project team faced a lot of difficulties as it was their first assignment, they were able to complete it within the desired time frame. This raised the confidence level and aspirations of the work force. (CEO of Company A)

"Seeding" by Recruitment

A move into a new area of application is a most sensitive moment from the point of view of human resources. As the director of Company B said, "In case an SME wants to change or add an area of application it needs to have domain expertise of some significant level to enter that area or else the effort may prove futile." Likewise, moving up the value ladder implies a dramatic change in the technical complexity of tasks and requires integration of subsystems and systems. With either aim, a firm can recruit an experienced person with the requisite competence, and then assign a team of talented and willing professionals whom the experienced person can guide and take along to achieve transition to the next stage of the value ladder. This "seeding" is likely to be more effective than starting with training existing staff. Knowledge of technology can be achieved with some efforts, but the domain expertise required to assess what is best for a particular project or for a particular client is something which comes only by experience. Company C laid great stress on merit as the grounds for selecting human resources. They took the view that although a highly meritorious professional may only stay with the firm for a short time, the amount the professional would accomplish would be sufficient to keep the firm going even if the professional left, as the professional would have motivated a lot of others to perform at that level. Company A and B were recruiting engineers who had the required competence and in a number of cases recruited postgraduates in engineering.

Training "On Demand"

Acquiring and upgrading competence requires certain formal and informal efforts on the part of the firm. It was found that all firms desired that individual professionals should be aware of the latest trends in technology and come up with ideas about the type of training the professional requires in order to perform better tasks. Companies A, B, and C all agreed on the importance of an individual professional having an important say in the type of training the professional needs to undertake.

The software professionals with us are aware of what they are doing on the job, with the help of their performance appraisal and discussions with the superior he knows what the areas where he can grow and perform are. He certainly needs to understand his requirement and to an extent the organization's requirement. (HR Manager of Company A)

When there was a question of the type of technologies available from which we had to choose on which we desired to proceed further in the work and career, the company did not pressurize us to make a certain choice, I made a specific choice and I have moved ahead with it. Our COO appreciated this fact. (GM projects, Company A)

Company B and C have incorporated items in their performance appraisal forms titled, "Area in which training is desired by the professional."

Communities of Practice

As software development projects are usually undertaken by teams, the interactions among team members are important to decide the outcome and timely completion of the project. Further to enhance the competence of the professionals, these interactions among team members are joined to interaction with clients in order to learn about new ways in which development can be performed and about new activities that can be undertaken. These interactions within and outside the firm with clients contribute to the learning and upgrading of competence of the professionals. Our software SMEs encourage such interaction on a regular basis. So far as purely internal communities of practice are concerned, they have been found in all our firms to arise naturally and informally within project teams but not so much across different project teams. Professionals have to be a part of different teams for different projects, therefore it can be said that such activities are there in firms but the level of activities can be enhanced. Accordingly our firms have institutionalized this phenomenon. Weekly meetings of all group members are organized where they are supposed to voice issues about technology, any new information about a product/process or technique that can help improve the functioning of an individual or group or the organization as a whole.

That [interchange on an informal basis] is the ideal situation. We did not see that happening so we institutionalized the meeting of all professionals to voice their problems, opinions, findings, whatever they had to say. (CEO, Company A)

Every Monday afternoon they have a meeting of all software professionals so that problems, new ideas, new learning, new methods, and so forth, can be discussed and shared. This platform has proved to be a strong point of company A, and they claim that it is an organization free of factions—people work in teams in the most efficient manner. Companies B and C have weekly meetings of team members for a similar purpose, as we were informed by the director of Company B and head of HR of Company C.

Commitment and Its Causes

Firms offer career paths which an individual can progress on depending upon their performance and experience in an area of application or domain expertise. Further to reward and motivate the workforce, all our software SMEs were using a mix of financial and nonfinancial incentives and programmes. Some nonfinancial incentives were recognition, promotion, public admiration of achievement, and holiday at company's expense.

It has been observed during these case studies that retention of workforce was a major issue for software SMEs in India. The aspiration of professionals to work for a large company where they can get high salaries is one of the reasons for this. The aspiration of software professionals to take up tasks that are inherently challenging is a characteristic that can help SMEs tackle this problem. The vision of the firm and the faith that professionals have in their top managers with regard to the direction the firm is moving in is of utmost importance to software professionals. This faith along with the nature of work and the culture of the organization builds a sense of belonging among the workforce.

It is an entrepreneurial spirit that we develop among the workforce, they feel that they are an integral part of the organization and are thus upbeat to perform and build the organization. We have witnessed steady growth and fairly low attrition rate since inception. (HR Head for Company C)

Both Companies A and B had similar stories to tell of such "affective commitment"; but they also mentioned continuance commitment, related to social and family factors keeping the individual in the locality.

The practice of assisting each other and going out of the way to help an individual or a teammate has been observed to be very common. Companies A, B, and C were of the view that for a firm to be dynamic it is essential that individuals go out of their way to help others, solve problems, and talk positively about other individuals, the team they are a part of and in general about the organization. All three firms had ample evidence of individuals behaving in such a way regularly (organizational citizenship behaviour directed at individuals, teams, and the organization). All three top managers stressed that the difference between a high-performing company and a not so high-performing company was at the level of how eager its workforce is in coming together to solve problems, helping each other, respecting the other team members and how cooperative a team and individuals can be when somebody is in need of help to perform. In the words of a professional at Company A:

If this spirit of togetherness and helping each other is not there, then probably we as a team or organization can never perform up to the required levels. Collective teamwork is the necessity to succeed.

Conclusion

We have seen that the Indian software development industry is mostly concentrated at the low end of the value ladder, as less developed country (LDC) exporters tend to be, and that there are factors tending to keep it there which are typical for LDC exporters: lack of lead customers at home, difficulty in getting orders at long distance for higher-value goods, and difficulty of learning from clients at long distance. These three inhibiting factors are likely to be even more problematic for SMEs than for large firms. The SMEs we have examined in this study do however show that there are other factors at work that we may call liberating:

1. **"Co-investment" from the Professional Workforce:** A central role is played by the workforce, who represent at the same time, in effect, the bulk of the capital stock of the firm. A comparison with manufacturing may be helpful here. For an LDC manufacturing firm the large bulk of its capital stock will consist of equipment and other physical capital. Any such firm which wishes to go up-market needs (we suppose) extensive re-equipment—a massive investment. The most optimistic assumption we can make about its workforce is that most of them are capable of being retrained to operate the new equipment. For an Indian software development SME seeking to move up-market, on the other hand, the requirements in terms of re-equipment are almost trivial. It is in the brains of the bulk of its workforce, the software professionals that the large bulk of the investment needs to be made. The usual problem in such an investment in human capital is that the firm does not own the capital and cannot therefore be sure of appropriating the returns. On the other hand, the employees in which the investment is made have a strong incentive to share in the inputs. What emerges from our SME case studies is that this is of particular significance for them. Their employees have every kind of financial and nonfinancial incentive to improve their skills in the context of their firm's moving up-market. By their own efforts at self-improvement, and by helping each other, they can play a vital role in such a move—in effect providing a massive co-investment that greatly lightens the funding burden on the firm. What they require, to provide them with the right incentives, is confidence that the firm is going to succeed. This is where faith in the firm's leadership comes in. That leadership has to get a number of things right: strategy, external relationships, and execution in terms of making the right demands of the right employees. The top managers of our three SMEs seem to have got all those things right. It would be absurd to suggest that this is typical, but our studies have at least indicated the factors of which intelligent managers can take advantage. We now review the favorable factors we found, first among external, then among internal relationships.

2. **External Relationships:** The literature on organizational learning and the development of competences does indeed stress the handicaps imposed by distance from the customer. These are, however, just that, handicaps, as opposed to absolute barriers: they can be countered by enough effort, part of which has to come from the customer. The incentive for that effort comes from the clear and large cost advantage of the Indian firm, which the customer can expect

to share, and would like to share over an ever-widening, ever more up-market, range of contracts. One factor which usually compounds the handicap is cultural distance, but here we may be confident that this plays little role: the foreign client, in the U.S. at least, is likely to have senior Indian employees who can operate on the interface, should that be necessary. Another related handicap arises from a low level of trust, when repeated face-to-face contact is not possible. Here in one of our firms the U.S. venture capitalists who had funded it clearly played a key role: if the firm was trustworthy enough for them to risk their money in, it was obviously trustworthy enough to buy from. All the handicaps mentioned can be much alleviated by strategic relationships with large software firms, and in all our firms they were. We have seen, moreover, that it does not follow that all they will pass on to the SME will be low-end work. The same can be expected of relationships with the major foreign firms—IBM, Accenture, EDS, GE, and so forth—now setting up in India.

The domestic market turned out to be capable of a positive role even when it did not contain lead customers. When a firm had moved into a new area on the basis of foreign contracts, it turned out to be able to find, or develop, a related market at home—giving protection against fluctuations in the export market and much increasing the return on the initial investment both by the firm and its employees.

3.   **Internal Relationships:** For a software development SME to move up-market involves a most delicate combination of investment and "co-investment." As we saw above, the employees who are "co-investing" have to have confidence in the firm's leadership—otherwise they will lose their investment. The confidence must be mutual, moreover the top managers must be sure they have picked the right people in whom to invest by training or recruitment, which means that they will be capable of doing the planned work, and that they will stay to do it. A small or medium enterprise has a range of advantages here: top managers will be better able to judge their juniors' capabilities, because they know them better; in a smaller unit it is easier to generate affective commitment (to keep the trained employee) and organizational citizenship behaviour (to leverage the investments and co-investments)

We have, thus, ended with optimism about the scope for Indian software SMEs to move up-market. We have derived it, however, from a very small sample, and using a research methodology that can only be appropriate to the development of hypotheses rather than being in any way capable of testing them. The extent to which Indian software SMEs are in general capable of exploiting the potential—of using, so to speak, the hand- and foot-holds which we have pointed out on the cliff-face of a move up-market—needs to be judged by investigations on a much larger scale.

References

Amit, R., & Schoemaker, P.J.H. (1993). Strategic assets and organizational rent. *Strategic Management Journal, 14,* 33-46.

Arthur, W.B. (1994). *Increasing returns and path dependence in the economy.* Ann Arbor: University of Michigan Press.

Athreye, S. (2002, June). (Cited in Krishnan, 2003). *The Indian software industry and its evolving service capability, mimeo.* Open University, UK.

Balasubramanyam, A., & Balasubramanyam, V.N. (1997). Singer, services and software. *World Development, 25*(11), 1857-1861.

Barney, J.B. (1991). Firm resources and sustainable competitive advantage. *Journal of Management, 17,* 99-120.

Blum, B.I. (1994). A taxonomy of software development methods. *Communications of the ACM, 37*(1), 82-94.

Brown, J., & Duguid, P. (1991). Organizational learning and communities of practice: Towards a unified view of working, learning and innovation. *Organization Science, 2*(1), 40-57.

Burns, T., & Stalker, G.M. (1961). *The management of innovation.* London: Tavistock Publications

Cohendet, P., Kern, F., Mehmanpazir, B., & Muneir, F. (1999). Knowledge coordination, competence creation and integrated networks in globalised firms. *Cambridge Journal of Economics, 23*(2), 225-241.

Coombs, R., & Hull, R. (1998). Knowledge management practices and path dependency in innovation. *Research Policy, 27*(3), 237-253.

Coyle-Shapiro, J.A., Kessler, I., & Purcell, J. (2004). Exploring organisationally directed citizenship behaviour: Reciprocity or it's my job? *Journal of Management Studies, 41*(1), 85-106.

D'Costa, A.P. (2000). Export growth and path dependence: The locking in of innovations in the software industry. Paper presented at the *4th International Conference on Technology Policy and Innovation*, Curitiba, Brazil.

D'Costa, A.P. (2002). Software outsourcing and policy implications: An Indian perspective. *International Journal of Technology Management, 24*(7/8), 705-723.

Gustafsson, H., & Metzner, M. (2002). *Innovation: The influence of venture capitalists on their portfolio companies.* Thesis, Institute of Economics, Linkoping University. Electronic Press.

Higashide, H., & Birley, S. (2000). *Value created through the socially complex relationship between the venture capitalist and the entrepreneurial team?* Frontiers of Entrepreneurship Research, Babson College.

Jassawala, A.R., & Sashittal, H.C. (1998). An examination of collaboration in high technology new product development processes. *Journal of Product Innovation Management, 15*, 237-254.

Krishnan, R.T. (2003, November 3-6). The evolution of a developing country innovation system during economic liberalization. Paper presented at *1st Globelics Conference*, Rio de Janeiro, Brazil.

Krishnan, R.T., Gupta, A., & Matta, V. (2003, March 3-5). (Cited in Krishnan, 2003). Biotechnology and bioinformatics: Can India emulate the software success story? Paper Presented at *Workshop on the Indian Development Experience, Department of Management Studies*, Indian Institute of Science, Bangalore.

Lam, A. (2002). Alternative societal models of learning and innovation in the knowledge economy. *International Social Science Journal, 171*, 67-82.

Lundvall, B.A. (1988). Innovation as an interactive process: From user-producer interaction to the national system of innovation. In G. Dosi, C. Freeman, R. Nelson, G. Silverberg, & L. Soete (Eds.), *Technical change and economic theory* (pp. 349-369). London: Pinter.

Mahoney, J.T., & Pandian, J.R. (1992). The resource based view within the conversation of strategic management. *Strategic Management Journal, 13*, 363-380.

Mariani, M. (2002). Next to production or to technological clusters? The economics and management of R&D location. *Journal of Management and Governance, 6*, 131-152.

Maskell, P., & Malmberg, A. (1999). Localized learning and industrial competitiveness. *Cambridge Journal of Economics, 23*(2), 167-185.

Meyer, J.P., & Allen, N.J. (1997). *Commitment in the work place, theory, research and application.* Thousand Oaks, CA: Sage Publications.

Nambisan, S. (2000). *Customer networks, entrepreneur strategy, and firm growth: Insights from the software industry.* Frontiers of Entrepreneurship Research, Babson College.

Nambisan, S. (2002). Software firm evolution and innovation-orientation. *Journal of Engineering & Technology Management, 19*(2), 141-165.

Narula, R. (2001). In-house R&D, outsourcing or alliances? Some strategic and economic considerations. In F. Contractor (Ed.), *Valuation of intangible assets in global operations,* pp. 101-122. Westport, CT; London: Quorum Books.

National Association of Software and Services Companies. (1999). *McKinsey study: Indian IT strategies.* New Delhi: National Association of Software and Services Companies.

National Association of Software and Services Companies. (2002). *The IT industry in India: Strategic review.* New Delhi: National Association of Software and Services Companies.

National Association of Software and Services Companies. (2003). *The IT industry in India: Strategic review.* New Delhi: National Association of Software and Services Companies.

National Association of Software and Services Companies. (2004). *Indian SME fact sheet* (p. 1). Retrieved July 14, 2006, from http://www.nasscom.org

Nilekani, N. (2001). *Indian Software Industry: Challenges ahead.* Presentation at the NASSCOM Information Technology Conference, Mumbai.

Nonaka, I., & Kono, N. (1998). Ba: Building a foundation for knowledge creation. *California Management Review, 40*(3), 40-54.

Organ, D.W. (1988). *Organizational citizenship behavior: The good soldier syndrome.* Lexington, MA: Lexington Books.

Panda, H., & Ramanathan, K. (1996). Technological capability assessment in the electricity sector. *Technovation, 16*(10), 561-588.

Pare, G., Tremblay, M., & Lalonde, P. (2001). Workforce retention: What do IT employees really want? *Proceedings of the 2001 ACM SIGCPR conference on computer personnel research,* (pp. 1-10), San Diego, CA.

Reddy, P. (1997). New trends in globalization of corporate R&D and implications for innovation capability in host countries: A survey from India. *World Development, 25*(11), 1821-1837.

Romijn, H., & Albaladejo, M. (2002). Determinants of innovation capability in small electronics and software firms in South-East England. *Research Policy, 31*, 1053-1067.

Romijn, H., & Albu, M. (2001, March). *Innovativeness in small high technology firms in the United Kingdom.* Technische Universiteit Eindhoven: Eindhoven Centre for Innovation Studies.

Sommerville, I. (1982). A pattern matching system. *Software: Practice and Experience, 12*(6), 517-530.

Torrisi, S. (1998). *Industrial organisation and innovation: An international study of the software industry.* New Horizons in the Economics of Innovation, Edward Elgar.

Vagasi, M. (2001, July 8-13). Integration of customers and other stakeholders in the product innovation process. In *Proceedings of the International Summer Academy on Technological Studies: User Involvement in Technological Innovation,* Deutschlandberg, Austria, 321-333.

Van Slyke, E.J. (1996). Busting the bureaucracy. *HR Focus, 73*(7), 15-16.

Visintin, F., Ozgen, B., Tylecote, A., & Handscombe, R. (2004). Italian success and British survival: Case studies of corporate governance and innovation in a mature industry. *Technovation, 25*, 621-629.

Von Hippel, E. (1988). *The sources of innovation.* Cambridge: MIT Press.

Wenger, E. (1998). *Communities of practice: Learning meaning and identity.* Cambridge: Cambridge University Press.

Wenger, E.C., McDermott, R., & Snyder, W.M. (2001). *A guide to managing knowledge: Cultivating communities of practice.* HBS Press.

Wynekoop, J.L., & Walz, D.B. (2000). Investigating traits of top performing software developers. *Information Technology and People, 13*(3), 186-195.

Yin, R.K. (1994). *Case study research, design and methods.* Sage Publications.

Zannad, H., & Rouet, V. (2003, June 3-6). Organizational commitment in innovative companies. Paper Presented at the *12th Annual Conference of the International Strategic Management Association*, Tunisia.

Appendix: Details of Questionnaire

Core Questions

- What are the challenges that Indian software SMEs face while attempting to move up market?

- What are the characteristics of a firm that help in predicting whether a firm is dynamic or not?

- Has your firm made any attempts to move up market (moving up the value ladder or enter new industry sector/geographic market or both)? If yes, were you successful?

- If yes, what and who would you give credit for the success?

- If no, what reasons do you attribute for the failure?

- Have the organizational policies and practices of the firm changed since its start?

- Has your experience of working in other firms influenced your choice of organizational policies and practices? If yes, how?

- Are you developing products of your own or is all work for clients only?

- How does your relationship with clients contribute to the performance of the firm? Other than spelling out the requirements for the products being developed for them, does client involvement contribute to any other aspect of business (like totally new product development, use of new process for software development and influence on organizational practices, etc.)?

- What sort of role does the Venture capitalist play in the firm?
- Are professionals in your firm using any informal efforts for problem solving and learning?
- If yes, do you recognize and appreciate such efforts by them? Would you allocate resources to foster such efforts and institutionalize them?
- Do you have regular user-developer meetings?
- Is the purpose of such meetings only for feedback and appraisal of work or is there any other aspect that is discussed?
- Do they offer suggestions for any other product or process that can be developed or used?
- Does interaction with clients help in developing new ideas for prospective products, services, and processes?
- Do clients have any influence on the organizational practices of the firm?

Questions Specifically for CEO/Director of the Firm

- How involved is the VC in the operations of the firm?
- Does (s)he provide help other than the funding that is provided by them? What sort of help is it?
- Is (s)he interested in financial returns only or is (s)he interested in the firm developing new and improved products as well?
- If the firm desires to develop some innovative products or use some innovative process for software development, does the VC offer support and encourage such an endeavour?
- When the firm came into being did the VC contribute in:
  - Devising an appropriate strategy for the firm
  - Technology to be used
  - Getting expert professionals
  - Contacts with prospective clients
  - Suggestions for organizational policies and practices

Questions Specifically for the Head of HR:

- What composition of HR policies and practices do you think Software SMEs need to have in order to move up market?
- What are the problem areas?
- What are your company policies for managing people? (no details, only response on dimensions)
- Do you involve the professional in activities like training needs assessment, appraisal, career planning? Does (s) he have a say in these or are they always directed towards the organization needs?
- What type of rewards and compensation system do you use? (Ask about the three levels model)
- Do you evaluate the performance of the professional on the basis of his/her individual performance only or do you incorporate Weightage for contribution to team performance and how the professional has engaged in team work?
- Are efforts put in to foster a sense of belongingness for the firm? If yes, how do you do it?
- Does a professional continue to work for a firm only because of the work and sense of belongingness for the firm?
- Have you observed professionals:
  - Helping individuals—when absent, when a new entrant joins the firm, when faced with difficulty, etc?
  - Place team goals above personal goals?
  - Work extra for their team to be able to achieve desired results
  - Help others within the team to ensure completion of assignment on time and with desired quality?
  - Work extra hours when working on multiple projects?
  - Always comply with organizational rules and regulations
  - Attend to tasks not essentially productive to the firm but that help to build the organizations image?

Chapter XIV

Comparing Expert Systems and Agent Technology for KM*

Tor Guimaraes, Tennessee Technological University, USA

Abstract

Agent technology offers a new means of effectively managing knowledge and addresses complex decision processes which heretofore appeared intractable. This chapter presents an overview and comparison of expert system and agent technologies, and shows the latter as a powerful extension in artificial intelligence for systems development. To illustrate, a system developed first using an expert system approach and then an agent-based approach are used to identify the strengths and weaknesses of the agent-based approach. Last, the practical implications of a company adoption of agent-based technology for systems development are addressed.

Introduction

Agent technology (AT) or expert systems (ES) can be useful tools for the emerging field of knowledge management (KM). KM is the process of creating value from an organization's intangible assets. It deals with how best to leverage knowledge internally in the organization and externally to the customers and stakeholders. The focus is on how to best share knowledge to create value-added benefits to the organization. Simply put, KM is the process of capturing collective expertise and distributing it in a manner that produces a payoff (Liebowitz, 1999a, b, 2000; Liebowitz & Beckman, 1998). The expert system, which provides a software representation of organizational expertise dealing with specific problems, is a useful mechanism to accomplish the knowledge-sharing task. However, as presented in Table 1, traditional ES development techniques have several shortcomings. These ES shortcomings are exactly what agent technology (AT) was developed to address. Today, as the system developer chooses between tools and techniques in addressing

Table 1. Comparing ES and AT advantages

Expert Systems	Agent Technology
Expert systems (ES) became the most important artificial intelligence technology since the early 1980s. Today, ES applications are found widely in business and government as ES development techniques and tool kits have multiplied. ES technology provides powerful tools to manage knowledge/expertise within specific domains	Operates without the direct intervention of humans and has some control over its own actions and internal state. It is capable of independent action. Agents share information, knowledge, and tasks among themselves and cooperate with each other to achieve common goals. The capability of an agent system is not only reflected by the intelligence of individual agents but also by the emergent behavior of the entire agent community. An agent learns from experience to improve its performance in a dynamic environment. Agents, as autonomous, cooperating entities, represent a more powerful and flexible alternative for conceptualizing complex problems. For problems characterized by *dynamic* knowledge, it is infeasible to predict and analyze all possible interactions among modules at design time. Flexible interaction among agents at run-time enables an agent-based system to effectively handle dynamic, unpredictable knowledge. Agents cannot only react to specific events but can also be proactive, polling the environment for events to determine the proper action in a given circumstance. An intelligent distributed agent architecture that allows flexible interactions among participating agents maps well to applications, like expert systems, that require seamless integration with humans.

new system requirements, careful consideration must be given to the advantages of using an expert system vs. enhancing it with an agent-based approach. The objective of this study is to analyze the added value of using AT, its significant features and characteristics that distinguish them from ES, and its strengths and weaknesses in systems development. The concepts are further illustrated through a case study in which the trade-offs between these techniques are explored.

Agent Technology and What It Can Do for You

While no standard definition of an agent has yet emerged, most definitions agree that agents are software systems that carry out tasks on behalf of human users. Intelligent agents generally possess three properties: autonomy, sociability, and adaptability.

Autonomy means that an agent operates without the direct intervention of humans and has some control over its own actions and internal state. It is capable of independent action (Wooldridge & Jennings, 1995). An agent does not simply act in response to its environment; it is able to exhibit goal-directed behavior by taking the initiative.

Sociability refers to an agent's ability to cooperate and collaborate with other agents and possibly human users to solve problems. Agents share information, knowledge, and tasks among themselves and cooperate with each other to achieve common goals. The capability of an agent system is not only reflected by the intelligence of individual agents but also by the emergent behavior of the entire agent community. The infrastructure for cooperation and collaboration includes a common agent communication language like the Knowledge Query Manipulation Language (KQML) (Finin, Labrou & Mayfield, 1998) or the Foundation for Intelligent Physical Agent (FIPA, 2000).

Finally, *adaptability* refers to an agent's ability to modify its own behavior as environmental circumstances change. An agent learns from experience to improve its performance in a dynamic environment. That learning can be centralized, as performed by a single agent without interaction with other agents, or decentralized, as accomplished through the interaction of several agents that cooperate to achieve the learning goal (Cantu, 2000).

Agent technology represents a new and exciting means of decomposing, abstracting, and organizing large *complex problems*. Agents, as autonomous, cooperating entities, represent a more powerful and flexible alternative for conceptualizing complex problems. As attention is increasingly placed on *distributed applications* like mobile and Web-based systems, applications will not necessarily run from a central location.

Communications can be costly in such environments. Direct routing of data to the recipient must be fast and efficient to make additional bandwidth available to others. Agent architectures provide a template for a distributed architecture that lends itself to many of these emerging applications. Agents can be used as mediators between heterogeneous data sources, providing the means to interoperate, using ontologies for describing the data contained in their information sources, and communicating with the others via an agent communication language (Broome, Gangopadhyay, & Yoon, 2002).

For problems characterized by *dynamic* knowledge, it is infeasible to predict and analyze all possible interactions among modules at design time. Flexible interaction among agents at run-time enables an agent-based system to effectively handle dynamic, unpredictable knowledge. Although knowledge of some problems is dynamic, the change is often local, affecting a subset of requirements. Therefore, some agents can be designated to deal with the dynamic knowledge of a problem, and the functionality of those agents can evolve, reflecting the changes encountered.

The inherent autonomy of agents enables the agent-based system to perform its tasks without direct external intervention. Agents cannot only react to specific events but can also be proactive, polling the environment for events to determine the proper action in a given circumstance. Despite the increased level of autonomy in an agent-based system, however, the system itself may not be able to automate all levels of intelligent activity. Human users may be required to perform higher-level intelligent tasks. An intelligent distributed agent architecture that allows flexible interactions among participating agents maps well to applications, like expert systems, that require seamless integration with humans. Further, agent technology offers mechanisms for knowledge sharing and *interoperability* between autonomous software and hardware systems characterized by heterogeneous languages and platforms. Agents can be used as mediators between these various systems, facilitating interoperability.

Enhancing Expert Systems with Agent-Based Systems

One way to better understand AT is to compare it with the more widely used expert systems. This does not imply that ES technology is obsolete or that ES development has nothing in common with agent-based system development. Tables 1 and 2 summarize AT and ES advantages and disadvantages, respectively. In general there are some important distinctions between ES and agent-based systems, which make the latter ideal for integrating individual ES with other ES and other system types. Probably the most important distinction is that expert systems rely on the user to initiate the reasoning process and to accomplish any action associated with the recommendations provided by the system (Yannis, Finin, & Peng, 1999). The integration of human interaction, then, is assumed and has been greatly facilitated by development tool kits and environments. Agents, on the other hand, are inherently autonomous. That does not mean that the integration of human interaction is necessarily complex. The human is simply another agent in the society of agents. While the user roles vary dramatically between the two paradigms, both readily accommodate human interaction.

Table 2. Comparing ES and AT disadvantages

Expert System	Agent Technology
Expert systems are typically brittle, dealing poorly with situations that "bend" the rules. Further, the components of an expert system are not typically intelligent enough to learn from their many experiences while interacting directly with users. Thus, the rules encoded initially do not evolve on their own but must be modified directly by developers to reflect changes in the environment. Expert systems are typically isolated, self-contained software entities. Very little emphasis is placed on tool kits that support interaction with other expert systems or external software components. As the system develops, functionality increases are accompanied by an ever-growing knowledge base in which inconsistencies and redundancies are difficult to avoid. Over time, portions of the process that initially required human intervention become well understood and could be totally automated, but there is no mechanism in place to support the transition from human-activated objects to autonomous objects.	Most AT weaknesses can be traced back to its lack of maturity. While agent concepts were under discussion as far back as 1985 (Minsky, 1985), applications have been slow to develop, due in part to a lack of mature system development tool kits that enable agents to represent and reason about their actions. A number of systems are now available or under development (Barbaceanu, 2001; Harvey, Decker, & Carberry, 2005; Rubenstein-Montano, Yoon, Lowry, & Merlau, 2005; Thomas, Redmond, Yoon, & Singh, 2005; Traverse, 2001), but they still suffer from general immaturity. Lack of software engineering techniques specifically tailored to agent-based systems. Although there are software development techniques such as object-oriented analysis and design, the existing approaches fail to adequately capture an agent's flexible, autonomous problem-solving behavior, the richness of an agent's interactions, and the complexity of an agent system's organizational structures; thus they are unsuitable for agent-based systems. If agents are to realize their potential, it is necessary to further provide software engineering methods for developing such systems such as DECAF (Graham, Decker, & Mersic, 2003). General difficulty associated with *decomposing goals and tasks* in ways that balance the computation and communication requirements, avoid or reconcile conflicts, and still achieve the initial objective. The issue of *privacy* is particularly relevant for a system in which software components act on independently across a distributed environment. While standards are under development for insuring that agents are locked out of systems where they are unwelcome, such standards generally require cooperative agents that do not intentionally attack an unreceptive host.

Another important distinction is that expert systems have a fixed set of rules that clearly define their reasoning process, while agents interact with their environment and adapt to new conditions. Thus, an application that characteristically incorporates dynamic changes in its data and rules are more naturally accommodated by agent-based techniques. Further, the expert system's knowledge base impacts the modularity and scalability of the system. As new functions are introduced into the system, the central knowledge base grows increasingly large. New rules risk conflicts with old, and changed rules potentially impact more functions than the developer may have planned. Agents, on the other hand, are extremely modular, like self-contained programs that can readily be reused across applications.

Finally, the social interaction inherent in agents facilitates mobile and distributed systems, with formal standards in place outlining interfaces between agents assumed to be heterogeneous in design. Expert systems, on the other hand, are fundamentally built as a cohesive product with a single overarching goal. Despite early emphasis on linking knowledge bases and integrating expertise, those goals are rarely achieved, perhaps because of the issues of combining knowledge bases without the benefit of a standard interface technique. Further, the system components are rarely reused outside the system for which they were built. In fact, it is quite common to throw away one prototype and completely rebuild the next version from scratch. Thus, tools are built with an emphasis on rapid prototyping rather than on facilitating component reuse.

As discussed by other authors (Lu & Guimaraes, 1989), whether or not to use ES technology in systems development is one major consideration. Once that decision has been made, various ES development approaches must also be considered (Yoon & Guimaraes, 1993). Further, the software developer must consider numerous issues in determining whether an agent-based approach is appropriate for a given application. In the final analysis, the system requirements must drive these choices. To illustrate the choice of using an agent-based approach over a strictly ES-based approach, a case study is presented next.

The Reverse Mortgage Advisor (REMA) Case Study

REMA Background

A reverse mortgage is a special type of home loan that allows a homeowner to convert the equity into retirement income. The equity, built up over years of home mortgage payments, can be paid to the homeowner in a lump sum, in a stream of payments, or a combination of the two. Unlike a traditional home equity loan or second mortgage, repayment is not required as long as the borrowers continue to use the home as their principal residence (HUD, 2001). While reverse mortgages have long been seen as a means of increasing the income of the poor or elderly, they have more recently been proposed as a mechanism for tapping home equity for a variety of options and at various stages in the life cycle (Rassmussen, Megbolugbe, & Morgan, 1997). In either case, "because each reverse mortgage plan has different strengths—and because fees and fraud can catch unsuspecting customers—experts say seniors should either shop smart with these tricky loans or not shop at all" (Larson, 1999, p. 2). The Internet already plays an important role in supporting the dissemination of information about reverse mortgages. In an effort to increase public awareness of this unique loan opportunity, federal regulators, consumer advocates, and loan companies have all developed Web sites (AARP, 2001; FannieMae, 2001; HUD, 2001; Reverse, 2001) to supplement the publications and training currently available through more traditional media. Such Web sites provide information on mortgage options and sources, answers to frequently asked questions, and even "calculator" functions to help "shoppers" estimate the amount of loan for which they are eligible. The use of Web sites, however, can be quite daunting, particularly for the potential reverse mortgage client who is over 62 and of limited income. The REMA project was initiated to increase the accessibility of reverse mortgage information.

REMA I: A Traditional Expert System Approach

REMA I is an expert system designed to provide a structured approach to determining whether an individual qualifies for a reverse mortgage. Unlike the traditional Web site, users are not left to their own devices as they sort through information to better understand their loan options. Instead, REMA I provides advice on Web sites to visit and recommended loan types. It is meant to supplement the Web-based technologies that precede it.

System Architecture

REMA I was developed using Multilogic's Resolver® and Netrunner® tools. Resolver® is a knowledge-based system development tool that combines a powerful rule editor with a flexible visual decision tree interface and inference engine. While it supports backward and forward chaining, linear programming, fuzzy logic, and neural net reasoning, REMA used the default goal-driven backward chaining technique. Resolver® greatly facilitated the coding process, supporting not only the encoding of the initial logic representation, but the debug process as well. Once REMA was developed, the executable was ported to Netrunner®, the engine that

Figure 1. REMA architecture

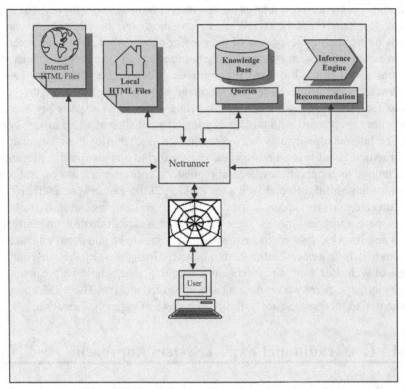

supports Web-top publication of Resolver® applications. Figure 1 provides a conceptual illustration of the final application, though, in fact, the knowledge base and inference engine are located in Resolver® and their output is located in Netrunner® at the time the application runs. The decision process was initially represented as a decision tree. One branch of that tree is depicted in Figure 2. The decision tree was then converted into a series of 34 "if-then" statements, similar to the sample rule in Figure 2. Each of the 34 rules resulted in the recommendation of one or more of 16 possible outcomes. The knowledge base represents the 34 rules the experts follow when providing advice to potential reverse mortgage consumers.

Queries provide links to local Hypertext Markup Language (HTML) files that provide reverse mortgage training. Those files may, in turn, reference additional information in HTML files at other sites provided by government agencies, consumer advocates, or loan companies. Those links are provided to the Web server through Netrunner®.

Figure 2. Decision tree illustrating generation of one of REMA's decision rules

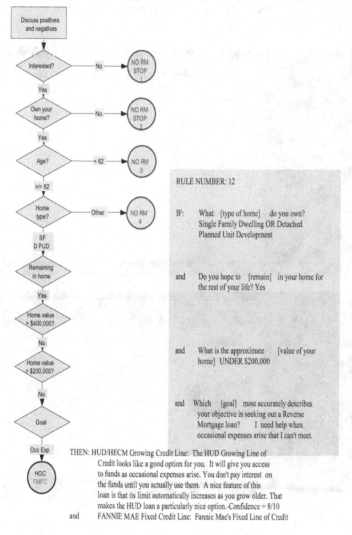

System Interface

Figure 3 illustrates a sample interface screen used to gather input for the system. Note that in addition to providing answers to fixed questions, the user may choose to view hypertext about home ownership issues (as illustrated in the bottom screen in Figure 3), view the rules associated with the question (by clicking on "Why are you asking this question?"), or return to a previous state by undoing the last answer. The undo option is useful if, for example, users find they are not old enough to qualify

Figure 3. The top screen illustrates a query screen used to gather input. The bottom screen illustrates the results of selecting the hypertext link while viewing the query screen.

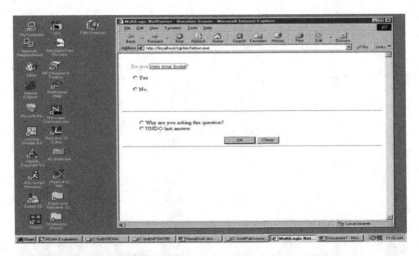

for a loan but would still like to continue the analysis. The user must backtrack and modify the age answer to continue.

REMA I Shortcomings

As is common in the life cycle of an expert system, upon completing REMA I, the current system's shortcomings were identified for improvement in future iterations. The current version is clearly at an early stage of development, so it was expected that the developer would want to "grow the system" by incorporating more than the initial three loan companies selected for Phase 1. However, several of the problems identified indicate that the expert system design may not be best for meeting overall project objectives. The "build a little, test a little" approach associated with expert systems was quite useful in facilitating discussions with experts, but the outcome of those discussions indicates an alternative design option should at least be considered before moving to the next development phase.

First, beyond the original assessment of loan qualifications, a cost-benefit analysis is the primary basis for selecting the optimal loan type. While many of the rules for determining whether a user qualifies for a given loan are easily expressed in symbolic terms, the cost-benefit analysis is a *computational* rather than symbolic algorithm. In order to take full advantage of the Resolver® tools, the cost-benefit analysis was replaced with a number of rules-of-thumb. For example, if the applicant's home is very expensive, the Freedom plan is usually best. Otherwise, the HUD and Fannie Mae options are best. One problem is that the concept of "expensive" varies from state to state. The REMA I rules were stated crisply (with "expensive" arbitrarily set to $400,000, for example), and at a minimum should be replaced with fuzzy rules. Ideally, however, the exact loan size, interest rates, application fees, and so forth, should be used to provide accurate assessments. These inaccuracies must be avoided in future developments. In some cases, systems (like FannieMae's MorNet) are available to compute exact costs and benefits. While the original objective of the project was not to replace these previously developed computational systems but to augment them with a training system, the longer term objective should most assuredly move toward a combination of the two types of systems. Otherwise, the advice portion of REMA will be inaccurate, which could have adverse legal implications. An agent-based design would more naturally accommodate the seamless integration of other software packages, while expert systems have very little support for interfacing with other expert systems.

Next, in generating REMA I, the developers discovered that both the rules for providing recommendations and the Web sites used for training users were extremely *dynamic*. A complete redesign of the decision tree and training files was required between building the baseline system, based on books and Web site information, and the current iteration, based on discussions with the experts. It was not just because tables of costs and benefits changed, though that did cause some system reconfiguration.

Additionally, over a very brief period, Congress passed new regulations regarding applicant qualification requirements; companies opted out of the list of reverse mortgage providers; other companies restructured their programs to focus on different target audiences; and, as always, Web pages appeared and disappeared across the Internet without notice to the sites that referenced them. Again, expert systems technology was not meant to accommodate such a dynamic environment.

Finally, the *training* aspect of the system was not as powerful as one might hope. This is due, in part, to the fact that the training simply took the form of instructional text. It certainly was an improvement over the baseline, in which users were on their own to wander the Web looking for relevant documentation. Instead, REMA I focused the Web searches addressing those specific issues of which a prospective applicant should be aware. An online system of this sort, however, has the potential of being a tutor, keeping up with the users previous searches and expressed preferences to even further tailor the training process. It has a potential for notifying the user as better options arise in this dynamic loan environment. But reaching this potential requires greater autonomy than is typical of expert systems.

The easiest choice for Phase II of system development would be to continue building the next iteration of the current expert system. The next iteration would require (1) an update of references to outside Web sites; (2) current system assessments from experts; (3) correction of any recently modified data for the HUD, FannieMae, and Freedom Plan options currently represented; (4) incorporation of at least one new loan source; (5) fuzzification of current crisp rules-of-thumb for loan source selection; and (6) incorporation of the MorNet expert system for calculating costs and benefits for those companies it covers. The general system architecture would continue as depicted in Figure 1. However, for the reasons outlined previously, instead of enhancing the current ES-based REMA, a decision was made to first explore the use of an agent-based approach to the problem.

REMA II: An Agent-Based Approach

System Architecture

Agents are specific, goal-oriented abstractions of task requirements in systems. From the discussion of the current REMA I system presented in this chapter, we derive a set of system requirements that agents must implement:

1. *Mediating* between multiple external agencies including HUD and FannieMae, to ensure that external information contained in the system remains current.

2. *Translating* between external information collected by the mediation with the external agencies (above) and the internal information on user characteristics and goals.

3. *Recommending* the appropriate course of action to the user based on rules and expertise contained in the system.

4. *Interfacing* with the user to guide them through collection of user characteristics and present the system recommendations to them.

5.   *Supervision* of the entire process to ensure that the asynchronous collection of information from external agencies is assimilated and incorporated in the recommendations of the system and the information presented to the user.

These system requirements, as derived from the design of the existing system, form the basis for an agent-based approach. The agent-based approach to REMA consists of multiple Mediator Agents, Tutor Agent, User Interface Agent, Recommender Agent, and Supervisor Agent, as shown in Figure 4.

Individual *Mediator Agents* are responsible for maintaining the most current information for calculating the costs and benefits of an individual company's reverse mortgage plan. These agents are responsible for interfacing with the external agencies that provide critical information about the programs available for REMA users and ensure that such information is available to the users of REMA. *User Interface Agents* collect and maintain information on the user's goals and personal characteristics, required for a reverse mortgage application. They are responsible for interaction with the user and provide guided input of user goals and characteristics in addition to presenting users with the final results and recommendations of the REMA system. The User Agent receives information from the user, through the user interface, and presents user characteristics and goals to the *Tutor Agent* to determine which internal and external information is most required to teach the principles of reverse mortgages. A *Recommender Agent* incorporates user characteristics and the most recent loan company information in performing a cost-benefit analysis to determine the best loan source of those available. This information is passed back to the User

Figure 4. Agent architecture for REMA

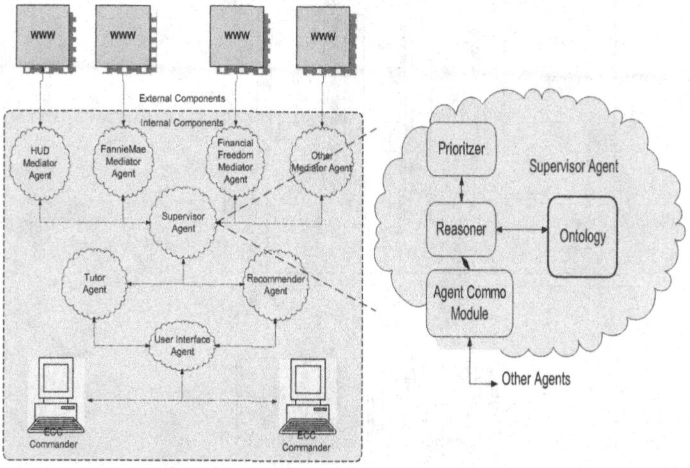

Interface Agent with information on options that are available to the users given their characteristics and goals. Finally, a *Supervisor Agent* is responsible for the overall function of the agent system and performs critical metafunctions to prioritize data requests, supply the most recent loan company data, and interpret terminology from heterogeneous sources to consistent internal agents by providing and interpreting a shared ontology of concepts contained in the REMA system.

Figure 5. Use-case diagram for agent based REMA

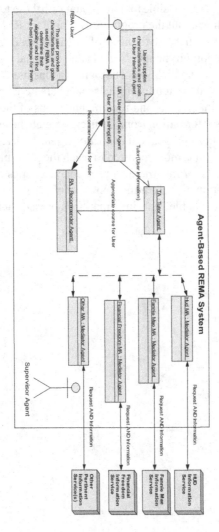

System Interface

REMA II is initialized with the user being assigned representation in the system through a User Interface Agent. This agent interacts with the user and collects information about the user through an interactive questionnaire. Information about the user is passed to the Tutor Agent who is responsible for matching the goals and characteristics of the user with information from the Mediator Agents to find the

Figure 6. Sample interface screen of agent-based REMA

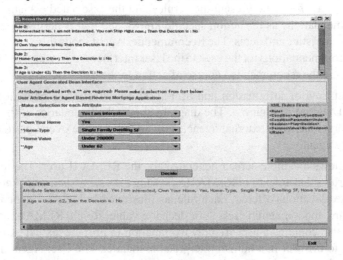

Figure 7. REMA II rule in eXtended Markup Language (XML) format

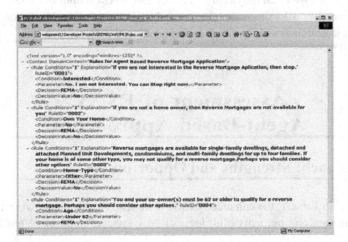

appropriate agency that may fulfill user needs. The Mediator Agents, under supervision of the Supervisor Agent, constantly and asynchronously, update their information of the most current programs that are available from the various agencies they interface with. Upon performing the matching, the Tutor Agent generates a match between the internal information provided by the user and the external information available from the financial agencies, through the Mediator Agents. These results are transferred to the Recommender Agent, which maintains the knowledge about courses of action based on specific information received by the Tutor Agent. The Recommender Agent maintains an active, in-memory representation of the decision tree illustrated in Figure 2. Upon receiving user-specific information, it can select the rules that are fired and present those rules and the associated explanations for the recommendations as the action specific knowledge that is pertinent given the users' characteristics and goals. The Recommender Agent sends this knowledge, as specific recommendations for the user, to the User Interface Agent who is responsible for presenting the recommended course of action to the user.

The overall flow of information and user-system interaction is presented in the Use-Case Diagram in Figure 5. The diagram shows the boundaries of the system and its interactions with external agencies, in addition to the oversight role of the supervisory agent.

Figure 6 shows a sample screen generated for the REMA II user. The top panel shows the rules that are part of REMA II, allowing the user to gain more knowledge about the explanations offered. Each rule, as illustrated in Figure 7, contains a set of conditions and a matching result, or decision value, for the REMA application. Each rule also contains a user friendly explanation to provide textual explanation of the rule to the user in a human interpretable manner. The User Agent Interface takes input from the user on various attributes, in terms of the parameters that are acceptable to REMA. For example, in answer to the question *"Do you own your own home?"* the user can only reply "Yes" or "No." After input of all required parameters, the user asks the system to advise by clicking the decide button and the rule space is searched and the result is displayed to the user.

Assessment of ES vs. Agent-Based Approaches

ES Approach: Strengths and Opportunities

As outlined in Table 1, the enhanced expert system approach is best when meeting quick turnaround requirements. Multilogic's Resolver® and Netrunner® tools greatly facilitate the system development process, and the consistency of design further insures efficiency. The resulting system will most certainly continue to support faster decision making and improved consistency, less demand on experts, and improved public understanding of the reverse mortgage process. Further, it will continue to support direct access to local HTML files or inserting new ones. Because of its Web emphasis, the system continues to broaden the audience for reverse mortgage training over previous brochure and booklet techniques. Finally, its "build a little, test a little" techniques have been shown to make effective use of the limited time of experts in the field, while essentially serving to formally document a process that is not currently well documented.

ES Approach: Weaknesses and Threats

The major shortcoming of this approach, however, is that it fails to resolve the three problem issues identified in developing REMA I. While a link to MorNet will improve the computational component of system recommendations as new loan companies are added, those insertions will continue to be computational, rather than symbolic, in nature. The value of the more established tool sets associated with expert systems will be less noticeable than if the entire task were heavily symbolic in nature. Further, while this approach will incorporate changes to the current data and rules, bringing the system up to date, it does not address the fact that the rules and data will change again. The static nature of the expert system limits its ability to adapt to the *dynamic* reverse mortgage process it represents or the dynamic Web environment in which it resides. Its lack of advanced communication or interoperability tools limits its ability to incorporate the functionality of other expert systems or Web sites into its knowledge base. As a result, the system will require frequent manual updates or risk providing inaccurate information that could cost its users money. Such losses may, in turn, carry negative legal implications. Finally, its lack of autonomy restricts the *training* function to the display of informational text rather than a full-blown tutor that learns about the user as it progresses or, on its own initiative, notifies the user of changes in loan options.

Agent-Based Approach: Strengths and Opportunities

Possessing the properties of autonomy, social ability, and adaptability, agent technology provides the potential for greatly enhancing the capabilities of the REMA system. As illustrated in Table 3, the strengths and opportunities of an agent-based system parallel in many ways those of the expert system approach. The system will most certainly continue to support faster decision making, improved consistency, less demand on experts, and improved public understanding of the reverse mortgage process. Further, it will continue to support direct access to a variety of loan sources

Table 3. Analysis of the strengths, weaknesses, opportunities and threats associated with the agent-based approach and the expert system approach

	Agent Based Approach	*Enhanced Expert System Approach*
Strengths	Faster decision making. Improved consistency. Less demand on experts. Improved reverse mortgage understanding. Supports better focused Web searches. Rules reflect changes in the environment. Other ES work more easily incorporated. Recommendations/training adapt to user.	Effective development tools. Faster decision making. Improved consistency. Less demand on experts. Improved reverse mortgage understanding. Supports better focused Web searches.
Weaknesses	Limited sites with XML/ontology standard. Limited agent development tool kits.	Accurately addressing the cost-benefit analysis will render the expert system tools less effective. Dynamic data and rules, controlled outside. Training limited to informational text. Knowledge base isolated from Web data. Does not incorporate other ES work.
Opportunities	Access information directly from source. Easily incorporate new training topics. Reach a broader audience. Formalize expert's process. Autonomous recommendations.	Access information directly from source. Easily incorporate new training topics. Reach a broader audience. Rapid prototype effective use of experts. Formalize expert's process.
Threats	Web sites volatile, with distributed control. Changing interface standards. Insufficient training data.	Inaccurate recommendations costly. Potential legal impact from misinformation.

by linking into their Web sites. Because of its Web emphasis, it continues to broaden the audience for reverse mortgage training over previous brochure and booklet techniques. The agent-based approach, however, has several additional strengths. First, it more specifically addresses the three problem areas identified at the end of Phase I. (1) Agent-based systems deal equally well with problems of a *computational* or symbolic nature. (2) It better addresses the *dynamic* nature of the reverse mortgage process, rather than establishing fixed rules that must be intentionally modified by the developer at regular intervals, information agents are established to seek and substitute relevant parameters from regulated Web sites as appropriate. (3) The learning component of agent-based systems supports incorporating a well-designed *tutoring* system that is both diagnostic, discovering the nature and extent of the user's knowledge, and strategic, planning its responses based on its findings about the learner. Also, while the three alternative loan sources are, in fact, representative of the available alternatives, future work must incorporate more companies.

The agent-based approach provides a natural mechanism for incorporating new loan companies with minimal impact on previous software components. The ontology component of the supervisor agent would require updates as new loan sites are added, but it minimizes the effort in mediating between heterogeneous data sources. Finally, the autonomous nature of the agent facilitates an ongoing search for the best possible loan. Thus, the agent can provide information about a new or improved loan source without waiting for the user to think of querying for improvements.

Agent-Based Approach: Weaknesses and Threats

While agent development environments are available, they are generally not as mature as those for expert systems; so system development will generally be more time consuming. The interface to remote Web sites could be facilitated by the use of the XML standard and an ontology to resolve varied terminology across heterogeneous formats; however, these standards are relatively new, and most of the sites of interest are HTML-based instead. It will, therefore, be important to establish a working relationship with sites across which data are shared; otherwise, the volatility of the data and the distribution of control will render the project ineffectual. Since the standards are relatively new and not widely in force, the developer risks having a new standard move in and replace the one on which the system is based. Finally, while the agent-based approach supports the development of an adaptive tutor/advisor, most learning algorithms require large amounts of data, which may be initially difficult to obtain.

Recommendation for
Next Phase of Development

Because of the dramatic increases in functionality associated with the agent-based approach, it is recommended that the fully functional system be built on the agent-based prototype, REMA II, rather than on the REMA I expert system. The only reason for selecting to an expert system approach would be to support a fast turnaround incremental improvement on the current system. Given current availability of a prototype system for immediate use, the plan that best incorporates the dynamic and heavily computational components of the advisor and the user-adaptive, self-initiating components of the tutor is preferred.

Practical Implications

A critical question for system development managers is under what circumstances would it likely be better to use AT instead of the presently more widely used ES technology for the development of specific applications? AT is extremely promising and it behooves all system development managers to understand its potential and limitations and perhaps begin to experiment with AT for possible adoption in the future. However, there are limitations. There are situations where the use of AT will not be efficient in terms of system development cost and implementation time. Systems development managers must remember that presently AT is still at a relatively early stage of adoption in industry at large. The availability of systems developers competent with the technology is relatively scarce. Also, there is a lack of systems development tool kits and shells, which today are commonly found for the development of ES. As discussed previously in the chapter, the fact that AT is useful for addressing relatively more complex application requirements, make the systems development analysis and design tasks correspondingly more complex and requiring software engineering methods that are still under development. In a similar fashion, the ability of AT to bridge the gap between distributed application components may raise questions about user privacy, data integrity, and human control over the agent-based system. Nevertheless, increasingly there are applications which will require the use of AT. The following conditions are likely to call for the use of AT in system development: (1) Applications requiring flexible decision making beyond fuzzy logic or the relatively strict rules required by ES. (2) Applications which require enough intelligence for direct system interaction with end users and for system learning from the experience itself, whereby the rules will evolve on their own without the need for modification by systems developers. (3) Applications that require a flexible and complex integration of two or more ES or systems of other types.

As the business community puts greater importance on the role of knowledge management in capturing collective expertise and distributing it in a manner that produces a payoff, the use of agent-based technology will have increasingly significant business implications. With the dramatic increase in Internet activity over the past five years, agents can play an important role in monitoring, filtering, and recommending information, using user profiles to personalize their support. Agent Mediators can facilitate the exchange of data among heterogeneous sites, maintaining an ongoing record of variable site formats and mapping information seamlessly into a format more easily understood by their users. Network Management Agents can focus on increasing throughput and minimizing delay by adapting protocols to the current hardware and workload environment. In general, complex problems can be decomposed into smaller, segmented problems that can be more easily resolved. All of these advances open decision support and e-commerce opportunities to a wider community and facilitate tapping more widely distributed knowledge bases to improve quality. Such advances are already within reach for many application areas. However, the ability to reach the full potential of these advances relies on continued development of software engineering methods specifically tailored to agent-based systems, software development tools, and security mechanisms that accommodate a widely distributed, mobile computing environment.

The effective use of agent technology enables developers to gain significant advantages over existing technologies in achieving their knowledge management goals. An increased level of software system autonomy limits the user burden for direct intervention and can relieve communication requirements in a bandwidth-limited environment. The distributed decision-making process can increase robustness and, because tasks are performed in parallel, overall system efficiency increases. The approach facilitates developing mediators that can integrate heterogeneous and legacy systems without requiring a single data representation structure. Further, the techniques support incremental development of complex systems via independent reusable components.

The REMA case illustrates some of the many powerful enhancements achieved by using agent techniques where expert systems were originally envisioned. To system designers/developers, one of the most compelling arguments for using only ES is the ready availability of software development tools to support this more mature development technique. Although there are many issues to be addressed for agent technology to realize its full potential, the technology has advanced at a fast rate due to the significant research effort in both academia and industry. Many of the components to build effective agents are moving beyond research communities and coming into common use in the immediate future. With their arrival we now have a powerful integrator for Web-based systems with the more traditional types of systems (including ES) thus providing a strong infrastructure for managing corporate knowledge.

References

AARP. (2001). Retrieved July 9, 2006, http://www.aarp.org

Barbaceanu, M. (2001). *The agent building shell: Programming cooperative enterprise agents*. Retrieved July 9, 2006, from http://www.eil.utoronto.ca/ABS-page/ABS-overview.html

Broome, B., Gangopadhyay, A., & Yoon, V. (2002, July 2002). *CAER: An ontology-based community of agents for emergency relief*. Paper presented at the 6th World Multi-conference on Systemics, Cybernetics and Informatics, Orlando, Florida.

Cantu, F. (2000). *Reinforcement and Bayesian learning in multiagent systems: the MACS project*. Technical Report CIA-RI-042, Center for Artificial Intellegence, ITESM.

FannieMae. (2001). Our business is the American dream. Retrieved July 9, 2006, from http://www.fanniemae.com

Finin, T., Labrou, Y., & Mayfield, J. (1998). KQML as an agent communication language. In J.M. Bradshaw (Ed.), *Software agents,* (p. 28). Boston: MIT Press.

FIPA. (2000). FIPA specification repository. Retrieved July 9, 2006, from http://www.fipa.org/repository

Graham, J., Decker, K., & Mersic, M. (2003). DECAF: A flexible multi-agent system architecture. *Autonomous Agents and Multi-Agent Systems, 7*(1-2), 7-27.

Harvey, T., Decker, K., & Carberry, S. (2005, July 25-29). Multi-agent decision support via user-modeling. In *Proceedings of International Conference of Autonomous Agents and Multi-Agent Systems* (pp. 222-229).

HUD. (2001). *Homes and communities*. Retrieved July 9, 2006, from http://www.hud.gov

Larson, M. (1999). *Shopping for a reverse mortgage: Few products, lots of tricky choices*. Retrieved July 9, 2006, from http://www.bankrate.com/brm/news/loan

Liebowitz, J. (2000). *Building organizational intelligence: A knowledge management primer*. Boca Raton, FL: CRC Press.

Liebowitz, J. (Ed.). (1999a). *Expert systems with applications: An international journal*. Amsterdam, The Netherlands: Elsevier.

Liebowitz, J. (Ed.). (1999b). *Knowledge management handbook*. Washington, DC: CRC Press.

Liebowitz, J., & Beckman, T. (1998). *Knowledge organizations: What every manager should know*. Boca Raton, FL: CRC Press.

Lu, M., & Guimaraes, T. (1989, Spring). A guide to selecting expert systems applications. *Journal of Information Systems Management*, 8-15.

Minsky, M. (1985). *The society of mind*. New York: Simon and Schuster.

Rassmussen, D., Megbolugbe, I., & Morgan, B. (1997). The reverse mortgage as an asset management tool. *Housing Policy Debate, 8*(1), 173-194.

Reverse. (2001). *Independent information on reverse mortgages for consumers, their families, professional advisors, and nonprofit counselors*. Retrieved July 9, 2006, from http://www.reverse.org

Rubenstein-Montano, B., Yoon, Y., Lowry, S., & Merlau, T. (2005). A multiagent system for U.S. defense research contracting. *Communications of the ACM, 48*(3), 93-97.

Thomas, M., Redmond, R., Yoon, V., & Singh, S. (2005). A semantic approach to monitor business process performance. *Communications of the ACM, 48*(12), 55-58.

Traverse, M. (2001). *Agent-based programming environments.* Retrieved July 9, 2006, from http://xenia.media.mit.edu/~mt/childs-play-pp.html

Wooldridge, M., & Jennings, N.R. (1995). Intelligent agents: Theory and practice. *The Knowledge Engineering Review, 10*(2), 115-152.

Yannis, L., Finin, T., & Peng, Y. (1999). Agent communication languages: The current landscape. *IEEE Intelligent Systems and Their Applications, 14*(2), 45-52.

Yoon, Y., & Guimaraes, T. (1993). Selecting expert system development techniques. *Information and Management, 24*, 209-223.

Endnote

* The authors gratefully acknowledge: the Fannie Mae Foundation, for the grant that supported the development of the REMA I prototype; Dr. J. Liebowitz, who led that prototype development effort; and Mr. Ed Szymanoski, for his constructive review and comments on the REMA I effort.

About the Editor

Mehdi Khosrow-Pour, DBA, is currently the executive director of the Information Resources Management Association (IRMA) and senior academic editor for
Idea Group Reference. Previously, he served on the faculty of The Pennsylvania
State University as an associate professor of information systems for 20 years. He
has written or edited more than 20 books in IT management, and he is the editor of
the *Information Resources Management Journal, Journal of Electronic Commerce
in Organizations, Journal of Cases on Information Technology,* and *International
Journal of Cases on Electronic Commerce.*

About the Authors

Tanya Bondarouk is an assistant professor of human resource management at the University of Twente, The Netherlands. She holds her PhDs in the fields of didactics and business administration. Her main teaching and research interests are in the area of social aspects of implementation of information technologies and human resource management, with a special reference to the interpretive research methods. More recently, she is involved in the research into e-HRM, conducting research projects in different private and public sector organizations.

Norman L. Chervany, Carlson professor of information and decision sciences at the Carlson School of Management, University of Minnesota, USA, received his doctorate in decisions sciences from Indiana University. His research interests focus on the human issues involved in the use of technology. His specific research revolves around the relationships among information technology/systems and organizational strategy, the role of trust in an organization's information management enterprise, work design issues in systems development, and the implementation of systems projects. Professor Chervany is widely published in such outlets as *MIS Quarterly, Management Science,* and *Decision Sciences.* He is a fellow of the Decision Sciences Institute.

Ronald Dattero is a professor of computer information systems at Missouri State University, USA. He holds a PhD from Purdue University. His research interests include applications development, knowledge management, database management, IT professional and personnel issues, and applied statistics. His work appears in such journals as *Journal of Management Information Systems, Information and Management, Information Systems, Information Resources Management Journal, Decision Support Systems, Communications of the AIS,* and *Communications of the ACM.*

Neil F. Doherty is a senior lecturer in information systems in the Business School at Loughborough University, UK. In addition to information security, his research interests include the interaction between organizational issues and technical factors in information systems development, understanding the reasons for failures of information systems projects, strategic information systems planning, and e-commerce. Neil has had papers published in a range of academic journals, including *European Journal of Information Systems, Journal of Information Technology, Journal of Strategic Information Systems, Information Resources Management Journal, IEEE Transactions in Engineering Management, Journal of Business Research, Journal of End User Computing, Information Technology & People, Behaviour & IT,* and *Information & Management.* Doherty is also an associate editor for the *International Journal of Electronic Business Research.*

Manal M. Elkordy is an assistant professor at Alexandria University, Egypt. She has a PhD from City University of London. Her research interests include information systems effectiveness and information systems management.

Deirdre A. Folkers has taught for The Pennsylvania State University's York Campus, USA, for more than 23 years. During this time, she has served as an instructor of computer science and curriculum developer (as well as coordinator and instructor) of Penn State York's noncredit computer seminar series. Currently, she teaches and advises students as an Instructor of Information Sciences and Technology. She holds degrees in computer science (The Pennsylvania State University), man-environment relations (The Pennsylvania State University), and information systems (University of Maryland, Baltimore County). She has written and presented on the topics of distance education and educational technology, including the use of course management software.

Heather Fulford is a lecturer in information systems in the Business School at Loughborough University, UK. Her research interests include security management in large and small enterprises, electronic commerce adoption, Web site design, and knowledge management. She is currently managing an EPSRC-funded project investigating the adoption of IT by UK SMEs, and has also gained government funding for an e-commerce adoption project. Fulford has had her papers published in a range of academic journals, including *Information Management & Computer Security, Information Resources Management Journal, International Journal of*

Retail & Distribution Management, and *Terminology.* She is also joint editor of the *Journal of Specialised Translation.*

Stuart D. Galup is an associate professor of IT at Florida Atlantic University, USA. He holds a DBA from Nova Southeastern University and is a certified computing professional. His professional work in the transformation of information technology organizations was featured in *Computerworld* and *Datamation.* His research appears in such academic journals as *Communications of the AIS, Communications of the ACM, Information Resources Management Journal, Communications Research, ACM Computer Personnel,* and *Journal of Computer Information Systems.* He is co-author of *Building the New Enterprise: People, Processes, and Technology* and *The IT Organization: Building a World-Class Infrastructure,* both published by Prentice Hall.

Tor Guimaraes has been rated by several independent sources as one of the top researchers in the world based on publications in the top IS journals. He holds the Jesse E. Owen Chair of Excellence at Tennessee Technological University, USA. He earned a PhD in MIS from the University of Minnesota and an MBA from California State University, Los Angeles. Guimaraes was department chairman and professor at St. Cloud State University. Before that, he was an assistant professor and director of the MIS Certificate Program at Case-Western Reserve University. He has been the keynote speaker at numerous national and international meetings sponsored by organizations such as the Information Processing Society of Japan, Institute of Industrial Engineers, Sales and Marketing Executives, IEEE, Association for Systems Management, and the American Society for Quality Control. Guimaraes has consulted with many leading organizations including TRW, American Greetings, AT&T, IBM, and the Department of Defense. He is on the board of directors of several national and international business organizations and is a senior strategic advisor to their CEOs. Working with partners in more than 30 countries, he has published over 200 articles dealing with the effective use and management of IS and related technologies.

William David Haseman is Wisconsin distinguished professor and director of the Center for Technology Innovation at the University of Wisconsin – Milwaukee, USA. He received his PhD from the Krannert Graduate School of Management at Purdue University and served previously on the Faculty at Carnegie-Mellon University. His research interests include groupware, Web services, decision support systems, services oriented architecture, and emerging Internet technologies. Dr. Haseman has published a book and a number of research articles in journals such as *Accounting Review, Operations Research, MIS Quarterly, Decision Support Systems, Information Management, Information Systems,* and *Database Manage-*

ment. He was conference chair for Americas Conference on Information Systems (AMCIS) in 1999 and conference chair for International Conference on Information Systems (ICIS) for 2006.

Omar E. M. Khalil is currently a professor of information systems at Kuwait University, Kuwait. He has a PhD in information systems from the University of North Texas. His research interests include information systems effectiveness, global information systems, information quality, and knowledge management.

Ned Kock is an associate professor and chair of the Department of MIS and decision science at Texas A&M International University, USA. He holds degrees in electronics engineering (BEE), computer science (MS), and MIS (PhD). Kock has authored several books, and published in a number of journals including *Communications of the ACM, Decision Support Systems, IEEE Transactions on Education, IEEE Transactions on Engineering Management, IEEE Transactions on Professional Communication, Information & Management, Information Systems Journal, Information Technology & People, Journal of Organizational Computing and Electronic Commerce, Journal of Systems and Information Technology, MIS Quarterly,* and *Organization Science.* He is editor-in-chief of the *International Journal of e-Collaboration,* associate editor of the *Journal of Systems and Information Technology,* and associate editor for information systems of the journal *IEEE Transactions on Professional Communication.* His research interests include action research, ethical and legal issues in technology research and management, e-collaboration, and business process improvement.

Laura Lally is an associate professor at the Frank G. Zarb School of Business at Hofstra University, USA. She holds a PhD in information systems from the Stern School of Business at New York University, and an MBA from Baruch College of the City University of New York. She has published articles in *Decision Sciences,* the *Journal of Global Information Management,* the *Journal of End-User Computing,* the *Information Society,* and the *Journal of Business Ethics.* She has received two National Science Foundation Grants to support her research in applying normal accident theory and the theory of high reliability organizations to information technology.

Margi Levy is a senior lecturer in information management at Warwick Business School, University of Warwick, UK. Before becoming an academic she worked as an IS consultant with Coopers and Lybrand in W. Australia, for a number of financial and software development organizations in London. Currently, she is researching into getting value from information systems for small and medium sized enterprises, information systems strategy, e-business for SMEs, and applicability of IS theory to SMEs. She has published in a number of journals: *Information and Management, Journal of Strategic Information Systems, European Journal of Information Systems, Information Resource Management Journal, International Journal of Technology Management,* and *Small Business Economics.* She is the Co-author with Philip Powell of the recently published book: *Strategies for Growth in SMEs: The Role of Information and Information Systems.*

D. Harrison McKnight is an assistant professor at the College of Business at Michigan State University, USA. He earned his PhD in MIS from the University of Minnesota. His research interests include trust building within e-commerce and organizational settings and the retention and motivation of information systems professionals. His work has appeared in such journals as *Information Systems Research, Journal of Strategic Information Systems,* and the *Academy of Management Review.*

Abhishek Nirjar (abhishek@iiml.ac.in) is an associate professor of strategic management at the Indian Institute of Management, Lucknow, India. He has served Malaviya Regional Engineering College, Jaipur, FORE School of Management, New Delhi, and Management Development Institute, Gurgaon. He has been the recipient of the Career Award for Young Teachers (research grant) instituted by the All India Council for Technical Education, New Delhi. He teaches courses on strategic management and entrepreneurship. He is currently researching innovation capability and firm performance, steps in new venture creation, and growth strategies of high-tech SMEs. Nirjar has a BS (Bundelkhand University), an MBA (Lucknow University), and recently completed his PhD at the University of Sheffield, UK.

Souren Paul is an assistant professor of MIS at the College of Business and Administration at Southern Illinois University Carbondale, USA. He holds a bachelor's degree and a master's degree in electronics and telecommunications engineering from Jadavpur University, India, and a PhD in MIS from the University of Wisconsin-Milwaukee. His current research interests include cognition and knowledge sharing in collaborative technology supported group work, virtual teams, and organizational knowledge management systems. He has published research articles in the *Journal of Management Information Systems, Decision Support Systems,* and *Information & Management.*

Alan R. Peslak is an assistant professor of information sciences and technology at Penn State University – Worthington Scranton, USA. He received his PhD in information systems from Nova Southeastern University, Fort Lauderdale, Florida. His research areas include information technology social, ethical, and economic issues as well as information technology pedagogy. Publications include the *Communications of the ACM, Information Resources Management Journal, Journal of Business Ethics, Journal of Computer Information Systems, Journal of Information Systems Education, Team Performance Management, Information Research,* and *First Monday.* He has over 25 years of diverse manufacturing and service industry experience.

Philip Powell is deputy dean, professor of information management and was director of the Centre for Information Management in the School of Management at the University of Bath, UK. He is also honorary professor of operational information systems at the University of Groningen. Formerly a professor of information systems with the University of London and director of the Information Systems Research Unit at Warwick Business School, he has worked and taught in Australia, Africa, the U.S., and Europe. Prior to becoming an academic he worked in insurance, accounting, and systems analysis. He is the author of six books on information systems and financial modeling. He has published numerous book chapters and his work has appeared in over 80 international journals and at over 100 conferences. He is managing editor of the *Information Systems Journal,* book review editor of the *Journal of Strategic Information Systems,* and on a number of other journal editorial boards. He is a past president of the UK Academy for IS. His research concerns the role and use of information systems in organizations especially issues of strategy and evaluation in the context of small firms. More recently he has contributed to research on e-business and knowledge management.

Jing "Jim" Quan is an assistant professor in the Department of Information and Decision Sciences in Purdue School of Business, Salisbury University, USA. He holds a PhD from the University of Florida and is an MCT/MCSE and CNI/CNE. His research interests include information technology (IT) and organizations, IT human resource management, and e-commerce. His work has appeared in such journals as *Journal of Management Information Systems,* the *Communications of the ACM,* the *Communications of the AIS, Information Resources Management Journal, International Journal of Information Management, Journal of Information Technology and Information Management,* and *Journal of Computer Information Systems.* He presented papers at the national and international conferences on information systems and technology.

Carol Stoak Saunders is a professor of MIS at the University of Central Florida, USA. She served as general conference chair of ICIS'99 and Telecommuting '96. She was the chair of the executive committee of ICIS in 2000 and inducted as an AIS fellow in 2003. Currently she is editor-in-chief of *MIS Quarterly.* Her current research interests include the organizational impacts of information technology, virtual teams, time, and interorganizational linkages. Her research is published in *MIS Quarterly, Information Systems Research, Journal of MIS, Communications of the ACM, Academy of Management Journal, Academy of Management Review,* and *Organization Science.*

Klaas Sikkel has an MSc in software engineering and a PhD in theoretical computer science. From 1994 he was involved in the design and implementation of groupware systems. At GMD, the German National Research Institute for Computer Science he was one of the founders of the project "Basic Support for Cooperative Work," one of the first to deliver Web-based groupware services. Currently he is an assistant professor with the Information Systems Group at the University of Twente. His interests include requirements analysis, evolutionary use of groupware and the use of ICT in higher education.

Monideepa Tarafdar is an assistant professor of information systems at the University of Toledo, Ohio, USA. She has an undergraduate degree in physics and a graduate degree in telecommunications and electronics engineering from the University of Calcutta, India. Her doctoral degree is from the Indian Institute of Management, Calcutta. Her current research and teaching interests are in the areas of strategic information systems management, management of IT, enterprise systems and organizational aspects of IS. Her teaching has been in the areas of management information systems, data management, data communications, and e-commerce. Her research has appeared in *Journal of Information Technology Cases and Applications, Journal of Global Information Technology Management, Information Resources Management Journal,* and *Journal of Cases in Information Technology.*

Andrew Tylecote (a.tylecote@shef.ac.uk) is a professor of the economics and management of technological change at University of Sheffield Management School, UK. He was educated at Oxford and Sussex in philosophy, politics, sociology, history, and economics. Most of his current work focuses on the impact on technological change of finance and corporate governance. During 1998-2002 he coordinated a six-country project finance by the European Union on corporate governance and product innovation in European firms. He is currently working with Economic and Social Research Council funding on corporate governance and technological development in China, and completing a book for Routledge on corporate governance and the technological advantage of nations.

Les Worrall (PhD, Liverpool, UK) is an associate dean (Research) at the University of Wolverhampton Business School, UK, where he leads the Management Research Centre. He is a council member of the British Academy of Management and a member of the Association of Business School's Research Committee. He has published extensively on regional economic analysis and has a particular research interest in the management of information and communications technology in UK local government. Professor Worrall is a member of the editorial boards of four journals and has published extensively in several areas of applied management research. He has also conducted research and consultancy for several "blue chip" companies and over 200 UK local authorities.

Jie (Jennifer) Zhang is an assistant professor of information systems at the College of Business Administration, University of Toledo, USA. She received her PhD in computer information systems from the Simon School of Business, University of Rochester. She employs analytical and empirical techniques to examine such issues as intermediation, advertising strategies for portal Web sites, online media concentration, software licensing, and consumer online searching and shopping behaviors in electronic commerce and management of information systems. Her research appears in *Journal of Economics and Management Strategies, Journal of Management Information Systems, Information Resources Management Journal,* and *Journal of Computer Information Systems.*

Index

theory of high reliability organizations
160
threats to the security of information
assets 46
top managers and external
relationships 307
traditional expert system approach 327
training "on demand" 310
translating 332
trust-building model 180
trust-building model for an unfamiliar
setting 180
trust and trust building 179
trust building 177
trust building model (TBM) 189
tutor agent 333
two extensions of normal accident
theory 163

U

unauthorised access 47
updating of the ISP 49
usability of Web sites 271
use-case diagram 336
use of executive informatin systems
(EIS) 89
use of IT as a weapon against terrorism
157
user interface agent 333
user involvement 96, 101

V

venture capitalist 304

W

Web-based system 200
Web site availability 285
Web site design parameters 271
Web site security and customization
271
Web sites with low usability 271
Web site usability 271

Web site usability 271
Web site usability (USAB) 281
WorkFlow system 15
Workload 81
World Wide Web (WWW) 272

Y

Y2K problem 157, 160